PUBLIC LANDS AND PRIVATE RIGHTS

The Political Economy Forum

Sponsored by the Political Economy Research Center (PERC)
Series Editor: Terry L. Anderson

PUBLIC LANDS AND PRIVATE RIGHTS

The Failure of Scientific Management

Robert H. Nelson

ROWMAN & LITTLEFIELD PUBLISHERS, INC.

ROWMAN & LITTLEFIELD PUBLISHERS, INC.

Published in the United States of America
by Rowman & Littlefield Publishers, Inc.
4720 Boston Way, Lanham, Maryland 20706

3 Henrietta Street
London WC2E 8LU, England

British Cataloging in Publication Information Available

Library of Congress Cataloging-in-Publication Data

Nelson, Robert H. (Robert Henry)
Public lands and private rights : the failure of scientific
management / Robert H. Nelson.
p.   cm.—(Political economy forum)
Includes index.
1. Public lands—United States—Management.   2. Land use—
Government policy—United States.   3. Public lands—West (U.S.)
I. Title.   II. Series.
HD216.N45   1995   333.1—dc20   94-46294   CIP

ISBN 0–8476–8008–8 (cloth: alk. paper)
ISBN 0–8476–8009–6 (pbk.: alk. paper)

Printed in the United States of America

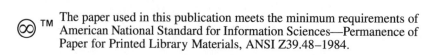

For Fred

Contents

Foreword

This is an extraordinary book, and we are lucky to have it. It is an indicator of Bob Nelson's many excellent qualities—and the high regard in which he is held by his colleagues—that we did not have to wait for him to retire or die for this rich collection to see the light of day. It is normal, on either of those occasions, generally the latter, for admiring friends to gather mostly unpublished pieces into a respectful pile and print them in honor of the departed, especially a distinguished academic. But this volume is not made up of castoffs of scholarly self-positioning on the publish-or-perish continuum. A number of these essays have been previously published, but in the main these are the working papers of a government policy analyst. Probably not since Harold Ickes' controversial diaries went public has there been so much perspective to be gained from perusing the insights of a Department of the Interior bureaucrat.

Nobody will agree with all of Nelson's conclusions and recommendations. Some may feel impaled by his lack of reverence for their own cherished rhetoric in the frequently theological debates that mire public lands policy. But no one is likely to come away from even a selective sampling of these rich morsels with their own assumptions and biases about public resources completely unrevised.

These prescient papers are not the work of a lifetime; they are quite precisely the analyses undertaken during a critical period of public land history. Nelson worked in the Office of Policy Analysis in the Department of the Interior from 1975 until 1993. During that period, Congress cleaned the barn of almost two centuries of public resource policies and imposed an unprecedented array of complex, frequently flaccid, but occasionally nondiscretionary mandates on federal land managing agencies. During the overhaul of federal forest and grazing land management, a major revision of federal coal programs, the ideological whiplash that Interior Secretary James Watt brought to the end of the "environmental decade," and finally, the rise of takings and ecosystem management issues, Nelson was a participant and an observer with an extraordinarily keen eye and clear voice. His analyses of how we got

ix

into the mess we are in and his recommendations for how to progress cast complex national patterns onto new and intelligible frames that challenge emotionally charged renderings of ancient and current disputes. They are also specific, laying out cleanly and without cant, the details and implications of policy choices in important public resource programs.

This volume is also not comprehensive. Although the history is broad and clear, Nelson's focus is on timber and grazing issues. He discusses the range wars, old and new, in about a third of the essays and timber management in slightly fewer pieces. He focuses unusual attention on agency analytical tools and the use and abuse of analysis in Forest Service and Bureau of Land Management planning efforts. He ends with a significant discussion of private rights on public lands.

As the book unfolds, Nelson's background in economics becomes increasingly clear—many of his proposals for reasonable next steps are anchored in his own profession—but Nelson is rarely if ever a mere economist. At their worst, Nelson's predilections are simply familiar. We know that an economist is going to point out that public land management agencies are not efficient and suggest somehow that some or all of the public lands ought to be managed with an emphasis on market incentives if not private ownership. In this, Nelson is true to the grape. But his treatment of decentralization of authority is unusual. Since Gifford Pinchot wrote his famous letter to himself from the Secretary of Agriculture, decisions arrived at locally have been the unfulfilled Tinkerbell of public resource agencies—we clap and the idea does not entirely die, but it never seems to get implemented either. Nelson's treatment of decentralization in the context of the interplay of private and local power gives his suggestions both a contemporary flavor and an interesting weight.

By placing national parks onto the block, Nelson also turns the tables on the normal set of range and timber program reformers' assertions and assumptions that shape a typical decentralization debate. This issue gets a different spin entirely when Nelson suggests that national parks, where more than 75 percent of the visitors are from the state where the park is located, ought to be turned over to the state for management. Even if we do not like that idea, wrestling it to the ground requires us to be clearer than usual about why the federal government owns land, who ought to be subsidizing whom to do what on that land, what requires national decision making, and which questions are more appropriately decided in a local or regional process.

However, the pleasure of this volume, and its usefulness, is not in its revolutionary prescriptions but in the clarity of its thought. Nelson's discussions—of the Sagebrush Rebellion, of agency analytic tools and biases, of an unlikely but intriguing near-total dismantling of the Department of the Interior—are not still another assault by a free-market partisan but an enlightening exposure to the ideas at play in many resource policy debates. Our capacity to think clearly about the assertions, assumptions, and commitments that underlie the apparently self-evident virtues of "scientific resource management" is sharpened perceptibly by Nelson's clean perspective and prose.

Nelson also brings to the analysis his life in a parallel universe as a student of urban and regional planning. His intelligent comparison of the traditions of that professional tribe with the efforts of forest and range managers to implement the planning mandates of the Resources Planning Act, the National Forest Management Act, and the Federal Land Policy and Management Act are informative and could be considered downright witty in spots if the consequences for the resources were not so tragic. His insistence on putting our public lands into the same categories with the eroding commitment to government-owned enterprises in western and central Europe has a striking pedagogical effect. Insightful juxtapositions abound, to wit: "Making a mining discovery is a lot like hitting the lottery. Even when the payoff to the lottery is far more than the price paid for the winning ticket, it obviously does not mean that the overall lottery is a bad deal for the government—even though a lot of politicians and the media seem to subject the operation of the mining law to a precisely analogous reasoning. They focus on a few big mineral discoveries—the mining law lottery winners—and ignore completely the far larger number of exploration failures." Political rhetoric to the contrary notwithstanding, the financial side of mining, and the expected returns to the average miner are, as Nelson points out, almost completely unknown.

Nelson's basic conclusions are also uncomfortably clear. Almost everything we have tried to accomplish on the public lands—from original, eighteenth-century efforts to sell the land and use the receipts to retire the Revolutionary War debt, to present efforts to charge equitable and efficient grazing fees—has failed. Nelson is a little bit fuzzier than we might wish about the standards for identifying failure, given the frequency with which that thought emerges in his essays. However, the basic notion—that judged by what Congress attempted to achieve, we have rarely come close to succeeding—is a reasonable basis for pause before embracing the next succulent slogan now on the platter: ecosystem management.

Ecosystem management is especially unappetizing given that the real culprit, according to Nelson, is the broad commitment of the progressive-era management agencies, their constituents, and their critics, to scientific decision making. The ethics of the paradigm are less at issue here than the implementation: It just does not work. Over and over again, Nelson demonstrates that under the guise of nonpartisan technical competence, land managers have manipulated analyses and misrepresented data to conceal costs and fabricate benefits. His discussion of bureaucrats serving their own interests in the guise of science is a far more complex and textured argument than the standard assertion that agency personnel lack proper incentives to serve the public interest rather than their own. Nelson makes a convincing argument that ideas we have regarded as self-evidently correct for about a century have fallen apart. What is interesting is that they have not eroded in the face of an alternate or competing paradigm. Rather, these ideas have collapsed under the weight of their own failures in spite of efforts by most of those involved to ignore shortcomings and rally 'round the party line. The result is that we are midstream without an alternative to replace the progressive-era's embrace of scientific management.

Nelson also points out, however, that our era is much like the period that preceded the progressive era—people are cynical and depressed about the potential for government. Over the next twenty or thirty years, he argues, new approaches that we cannot fully discern will gradually emerge to replace the failed system. Nelson tries to appear optimistic, but given what he has told us about the last two centuries it is not clear why.

This volume is both familiar and challenging. We have heard most of these stories before, but rarely has the ground been plowed to produce so much fresh detail, insight, and understanding. At the end, perhaps the most troubling issue Nelson raises concerns our capacity for governing ourselves. How is it possible that insightful analysts—even ones as pesky and thoughtful as Nelson—can prosper and find encouragement in the catacombs of the Interior Department, while the policies produced there, and the debate that surrounds them, continue to be so witless? Nelson demonstrates that we do not lack for insight at the highest levels. If federal land policy is guided by analysts so sharp and honest, why does it turn out so poorly so often?

Sally K. Fairfax
College of Natural Resources
University of California, Berkeley

Preface

In May 1975 I joined the economics staff of the Office of Policy Analysis, located in the Office of the Secretary of the U.S. Department of the Interior.[1] I stayed in this office until August 1993, when I left to become a member of the faculty of the School of Public Affairs of the University of Maryland. My eighteen years at the Interior Department gave me an excellent education in the workings of American government and were on the whole a fascinating experience.[2]

For the first ten years my principal assignment was the public lands.[3] (After that, although I continued to work on public land issues, I also spent large amounts of time in other areas of Interior responsibility such as American Indian affairs.) On arriving at Interior, my first task was to design a benefit-cost system to analyze the adequacy of economic returns to public rangeland investments. In 1977 I was involved in a major study of the appropriate fee to be charged for grazing livestock on public lands—an experience I would eventually repeat several times. In the late 1970s I studied the methods for setting the levels of public timber harvests then being employed by the federal land management agencies.

Beginning in 1976, I commenced almost a decade of close involvement with the management of the coal reserves owned by the federal government in Wyoming, Montana, and other western states. Although little developed before 1970, federal coal by 1993 had become the source of 27 percent of total U.S. coal production. Reflecting the intense economic and environmental controversy surrounding the leasing of this coal for development, I would eventually participate in four comprehensive reviews and redesigns of the federal coal program. In the last one, my role was that of senior economist for the Commission on Fair Market Value Policy for Federal Coal Leasing (concerning which

James Watt would make some infamous remarks about the makeup of the Commission members, leading directly to his departure as Interior Secretary).[4] I described the first five years of these experiences in a 1983 book, *The Making of Federal Coal Policy*.[5]

In 1978 I was encouraged by the Office of Policy Analysis to devote a portion of my time to thinking and writing about the longer-term policy issues and government strategy relating to the public lands. I have always enjoyed the study of history, partly in the conviction that the past often holds the key to understanding the present and future. Thus, a number of my papers addressed the history of government policies for the public lands. For some of the more recent episodes in that history, I was able to draw on my own experiences at Interior and/or on government sources that became available to me through my own work efforts (in most cases sources that were publicly available but often little known outside the government).

I continued to write on public land issues throughout my years at Interior. Although some of my articles and papers are found in publications easily available to interested professionals, a number appeared in little-known outlets and still others were distributed within the government but never published for outside audiences. Given the continuing— indeed, it may well be growing—interest in the subjects examined in these writings, it seemed to me that it might be helpful to assemble them in one place. In this book I thus make available a selection of past articles and papers of mine on public land policy, organized by subject matter and, to some extent, by chronology.

The material is included mostly as it was originally written. I did heavily edit several papers that had not previously been published, although their basic content was little altered. I revised introductory and concluding sections of most papers in order to better relate them to the larger themes of this book. A number of sections of individual works that either seemed of less interest or were duplicative of subjects covered elsewhere were deleted. I added a few key facts and dates here and there, but for the most part did not try to update the articles and papers to reflect events subsequent to their writing.

Before starting at the Interior Department in 1975, I was trained professionally in economics. I had also previously studied land use problems in urban settings, resulting in a 1977 book titled *Zoning and Property Rights*.[6] Over the years I have been impressed with the many common elements in the histories of the urban private lands and the public lands of the United States. In both areas of land use, it was in the progressive era that the ideas and institutions that would dominate developments in the twentieth century took shape. Great hopes were invested in the expert planning and scientific management of land use. However, as with most of the hopes in the twentieth century for the scientific management of society, the reality of private and public land management over the course of the century turned out to be much less than expected. This book continues a larger project of mine that is now approaching a quarter century in length: the study of the failure, in many fields, of the progressive ideals and the search for a new guiding vision for American government.

I should emphasize that the conclusions, analyses, and opinions in this book are my own. They do not necessarily represent the views of the Office of Policy Analysis or the U.S. Department of the Interior. To a degree perhaps unusual for a career government employee, I had the benefit during my years at Interior of substantial freedom to address controversial topics in the fashion that seemed to me to be most enlightening. I like to think that this freedom lasted over the terms of five presidents and eight secretaries of the interior at least in part because I succeeded in clarifying important public land issues in a way that many people of diverse views—while not agreeing with me in every respect—found on the whole to be illuminating.

There were many people at the Interior Department who encouraged me to write about public land issues and offered valuable comments and criticism. Former directors of the Office of Policy Analysis, including William Moffat, Heather Ross, Lester Silverman, Donald Sant, Martin Smith, and Richard Stroup, gave me the time and support necessary for such pursuits. Robert K. Davis and Theodore Heintz, successive directors of the economics staff within the office while I was on the staff, both provided particularly strong encouragement and other assistance. Donald Bieniewicz, a fellow member of the economics staff, was an unfailing source of constructive criticism (as well as the co-author with me of the article on which chapter 13 of this book is based). Many other staff members with whom I served in the Office of Policy Analysis, including Austin Burke, Larry Finfer, Indur Goklany, Jon Goldstein, Abraham Haspel, Lou Pugliaresi, Marshall Rose, Donald Rosenthal, Willie Taylor, and Richard Wahl, were frequent companions in many enjoyable discussions of the problems and the future of the public lands. I thank them all.

Notes

1. I describe the workings of this office in Robert H. Nelson, "The Office of Policy Analysis in the Department of the Interior," *Journal of Policy Analysis*

and Management (Summer 1989); reprinted in Carol H. Weiss, *Organizations for Policy Analysis: Helping Government Think* (Newbury Park, Calif.: Sage Publications, 1992).

2. For reflections on the federal policy-making process, see Robert H. Nelson, "The Economics Profession and the Making of Public Policy," *Journal of Economic Literature* (March 1987).

3. See Robert H. Nelson, "The Public Lands," in Paul R. Portney, ed., *Current Issues in Natural Resource Policy* (Washington, D.C.: Resources for the Future, 1982).

4. Commission on Fair Market Value Policy for Federal Coal Leasing, *Report of the Commission* (February 1984).

5. Robert H. Nelson, *The Making of Federal Coal Policy* (Durham, N.C.: Duke University Press, 1983).

6. Robert H. Nelson, *Zoning and Property Rights: An Analysis of the American System of Land Use Regulation* (Cambridge, Mass.: MIT Press, 1977).

Introduction

In the 1970s Congress enacted the Endangered Species Act of 1973, the Forest and Rangeland Renewable Resources Planning Act of 1974, the National Forest Management Act of 1976, the Federal Land Policy and Management Act of 1976, the Federal Coal Leasing Amendments Act of 1976, the Surface Mining Control and Reclamation Act of 1977, the Outer Continental Shelf Lands Act Amendments of 1978, the Public Rangelands Improvement Act of 1978, and still other legislation with important consequences for the public lands. It was the greatest burst of legislative activity in the two-hundred-year history of public lands.[1]

Congress mandated for the public lands a process of rational decision making based on comprehensive land use planning. There would be wide consultation with the public, including ample opportunities to review and comment on all elements of the planning process. After all the information was gathered, the standard of decision making would be, in essence, science as documented in the land use plan.

The 1970s legislation represented an effort to revitalize the founding vision for public land management as it had been developed in the progressive era of the late nineteenth and early twentieth centuries. The progressives sought to curb the subservience to special interests that in their view had all too often corrupted the activities of the federal government in the second half of the nineteenth century. On the public lands this task required that the responsibility for the management of the lands should be turned over to professional forestry, rangeland science, wildlife, and other experts. The turn-of-the-century ideal was efficient management guided by scientific knowledge. It was, as historians have written, a period in which the progressive "gospel of efficiency" was spreading with a religious zeal throughout all areas of American life.[2]

By the 1960s, however, much of the original enthusiasm had been lost. The management of the public lands had returned to its old interest-group ways. The public land agencies often seemed most concerned with trying to conciliate every user group possible. Indeed, to a considerable degree that was what "multiple-use" management as formally mandated by the Multiple-Use and Sustained-Yield Act of 1960 meant in practice.

Then came the 1964 Wilderness Act, which signaled the emergence of a powerful new force in public land management. Like the conservation movement early in the century, the environmental movement brought a moral vision and a crusading spirit to public land issues. Long-standing practices of the land agencies now came under strong attack. Demands for reform were pressed in many areas. Environmentalism provided much of the impetus to enact the new legislative foundation for the public lands in the 1970s.

Yet the 1970s laws reflected more a demand for moral renewal and for better results than a clear diagnosis of why the original progressive scheme had failed. Indeed, from the beginning the reality of scientific management had fallen well short of the goal. In part the failures had occurred because ideas of scientific management would always be utopian. The thinking behind scientific management, for example, tended to assume that all necessary supply and demand and other economic information would be readily available to decision makers. In practice, though, important details would almost always be missing, perhaps because they were too costly to justify obtaining. The central planning role envisioned by the theorists of scientific management was in practice much more difficult to accomplish than the progressives ever understood.

The proponents of scientific management also had a flawed understanding of the relationship between science and politics. The progressive scheme assumed that society would set clear goals in the political process, and then expert managers would separately and efficiently realize these goals in the administrative process.[3] But what if society could not agree on any clear values in advance? What if decisions about means and ends could not actually be separated? In one of the most famous articles of post–World War II social science, Charles Lindblom made just this argument. He found that government worked by a process of "muddling through."[4] The ends did not precede the means, as rational models of government decision making supposed; rather, in practice the ends were typically determined jointly with the means. Hence, it seemed that science could not operate in a separate domain from value decisions; instead, the science and the values must somehow be worked out together.

By the last quarter of the twentieth century, scientific management was also out of touch with new social values emerging in American society. Early in the century the progressives saw in scientific and economic progress the virtual salvation of mankind, the route to heaven on earth.[5] These hopes were significantly dashed by the world wars, genocides, Siberian prison camps, and other dismal events of the history of the twentieth century. By the 1970s the environmental movement was becoming a leading vehicle for expressing new doubts concerning the actual gains to the world from the economic growth and technological advance of the modern age. The benefits for the human spirit were increasingly questioned, despite the vast expansion of material abundance. Some radical environmentalists went much further, asserting that the pursuit of economic progress was a basic threat to the earth and one of the grave evils of our time. In short, the very core of the progressive value system—its secular "theology" if you will—was being rapidly undercut by events as well.

It has become apparent in recent years that the prospects for the progressive governing scheme actually depended on something the progressives mostly took for granted: the existence in American life of a set of common values and a strong sense of national community. This sense of community probably reached its peak in the United States during World War II, when a unified nation was able to undertake complex administrative tasks that would have been impossible in normal times. However, as the old value consensus in American society today gives way to a new pluralism, the progressive governing scheme tends to become less and less workable. The idea of one set of values and one administrative design for all the United States is not only flawed but increasingly seems an outright impossibility.

The fragmentation of the body politic in turn has encouraged local groups and private parties to assert new "rights" to government benefits. On the public lands the result is the creation of private rights to these lands, ranging from ranchers with grazing rights, to commercial outfitters with hunting and other recreation use rights, to wilderness advocates who successfully pressure the government to set aside their own private playgrounds. The public lands have been carved up into many domains whose beneficiaries fight as fiercely as any private property owner to defend existing entitlements. It is a new form of range war, now fought in the political and judicial arenas, but with control over the use of the land still the object of the struggle.[6] Like the old contests among homesteaders, cattlemen, and sheep herders, the new range wars not only damage the land itself, but are economically inefficient as well.

For all these reasons, and still others that will be examined in this book, the scientific management mandated by Congress in the 1970s legislation for the public lands already rested at the time of its enactment on a weak foundation. It was not long before the whole edifice began to totter. This has not been an unusual outcome over the two-hundred-year history of public land legislation, most of which has failed to realize its purposes. As of this writing in 1994, there is deep discontent on virtually all sides with the workings of the planning and management systems for the public lands. The former director of the Bureau of Land Management during the Carter administration, Frank Gregg, summarized the discussion at a recent public lands conference with the conclusion that "we have now amassed a considerable history in participating in and judging the revised system, and we agree that we are in another generation of dissatisfaction. We have characterized the present as gridlock, polarization, so extreme as to suggest extraordinary urgency in pondering what needs to be done.''[7]

As in the West of the old range wars, the solution to current problems will require defining more clearly the rights to the use of the land. In many cases formal recognition of existing private rights on public lands will be appropriate, much as the Taylor Grazing Act of 1934 codified the existing division of the rangeland forage use among livestock operators, a division that had developed informally over the previous half century. Today, however, there are many more users and many more informal rights that can be grounded in historic experience. Private rights can be collective as well as individual, and new formal private rights thus might as well be assigned to an environmental or recreation group as to a rancher.

The great advantage of privatization is that it creates a set of people with strong personal stakes in achieving good results on the land. Management in the name of all the people may in practice be management by no one. The progressives sought to deny legitimacy to the "special interests,'' but private motives and self-interest have hardly disappeared from public land management. Yet in refusing to give these forces greater legitimacy the progressives offered no means to channel them constructively. Operating mainly through the political process, the pursuit of self-interest then often yielded economically wasteful and environmentally destructive results. The market is a way of recognizing private interests and then creating a structure of incentives that directs these interests to serve a greater social purpose. In an era when the moral grounds for coercion seem particularly doubtful, the voluntary character of market exchanges is also a powerful attraction.

To be sure, as many economists and others have pointed out, there are numerous ways in which the market can fail, even by a narrowly defined objective of economic efficiency. As economists have been less candid in acknowledging, the operation of a market acts to shape the values of society, and, indeed, a decision to rely on a market reflects a number of heroic value choices. So politics and government will have to become involved to some degree. Even in these areas, however, the issues at stake may be mostly matters of state and local concern.

In that case the governing responsibility perhaps should be placed at the state and local level. If local taxpayers provide the revenue, they are more likely to want to spend it wisely. By contrast federal responsibility encourages financial promiscuity; from the perspective of any one locality, virtually any expenditure of federal money is seen as a net benefit to its citizens. The federal budget is in some sense a "common pool resource"; the problem of overgrazing the budget commons is likely to be less severe as the size of the government jurisdiction decreases.

This book proposes a major decentralization of responsibility for the management of the public lands. Other economists—such as Alice Rivlin, current director of the federal Office of Management and Budget in a recent book—have reached similar conclusions on a much broader basis with respect to the activities of the federal government.[8] For some areas of the public lands, privatization would often be appropriate when it consists of the formal recognition of rights that already exist on a de facto basis. For other areas the better answer is to keep the lands in public ownership but to turn the responsibility for their management over to state and local governments. Still other areas—those with genuine significance to the whole national community, such as the "crown jewel" national parks—are best kept in federal hands.

A major redirection of public land management in this fashion would be consistent with other trends of recent years. All around the world nations have been privatizing inefficient and poorly run government businesses. In the United States many large corporations have cut out layers of middle management, curtailed the headquarters staff, and decentralized decision-making authority. By contrast the Interior Department contains a number of bureaucracies, created in many cases in the late nineteenth or early twentieth century, whose mission, organization, and general mode of operation have not been changed in any substantial way for decades.

As the end of the twentieth century approaches, the current period has many similarities to the progressive era. There is once again great discontent with existing institutions. A new set of ideas and a new institutional framework are required, just as the progressives saw such a need one hundred years ago. Today, however, it is the legacy of progressivism that is holding back change. Although the progressive model has been undermined by events, its lingering influence still continues to exert a powerful restraint on the ability to adopt new land management approaches. Once a force for radical change, progressivism has become the defender of the status quo, in this sense the true "conservatism" of our time.

Nevertheless, for the reasons that will be examined in this book, a whole new public land system is likely to emerge in the next century. It may require twenty or thirty years, as the developments in the progressive era are typically considered to span 1890 to 1920, but a new set of values, a new organizational structure, a new guiding vision applied to the public lands can be expected.[9] One hundred years ago the disposal philosophy of the nineteenth century was abandoned for the progressive vision of the scientific management of the public lands. This book explores the search for a new guiding vision to take its place.

Notes

1. See Samuel Trask Dana and Sally K. Fairfax, *Forest and Range Policy: Its Development in the United States* (New York: McGraw-Hill, 1980).

2. See Samuel P. Hays, *Conservation and the Gospel of Efficiency: The Progressive Conservation Movement, 1890–1920* (Cambridge, Mass.: Harvard University Press, 1959).

3. See Dwight Waldo, *The Administrative State: A Study of the Political Theory of American Public Administration* (New York: Holmes and Meier, 1984, 1948).

4. Charles E. Lindblom, "The Science of 'Muddling Through,' " *Public Administration Review* (Spring 1959).

5. See Robert H. Nelson, *Reaching for Heaven on Earth: The Theological Meaning of Economics* (Lanham, Md.: Rowman and Littlefield, 1991).

6. See Terry L. Anderson, ed., *Multiple Conflicts over Multiple Uses* (Bozeman, Mont.: Political Economy Research Center, 1994).

7. Frank Gregg, "Summary," in *Multiple Use and Sustained Yield: Changing Philosophies for Federal Land Management*, Committee Print No. 11 of the Committee of Interior and Insular Affairs, U.S. House of Representatives (1992):311. This publication contains the proceedings and summary for a work-

shop convened on March 5 and 6, 1992, in Washington, D.C., organized by the Congressional Research Service.

8. Alice M. Rivlin, *Revising the American Dream: The Economy, the States and the Federal Government* (Washington, D.C.: Brookings Institution, 1992).

9. See also Robert H. Nelson, "Government as Theatre: Towards a New Paradigm for the Public Lands," *University of Colorado Law Review* Vol. 65, No. 2 (1994).

Part I

Intentions Are Not Good Enough

Introduction

The history of the public lands is filled with laws that had lofty purposes and achieved dismal results. Partly it has been a matter of congressional ignorance. The typical congressman has known little of the actual circumstances on the ground in which the laws would be applied. Instead, the public lands offered an opportunity for legislators to decree that their pet economic theories or social ideals should be realized. Rather than helping, Congress has typically created new obstacles to practical solutions. History shows that in the end the citizenry has often chosen to ignore the laws. Despite many pious outcries against "fraud and illegality," local actions have often been taken more from necessity than from any criminal intent.

Whenever the public land laws became entirely out of touch with actual needs, Congress was eventually forced to make changes. Frequently the result was to ratify institutions already well developed informally. The mining laws of the nineteenth century, for example, were enacted into legislation about twenty years after their methods had been developed in the mining camps of California.

If the world were static, this approach might have worked well. However, the slow pace at which Congress moves has often meant that it has finally put its blessing on a practical solution that was no longer the most effective for the circumstances at hand. The Homestead Act of 1862, for instance, gave a formal congressional acceptance of the widespread squatting of the first half of the nineteenth century in Iowa and other fertile Midwest areas. It thereby legalized a practice that the government had strenuously opposed but never been able to stop. Yet the Homestead Act worked poorly in the arid environment of the Rocky Mountain West, where it would be applied through much of its history. Over the course of the nineteenth century, it was due in large part to

3

the unworkability of the public land laws that perhaps less than 50 percent of the land disposal to the private sector ever took place within the law.

In the twentieth century legislators and administrators typically believed that a new era had arrived. Now they finally knew enough and had the wisdom actually to solve the problems of the public lands. Science was transforming human knowledge and capabilities. Yet as the twentieth century draws to a close, probably the most accurate assessment is that Congress in the past one hundred years has been no less but no more successful than its nineteenth-century predecessors. If squatters no longer physically take possession of the land, there has been a proliferation of many new private rights to public lands. As in the nineteenth century, Congress has alternately tried to cancel or affirm these rights, but with little understanding of the problem and doing little good in either case.

To be sure, the failures of the past cannot be taken as a recipe for doing nothing; events will surely move forward for better or worse. One important lesson is that a single ''solution'' designed at the national level is not likely to succeed. There is a strong case, as later chapters of this book will examine, for institutional arrangements that allow much greater room for state and local flexibility and experimentation. The people most directly affected by public land management, the local governments and the private users, must have a much greater ability to devise their own practical ways to manage and to protect the lands.

Chapter 1

Ineffective Laws and Unexpected Consequences: A Brief Review of Public Land History

Henry Clay commented, "No subject, which has presented itself to the present, or perhaps any preceding Congress, is of greater magnitude than that of the public lands."[1] The acquisition of the Louisiana Territory, the railroad land grants, and the Homestead Act were all landmark events in the history of the United States in the nineteenth century. At the opening of the twentieth century the adoption of a reclamation program and the creation of the national forest system under Forest Service management were leading elements in the progressive program of President Theodore Roosevelt. Conservation of public resources was a prominent theme in the New Deal of President Franklin Roosevelt. In the past quarter century the designation of wilderness, the protection of the spotted owl in public forests of the Pacific Northwest, and the setting aside of public lands in new national parks and wildlife refuges in Alaska have been defining moments for the environmental movement.

The public lands are thus engraved in the American imagination, playing a central part in shaping American culture. Yet the rich symbolism has not yielded corresponding benefits for the land. Regarded from a merely practical perspective, there has been one bad public land policy after another. However noble the intent may have been, in more than two hundred years of public land history the high hopes of legislators seldom have been realized. Time after time public land laws enacted

This chapter is a newly edited version of an unpublished paper, "Policy Lessons from the History of the Public Lands," prepared for the Office of Policy Analysis, U.S. Department of the Interior, July 1979.

only a few years before were already in need of replacement. Where policies had been most successful, they were often adopted as desperate expedients. Unable to achieve its own lofty and moralistic aims, Congress was eventually forced to concede to and grant legitimacy to practices that had previously developed as practical responses on the ground—sometimes outside the law—to immediate needs. Indeed, in retrospect we can now see that policies not first successfully tested by such a process of trial and error have not stood much chance of success.

This chapter reviews this history. Its message is one of caution and modesty: If we are sure we know the answer, we are probably wrong. But such a conclusion does have one important policy implication—that it will be a mistake to require the same management regime and the same policies everywhere. Not only will there be a great difference in geographic, economic, political, and other circumstances from one part of the public lands to another, but any attempt to impose uniformity will cut off the learning process. Yet the progressive design for the public lands sought to do just that; it was based on the assumption that one national organization grounded in one scientific approach to managing the public lands would yield the best answers everywhere.

Origins of the Public Land System

When the War of Independence was concluded in 1781, several of the thirteen original states had large western territories. The state of Virginia had the largest, a huge area including the current states of Michigan, Ohio, Indiana, Kentucky, Virginia, and West Virginia. Georgia held claim to Alabama and Mississippi, North Carolina to Tennessee.

Other states such as Maryland and New Jersey, however, had no territories in the west. These states feared that the political balance of the new nation would be upset if the large western areas were to be developed as sections of the states then holding them. Beginning with Virginia in 1783 and concluding with Georgia in 1802, each of the states with western holdings ceded them to the national government. The Northwest Ordinance in 1787 incorporated the basic decision that these western areas would be held by the national government as territories until a certain level of population and development had been reached, at which point new states would be formed.

The acquisition by the national government of a huge new western domain raised the question of policies for these territories. The precedents from the colonial era offered three basic modes of settlement. In New England the land system was the most developed, involving elements of town planning and public control over the shape of new settlement. Substantial grants of land (six square miles at one stage) were made available to religious and other groups to form new communities. Prior to settlement the land in the planned community was surveyed and certain lots were set aside for religious, educational, and other purposes. New settlers received free title to land in exchange for services in building the community.

In the southern colonies new immigrants received free land on arrival as a matter of right—in Virginia at first one hundred and later fifty acres, and similar amounts in North Carolina. In the Mid-Atlantic states proprietors such as William Penn were granted huge lands and exercised control over their development. They typically attempted to derive large revenues from sale of the land to new settlers, although often they were frustrated by squatting. In Virginia as well there was widespread squatter occupancy of the land, in many cases because settlers seeking to exercise their rights to free land could not determine whether it already belonged to someone else. Because of this problem Virginia and other states eventually established a practice that would later be a major source of controversy on the federal lands, the right of preemption. Preemption gave squatters the right to purchase at the going price the land they had already occupied and developed.

The colonial era thus was characterized by a land policy designed to promote settlement, very often including the offering of free land as an inducement. Attempts to impose high prices and capture substantial revenues were often defeated by the many squatters—about which very little could be done in distant places on the frontier.

However, the new United States government rejected a policy of cheap land to promote settlement of the western territories. Without taxes such as the income tax, the only major revenue sources for the national government were tariffs and sales of public lands. In forming a public land policy, this financial consideration was paramount. Until just before the Civil War the basic policy of the federal government was that public lands should serve as a significant source of revenues. Although sales of public land were quite variable, they did in fact play this role in certain periods. For the six decades from 1800 to 1860, land sales represented 6, 19, 6, 26, 7, and 7 percent, respectively, of total federal revenues.

One might have expected that Thomas Jefferson, with his agrarian ideals, would have advocated policies favoring settlement. He had in fact at one time accurately foreseen the problems of placing financial and other obstacles in the way of settlers, observing that "by selling the lands to them, you will disgust them, and cause an avulsion to them from the common union. They will settle the lands in spite of everybody."[2] Yet by the late 1780s Jefferson had joined the majority favoring a revenue raising strategy. Alexander Hamilton, Henry Knox, and others had little tolerance for squatting, the latter regarding it as a "usurpation of the public lands" and an "audacious defiance" of the national government.[3] In his report on federal land policies, Hamilton explained the objective of the government.

> In the formation of a plan for the disposition of the vacant lands of the United States there appear to be two leading objects of consideration: one the facility of advantageous sales, according to the probable course of circumstances; the other the accommodation of individuals now inhabiting the western country, or who may hereafter emigrate thither. The former as an operation of finance claims primary attention.[4]

The decision to offer the public lands for sale raised a number of important questions: Should competitive bidding be employed; what should be the minimum price of the land; in what sizes should parcels of land be offered; should government credit be provided; should there be any restrictions on the amounts any one buyer could acquire; and at what rate should new lands be sold? The Land Ordinance of 1785, a landmark in the history of public land policy, was the first comprehensive attempt to answer these questions, even before the adoption of the federal constitution. It established the rectangular survey system (dividing the land into townships each composed of thirty-six-square-mile sections) that is still employed. It also set the requirement that lands be surveyed before being sold, following the New England practice in this regard, and established the policy of setting aside land for the support of schools.

The method of sale was to be competitive bidding with a minimum acceptable price, initially one dollar per acre. If the land was not sold when offered, it would subsequently be available for purchase by anyone at the minimum price. No restrictions were to be placed on the size of individual parcels or on the total amount of land that could be owned by any one individual. Squatters were regarded with disfavor and were to be given no special opportunities. Another provision of great future importance was the reservation of one section per township to be used for the support of education.

The 1785 Land Ordinance had little immediate impact as land sales at first moved at a slow pace. The overall question of land sales did not receive much further attention until the Land Act of 1796, the first significant action by the new Congress with respect to the public lands. This act represented an attempt to stimulate a more rapid pace of sales and to collect higher revenues to meet government obligations. Over the next sixty-five years, as maximizing revenues proved impractical in practice and in growing conflict with other important objectives, Congress would be required over and over again to back away from its revenue objectives.

Credit and Relief: The First Step toward Free Land

The congressional expectation that large revenues would be obtained from public land was frustrated by a number of hard realities. There were large areas of land within the existing states still available for settlement at prices significantly below the price of federal lands. Congress had created military districts where revolutionary war veterans were entitled to free land. Veterans often preferred to sell their entitlement cheaply, undercutting federal land prices. New settlers in the West typically arrived with few financial resources and thus could not afford to pay much, especially in advance, as Congress was asking. They would always be tempted simply to pick out and settle on a choice piece of land without permission. The vastness of the lands on the western frontier and the small presence of the federal government meant that the ejection of squatters was unlikely.

In the years immediately following the Land Act of 1796, these factors combined to hold land sales at low levels. In 1799 the federal government received only $843 from this source. By 1800 Congress had decided that changes were necessary. Additional land sale offices closer to actual areas of settlement were authorized. The size of parcels offered was reduced, in the hope of making them easier to afford. The most important step was to grant government credit, allowing equal payments over four years. Henceforth, settlers would be able to move onto the land after paying one-quarter of the government selling price. To be sure, once there, it would prove very difficult to remove them, whether they met their payments or not. The credit system was strongly opposed by Secretary of the Treasury Albert Gallatin, who predicted that many settlers would never pay. Gallatin proposed instead full cash sales but with a substantial reduction in the price of land. The resulting increase in land sales, he believed, would generate more revenue over the long run.

As many had predicted, by 1806 a substantial number of settlers were seriously in arrears and faced eviction. Congress now had to decide between revenue and other objectives. Granting relief would create a precedent almost certain to lead to new occupancy by settlers with poor prospects and to further demands for relief. In the end Congress put aside its revenue objectives and granted settlers prior to the Land Act an extension of their payment period. A much broader relief act was passed in 1809, and by 1820 a total of eleven relief acts had passed. As historian Roy Robbins observed, "After 1806, in fact, relief acts came to be passed almost as regularly as annual appropriation bills."[5]

Granting of credit was finally abolished in 1820. Congress, however, would still have to pass a series of further relief acts for settlers who had bought land prior to 1820 and who now faced forfeiture. Under a general 1821 relief act, settlers were given as many as eight years to complete payment on the land, interest was forgiven, and those who immediately paid the balance received a 37½ percent discount. A final relief act in 1832 abandoned altogether the pretense of holding debtors due. It granted anyone who had previously forfeited land an entitlement to new lands to make up for whatever had been lost. Thus in the end the federal government simply made land fully available without charge to those who could not or would not pay for it.

The credit experience had required the federal government to face the first major challenge to its professed objectives. Despite earlier proclamations, when confronted with the actual necessity of evicting settlers, the government had capitulated. Settlers had often taken large risks and made valiant efforts against Indians, hunger, disease, isolation, and other obstacles. To deprive settlers of the lands they had occupied, where this land was surrounded by a huge expanse of still-vacant public land, simply because the settler could not pay, seemed cruel and unfair. As a practical matter, it could not be done. Far from Washington, on a frontier occupied by many other settlers in similar circumstances, eviction of squatters was an impossibility. Moreover, two new considerations were emerging, a growing recognition that the East could benefit economically from western settlement and a developing sense of pride in westward movement that was to become the belief in a manifest destiny of the United States.

The Establishment of Preemption Rights

Learning from these experiences, Congress might have faced up to the impracticality of its previous policy, abandoned its hopes for high revenues, and adopted a policy to enhance the rights of the settler in the interest of western development. However, Congress never seriously considered such a course. Lawmakers, especially those from eastern states, still regarded the squatter as a lawbreaker. Congress also objected to the acquisition of lands for speculative purposes, which it regarded as giving away the value of the land to private parties. Given the continuing need for revenues, Congress turned back to a straight cash system of land sales. However, finally following the advice of Gallatin fifteen years earlier, the price was reduced from $2 per acre to $1.25, a level at which it would be fixed for seventy years.

Settlers didn't much care; they still continued to move onto the land without permission. Since the federal government had little power to remove them, and little inclination to try, the greatest threat to the squatter was the possibility that the government might sell the land to someone else. To ensure against this possibility, settlers pressured the government in various ways. For example, land could be sold only after it had been surveyed, so preventing a survey became an important settler objective in many areas.

The most effective device was to form extralegal organizations to control the outcome of government land sales. Potential outside bidders faced attacks on their person and property. Eventually these practices were so widely employed that they would become the accepted code of the frontier; no self-respecting westerner would bid against a squatter who had already occupied a piece of federal land. In some areas squatter rights were formalized, albeit outside regular legal institutions. The initial settler on the land established a claim that gave him the right to buy the land—frequently up to a maximum of 160 acres—for the minimum government price when the land was eventually put up for sale. Such claims were sellable and were recognized by banks and in some cases even by state laws. Historian Roscoe Lokken describes one Iowa claims association in action:

> On one occasion a man named Crawford located a claim north of Iowa City and built a cabin on it. But William Sturgis had already registered this tract with the secretary and therefore had the support of the claim association in ejecting the trespasser. In response to a meeting called for that purpose, a group of men proceeded to Crawford's cabin. He was given an opportunity to leave peaceably and was offered payment for his labor. His refusal of both resulted in the destruction of his cabin "in fifteen minutes." The claim jumper found himself, ax in hand, "in the center of the vacant space once occupied by his cabin." The association had to take action a second time before the matter was finally settled. Crawford later tried to secure legal redress, but since "it was almost impossible to find a

judge, lawyer or juror in Iowa who was not a claimholder, his effort was not crowned with much success."[6]

Seeking to achieve a formal legal status for these arrangements, westerners regularly requested that Congress grant preemption rights. As noted above, preemption gave a squatter a preferential right to purchase the land that he had already occupied and developed. By 1820 Congress had already passed twenty-four limited statutes for particular areas that retroactively granted preemption rights to existing settlers. Between 1820 and 1837 another fifteen preemption laws were enacted, two of a general nature, but all still limited to squatters who had occupied land prior to passage of the laws. Congress steadfastly refused to give new settlers the same rights in advance.

Finally in 1841 a general preemption law was enacted guaranteeing to future settlers as well the right to occupy and then later to purchase 160 acres of surveyed land at the minimum government land price of $1.25 per acre. As has happened so often in the history of the public lands, Congress was formally recognizing a right that as a practical matter had already been well established through extralegal means. The leading historian of public land policy, Paul Wallace Gates, comments that informal claims associations were so successful in preventing competition at government land sales that "it is doubtful whether any important sales of public lands were held between 1835 and 1860 at which such combinations did not function, and almost invariably they accomplished their objectives."[7] The preemption legislation thus was regarded in some areas more as a legal nicety than an essential requirement. One Iowa newspaper commented in 1841 that "to be sure, it is far better to have the law, as it legalizes a course which, although universally in vogue, was in fact unlawful."[8]

Military Bounties and Reduced Prices: Further Steps toward Free Land

After the squatter finally obtained a full legal right to buy the land he had already occupied, western attention turned to the price of land. At a price of $1.25 per acre, many settlers found it difficult to raise the $200 required to buy 160 acres of land. Moreover, there was a wide range in the quality of land. In some areas poor land had gone unsold for ten or twenty years because the uniform price of $1.25 per acre exceeded its real value.

By the 1840s westerners had been pressing for two decades for a policy of reduced land prices on lower quality land—so called "graduation" of land prices. The famous defender of western interests, Senator Thomas Hart Benton of Missouri, had unsuccessfully introduced legislation for a graduation policy since the 1820s. Easterners always opposed the idea on the grounds that it represented an unwarranted western attempt to acquire cheap land and would undermine the government's objective to achieve significant land sale revenues. Finally, however, in the late 1840s Congress took actions that had the practical effect—if not the intent—of implementing such a policy.

Since the American Revolution, Congress had used grants of free land to attract soldiers and to reward veterans—a precursor to current veterans benefits. This policy was also adopted in the Mexican-American war of 1846–48. An 1847 act authorized free grants of 160 acres to veterans who served more than one year and forty acres to those who served less. The Bounty Land Act of 1850 generously extended these benefits to veterans of military service at any time since 1790 and reduced to nine months the time required to gain full benefits.

Many veterans, however, had little interest or inclination to move to the West, which made it necessary for Congress to allow the sale (technically "assignment") of veterans' rights. Active markets sprang up in the military land scrip issued to veterans. The bearer of such scrip could use it only for those lands that had already been offered for sale but had not been purchased. Because of this limited scope for use, because the scrip was typically offered for sale in the East far from land sale areas, and because fraudulent scrip was a risk, military scrip sold at a substantial discount—typically 30 to 40 percent off the government land price.

In this way military bounties provided for graduated land prices, making available at a lower price land that was less desirable and had not been sold when originally offered. This graduation measure was adopted, however, as a military measure, not as a deliberate policy of reduced prices. Gates comments that "in considering new bounty land legislation, Congress gave little thought to the effect this would have upon land policies then in operation, except that such a step would reduce revenue from the lands."[9]

The West in fact resented military bounties, partly because the low prices fostered widespread speculation, and partly—and more importantly—because bounties were promoted by eastern interests to benefit eastern veterans. As westerners continued to push for a formal graduation policy, Congress finally enacted the Graduation Act in 1854. The price for lands that had gone unsold for ten to fifteen years was reduced to one dollar per acre. Prices for lands unsold for longer periods were further reduced in proportion to the length of time they had gone unsold. Lands on the market for more than thirty years were offered at 12½ cents per acre. The maximum amount of land that could be purchased under these provisions was 320 acres.

Together military bounties and graduation sales significantly reduced the effective selling price for public lands. Between 1855 and 1862 a total of 72.1 million acres of public land was sold, either for straight cash payment or for military scrip. Of this acreage only 23 percent was for the full price of $1.25 per acre. Graduation sales represented 36 percent and military scrip sales 41 percent of all land sales.

Free Land to Railroads and Homesteaders

The next logical step after preemption and lower land prices was to make land available for free. It would represent the full triumph of policies favorable to settlers and rapid western development, entirely abandoning the old government objective of raising revenues. In the mid-nineteenth century strong forces were building in addition to the traditional western interests favoring such a policy. Many easterners now recognized that much could be gained from rapid economic development of western lands. The West could supply raw materials for the finished goods of the East, which could then be sold in the growing markets of the West. Massive foreign immigration was alleviating the long-standing eastern fear that western settlement would depopulate the East. Thus, Horace Greeley of "Go west, young man" fame was a leading proponent of free land, trumpeting from the pages of the New York *Daily Tribune*: "Every thousand hardy, efficient workers who flow West on free lands would leave places open for as many others; and these taking a step upward, would leave room for advancement of as many more and so on. Even to those workers who will never migrate, free land at the West would be a great and lasting benefit."[10]

Until the Civil War policies favorable to western development had to overcome strong Southern resistance. Although at first allied with the West and supportive of federal land grants for the building of canals and roads, the South had later come to see further western growth as a greater benefit to the industrial North than the agricultural South. Moreover, admittance of too many western states would make it impossible to maintain the political balance on slavery.

In 1850 the first railroad land grant could pass Congress only because the line ran from Chicago, Illinois, to Mobile, Alabama, and thus received both Northern and Southern support. Under this grant, the Illinois Central and Mobile and Ohio railroads obtained the even-numbered sections within six miles of the line. For the remaining alternating government sections, the price was doubled to $2.50 per acre, a policy adopted with future railroad grants. Proponents of railroad grants asserted that the grants were really costless, because the government's remaining half of the land produced the same revenues that could have been received from the sale of all the land in the absence of the railroad. More railroad grants followed in the next few years. By 1856 a total of nineteen million acres of public land had been granted for the construction of 8,647 miles of railroad lines. These early grants differed from later grants in that the land was first given to states, which then transferred it to the railroads.

Prior to the Civil War, disputes between the North and the South as to the best terminal point blocked the granting of land for a transcontinental railroad. Finally, in 1862, the Pacific Railroad Act authorized a grant to the Union Pacific Railroad of the odd-numbered sections within five miles on both sides of a line that went from Omaha to San Francisco. In 1864 Congress increased the grant to the Union Pacific to ten miles on each side and also authorized a vast grant—by far the largest ever made—to the Northern Pacific Railroad for a route from Lake Superior to Seattle. The Northern Pacific received alternating sections for twenty miles on each side in existing states and for forty miles in the territories, amounting to forty-five million acres in all for 2,100 miles of railroad. The grant to the Northern Pacific included 23 percent of the land in the state of North Dakota and 15 percent of that in Montana. The huge size of such grants, the slowness of the railroads in disposing of the lands to settlers, predatory pricing policies, and other resentments stirred strong opposition to further railroad grants. The last such grant was made in 1871. All told, a huge domain of 212 million acres of public land (37 million of which were later forfeited) had been transferred to the railroads.

The immediate purpose was to provide financial assistance to the railroads for construction. The railroads also became huge proprietors responsible for development of vast areas, a corporate throwback to William Penn and other colonial proprietors of vast land grants from the English crown. The proprietorship system had been firmly rejected by early Congresses but, as has happened often in the history of public land policy, eventually returned in a new guise.

In promoting settlement of their lands, the railroads' performance on the whole has been judged favorably. Although large areas of checkerboard lands remain to this day in railroad ownership, in many cases the railroads actively sought land sales and settlement. They were generally restrained in their pricing and credit policies, out of fear of political retaliation, among other reasons. The Harvard University historian of western settlement, Frederick Merk, reported that in the Great Plains the railroads "advertised with extraordinary enthusiasm. The Northern Pacific Railroad kept 800 agents in various European countries distributing literature and assisting emigrants."[11]

Although there was wide support, passage of a homestead act also was blocked for many years by Southern opposition. In 1860 the Republican Party made homesteading a leading plank in its campaign platform. On May 20, 1862, after the South had seceded, Congress enacted the Homestead Act. It provided that each homesteader could acquire 160 acres of free public land by residing on and cultivating this land for five years. The settler could also commute his homestead right after six months through a purchase at the going price of $1.25 per acre, similar to preemption.

Incongruously, the two private recipients of free land in the West thus were the railroad—the public symbol of monopoly and concentrated power—and the homesteader—the symbol of the self-made individual. There was in fact a substantial conflict between the interests of the two groups. The bulk of railroad grants had been made before homesteading reached high levels, and thus the railroads in many instances had already selected the most desirable lands. Large areas committed to Indian reservations and state land grants also restricted the lands that were available for homesteading. The pickings were often slim by the time settlers arrived. Gates comments that:

> With over 125,000,000 acres of railroad lands, 140,000,000 acres of state lands, 100,000,000 acres of Indian lands, and 100,000,000 acres of federal lands for sale in large or small blocks, and with the opportunities for evasion of the Homestead and Pre-emption laws and their variations outlined above, it is obvious that there were few obstacles in the way of speculation and land monopolization after 1862. As before, it was still possible for foresighted speculators to precede settlers into the frontier, purchase the best lands, and hold them for the anticipated increase in value which the succeeding wave of settlers would give to them.[12]

The Homestead Act embodied the lessons of the settlement of the humid Middle West farming areas over the half century previous to its passage. By 1862, however, few of these areas were still available to homesteaders. For example, the extremely fertile lands of Iowa, the ideal setting for homesteading, had already been largely transferred to private ownership by 1862. Only 2.5 percent of Iowa lands were homesteaded. In the 1860s and 1870s the frontier had reached the states of North and South Dakota, Nebraska, and Kansas.

In the eastern parts of these states there still remained good farm land that received adequate rainfall. For these lands the Homestead Act was well suited and on the whole worked satisfactorily. However, as the frontier moved farther westward, it would reach much more arid regions less suitable for farming. Indeed, within fifteen years after the passage of the Homestead Act it was becoming clear to the most observant students of the public lands that the Act was gravely flawed for the new areas where western settlement would be taking place.

John Wesley Powell and the Public Land Commission of 1879

John Wesley Powell was one of those who saw most clearly the problems of the Homestead Act. Powell had become famous as an explorer of the Colorado River and for his scientific reports on western geology, climate, and Indian culture. He knew full well that much of the West was in fact a desert. While the average rainfall in the Midwest was thirty-five inches per year, it was as little as five inches in some areas of the West and in normal years exceeded fifteen inches only in the higher mountain regions.

Powell reported such findings in 1878 in his classic *Report on the Lands of the Arid Region* of the United States.[13] He proposed a comprehensive redesign of public land policies west of the 100th meridian, the approximate dividing line between humid and arid regions. The departure point for Powell's analysis was that without irrigation most of the West was not suitable for farming. The best and often the only feasible use for most of the land was livestock grazing. In this use much larger acreages were required for an economical ranch operation than the 160 acres allowed under the Homestead Act.

Powell cautiously proposed 2,560 acres—huge by eastern standards—as a suitable ranch size, even though he was concerned that this was probably not enough. In the West fifty to one hundred acres are normally required to obtain sufficient forage to feed one cow for one year. A ranch of 2,500 acres thus could support thirty-five to fifty cows, hardly a large operation. In some desert areas of the Southwest, each cow requires five hundred acres—almost a square mile—to supply it with forage for a single year. In such circumstances viable ranches would have to be fifty thousand to one hundred thousand acres, and a large ranch would need even more land. By contrast, in those areas of the West that could be irrigated, Powell believed that 160 acres was more than adequate for a farm. Indeed, he proposed eighty acres.

Other areas were suitable for mining and timber, more valuable uses than livestock grazing. Powell recommended that public land laws be tailored to each use. A comprehensive system of land classification was proposed to allocate specific areas of land to uses appropriate to these areas.

Powell also saw the need to abandon the rectangular layout of farms and ranches that was based on the use of survey methods dating back to the eighteenth century. In the West, access to river and stream banks, water holes, and other water sources was often the key to the use of the land. Powell recommended that each rancher have access to water, requiring the flexible design of ownership boundaries. He sought to avoid giving the owner of a single water hole, or points of access along the shores of a river, the effective control over all the surrounding rangelands. Powell argued that the best way to achieve this goal would be to establish collective ownership of the water and surrounding range. He recommended the formation of grazing cooperatives for this purpose.

Powell was a persuasive spokesman for his views and an influential figure in Washington governing circles. At his urging, and with the strong support of the recently formed National Academy of Sciences and of the Secretary of the Interior Carl Schurz, the Congress in 1879 authorized the creation of a commission to study the public lands. The commission work clearly reflected the thinking of Powell, who was a member. Its 1880 report stated that:

There was a kind of homogeneity in the quality and value of the land of [the old Northwest Territory]. It was all valuable for agriculture and habitation, but in the western portion of our country it is otherwise. Its most conspicuous characteristic from an economic point of view is its heterogeneity. One region is exclusively valuable for mining, another solely for timber, a third for nothing but pasturage, and a fourth serves no useful purpose whatever. . . . Hence, it has come to pass that the homestead and preemption laws are not suited for securing the settlement of more than an insignificant portion of the country.[14]

The commission recommended repeal of the preemption law and a gradual reduction in the price of rangeland to 12½ cents per acre, reflecting its low value in grazing use. It suggested 2,560 acres as the basic size of units for homesteading or other disposal on lands used for grazing. The commission also recommended the classification of the public lands according to timber, grazing, mineral, or other best use and the development of public land policies specifically designed for each type of land.

An Era of Fraud and Abuse

Powell's arguments were scientifically correct but unpersuasive to Congress. Few of the recommendations of the 1880 commission were accepted. It had taken seventy-five years for the nation to overcome its antipathy to the squatter and to accept the principles of the Homestead Act. Once accepted, they became the new gospel. The Republican Party of the time saw the Homestead Act as one of its great historic accomplishments, a triumph for the little man, free-market individualism, and personal initiative. The development of the West, with which the Homestead Act was closely associated in the public mind, was seen as contributing importantly to the rapid industrial growth of the United States after the Civil War.

Thus Powell's ideas faced formidable obstacles. Most of his recommendations would eventually be followed in some form, but this would typically occur only much later. Instead, there was widespread farm failure in the arid West; large waste of timber, minerals, and other natural resources; and massive land-law fraud and abuse. It was only after overwhelming evidence had accumulated that it was possible to penetrate the aura of the Homestead Act. The vindication of Powell's views did not occur until fifty years later with the passage of the Taylor Grazing Act in 1934.

In the meantime the nation was saddled with a system of public land laws that could not work for the lands on which they were being applied. There was no legal way to acquire the large acreage required for a viable ranch, timber operation, or other production unit in the West. The momentum of westward movement, however, was much stronger than the obstacle of ill-conceived land laws. The resulting collision yielded a system that institutionalized massive fraud and abuse of the public land laws, which eventually came to be seen widely in the West as objects of ridicule. It was understood and accepted that they would simply have to be ignored.

As we have seen, this was not the first such instance of unworkable laws that had to be circumvented in one way or another. Squatters had already colluded to control government land sales prior to the enactment of the preemption law in 1841. However, the practices of the late nineteenth century were perhaps still more flagrant, involving wider lying and misrepresentation by settlers and speculators alike.

One early demonstration of how to circumvent the public land laws was provided by officials of state government. Overall, the states were the largest single recipients of federal grants of land. Until 1848, on admittance to the union, states received one section per township for educational purposes. Later new states received two sections, and after 1894 this was increased again to four sections. States also received a variety of other grants for educational and economic development. Some of the largest grants to states were made under the infamous Swamp Act of 1850, close to fifty million acres in all. To obtain these grants of land, state officials resorted to perjury and outlandish misrepresentation, a precedent for a style of flagrant fraud that the private sector was to emulate later in the century.

The rationale for the Swamp Act was reasonable enough. Many states had large swamp areas (now called wetlands), which in that era were regarded as of no value until they were drained. The federal government was not prepared to undertake this task itself. Hence, Congress authorized the transfer to state governments of swamplands within their boundaries. The theory was that the states would drain the lands in order to capture sizeable revenues from their sale.

In administering the Swamp Act, federal authorities let the states themselves identify swamplands, requiring them to submit confirming testimony and other evidence of swamp character. Tempted by the prospect of acquiring large new federal lands, the states stretched and then went beyond any conceivable notion of legitimate swampland. A special study of more than one million swamp acres selected by the state of Missouri found only sixty-four thousand acres that could reasonably be classified as wet; the rest were clearly dry and arable. Mountainous regions were included in some state selections. Numerous conflicts arose between state selections and land already claimed by settlers— and thus unlikely to be legitimate swampland. It was, interestingly enough, a predecessor of current wetlands disputes, except that today it is the federal government that is attempting to assert new public control over private swamps (wetlands) that seem to many to lack true swamp-like qualities.

The Swamp Act promoted widespread public cynicism. Stories were circulated such as the Mississippi selection agent who carried his boat in a horse-drawn trailer over a large pine tree acreage and then swore that the lands were navigable. Roy Robbins described the Swamp Act as "one of the greatest land-grabs in the history of the public domain. Only a small part of the proceeds of the original grants ever went to the purposes for which they were intended."[15]

In the 1870s Congress authorized several new methods of transferring land from federal to private ownership. None worked as intended. Enacted in 1873, the Timber Culture Act had the stated purpose of increasing the number of trees on western lands. The act authorized grants of 160 acres to settlers who would cultivate forty of these acres with trees for ten years. However, in practice a main use of the act was to obtain additional acreage beyond the 160 acres available under the Homestead Act. Simply by making a statement of intent (formally, an "entry"), a settler could control 160 acres for ten years, whether that settler ever intended to plant trees or not. In many cases, before the ten years were up, entrants would relinquish control for a price, and an active market developed in relinquishments. The commissioner of the General Land Office reported in 1883 that "my information leads me to the conclusion that a majority of entries under the Timber-Culture Act are made for speculative purposes and not for the cultivation of timber. . . . No trees are to be seen over vast regions of country where Timber-Culture entries have been most numerous."[16]

The Desert Land Act of 1877 authorized the sale of 640 acres to settlers who irrigated the lands within three years. However, in practice there was little an individual settler could do to build irrigation works; costly systems covering sizeable areas were generally necessary. From Arizona a report was received that "more perjury is committed" under the Desert Land Act than was ever seen before.[17] In 1884 the commissioner of the General Land Office reported that "hearings in contested cases and examinations by special agents have disclosed a want of any attempt to irrigate the land in many instances, that desert entries are frequently made of lands not desert in character, . . . that lands taken up under this act are often used for stock-grazing."[18]

The Timber and Stone Act of 1878 allowed settlers in the states of California, Oregon, and Washington to buy 160 acres at a minimum price of $2.50 per acre. The law was intended to make available only small amounts of timber for local use. Purchasers were required to swear that the timber was in fact for nearby use and that they had no intention to sell the lands to speculators. Any such statements were in practice widely ignored. The Timber and Stone Act was used by timber companies to accumulate large blocks of prime forest lands in the Pacific Northwest. Public land historian Benjamin Hibbard reports that "within five years the practical effect of this law in transferring public timberlands almost directly to large corporations and timber speculators was recognized in official reports, and its repeal was strongly urged."[19]

The new laws in the 1870s supplemented the continuing mainstays of the public land system, the Preemption Act and the Homestead Act. These laws were themselves subject to wide circumvention. The purpose was generally either to obtain land for speculation or to obtain the large acreage required for economical timber harvesting, mining, ranching, and other enterprises in the West. A company might, for example, gather its employees together and have each worker make an entry for 160 acres, testifying that they had occupied and improved the land. On making payment to the government, these employees would transfer the land to the company. In 1882 the report of the commissioner of the General Land Office, which recommended repeal of the preemption law, described abuses of "great magnitudes—a material portion of the preemption entries now made are fraudulent in character, being chiefly placed upon valuable timber or mineral lands, or water rights, and made in the interest and by the procurement of others, and not for the purpose of residence and improvement, by the professed preemptor."[20]

The Homestead Act was the object of similar manipulations, especially the commutation provision of the act. Other frauds occurred in making the obligatory demonstration that 160 acres had been occupied and cultivated for the required five years. The General Land Office had so few personnel and was so overworked that it was typically impossible to make inspections on site. Settlers frequently lied outright or resorted to conscience-soothing tactics as described in the following public lands report.

It is common knowledge in the city of Duluth, Minnesota, that in 1892, 1893, and 1894 persons desiring to commute would take an ordinary dry goods box, make it resemble a small house with doors, windows and a shingled roof. This box would be 14 by 16 inches, or larger, and would be taken by the entryman to his claim. On the day of commutation proof he would appear at the local office, swear that he had upon his claim a good board house, 14 by 16 with shingled roof, etc. The proof on its face would appear excellent and was readily used by the local officers.[21]

The evasions employed by timber companies to acquire large forest areas were particularly important in that the later counterreaction would be instrumental in building public support for creating a national forest system. The General Land Office reported that "in all the pine region of Lake Superior and the Upper Mississippi, where vast areas have been settled under the pretense of agriculture under the Homestead and Pre-emption laws, scarcely a vestige of agriculture appears. The same is true on the Pacific Coast and in the mountain regions of Colorado, Utah, Montana and Idaho."[22]

The Adoption of Reforms

By the 1880s the pervasive evasions of the public land laws were attracting national attention. The appointment in 1885 of William Sparks to be commissioner of the General Land Office helped to make the whole country aware of these problems. In his first report as commissioner, Sparks lamented that "the idea prevails to an almost universal extent that, because the government in its generosity has provided for the donation of the public domain to its citizens, a strict compliance with the conditions imposed is not essential. Men who would scorn to commit a dishonest act toward an individual, though he were a total stranger, eagerly listen to every scheme for evading the letter and spirit of the settlement laws, and in a majority of instances I believe avail themselves of them."[23]

Such criticism of western practices of long standing alienated powerful groups in the West. Sparks was forced to resign in 1887. However, his efforts helped to create pressures that would soon bring significant changes in the public land laws. In 1891 Congress enacted the General Revision Act, which repealed the Preemption Act and the Timber Culture Act. The minimum time for commutation under the Homestead Act was raised from six to fourteen months.

Another important congressional action was to eliminate cash sales of land. After the Civil War, land that had previously been surveyed and unsuccessfully offered for sale was still available for cash purchase. Small settlers opposed cash sales because they preferred to have all lands reserved for homesteading and other less expensive ways of acquiring land. Settlers also preferred to manipulate poorly designed laws to their benefit, rather than actually paying the government directly for land.

However, the attempt of Congress in the 1891 legislation to remedy the basic deficiencies of the public land laws proved largely counterproductive. Congress was unable or unwilling to take on the task of designing a new land system that would be workable in the actual circumstances of the West. Instead, Congressmen preferred to condemn western behavior in evading the laws and attacked the symptoms of the system by abolishing some of the sources of greatest fraud and abuse. However, the result was not to reduce the total amount of fraud and abuse, but to redirect it.

In some ways extralegal activities became even more necessary. The Preemption Act and Timber Culture Act had provided a vehicle for legally obtaining an extra 160 acres beyond the 160 acres already available to the homesteader—or by using both laws to obtain an additional 320 acres. Cash sales had made substantial additional areas available for purchase legally. Gates comments that the 1891 repeal of these provisions of the public land laws "eliminated much of the flexibility that had enabled persons in the High Plains to acquire control over if not ownership of 320 or 480 acres." As a result, "Congress made it even more necessary for ranchers and others seeking to gain ownership of economic units to resort to fraud in a more systematic way than they had before 1891."[24]

With the public land laws still widely criticized, President Theodore Roosevelt formed a second public land commission in 1903. This commission came to conclusions similar to its predecessor in 1880. Once again drawing heavily on Powell's ideas, the cornerstone of its recommendations was classification of lands for their proper use and the adoption of different land policies appropriate to each type of use. For lands suited for livestock grazing, the commission recommended implementing grazing districts with controls on livestock numbers and imposing a grazing fee. Repeal of the Timber and Stone Act, combined with new authority for the sale of timber, was recommended for lands suited for timber harvesting. The commission proposed the creation of thirteen new forest reserves. It also favored further extending the commutation period under the Homestead Act to three years and changes to end abuses in the Desert Land Act.

The First Reservations in Public Ownership: The National Parks

By the end of the nineteenth century a new public land system was taking shape. The view took hold that retention and government management of public lands were the best policy. Partly it was a matter of public revulsion against the continuing fraud and abuse under the disposal laws. Few people outside the West understood that the objectionable practices were often unavoidable symptoms of a clumsily designed and in many ways misconceived land disposal system. The shift to a retention philosophy was also part of a much broader turn to government to solve the problems of the nation. During the progressive era many leading American intellectuals concluded that scientific management of the resources of the nation was necessary and that on the public lands the federal government was the best available instrument for achieving this purpose.

The first large areas set aside for permanent public ownership were for the purpose of preserving unique scenic and otherwise attractive sites in national parks. Yosemite Valley was given to the state of California for a park in 1864, adjoining federal lands were designated a national park in 1890, and the two areas were subsequently combined to form the current Yosemite National Park.

Yellowstone is generally considered to be the first national park. Its history is similar to several other early parks. The public knew little about Yellowstone until an explorer's report in 1868. Shortly thereafter, two more groups visited the park, the second of which included two prominent Montana citizens, Nicholas Langford and Cornelius Hedges. They were so impressed by what they saw that they are said to have agreed on the spot to seek preservation of the area for the whole nation. A bill was quickly introduced in Congress to remove two million acres from the possibility of any private land acquisition. It passed on March 1, 1872, with no great discussion or controversy. The Yellowstone area was so isolated at the time that no important commercial interests opposed creation of the park. Indeed, the one private party with a substantial stake in the matter was the railroad; it supported the park in hopes of greater tourist traffic and hotel business.[25] Congress had no idea that it was taking the first step in what would become the National Park System. John Ise, a historian of the national parks, considered passage of the bill to be ''so dramatic a departure from the general public land policy of Congress that it seems almost a miracle.''[26]

No money was appropriated to administer the new park until 1878 and in that year only $20,000 was set aside, mainly for roads. Because of political scandals and inadequate protection, the army was summoned in 1886 to run the park and remained there in this capacity for 30 years. The secretary of the interior prohibited hunting in 1880, but the ban was ineffective because the only penalty faced by poachers was ejection from the park area. Congress did not provide for prosecution of poachers until 1894. The contemporary features of a national park thus were evolving slowly, not as part of any grand design, but case by case as specific measures were adopted to address immediate problems.

In 1875 Mackinac Island in Michigan was designated to be the second national park, but it did not survive. The next parks were Yosemite (supplementing the existing state park), Sequoia, and General Grant (now Kings Canyon), all created in California in 1890. Spurred by intense national publicity concerning the plight of the giant trees, Congress authorized the Sequoia park to protect them and to function as a "public pleasure ground." Of the other two parks, at first Congress thought of the new areas as forest reservations.[27]

The last national park created in the nineteenth century was Mount Rainier in Washington State in 1899. Other important new parks were Crater Lake in 1902, Mesa Verde in 1906, and Glacier in 1910. In 1916 the modern park era commenced as Congress established the National Park Service to run a single national system of parks.

The setting aside of the early national parks was one of the success stories in the history of the public lands. In this case Congress acted ahead of its time, although less out of great foresight than because of the energetic efforts of a few preservationists, supported in some cases by railroad and hotel interests. A key factor was that a park generally did not involve a conflict with existing agricultural, timber, mining, and other commercial interests.

The Creation of the National Forest System

As noted above, in 1891 Congress enacted a broad reform of the public land laws, the General Revision Act. This act contained a section authorizing the president to "set apart and reserve in any State or Territory having public land bearing forests, any part of the public lands wholly or in part covered with timber or undergrowth."[28] This authority created the basis for the present system of national forests. Under the act President Benjamin Harrison soon proceeded to withdraw the first fourteen million acres of forest reserves.

The impetus for forest reservations arose from much the same popular pressures that in the year before had led to the creation of the Yosemite and General Grant forest reserves (only later to be designated national parks). No explicit provision for the presence of commercial activities was included in the 1891 legislation. Many proponents of creating reserves hoped that they would in fact be preserved in the manner of national parks.

However, given the large acreage and the opposition in the West to removal of so much land from active use, preservation probably was never a real option. Pressures intensified during the 1890s for public management for utilitarian purposes, resulting in 1897 in the passage of the Forest Management Act, the basic charter for the existing national forest system. Although this act did not provide an unambiguous mandate for management of the forests reserves, it did allow the government "to regulate the occupancy and use," a power that would later be construed broadly. Harvesting of timber was confined to "dead, mature, or large growth of trees," a limitation that also was to be interpreted flexibly in the future.

The enactment in 1897 of the Forest Management Act reflected the rising influence of the conservation movement, led by Gifford Pinchot. The act followed the publication of the recommendations of the National Forest Commission on which Pinchot served. Pinchot was later to be one of President Theodore Roosevelt's closest advisors, the founder of the Forest Service, and the leading conservationist spokesman for several decades. Pinchot's professed mission was to bring scientific management to the forests of the United States. In the late nineteenth century the scientific revolution was having a profound impact on American life. Steam power, railroad transportation, the telephone, the elevator, electricity, and many other inventions were transforming American society. There was evidence everywhere of the extraordinary consequences of concentrating the scientific skills of technical experts on the problems of society. Scientists were themselves organizing to provide this knowledge. The National Academy of Sciences was formed in 1863 and many other professional organizations were founded in the second half of the nineteenth century.

This movement reached forestry as well. The American Forestry Association was organized in 1876 and, although initially oriented toward preservation, "during the 1890s the organized forestry movement in the United States shifted its emphasis from saving trees from destruction to promoting sustained-yield forest management."[29] As a result, a major schism opened between old-style preservationists and the new breed of forest professionals led by Pinchot.

Even today the large differences between the groups are often not fully appreciated. This is probably because both preservationists and conservationists strongly favor public ownership of large land areas and vigorously oppose private influences in the administration of the public lands. Nevertheless, the basic objectives of the two movements frequently have been much different. The preservationist goal was to set aside the most important scenic, historic, geologic, and other special attractions of the nation to be maintained in a natural state. The conservation movement, by contrast, favored full use of land and natural resources for productive purposes. Private management was opposed by conservationists only because they believed it to be less efficient and effective in this respect than public management. Private timber operators, for example, were faulted not because they harvested the timber, but because they wasted large amounts of usable timber and made little effort to restock the forest for long-run sustainable yields. As Pinchot stated in 1903, "the object of our forest policy is not to preserve the forests because they are beautiful . . . or because they are refuges for the wild creatures of the wilderness . . . but . . . the making of prosperous homes. . . . Every other consideration becomes secondary."[30] Pinchot favored the inclusion of the national parks in the national forest system, where both timber harvesting and grazing would be allowed.

Pinchot and other conservationists rejected both political influence in management and free-market decisions. The nation's forests were instead to be managed by an elite group of professionals employing the principles of scientific forestry. In his insightful study of the conservation movement, Samuel Hays states:

> The deepest significance of the conservation movement, however, lay in its political implications: how should resource decisions be made and by whom? Each resource problem involved conflicts. Should they be resolved through partisan politics, through compromise among competing groups, or through judicial decision? To conservation such methods would defeat the inner spirit of the gospel of efficiency. Instead, experts, using technical and scientific methods, should decide all matters of development and utilization of resources, all problems of allocation of funds. Federal land management agencies should resolve land-use differences among livestock, wildlife, irrigation, recreation, and settler groups. National commissions should adjust power, irrigation, navigation, and flood control interests to promote the highest multiple purpose development of river basins. The crux of the gospel of efficiency lay in a rational and scientific method of making basic technological decisions through a single, central authority.[31]

Modifying the Homestead Act

Besides the repeal of failed laws and the setting aside of national parks and forests, a third type of reform was to modify some existing laws to try to make them more suited to the actual circumstances in the

West. The most important of these efforts was to increase the size of the basic land unit granted under the Homestead Act.

The first such increase was included in the Kinkaid Act in 1904, which authorized homesteading of 640 acres in arid western sections of Nebraska. In 1909 the Enlarged Homestead Act raised the acreage for homesteading to 320 acres of nonirrigable land throughout the West. A 1912 amendment reduced the required period of settlement from the traditional five years to three years. The Enlarged Homestead Act did stimulate much new homesteading. In 1910, 98,829 entries were filed for fourteen million acres of land, the second-highest amount ever. The final attempt to achieve a workable homestead law was the Stock-Raising Homestead Act of 1916. It was designed expressly for grazing lands and provided for acquisition of 640 acres.

The Kinkaid, Enlarged Homestead, and Stock-Raising Homestead acts proved to be the last gasps of the homestead approach. Many westerners still hoped for an infusion of people and economic development such as had occurred earlier in the Middle West. One strong supporter of the Stock-Raising Homestead Act, Congressman Harvey Fergusson of New Mexico, compared his state to Iowa except that "a full section, not a 160 acre homestead, would be necessary to a successful farm in New Mexico."[32]

In the end all three acts were failures. Except where irrigation was possible, 320 or 640 acres was still much too small for an economic farming or ranching operation in most of the West. The Great Plains historian Walter Prescott Webb commented acidly on the realism of the Enlarged Homestead Act. Referring to the Congressional reduction from five years to three in the required settlement period under the act, he noted that "[this reduction] seemed to grow out of the realization that on the remaining land the average family could not hold out for five years. The point of starvation was reached short of that, and consequently it would be humane to shorten the required time of residence to three years."[33]

In 1925 the secretary of the interior acknowledged what was becoming obvious to all when he declared that "stock raising on a tract limited to 640 acres is not practicable" and as a result "homesteads for stock raising are rapidly reverting to the open range."[34] A later study of the Stock-Raising Homestead Act found that under it "50 million acres of land, relatively good for grazing but submarginal for crops, had gone to private ownership. Of this quantity 25 million acres had been abandoned for cultivation and 11 million acres additional now constituted acute problem areas. On all of this area the range had been destroyed and will be of little use for years to come unless reseeded."[35]

The attempt to make homesteading applicable to the West had a huge cost in human terms in addition to the ordinary economic losses. Many thousands of settlers, with the encouragement of the federal government, tried to build viable farming units on the arid western rangelands. For a time between 1910 and 1920, unusually high rainfall offered false hopes; it seemed that many settlers might be succeeding, especially those using methods of dry-land farming. However, the return of normal weather patterns involving less rainfall and periods of severe drought forced large numbers of these settlers to leave the land. Abandoned farms left in their wake a rangeland stripped of natural vegetation and exposed to wind and water erosion. The unfortunate consequences are still visible in many portions of the western rangelands today.

On the poorest quality rangeland, as many as sixty thousand acres could be necessary for a one-hundred-cow operation. Ranches of larger herd sizes required correspondingly larger acreage. Even with the many informal methods for getting around the laws, it was not usually possible to assemble lands of such large acreage under private ownership. Large areas of western range therefore remained in public ownership, at least nominally open to any party wanting to use them.

The public rangelands were a grazing commons and they had the usual problems of a commons. Without controls on use, the benefits of sound practices would not accrue to any one rancher. Indeed, each rancher's incentive was to maximize the number of his own cattle. If each rancher followed this incentive, the result would be severe overgrazing.

To meet this threat, western ranchers once again had to devise solutions outside the law. In an initial attempt in the 1880s ranchers followed the example of earlier squatters on public lands and simply fenced in their own areas of public rangeland as their own property. Fifty years earlier, when the federal government was smaller, public attitudes were different, and when transportation and communications were poorer, nothing much might have been done. The federal government might well have ended up affirming rancher ownership rights to the rangelands, as it had done for legions of squatters before. However, western ranchers generally had to fence in acreage that to most easterners seemed to be an enormous amount of land. Moreover, a number of owners of large ranches were from Great Britain, arousing strong feelings against foreign ownership. Finally, the rangeland areas fenced in by ranchers were also sought by homesteaders. With populist sentiment on the upswing in American politics, the fences erected by big ranchers over wide areas of the West provoked outcries of scandal and a clamor for their removal. In 1885 Congress enacted legislation compelling removal of the fences. The reform commissioner of the General Land Office, William Sparks, acted promptly, tearing down many fences and, in 1887, even obtaining the assistance of the army in this task.

The scarcity of water in the West meant that over large areas of rangeland there were only a few available water sources. By making homestead or other entries, ranchers could frequently acquire these water sources. In this manner they obtained effective control over all the surrounding rangeland. In other cases access to public rangelands could be secured only by crossing particular lands. By acquiring these lands ranchers could control use of the much larger area of surrounding public rangeland.

Local ranchers also organized informally among themselves to control grazing levels. If necessary, their mutual agreements could be backed up by threats of violence. One student of grazing policy reports that ''by control of water sources, by legal fencing of their own properties and illegal fencing of federal property, by grazing-territory agreements among themselves, and by extralegal threats and pressures to fend off intruders, most ranchers were able to evolve a fairly satisfactory system for using the forage resources of the public lands to support their ranching operations.''[36]

By the mid 1920s it had become apparent even to the staunchest diehard that homesteading was not working in the arid West. The Hoover administration proposed to cede the lands to the western states in order to let them resolve how to manage the lands. A hundred years earlier John C. Calhoun had fought vigorously for cession of the public lands to the states. He argued that the Constitution required all states to enter on equal terms, yet the thirteen original states had owned all the public lands within their boundaries. Hoover's offer was a partial one, however, in that he wanted to retain the mineral rights for the federal government. The western states, concluding that without the mineral rights the remaining public lands were not worth much, showed little interest.

In the 1930s drought and overgrazing were causing mounting rangeland erosion and loss of the better vegetation. The poor economic condition of the livestock industry heightened pressures to run more cattle on the range. Virtually compelled to act, Congress in 1934 finally ended fifty years of agitation for formal rangeland controls by enacting the Taylor Grazing Act. This act basically extended the existing national forest system of grazing controls to the remaining public domain. Permits were required for grazing on public lands; ranchers were assigned to graze on specific areas ("allotments") where a specific level and time for grazing was prescribed; the amount of grazing allowed was based on a rancher's historic level of use; ranchers were required to own complementary base property; and a small grazing fee was assessed. Under the new law grazing districts were formed with rancher advisory boards. These boards were to play a large role in determining allocations of public land grazing among ranchers—and generally in making the new grazing system work. At the federal level a new agency, the Grazing Service, was formed in the Department of the Interior to administer the Taylor Grazing Act.

The Taylor Act largely ended private acquisition of the public domain.[37] The Homestead Act and other disposal laws were suspended. At first the act was limited to 80 million acres but soon it was extended to 142 million acres, containing the bulk of western rangelands still part of the public domain. Seventy-two years lay between the Homestead Act and the Taylor Grazing Act. Within fifteen years of enactment, it had already become clear to many that the Homestead Act was not suited to the Mountain West. Yet it proved impossible to achieve a decisive breakthrough to a new and workable land system. Instead, over the next decades a variety of halfway measures were adopted that failed as well. Settlers on the ground could only try as best they could to make practical adaptations, often outside the formal requirements of the law. In this manner the public land system moved small step by small step toward the eventual formalization of a system of grazing controls in the Taylor Act. The outcome was, in a number of key respects, the arrangement originally proposed by Powell in 1878.

Despite the prosettler land policies of the Colonial era, the Land Ordinance of 1785 had established high revenues from public land sales as the main objective of the public land system. Within fifteen years the possibility of achieving that objective was very much in doubt. Yet in that earlier era as well it had taken another sixty years for the land-law system to recognize the realities of western settlement and to evolve into the Homestead Act. In short, the nation had twice required more than sixty years of circumvention and illegality before a point could be reached where public and congressional understanding would allow a failed set of public land laws to be fully and explicitly discarded.

Lessons from Public Land History

The first 150 years of public land history saw a vast area of public land transferred to private ownership where it could be put to productive use. By this measure these policies were a great success. Those who benefited saw little reason to complain or to seek new laws. By another measure, however, the policies were a major failure. The public land laws were consistently based on flawed understandings of the circumstances of the lands; they prescribed inappropriate systems of disposal; and they seldom achieved the results intended by Congress.

The Preemption, Homestead, and Taylor Grazing acts ratified and gave further impetus to squatting and other practices that had already developed outside the law. There were thus two systems of public land management. One was an informal system that worked reasonably well enough. The second was the legislatively mandated system, which was mainly an obstacle to be overcome, often causing much economic waste and damage to the land. A leading student of the public lands, Benjamin Hibbard, observed in 1924 that "while therefore, there were many individuals with interesting, even excellent ideas on how the public domain should be administered, it cannot be said that a conscious policy worthy of the name existed. It was rather a series of expedient actions put into practice from time to time which must perforce be gathered together, classified as best they may be, and called the public policies."[38]

The history of the public lands offers a basic challenge to today's widely accepted ideas about government policy making. According to many people, public policies are, or at least should be, formed through a rational process in which the government first identifies a problem, develops and analyzes alternative policy solutions, and then selects the best from among the policy alternatives. This concept involves a "top-down" policy-making process. Historically, however, where public land policies have been successful, they have almost always been "bottom up." They arose first in common practice, very often at odds with the intentions of members of Congress and the executive branch. In many cases the steps required to meet the practical needs of the frontier involved steps that were not only inconsistent with congressional intentions, but also illegal. The public land laws in fact left settlers in the West with few other options. Eventually the common practice would gain greater official acceptance and then would finally be incorporated into the law. The process of evolution from practical action on the ground to new public land law has commonly taken many years to complete—on some occasions more than half a century. The ultimate result has often been the official recognition of a private practice or right that had developed long before on the public lands.

Why were the legislators in Washington so consistently out of touch with the actual circumstances on the land in the West? One explanation seems to lie in the great difficulty of changing public thinking once it had fixed on an idea. The American public as a whole was not willing to abandon ideas until they had failed repeatedly. This rigidity was reinforced by the moralistic quality of public land debates, the tendency to perceive public land mangement as one important element in saving the world. In many cases, by the time public opinion caught up and the public was willing to accept new practical solutions, the circumstances of the public lands had changed again. The public and the legislature thus were caught in a cycle of always mistakenly applying the lessons of the past to new and different problems in the present.

Another important factor was the large distance of the policy makers in the nation's capital from the lands on the western frontier. The majority of congressmen from the older eastern states lacked firsthand knowledge of conditions on the lands. With little direct contradiction offered by personal experience, it was easy for them to continue to believe what was consistent with their own ideological preconceptions. They may well have believed they were doing good in the world, and they probably felt good about this, and they had no way of knowing any better. The people of the West thus became pawns to the romantic imagination of the East.

That the issues involved matters of land ownership and the exercise of property rights contributed further to this tendency. In other nations whole Marxist revolutions were fought in the name of perfecting society through abolishing the selfish motives of private property. The depth of feeling about property—whether favorable or unfavorable—tends to inflame thinking on the subject. For years easterners could not accept that settler squatting should be given formal legitimacy, whether through preemption rights or homesteading. For them squatting was simply a morally and legally unacceptable infringement on the property rights of the government.

The Homestead Act survived long after it clearly began doing major damage to the land and had become subject to widespread fraud and abuse because the idea of the small farmer acquiring his own plot of land through his own initiative and hard work had such immense popular appeal to easterners and westerners alike. In the face of this romantic ideal a contrary reality on the land, even when it was pointed out by people who really knew the West, carried little weight.

There have always been a few realistic individuals who recognized the deficiencies of current policies and proposed improvements. In 1804 Albert Gallatin explained why credit policies would lead inevitably to widespread settler defaults sixteen years before defaults became so pervasive that Congress was forced to abolish credit. John Wesley Powell pointed out the policy significance of the arid conditions throughout much of the West sixty years before Congress could accept this hard reality. Such people had stature and prominence in their time and their views were widely known. Yet until the correctness of their thinking could be proven by hard and bitter experience, rational arguments were not enough. When they could not change the law, people in the West simply adapted as best they could. To the extent that they succeeded, they also diminished the urgency of change.

Conclusion

Matters have not changed all that much today. The West still complains about a lack of understanding in the East of its true circumstances. Westerners are still being forced to circumvent faulty laws. Debates about public land policies are frequently charged with a level of emotion suggesting that issues of ideological correctness, if not of religious conviction, are the primary matter at stake. Members of Congress still deliver moralistic sermons on the transgressions of the West. In the past such infusing of public land issues with broader symbolic significance frequently blocked the practical thinking necessary to devise effective policies. And today it is most of all the old scientific management theories of the progressive era that stand as a barrier to the development of new institutions for the public lands.

The thinking of the progressive era provided the grounds for retention of lands in federal ownership, comprehensive land use planning, land management agencies to be run by expert professionals, and many other features of the current public land system. But if scientific management has failed, then this whole system comes into question. The central problem on the public lands in the twenty-first century will be to find a new set of institutions shaped by a new set of ideas—a new paradigm, if you will—in place of the old progressive vision. Yet this new vision will have to answer an old question: Who will have control over the land? That is to say, who will exercise the rights to the use of the land?

Notes

1. Quoted in Frederick Jackson Turner, "The Significance of the Frontier in American History," in George Taylor, ed., *The Turner Thesis: Concerning the Role of the Frontier in American History* (Boston: D. C. Heath, 1956): 13.

2. Julian P. Boyd, *The Papers of Thomas Jefferson*, quoted in Paul W. Gates, *History of Public Land Law Development* (Washington, D.C.: Government Printing Office, 1968): 62.

3. Quoted in Gates, *History of Public Land Law Development*: 122.

4. From *American State Papers, Public Lands*, quoted in Benjamin Horace Hibbard, *A History of the Public Land Policies* (Madison, Wis.: University of Wisconsin Press, 1965): 2.

5. Roy M. Robbins, *Our Landed Heritage: The Public Domain 1776–1970* (Lincoln, Nebr.: University of Nebraska Press, 1976): 25.

6. Roscoe L. Lokken, *Iowa: Public Land Disposal* (Iowa City, Iowa: Historical Society of Iowa, 1942): 73.

7. Gates, *History of Public Land Law Development*: 236.

8. *Ibid.*: 236.

9. *Ibid.*: 271.

10. New York *Daily Tribune*, May 6, 1852, quoted in Robbins, *Our Landed Heritage*: 108.

11. Frederick Merk, *History of the Westward Movement* (New York: Alfred A. Knopf, 1978): 472.

12. Paul W. Gates, "The Homestead Law in an Incongruous Land System," in Vernon Carstensen, ed., *The Public Lands: Studies in the History of the Public Domain* (Madison: University of Wisconsin Press, 1963): 323.

13. John Wesley Powell, *Report on the Lands of the Arid Regions* (Washington, D.C.: 1878).

14. Report of the Public Lands Commission, 46th Cong., 2d sess., 1880, H. Ex. Doc. 46: 9, quoted in Robbins, *Our Landed Heritage*: 290.

15. Robbins, *Our Landed Heritage*: 155.

16. Land Office Report, 1883: 7–8, quoted in Hibbard, *History of Public Land Policies*: 417–18.

17. Government Land Office Annual Report, 1887, quoted in Gates, *History of Public Land Law Development*: 640.

18. Land Office Report, 1884: 8, quoted in Hibbard, *History of Public Land Policies*: 429.

19. Hibbard, *History of Public Land Policies*: 466.

20. Land Office Report, 1882: 8, quoted in Hibbard, *History of Public Land Policies*: 169.

21. Quoted in Merk, *History of the Westward Movement*: 455.

22. Report of the Land Commission, 1876: 8, quoted in Robbins, *Our Landed Heritage*: 246.

23. Land Office Report, 1885: 20, quoted in Gates, *History of Public Land Law Development*: 472.

24. Gates, *History of Public Land Law Development*: 486.

25. See Terry L. Anderson and Peter J. Hill, "Rents from Amenity Resources: A Case Study of Yellowstone National Park," in Anderson and Hill, eds., *The Political Economy of the American West* (Lanham, Md.: Rowman & Littlefield, 1994).

26. John Ise, *Our National Park Policy: A Critical History* (Baltimore: Johns Hopkins University Press for Resources for the Future, 1961): 17.

27. *Ibid.*: 55.

28. Quoted in Gates, *History of Public Land Law Development*: 565.

29. Samuel P. Hays, *Conservation and the Gospel of Efficiency: The Progressive Conservation Movement, 1890–1920* (Cambridge, Mass: Harvard University Press, 1959): 28.

30. Gifford Pinchot, *Breaking New Ground* (New York: Harcourt Brace and Co., 1947): 326, quoted in Orris C. Herfindahl, "What is Conservation?" in Dennis Thompson, ed., *Politics, Policy and Natural Resources* (New York: The Free Press, 1972): 174.

31. Hays, *Conservation and the Gospel of Efficiency*: 271.

32. Gates, *History of Public Land Law Development*: 512.

33. Walter P. Webb, *The Great Plains* (Boston: Ginn, 1931): 423.

34. Quoted in Gates, *History of Public Land Law Development*: 251.

35. *The Western Range*, 74th Cong., 2d sess., 1925, 199, quoted in Gates, *History of Public Land Law Development*: 528–29.

36. Wesley Calef, *Private Grazing and Public Lands: Studies of the Land Management of the Taylor Grazing Act*, (Chicago: University of Chicago Press, 1960): 50–51.

37. See E. Louise Peffer, *The Closing of the Public Domain: Disposal and Reservation Policies, 1900-1950* (Stanford, Calif.: Stanford University Press, 1951).

38. Hibbard, *History of Public Land Policies*: 548–49.

Part II

The Failed Promise of Scientific Management

Introduction

A central question for the public lands—as for any part of government—is the basis on which decisions will be made. What information must be available? What are the appropriate decision criteria? What will establish the legitimacy of a government decision?

Dating back at least to the early part of the twentieth century, the correct answer for public land management has been the scientific answer. Yet despite the constant invocation of scientific authority, the methods of science have often had little to do with public land decisions. Even in those areas where well-defined technical answers have been possible, the scientific process itself has been thoroughly politicized. Most public land decisions in any case intermingle scientific and value considerations in ways that are impossible to separate. Society, reasonably enough, is not prepared to delegate the determination of its basic values to scientists.

Chapter 2 reviews the management of the national forests over the course of the twentieth century, showing how the scientific professionalism sought by the progressive movement early in the century has typically fallen well short in its appointed task. As a result, the Forest Service today faces a crisis of agency purpose. Some students of the public lands argue that benefit-cost and other economic methods provide the necessary scientific basis for public land decisions. Chapter 3 examines the failed efforts to introduce greater economic expertise into the management of the public rangelands, as attempted by the Bureau of Land Management in the Department of the Interior. Chapter 4 describes how the statutory mandates for comprehensive land use planning of the mid-1970s sought to revive scientific decision making but in practice have been unable to accomplish this goal. Instead, as later chapters of this book will explore, the development of formal systems of land use planning may represent the last gasp of the progressive concept on the public lands.

Chapter 2

Mythology Instead of Analysis: The Story of National Forest Management

The national forests have been the showcase for public land management. The first chief of the Forest Service in 1905, Gifford Pinchot, was also the most prominent figure of the American conservation movement. Millions of Americans remember with great fondness their visits to the national forests for hiking, fishing, and other pursuits. The national forests contain snow-capped mountains, deep canyons, rivers, and other features of striking natural beauty. When Herbert Kaufman published his classic of public administration in 1960, *The Forest Ranger*, he spoke of the Forest Service in the most enthusiastic of terms.[1]

The Forest Service is today a beleaguered agency. Many of its old friends in the environmental movement have abandoned it, a few even calling for its abolition. Critics of longer standing, who see the Forest Service as an unwelcome assertion of federal power over the West, continue their harsh attacks. Such developments reflect in part the fading power of the progressive gospel in American life.

Indeed, the Forest Service today illustrates better than any other land management agency why scientific management has failed to keep its promise. Even in the heyday of the agency, the national forests were never managed scientifically; the claims to scientific management were mostly a matter of rhetoric. They were an effective political device to marshal public support for the Forest Service in an age that worshipped

---

This chapter was first published in Robert T. Deacon and M. Bruce Johnson, eds, *Forestlands: Public and Private* (San Francisco: Pacific Institute for Public Policy Research, 1985). A new introduction has been added, a few paragraphs have been omitted, and a few other minor changes have been made to the original.

science. Today, however, this same rhetoric—the myths and images that the Forest Service offered up so successfully to the American public through most of the twentieth century—has lost much of its appeal. Science has a diminished moral standing in American life; economic progress grounded in the efficient use of resources no longer seems capable of solving the problems of American society. The Forest Service has struggled to find a new gospel to suit a new age. Thus far, however, it has not been successful.

This chapter reviews the history of the national forests and shows how the Forest Service preached scientific management but generally behaved otherwise and today faces an uncertain future without any real guiding vision.

The Movement for Forest Reserves

The story of the national forests begins in the 1860s and 1870s, when widespread uncontrolled harvesting of timber on the public domain began to attract national attention. An 1869 report of the Michigan legislature warned that "generations yet unborn will bless or curse our memory accordingly as we preserve for them what the munificent past has so richly bestowed upon us, or as we lend our influence to continue and accelerate the wasteful destruction everywhere at work in our beautiful state."[2] Commissioner J. A. Williamson of the General Land Office stated that "a national calamity is being rapidly and surely brought upon this country by the useless destruction of the forests."[3] The warnings of George Marsh's famous study, *Man and Nature*, especially the critical influence of forests in controlling erosion and preserving water flow, were widely discussed.[4] In 1875 growing interest in forestry led to the founding of the American Forestry Association.

By this time there was also greater recognition of the need for new laws to control the disposal of public lands valuable chiefly for timber. In 1878 Congress passed the Timber and Stone Act. The act allowed sale of 160 acres of timberland in the states of California, Nevada, Oregon, and Washington but limited use of the timber to the purchaser. Not surprisingly, this limitation proved virtually impossible to enforce; there was widespread acquisition of timberlands for speculation and sale to timber companies. In some cases timber companies would round up a crowd from a tavern or other gathering place, shepherd the enlistees down to the land office to purchase tracts, and have them sign over the timberlands immediately thereafter. Around fifteen million acres were eventually sold under the Timber and Stone Act, most of it ending up in the hands of timber companies. The Preemption Act and the commutation provision of the Homestead Act were also subject to similar manipulations.

The failure of timber disposal laws would lead ultimately to the retention of public timber in the national forests. The first small step in this direction occurred in 1876 when a rider was attached to an appropriations bill providing $2,000 for the Agriculture Department to collect statistics and report to the Congress on forestry problems. Also in 1876, legislation to set aside national forest reserves was first introduced. In 1882 the third report on forestry by the Agriculture Department recommended that "the principal bodies of timber land still remaining the property of the government . . . be withdrawn from sale or grant under the existing modes for conveying the public lands, and that they be placed under regulation calculated to secure an economical use of the existing timber, and a proper revenue from its sale."[5] Finally, after years of inaction a short section providing for the creation by the president of forest reserves was added to the General Reform Act of 1891. Others have disagreed, but the early historian of federal forest policy, John Ise, was of the view that "it is fairly certain that no general forest reservation measure, plainly understood to be such, and unconnected with other measures, would ever have had the slightest chance of passing Congress."[6]

Within two years President Benjamin Harrison had established the first forest reserves, which contained thirteen million acres. President Grover Cleveland added another 4.5 million acres in 1893. At this point, however, additions were halted until the question of management policy for the reserves could be decided.

The Creation of the Forest Service

Until 1891 lands had been set aside in reserves for the purpose of preserving them in their natural condition. Indeed, much of the support for the 1891 forest reserves legislation had come from preservationists seeking to enlarge the area in which timber harvesting and other commercial activities were precluded. According to one observer, the main forces behind the creation of the forest reserves were "the drive by wilderness groups to perpetuate untouched large areas of natural beauty, by eastern arboriculturists and botanists to save trees for the future and by western water users, both large corporations and small owners, to preserve their water supply by controlling silting."[7]

However, in a forerunner of current wilderness controversies, many in the West strongly opposed taking large new acreages out of productive use and including them in forest reserves. In 1896 the National Academy of Sciences appointed a commission to study the future of the forest reserves. The commission included Gifford Pinchot, then a young and little-known forester. Pinchot strongly opposed pure preservation and instead favored a policy of maximum use; the forest reserves, he believed, were "made to be used, not just to look at."[8] The commission supported Pinchot's ideas and issued a report in 1897 that firmly backed the management of the reserves for productive uses including timber harvesting. Moreover, it considered that charging users of the forest a fee might be appropriate.

In June 1897 President William McKinley signed the Forest Reserve Act, the "organic" act of the Forest Service. The act provided authority to establish necessary rules and regulations for forest reserves in order to "regulate their occupancy and use." Sale of timber was specifically allowed for the appraised price, although limited to "dead, matured or large growth of trees." Gradually, as Forest Service harvesting increased, this restriction was to be interpreted very flexibly by the Forest Service, until sued on the matter in the 1970s. Further forest reserves could be created where the creation served the purpose either of "securing favorable conditions of water flows" or "to furnish a continuous supply of timber."[9]

Administration of the forest reserves was assigned to the General Land Office in the Interior Department, which had a staff with little knowledge of forestry. Pinchot became chief of the Division of Forestry in the Agriculture Department in 1898, and he soon decided that efficient administration of the forest reserves could be achieved only by their transfer to his division.

When Theodore Roosevelt became President in 1901, he quickly set about defining the themes of his administration. Pinchot met with Roosevelt and persuaded him to propose in his first message to Congress that timber management "should be united in the Bureau of Forestry" in the Agriculture Department.[10] But Congress was not yet ready to go along with this idea, in part because it was not yet prepared to agree with Pinchot that the national forests should be given over to such intensive forestry management. Pinchot thereupon embarked on an energetic campaign to secure the transfer of the reserves. At Pinchot's suggestion Roosevelt created a committee to study the organization of government scientific efforts; Pinchot served on the committee, which indeed endorsed the transfer. In 1905 the American Forest Congress, which provided the final impetus, was held in Washington, D.C. The congress brought together a wide range of concerned parties, including the National Lumber Manufacturers and the president of the Northern Pacific Railroad. Strong support across a wide spectrum of opinion spurred passage of the Transfer Act, signed on February 1, 1905.

In a famous statement actually drafted by Pinchot, Secretary of Agriculture James Wilson laid out the broad directions of the new Forest Service. The letter captures much of the spirit and philosophy that would guide the Forest Service through the twentieth century.

In the administration of the forest reserves it must be clearly borne in mind that all land is to be devoted to its most productive use for the permanent good of the whole people, and not for the temporary benefit of individuals or companies. All the resources of forest reserves are for use, and this use must be brought about in a thoroughly prompt and businesslike manner, under such restrictions only as will insure the permanence of these resources. The vital importance of forest reserves to the great industries of the Western States will be largely increased in the near future by the continued steady advance in settlement and development. The performance of the resources of the reserves is therefore indispensable to continued prosperity, and the policy of this department for their protection and use will invariably be guided by this fact, always bearing in mind that the conservative use of these resources in no way conflicts with their permanent value.

You will see to it that the water, wood, and forage of the reserves are conserved and wisely used for the benefit of the home builder first of all, upon whom depends the best permanent use of lands and resources alike. The continued prosperity of the agricultural, lumbering, mining and livestock interests is directly dependent upon a permanent and accessible supply of water, wood, and forage, as well as upon the present and future use of their resources under businesslike regulations, enforced with promptness, effectiveness, and common sense. In the management of each reserve local questions will be decided upon local grounds; the dominant industry will be considered first, but with as little restriction to minor industries as may be possible; sudden changes in industrial conditions will be avoided by gradual adjustment after due notice; and where conflicting interests must be reconciled the question will always be decided from the standpoint of the greatest good of the greatest number in the long run.[11]

Many of the basic issues of federal timber management had already emerged by the time the Forest Service was created in 1905. The leading controversy of the 1890s had been whether the forest reserves should be preserved in their natural state or utilized for various productive purposes. Preservation had seemed for a moment to win out, but Pinchot stood solidly for utilization, and under his leadership this philosophy was firmly established. A separate organization, the National Park Service, was eventually formed in 1916 to manage the most scenic and wild areas for recreational and other noncommercial uses.

Pinchot himself had little interest in recreational use of the national forests. His belief that timber in the national parks should be harvested embittered many preservationists, as did his support for the construction of Hetch Hetchy Dam in Yosemite National Park. He considered forestry to be ''tree farming'' and the basic purpose of the forests to be provision of wood for homes: ''The object of our forest policy is not to preserve the forests because they are beautiful . . . or because they are refuges for the wild creatures of the wilderness . . . but the making of prosperous homes. . . . Every other consideration comes as secondary.''[12]

Pinchot considered the preservationist cause to be romantic sentimentalism. He portrayed himself instead as a hard-boiled scientist, one of the first practitioners of the science of forestry in the United States. As a young man Pinchot had studied forestry in France and upon his return to the United States he sought to promote the lessons he had learned. He was a founder in 1900 of the Society of American Foresters, whose mission was to spread scientific forestry.

In his scientific orientation Pinchot was very much a man of his time. Frederick Taylor was spreading the principles of scientific management to the business and government world. Belief in the great powers of science to solve the problems of mankind was widespread. Faith in science had become much like a religion for many, and Pinchot was the apostle of this faith for forestry. Samuel Hays, in particular, has emphasized the critical role played by science in the conservation movement.

Conservation, above all, was a scientific movement, and its role in history arises from the implications of science and technology in modern society. Conservation leaders sprang from such fields as hydrology, forestry, agrostology, geology, and anthropology. Vigorously active in professional circles in the national capital, these leaders brought the ideals and practices of their crafts into federal resource policy. Loyalty to these professional ideals, not close association with the grass-roots public, set the tone of the Theodore Roosevelt conservation movement. Its essence was rational planning to promote efficient development and use of all natural resources.

The idea of efficiency drew these federal scientists from one resources task to another, from specific programs to comprehensive concepts. It molded the policies which they proposed, their administrative techniques, and their relations with Congress and the public. It is from the vantage point of applied science, rather than of democratic protest, that one must understand the historic role of the conservation movement.[13]

Science is of course not the domain of the layman; it requires special training to acquire technical knowledge. Politics should not become involved; rather, scientific knowledge is to be applied by the experts in the field. Such a vision underlay not only the development of the Forest Service, but much of the growth of government under the progressive banner during the first two decades of this century.

The conservationists saw in science the ability to provide objective answers to social issues. Conflicts should be resolved, not through political combat among special interests, but by appeal to what was right, that is to say, what science and technical expertise determined. Theodore Roosevelt, one of the most optimistic of all Progressives, epitomized this philosophy. He believed that "social and economic problems should be solved, not through power politics, but by experts who would undertake scientific investigations and devise workable solutions."[14] The view that forestry was a science meant such objectivity could be attained and could serve as a guide for managing the national forests in the public interest.

These convictions have motivated the Forest Service to fight fiercely to retain political independence. Their wide acceptance has also made outsiders much more willing to grant such independence. Until the 1990s, all the chiefs of the Forest Service had come from within the service and had served through changes in the presidency. Pinchot proudly remarked that "from the day I entered the Division of Forestry under President McKinley till I was dismissed from the Forest Service by President Taft, not one single person in the office or the field was appointed, promoted, demoted, or removed to please any politician, or for any political motive whatsoever."[15]

The scientific influence also explains other features of the Forest Service. It has included three basic divisions: the best-known division manages the national forests; the other two conduct forestry research and provide technical forestry assistance to state and private forest owners. The Forest Service has collected and distributed information on trends in timber markets and has promoted adoption of more scientific forestry practices. In general it has functioned as the leading planner for long-term timber production in the United States.

The creation of the Forest Service can in fact be seen as one of the important steps in a much broader social development: the displacement of small, decentralized, competitive institutions (such as individual lumbermen) by large, scientific, planned institutions. In most cases this occurred within the private sector as a small number of large corporations took the place of many smaller firms. This happened, for example, to some degree in timber with the assembly of the Weyerhaeuser holdings. The Forest Service was unusual for its time primarily in that it was a public agency.

The Moral Crusade

Good science constantly questions old answers and challenges conventional wisdom. On the one hand, the best scientists maintain an attitude of habitual doubt and skepticism; strict requirements must be met for scientific proof before any final answer will be accepted. On the other hand, these same characteristics are at odds with the successful conduct of politics. A good politician typically must maintain a posture of certainty even when he may harbor many private doubts. Confessions of doubt are likely to be seen as signs of weakness and inability to lead. They erode the commitment of supporters and undercut the necessary solidarity.

Although Gifford Pinchot considered himself a scientist, most of his life was spent in the political arena, where he was a great success. Similarly, while conservationists promoted scientific management, they sought to incorporate its use by restructuring political institutions and enlarging the role of government. In essence the conservation movement espoused a set of political rather than scientific ideas; conservationism was, in short, a political ideology. Like other ideologies, it faced the need to attract and sustain popular support. The political requirements of conservationism were bound to conflict with the scientific methods that conservationists sought to advance.

Indeed, there was a religious quality to the progressive and conservationist faith in applied science, a point that Dwight Waldo has stressed.[16] Hays later echoed this theme when he characterized conservationism as the "gospel" of efficiency. According to conservationist tenets, improvement would occur steadily in the human condition, eventually making it possible for all mankind to achieve "the good life." This vision of human progress—leading toward a secular "heaven on earth"—produced a widely held sense of virtue and important purpose.

In the progressive era a new ethic of human progress replaced the Protestant ethic as the motivator of good works. From the very beginning Pinchot instilled such attitudes in the Forest Service. He himself commented that Forest Service employees were not to be motivated by "the desire to earn good money"; rather, they were doing "good work in a good cause."[17]

The Forest Service was all the more virtuous when contrasted with the self-seeking, mercenary attitudes of its opponents. In the service of the good cause, the Forest Service had to overcome the "special interests" who "go on creating baronies for themselves out of the resources that belonged to all the people. We denied and opposed their profound conviction that money and profits are all important and must control."[18] Pinchot and the men of the Forest Service saw themselves as fending off the "vast power, pecuniary and political [of the] . . . railroads, the stock interests, mining interests, water power interests, and most of the big timber interests."[19] The basic reason that the Forest Service could win, Pinchot stated, was that "in the long run our purpose was too obviously right to be defeated."[20]

The elevation of applied science from a practical tool to a new form of religious faith was characteristic of the progressive era. But the roles of science as practical problem-solving technique and as theology are very different. The future of the Forest Service included much tension between these elements. The demands of political mobilization as well as organizational discipline and morale were often to place a greater premium on the theological than on the problem-solving role of science.

Crying Wolf

Predictions that the country would soon run out of timber—experience a "timber famine"—have recurred throughout American forestry history. The commissioner of the General Land Office in 1868 predicted that "in forty or fifty years our own forests would have disappeared and those of Canada would be approaching exhaustion."[21] Matters appeared to be getting worse when in 1876 a forestry student purported to prove that within ten years there would be "a clean swoop of every foot of commercial wood in the United States east of the Pacific slope."[22] In 1889 former Secretary of the Interior Carl Schurz feared that "if the present destruction of forests goes on for twenty-five years longer, the United States will be as completely stripped of their forests as Asia Minor is today."[23]

This refrain was taken up by Pinchot, who was sure that a timber famine was imminent: "The United States has already crossed the verge of a timber famine so severe that its blighting effects will be felt in every household in the land."[24] Counseled by Pinchot, President Theodore Roosevelt had warned, "If the present rate of forest destruction is allowed to continue, with nothing to offset it, a timber famine in the future is inevitable."[25] It was not until the energy crisis of the 1970s that public alarms over natural resource depletion were again driven to such heights.

The specter of timber famine was raised anew in the battle over public regulation of private timber harvests. A committee of the Society of American Foresters, chaired by Pinchot, forecast in 1919 that "within less than 50 years, our present timber shortage will have become a blighting timber famine."[26] To prevent such an occurrence, the committee advocated federal regulation of private timber harvesting. The report of this committee set off a bitter struggle over public regulation of private forests that continued for thirty years.

The possibility of running out of timber naturally aroused strong public fears, and playing to these fears was an effective way of mobilizing public support. But one cannot give false alarms too many times; a timber famine cannot be forever looming. By the 1930s it was becoming necessary to explain where the timber famine had gone. Although Pinchot still raised the cry, for many others, "The bogey of timber famine was ceasing to be a pivotal issue and was even becoming an embarrassment."[27]

The timber famine episode raises the question: How could an organization based on special expertise and the application of science go so far wrong? The hallmark of science is accurate prediction; to make an unqualified prediction that does not materialize casts serious doubts on the scientific credentials of the predictor. Pinchot and others in the Forest Service concluded that a timber famine was inevitable on the basis of their projections of future timber demands, which were greatly in excess of projected timber supplies. But demand, of course, is not independent of price, a matter then generally neglected. As timber comes into shorter supply and prices rise, purchasers find new ways to economize on the amounts they use. Similarly, the effective supply is not independent of price but can be increased by better utilization, shifts to lower grades of wood, wood treatments, and various other means.

Pinchot believed the only way to avoid a timber famine was through more scientific management of the forests to produce much greater supplies of timber. As Sherry Olson has observed, however, the actual historical solution to the timber problem was achieved mostly by lowering demand through conserving on wood use.[28] Wood users learned how to substitute other materials for wood and how to utilize available wood supplies more efficiently. For example, pushed by rising timber costs, the railroads in the decade from 1900 to 1910 developed a host of new conservation techniques, among the most important of which were the adoption of wood-preserving methods, substitution of new species and materials, and the more efficient allocation of timbers to various uses. Railroad foresters had initially looked to the Forest Service for help but were gradually put off by the "dogmatic character of their publications. . . . They were advised to adopt practices in line with an idealized concept of 'good forestry,' instead of forest practices that would actually promote railroad economies."[29]

Indeed, the Forest Service was apparently preoccupied with its moral crusade to the extent that it actually neglected in many cases the scientific management of the nation's timber supplies. The Forest Service was often more concerned with a favorable public reaction and with expanding its domain than with scientific research. Pinchot believed that the answers were already known and "research was practically eliminated in the first few years of his administration."[30] Pinchot's role in almost single-handedly bringing about creation of the national forests has established his place in history. But in this task his greatest skills, ironically, were as a propagandist and politician. By selling the idea of scientific management of the forests to an enthusiastic public and by promoting the virtue of the Forest Service, Pinchot succeeded in gaining the influence needed to overcome that agency's many determined opponents.

Science in the Forest Service

Ashley Schiff has conducted a major study focused on the question of whether the Forest Service was a suitable agency for the management of forestry research.[31] The Forest Service was often faced with strong opposition, and it had to fight strenuously for its political aims. Could the Forest Service afford to show a scientific questioning attitude toward its own policies in the face of strong outside challenges? Instead, the tendency might well be to circle the wagons and defend established policy. Science would be enlisted for the defense rather than left free to inquire in any direction.

The highly moralistic tradition of the Forest Service likely enhanced this tendency. As a former chief declared, the Forest Service was "born in controversy and baptized with the holy water of reform."[32] As a result, according to Schiff, there was a "danger . . . that moral righteousness when embroidered with scientific technology would be too attractive in a science worshipping age. Moral appeals might even lead 'researchers' astray by encouraging tendencies to oversimplify and overgeneralize complex problems. Worse yet, their thinking might become rigidified, thereby losing the best qualities of the research mind."[33]

The tendency to make unrealistic and exaggerated claims has been most in evidence when the Forest Service has sought to expand the scope of its authority—usually in the face of much resistance. In the debate prior to the passage of the Weeks Act in 1911, which authorized acquisition of private lands for eastern national forests, a question arose as to whether the federal government actually had constitutional authority to make such purchases. In fending off this challenge the Forest Service argued that forests were a critical factor in determining river flows; thus, forest land purchases by the federal government could be justified under the federal power to regulate navigation in waterways.

The public then, as now, was greatly concerned about the problem of flooding; severe floods in the Ohio, Mississippi, and other river valleys had caused damage on a vast scale. Pinchot, abandoning scientific caution, agreed that "the great flood which has wrought devastation and ruin in the Upper Ohio Valley is due fundamentally to the cutting away of the forests on the watersheds of the Allegheny and Monongahela Rivers."[34] The Weather Bureau and the Corps of Engineers immediately challenged Pinchot's claim, but with little consequence. The Weeks Act passed with the inclusion of the provision that new forest lands could be acquired for the purpose of improving downstream navigation. Not surprisingly, the Forest Service was unreceptive toward scientific studies that questioned the actual importance of forest influences on river flows.

During the New Deal the Forest Service sought to expand its domain by acquiring large new public holdings of private forests and by imposing federal regulation on private forests. Once again there was wide opposition, and again the Forest Service responded with a campaign of exaggerated claims. Scientific objectivity had to make way for the political advantages of strong emotional appeals. The National Plan for American Forestry, released in 1933, repeated the claim that denuded forests were "major contributing causes of excessively rapid runoff and destructive floods."[35] Such statements by the Forest Service again were severely criticized by other scientific organizations. According to the

Geological Survey, the leading government agency for hydrologic research:

> the changes which have been brought about by streamflow regulation through agricultural and forestry practices over broad areas are in general, so insignificant and tenuous that they are indeterminate. It is a sad commentary on a so-called scientific organization like the Forest Service that during its existence it has never published a report on the role played by vegetal cover on the hydrologic cycle which was in accord with well established hydrologic principles.[36]

Confronted with such statements, the chief of the Division of Silvics replied, "All that may be true, but I think with my heart as well as my head."[37]

Schiff suggests that the Forest Service may have actually recognized that its position lacked scientific merit but deliberately failed to conduct its own research as a way of delaying the necessity of formally acknowledging the situation. By the mid-1940s it was widely recognized that the Forest Service had greatly overstated the importance of forest condition in controlling floods. Acceptance of such views within the Forest Service could be achieved only because the old guard was now leaving. Pressed to return to the old crusading spirit, a representative of a newer era, Forest Service Chief Richard McArdle, responded in 1955: "We live in different times. We cannot recreate the initial crusade for forestry anymore than we can rediscover America. That crusade was pointed toward creating a widespread public awareness of our need for the products and services of forest lands. I think our task in the next half century is more concerned with action than with publicity."[38]

Fire prevention is another area in which the Forest Service refused for many years to accept scientific evidence conflicting with its policies. From its inception the Forest Service had promoted this issue as another moral crusade. In the 1920s, however, scientific evidence began to accumulate that in the South use of fire was necessary to promote regeneration of the longleaf pine. The Forest Service refused to heed this evidence, insisting that its policies were correct; yet, the longer the agency ignored its critics, the more difficult a later reversal became. In the end outside scientific opinion became so united that the Forest Service had to give in.

Based on the fire and water cases as well as other Forest Service history, Schiff concludes that the Forest Service was often all too willing to sacrifice scientific objectivity for public appeal. This produced not only poor science, but much less effective management of public forests. "In the end, therefore, administration itself suffered because research was too closely identified, from a spiritual and structural standpoint, with 'the cause.' "³⁹

An Era of Custodial National Forest Management, 1905 to 1945

Pinchot had envisioned that the Forest Service would intensively manage the national forests for timber and other uses. He also expected that the national forests would be profitable, that their revenues would exceed their costs. In his view the main reason for creating the system of national forests was to introduce greater efficiency in forest management. In each of these beliefs events were to prove him wrong.

For the first forty years management of the national forests was mainly custodial. The effect of creating a national forest in an area was to curtail timber harvesting rather than to stimulate it. In the earlier part of this century there were still huge supplies of timber available on both private and public lands. Timber prices were held at low levels by this vast supply, and many timberland owners found it difficult to cover payments on their land. The private sector thus pressured the Forest Service to limit harvesting in order to avoid further depressing prices. Seeking to create greater stability in the timber industry and not wanting to antagonize western timber interests, the Forest Service generally obliged. Among the objectives of its policy the Forest Service sought to "avoid competing with private enterprise by withholding federal timber until private supplies were exhausted; sell only to meet purely local shortages; protect the national forests from fire and other disasters."⁴⁰

In 1910 the timber harvested from Forest Service lands was around five hundred million board feet, less than 2 percent of national lumber production. By 1929 the Forest Service harvest had risen to around 1.6 billion board feet, but this was still small compared with national lumber production of 36.9 billion board feet. At the time the total timber inventory on Forest Service lands was 552 billion board feet, around a third of the national public and private timber inventory. The Forest Service harvest never exceeded a few percent of national timber production until heavy demands in the aftermath of World War II forced the nation to turn to the national forests for timber supplies.

The pattern of harvesting private lands first and Forest Service lands later was politically popular because "harvesting it would have lowered stumpage prices on private lands."[41] Nevertheless, it was also economically rational. The private lands were generally the better timberlands, having higher volumes of timber per acre and being located closer to roads and other transportation. Because future returns are discounted, the long-run value of timber is maximized by taking the lowest cost timber first, just as the highest grade and lowest cost mineral deposits are taken first.

While timber was being harvested on private lands, the national forests were becoming a major source of recreation, a use in which Pinchot had shown little interest. The national forests contain much of the higher elevated scenic areas west of the Mississippi, as well as many other attractions. Although mountainous terrain and steep slopes made the lands less valuable for timber production, these features made them more desirable for recreation. In contrast to the circumstances of timber production, the national forests held the most desirable recreational areas and were appropriately brought into recreational use ahead of private lands. The numbers of recreational visits to the national forests grew rapidly from 4.7 million in 1924 to 16.2 million in 1940. By 1950 recreational visits had further climbed to 27.4 million, almost six times the level twenty-five years earlier.

Despite the rapid growth in recreational use of the national forests, Pinchot and his successors in the Forest Service were unsympathetic to the idea of setting aside certain lands solely for recreation. They contended that recreation and other uses could be accommodated together without great loss to either. They generally resisted creation of any areas in which one or another use was automatically precluded. Rather, it was thought that the land manager should exercise his professional judgment in deciding the best overall use of the land in light of the particular circumstances at hand. In some cases a use such as timber harvesting might prove to be incompatible with recreation, but why prejudge the issue?

The Forest Service thus showed little sympathy toward the creation of national parks and found it difficult to understand that park proponents distrusted the exercise of professional judgment and wanted ironclad guarantees that an area would be protected. In retrospect it is ironic that one of the most important functions of the national forests for their first forty years was to serve as a holding zone from which the national parks and monuments, wilderness areas, back-country areas, and other special recreational areas could later be formed. A host of important national parks—including Olympic, Grand Canyon, Grand Teton, Glacier, North Cascades, and others—were created entirely or in part from land originally in the national forests. If these lands had previously passed into private ownership, many of these parks and recreation areas might never have been created or might have been much smaller; in any case, the task would have been much more difficult, as the problems in the 1970s in assembling the land for the Redwood National Park demonstrated.

The Forest Service greatly resented the loss of some of its most attractive lands to the national park system, and it resisted the formation of most of the national parks noted above. Eventually, however, it perceived that it would have to move with the tide, if for no other reason than to protect its domain. Moreover, some Forest Service staff were becoming strong enthusiasts for wilderness protection—young Aldo Leopold, for one. The first wilderness area was established in 1924 and by 1939 about 13 million acres had been set aside in "primitive areas" with restricted commercial use.

In short, up until World War II the guiding principles of the Forest Service concerning the proper management of the national forests had not been put to much of a test. The Forest Service espoused active management to maximize use, but actual management activities to that point had been fairly minimal. The public saw the national forests as a vast recreation area, a lot like a national park, although lacking the natural wonders. The Forest Service had become popular by making available its 180 million acres for public pleasure and by promoting good causes such as fire prevention. But matters would become much more complicated after World War II. New economic pressures would bring about a shift to much more intensive use of the national forests.

The Campaign for Federal Forest Regulation

For most of American history, timber companies simply cut and moved on to the next virgin stands. This pattern made much economic and other sense at the time. There were vast forests rich in timber; transport costs might rise, but it would still be cheaper to move to new stands, as long as they were available, than to regrow the forest. The long time required for timber to reach harvesting age—forty to one hundred years—made it especially difficult to achieve an adequate return from reforestation.

Pinchot and other early members of the forestry profession had learned their forestry in the European tradition. There was little old-growth timber available in Europe; instead, European forestry was conceived for circumstances in which harvesting had gone on for centuries. The forests had typically been through many cycles of cutting, regrowth, and cutting once again. Given these circumstances, it was logical that maintenance of a sustained yield of timber was a central principle in European forestry.

Pinchot and many others in the new American forestry profession directly adopted the idea that sustained-yield forestry represented proper and "truly scientific" forest management. Other forestry practices were considered wasteful and unscientific. Accordingly, the Forest Service released a continuing flow of data and statistics on the number of forest acres that had been harvested but not reforested. In graphic terms it described the extent of "forest devastation" on these lands.

Given private unwillingness to reforest, Pinchot came to the conclusion that either public ownership or public regulation of private forests was necessary to achieve sustained-yield timber management for the United States. Recognizing that public acquisition of private timberlands would be extremely expensive, and would on any wide scale be likely to generate fierce resistance, Pinchot came to advocate federal regulation of private timber harvests.

As noted earlier, in 1919 the president of the Society of American Foresters designated Pinchot to be chairman of a committee whose purpose was "to recommend action for the prevention of devastation of privately owned timberlands in the United States."[42] The committee subsequently reported that drastic steps were required to head off a timber famine. It proposed that the federal government be authorized "to fix standards and promulgate rules to prevent the devastation and to provide for the perpetuation of forest growth and the production of forest crops on privately owned timberlands for commercial purposes."[43]

The necessity of government regulation was widely accepted among professional foresters. There was strong disagreement, however, as to whether the federal government or the states should be the primary regulator. Pinchot favored federal regulation, but his two successors as chiefs of the Forest Service, Henry Graves and William Greeley, both favored state responsibility. In the American tradition of decentralization many other professional foresters agreed that, whenever possible, the state level was the better choice. The timber industry itself did not dispute the fact that private owners were not reforesting. The National Lumber Manufacturers Association in fact supported public reforestation.

The concerns about forest devastation and the drive for regulation did not produce much legislative movement toward direct regulation, but these pressures helped to spur the passage of the Clark-McNary Act in 1924 and the McSweeney-McNary Act in 1928. These two acts created the basis for federal assistance to state and private forestry and a major federal program of forestry research. Rather than compulsory regulation, voluntary cooperation became the byword.

The depression of the 1930s encouraged radical views, and in many fields the New Deal brought about major changes in policy and legislation. This failed to occur in forestry, but not for lack of Forest Service effort. In 1933 the Forest Service released its most comprehensive study of forestry up to that time: the National Plan for American Forestry (also called the Copeland Report). The plan recommended a massive acquisition program to more than double the area of public forests. In the spirit of the times the Forest Service made a harsh attack on the effects of private ownership and profit incentives.

Laissez faire private effort has seriously deteriorated or destroyed the basic resources of timber, forage, and land almost universally. It has not concerned itself with the public welfare in protection of watersheds. It has felt little or no responsibility for the renewal of the resources on which its own industries must depend for continued existence and much less for the economic and social benefits growing out of the perpetuity of resources and industry.[44]

The Forest Service also argued that public ownership of the forests was required to expedite forestry planning for the whole nation. At that time the idea of public ownership and national planning was being widely proposed not only for the forests, but for much of the U.S. economy. During the 1930s and 1940s the Forest Service also campaigned vigorously for federal regulation of private forests where public ownership was not achieved. In 1935 the chief of the Forest Service, Ferdinand Silcox, set the official Forest Service position, which was not changed until the early 1950s.

1. The primary objective of forestry is to keep forest land continuously productive. This must take precedence over private profit.
2. Forest devastation must stop, and forest practice must begin now, not in the nebulous future.
3. Public control over the use of private forest lands which will insure sustained yield is essential to stabilize forest industries and forest com-

munities. The application of the required practices on private lands must be supervised by public agencies and not left to the industry.[45]

The drive for public regulation was gradually being undercut, however, by the spread of private industrial forestry. Industry reforestation and management for long-term sustained yields emerged in the 1930s and spread rapidly. One of the earliest full-fledged ''tree farms'' was on the Clemons tract of the Weyerhaeuser company, set up in 1941. By 1950 a University of Michigan forestry professor remarked, ''Millions of tree farm acres are already getting more intensive forest management than is available to most of the publicly owned lands.''[46]

Surprisingly, the Forest Service sometimes reacted to this development with suspicion and distrust, even though it had promoted it for many years. The Forest Service feared that improvements in private forestry practices might be an industry ploy to defeat Forest Service objectives of regulation or large-scale public forest acquisition. Lyle Watts, chief of the Forest Service, complained in 1943 that ''it is unfortunate that a well-financed publicity campaign sponsored by the forest industries during the recent past should tend to cultivate public complacency when the situation with respect to our forest resources is so unsatisfactory.''[47]

Any real prospects of federal forestry regulation withered with the coming of World War II. The nation was too absorbed with the conflict to embark on major domestic reforms. In the next several decades private industry would surpass the Forest Service in the sophistication of its timber management. Ironically, after the Forest Service finally began to harvest timber on a large scale in the 1950s, one of the main criticisms aimed against it would be its failure to achieve reforestation.

The Forest Service made another pitch for federal regulation in the early 1950s. As expressed in 1951 by the assistant chief of the Forest Service, Edward Crafts, one argument for public regulation was a sophisticated version of the old timber famine theme: ''Latest surveys show—and practically all authorities agree on the basic figures—that the drain of sawtimber trees substantially exceeds growth. Thus, we have a situation in which we are gradually using up our capital growing stock of the larger and better trees.''[48]

The Forest Service proposals for regulation, however, were incompatible with the philosophy of the Eisenhower administration then coming into office. The Forest Service was concerned that the new administration might abandon the traditional nonpolitical tenure of its chiefs and, more broadly, feared compromise of its traditional freedom from heavy-handed political interference. To head off this threat, the Forest Service modified some of its positions to fit the views of the new administration, most notably dropping the idea of establishing federal forest regulation.

This campaign for regulation once again showed the Forest Service making strong, unqualified predictions only to be proved wrong by actual events. It officially stated for many years that private forest owners could never be expected to practice sustained-yield management and other forms of intensive forestry. Yet within a few decades industry was in many cases applying a more scientific forestry than was found in the national forests.

One reason for the Forest Service's miscalculation can be traced to a lack of interest and sophistication in using economic analysis. The Forest Service viewed sustained-yield management as a desirable end in itself, not something to be employed because it made economic sense. Private industry had a more pragmatic view: it would practice good forestry when it could make money in doing it. The Forest Service, however, failed to grasp that industry behavior was dependent on economic calculations. Because it tended to see actions in terms of good and evil, it viewed early industry failure to reforest as a moral fault. The private sector was portrayed as irresponsible and destructive in its refusal to save the forests from "devastation." With this outlook the Forest Service did not recognize that when old-growth became less available and timber prices rose, reforestation would become economically profitable and industry would then move rapidly to undertake it.

Demands for Forest Service Timber after World War II

As noted above, in meeting national timber demands, the highest quality and most accessible timber was the first to be cut. Timber production in the United States thus started in the East and moved westward. By 1870 the Great Lakes states with their vast forests of white pine had displaced the middle Atlantic area as the most important timber-producing region. In 1889 the Great Lakes states produced 35 percent of the nation's lumber. But as these supplies became depleted, new sources had to be found. By 1899, with 32 percent of the nation's production, the South had already passed the Great Lakes states as the largest lumber producer. The Pacific Coast and Rocky Mountain regions were just beginning to become important; their combined lumber production had not yet reached 10 percent of national production. Thus, at the time the national forests were being established, the West was not a major source of timber supply. This was no doubt an important factor facilitating creation of the national forest system.

By 1929, however, the Pacific Coast region, along with the South, had become one of the two major sources of timber for the nation. As production shifted westward, the national forests in the West became a potentially important source of timber. But, as noted earlier, public timberlands were generally the poorer timber-producing lands. In the Pacific Coast region, for example, the old-growth forests owned by private industry contained more than twice as many board feet per acre as publicly owned forests. Moreover, public forests tended to be located farther from transportation, on steeper slopes, and in otherwise more difficult terrain. In 1929 the total Forest Service harvest was still only 4 percent of national lumber production, and during the depression years the overall Forest Service harvest declined.

World War II marked a turning point; between 1939 and 1945 the harvest from the national forests doubled and continued to rise thereafter. In 1952 the Forest Service harvest reached 6.4 billion board feet, 13 percent of the U.S. timber supply. It rose further to 10.7 billion board feet in 1962, supplying 22 percent of the national timber supply. At this point the Forest Service harvest stopped growing and stayed roughly at the same level for several decades.

The Forest Service's share rose rapidly because, while Forest Service harvests themselves were increasing steadily, there were only modest increases in total national timber production. In 1976 total U.S. lumber production was thirty-six billion board feet, eight billion less than it had been in 1909. Likewise, per capita use of lumber had fallen steadily from 539 board feet in 1900 to 199 board feet in 1976. Although plywood and veneer have replaced lumber in many wood uses, combined use of lumber and plywood is still well below the levels of wood use per capita reached earlier in this century.

The need to draw upon stands of old-growth that are progressively more difficult to harvest and more costly, together with a gradual dwindling of these supplies, has caused the real price of timber to rise rapidly. Between 1900 and 1954 the nominal price of lumber rose nine times, and the real (inflation-adjusted) price almost tripled. The continuing rise in prices largely explains the sharp reductions in per capita use of timber as well as mounting pressures for greater timber production on the public forests.

In 1952 the Forest Service began a major study of the timber situation, eventually to be released in 1958 with the title *Timber Resources for America's Future*.[49] The report described the much greater efforts being made to utilize Forest Service timber. For example, whereas very little road construction for timber harvesting had occurred prior to 1940 in the West, from 1940 to 1951 construction rose to almost eight hundred miles of roads per year. Then in 1952 and 1956, respectively, construction reached 1,650 and 2,600 miles; a further need for thirty thousand miles of new roads was projected. The study also warned that a major commitment of new resources to forestry was necessary to avoid future timber shortages.

In the late 1950s the Forest Service had begun to shift its timber harvesting into high gear, but it did not anticipate the strong opposition among recreationists that was about to develop. It still tended to regard recreation as an incidental activity, a logical use of large areas of often scenic forest land, but one that did not require much special attention. Whereas the dominant event of the fifteen-year period from 1945 to 1960 was the major expansion in timber production, the next twenty years would be dominated by a counterthrust of recreational users of the national forests that prevented further harvest increases.

Forest Service Timber Predictions

After so many false alarms, the term "timber famine" came into disrepute in the 1930s, and few predictions of a timber famine have been made since. But to some extent the mentality did not really disappear, but rather took on new, albeit less extreme, forms. Instead of a famine, the prediction became a "timber shortage," and the suggestion was made that unacceptable social consequences—such as rapidly rising timber prices—would afflict the nation.

Since 1933 the Forest Service has undertaken a number of comprehensive studies of future demands and supplies for timber in the United States.[50] These include the two assessments mandated under the Forest and Rangeland Renewable Resources Planning Act of 1974 (RPA) prepared for 1975 and 1980. Each of these timber studies has concluded that a major shortage of timber was likely to develop, sooner in some cases than in others.

Sufficient time has passed that some of the earlier predictions of timber shortages can be assessed in retrospect. It is significant that in light of actual events, all were too pessimistic. The shortage proved to be almost as elusive as the earlier famines were. Table 2–1 shows Forest

Service predictions for two years, 1950 and 1975, plus actual figures for the nearest years available.

Table 2-1. Comparison of Predicted and Actual Total U.S.
Sawtimber Growth, Volume, and Harvest (billions of board feet)

	1933 Prediction for 1950	Actual 1952	1958 Prediction for 1975	Actual 1976
Timber growth	12.8	47.2	58.6	74.6
Inventory volume	1,207.2	2,507.0[1]	1,934.0	2,578.9
Timber harvest	33.7	48.8	65.4	62.9

[1] Inventory data are for 1953.

Sources: USDA, Forest Service, *A National Plan for American Forestry: The Report of the Forest Service of the Agriculture Department on the Forest Problem of the United States* (Washington, D.C.: Government Printing Office, 1933); USDA, Forest Service, *Timber Resources for America's Future* (Washington, D.C.: Government Printing Office, 1958); and USDA, Forest Service, *An Assessment of the Forest and Rangeland Situation in the United States* (Washington, D.C.: Government Printing Office, 1980).

The difficulties of projections become greater as the projections become more disaggregated. This is an important point because recent public land planning has required greater use of projections broken down in considerable detail, especially in the RPA effort. The predictions in 1958 for 1975 and the actual 1976 outcomes are shown in Table 2–2 for some highly specific items. As can be seen, in one case the prediction proved almost exactly correct, but in most cases the predictions were far off, in two cases by as much as a factor of six.

Relying on its future demand projections, the 1958 Forest Service study estimated needed forest growth and showed it to be much above projected growth, leading to a major shortage. The study reported that "the interpretations given to these projections of future growth are perhaps the most important in the entire timber resource review. The projections indicate that if medium levels of timber demand are met each year, sawtimber growth by 1965 would show a 14 percent deficit in relation to needed growth and a 76 percent deficit by the year 2000."[51] The study then warned:

Prompt and very substantial expansion and intensification of forestry in the United States is necessary if timber shortages are to be avoided by 2000. . . . The necessary intensification in forestry will have to be in addition to what could be expected by extending the trends in forestry improvements in recent years. This acceleration in forestry will have to come soon, and very largely within the next two decades, because otherwise it will be too late for the effects to be felt by 2000. The degree of forestry intensification needed is much larger and far greater than the general public or most experts are believed to have visualized.[52]

Table 2-2. Comparison of Predicted and Actual Total U.S. Demands for Selected Items

Item	Units	1958 Predicted for 1975 (millions)	Actual 1976 (millions)
Cooperage	board feet	600	94
Piling	linear feet	59	39
Poles	pieces	6.5	6.3
Posts	pieces	400	60
Mine timbers	cubic feet	105	24

Sources: USDA, Forest Service, *Timber Resources for America's Future* (Washington, D.C.: Government Printing Office, 1958); and USDA, Forest Service, *An Assessment of the Forest and Rangeland Situation in the United States* (Washington, D.C., January 1980).

Only seven years later a third set of future projections for timber was made by the Forest Service as shown in Table 2–3. Once again the Forest Service did not anticipate future timber growth. Projecting only five years ahead, the Forest Service underestimated 1970 growth by 11 percent. By 1976 actual timber growth already exceeded the Forest Service projection for 1980 by 16 percent. Somewhat smaller differences between the predicted and actual results occurred for timber harvests.

Regarding the underestimation of growth potential, Marion Clawson has commented that "timber growth potential has been repeatedly and seriously underestimated" by the Forest Service. The agency failed to take proper account of the impact of ongoing harvesting on future growth; the "great increase in annual net growth of timber was a direct consequence of the decline in standing volume. . . . Net growth was possible only as original stands of timber were opened up by harvest."[53] The older stands grew little if at all; harvesting them more quickly made way for rapidly growing young stands.

The agency's tendency to overstate projected timber shortages again displayed its weak understanding of economic forces. Price changes operate to bring demand and supply into equilibrium; an impending

Table 2-3. Comparison of Predicted and Actual Total U.S. Sawtimber Growth, Volume, and Harvest (billions of board feet)

	1965 Prediction for 1970	Actual 1970	1965 Prediction for 1980	Actual 1976
Timber growth	59.6	66.2	64.5	74.6
Inventory volume	2,586.0	2,538.6	2,645.0	2,578.9
Timber harvest	53.6	58.5	60.4	62.9

Sources: USDA, Forest Service, *Timber Trends in the United States* (Washington, D.C.: Government Printing Office, February 1965); and USDA, Forest Service, *An Assessment of the Forest and Rangeland Situation in the United States* (Washington, D.C., January 1980).

shortage calls forth a higher price, which both reduces demand and stimulates additional supply.

The Multiple-use Sustained-yield Act of 1960

Recreation does not necessarily conflict with timber harvesting; many game animals, for example, require a diversity of habitat, which timber harvesting can provide. Timber harvesting substitutes to some degree for fire, insects, and disease in providing areas of brush and browse. For the bulk of recreation, however, especially ordinary hiking and camping, most recreationists prefer uncut old-growth forests to the much smaller, less imposing trees in reforested areas. Almost all recreationists find the immediate aftermath of clear cutting to be visually unattractive or worse.

When demands for recreational uses surfaced, there was little in the background of the Forest Service to prepare it for the problem of resolving competing uses. Pinchot had been concerned with building political support for the Forest Service. He sought the backing of all national forest users and preferred to avoid what were then only abstract questions of allocation among competing uses.

When conflicts began to arise, the Forest Service did not respond with fresh thinking. Rather, it continued to employ the basic tactics of Pinchot, giving a commitment in very general terms to accommodate all the different kinds of uses but leaving the specifics for later resolution. This approach was embodied in the Multiple-use Sustained-yield Act of 1960.

The act did not actually create any new authority, as the Forest Service conceded; nevertheless key members of the Forest Service argued that an explicit congressional endorsement of its previous practices was needed. The main tenet of the act was its requirement that the national forests be managed according to the principles of "multiple use" and "sustained yield." These terms were defined in the legislation as follows:

> "Multiple use" means: The management of all the various renewable surface resources of the national forests so that they are utilized in the combination that will best meet the needs of the American people; making the most judicious use of the land for some or all of these resources or related services over areas large enough to provide sufficient latitude for periodic adjustments in use to conform to changing needs and conditions; that some land will be used for less than all of the resources; and harmonious and coordinated management of the various resources, each with the other, without impairment of the productivity of the land, with consideration being given to the relative values of the various resources, and not necessarily the combination of uses that will give the greatest dollar return or the greatest unit output.
>
> "Sustained yield of the several products and services" means the achievement and maintenance in perpetuity of a high level annual or regular periodic output of the various renewable resources of the national forests without impairment of the productivity of the land.[54]

Clearly, the Multiple-use Sustained-yield Act in practice provided little specific guidance to Forest Service land managers. Because of its vagueness, the definition of multiple use is subject to many interpretations. The Public Land Law Review Commission concluded from its investigations that "multiple use has little practical meaning as a planning concept or principle."[55] Even Edward Crafts, one of the key Forest Service officials responsible for the Multiple-use Sustained-yield Act, later conceded, "Everything fell under multiple use, and who can argue against multiple use because it is all things to all people. They used it as a justification for whatever they wanted to do."[56]

The definition of sustained yield in the act similarly allows many interpretations. For example, the question of area is critical. Obviously, sustained yield is not achieved in a small area that is clearcut. Then how large must the area be? Can sustained yield include yields from nearby private or other public agency lands? Must a sustained yield be achieved every day, year, decade, or century? The legislation provides little guidance on these and other critical questions.

The true significance of the Multiple-use Sustained-yield Act is symbolic. It gave a boost to recreation and certain other uses by providing explicit "authority to manage the lands for recreation and other purposes for which prior authority was lacking or unclear."[57] The act also represented for the Forest Service a congressional pat on the back for its traditional ways of doing things. The Forest Service hoped to fend off attempts by outside groups—both industrial and recreational—to box the Forest Service into specific policies in particular areas. The Forest Service instead preferred its traditional administrative discretion, which allowed it to deal equally with all the multiple uses in each forest area.

At the time, the Forest Service was upset by losses of its land to the National Park Service and was also unhappy with the loss of administrative discretion entailed in proposals for statutory designation of wilderness areas. According to some observers, the Multiple-use Sustained-yield Act was an attempt to forestall creation of further national parks. The Forest Service agreed to go along with formal congressional wilderness designations only "in exchange for congressional ratification of its long standing multiple use philosophy in the Multiple-Use Sustained-Yield Act of 1960."[58] The Sierra Club in fact was about the only prominent organization to oppose the bill, because it saw multiple use possibly limiting further creation of national parks and wildernesses.

An Economic Interpretation of Multiple Use

Under the pressure of increasing use conflicts an attempt was made in the 1970s to give the multiple-use concept a more concrete meaning. The impetus came also in part from the need to work out the implications of the Forest and Rangeland Renewable Resources Planning Act of 1974 and the National Forest Management Act of 1976.

John Krutilla, a leading environmental economist, in 1979 criticized the Forest Service, and in fact the whole forestry profession, for never facing up to the question of multiple use. Where foresters had "appreciated that there is need to provide the 'correct' level and mix of the various resource services which the national forests are capable of producing, up until the present the instincts and proper impulses of the profession expressed themselves somewhat more as high motives and sincere exhortations than as the application of operational criteria."[59] Partly because objective criteria for allocating the services of the national forests were never developed, the forestry profession was forced to suffer "indignities at the hands of one or another group insisting that the national forests satisfy their mutually incompatible demands."[60] To resolve this undesirable situation, the Forest Service had to recognize the "need to bring into its management frame of reference the developments which have advanced in other scientific or management disciplines which, while not required of the forester during the 'golden age of forestry,' have elements of direct applicability to national forest management today."[61] In short, Krutilla argued that the time had come to make good on the original promise of Gifford Pinchot, who preached only scientific management.

In developing a more scientific approach the critical first step should be to define a precise goal. Krutilla considered that there might be three basic types of goals for the Forest Service: (1) to promote economic efficiency, (2) to improve the distribution of income, and (3) to help stabilize the economy. There was little disagreement that the third of these is not the job of the Forest Service. But he also went on to dismiss social equity as a legitimate Forest Service mission; as a practical matter, "it is a bit quixotic for the Forest Service to attempt to ensure 'community stability' when the means to do so are not available to it."[62] Krutilla was also concerned that public participation could cause forest outputs to be distributed not on the basis of economic efficiency, but to the greatest number of votes. As a consequence, then, Krutilla argued that the goal should be "to manage the national forests in order to maximize benefits"—in short, to "pursue economic efficiency."[63]

To pursue efficiency in this sense means seeking the maximum possible net value of the outputs of the national forests. Where market prices exist, outputs should be valued at these prices. Where no markets exist, estimates should be formed of the prices that would otherwise have existed: simulated market prices. Clearly, such prices may be difficult to estimate; yet according to Krutilla, the difficulties were not so great as to preclude this approach. Economics thus provides a specific definition of multiple use. Given different combinations of possible outputs, the only way to compare apples and oranges is to establish a set of relative values—that is, prices. Using these prices, the agency course of action is that which maximizes total net value.

Despite some very substantial difficulties in estimating nonmarket values, this approach represents the most scientific way available to make management decisions for public forests. Yet historically the Forest Service never considered such a procedure. While the term "multiple use" was offered as a principle for making public forest decisions, it was essentially left undefined. Thus, as noted above, multiple-use decision making in practice meant decision making by administrative discretion—the absence of any binding objective standards.

Rejecting economic analysis, the Forest Service did not offer any other type of analysis in its place. Instead, the Forest Service response has been to muddle. In the end this left decisions to be determined mainly by the forces of interest-group politics, ironically the very antithesis of the original conservationist ideal. Multiple-use decision making might more accurately be described as multiple-interest-group decision making.

The Wilderness Act of 1964: A Contradictory Step

The Forest Service began designating wilderness areas in 1924 when Aldo Leopold persuaded the local forest supervisor to set aside seven hundred thousand acres of the Gila National Forest in New Mexico as the first wilderness area. The early designation of a wilderness area (then called "primitive area") was not very restrictive. Roads were not necessarily excluded and timber harvesting was often allowed. In 1939 new wilderness regulations were issued that greatly tightened the restrictions. A procedure was established to review existing wilderness areas for permanent inclusion in a new wilderness system. Subsequently, however, the Forest Service moved very slowly, and in 1960 many areas still had not been reviewed.

After 1939 wilderness designation effectively committed an area to one particular use. Except where other nonwilderness uses were already present, these uses were allowed only to the extent that they did not detract seriously from the wilderness character. The explicit identification of one primary use, of course, violates the multiple-use principle. In fact, the purpose of wilderness designation was precisely to eliminate the discretion to consider all uses. Wilderness proponents wanted a formal and permanent commitment to each wilderness area; they were not willing to trust the discretion of individual Forest Service field managers.

With tighter restrictions little acreage was added to the wilderness system after the 1930s, and in some cases areas with high timber or other commercial value were taken out of wilderness status. This created opposition both inside and outside the Forest Service to the agency's wilderness policies.

Not only the pace of reclassification but its results were challenged by preservationists. . . . There was, too, growing skepticism among preservationists that the Forest Service would, or even could, maintain permanent reservation for lands classified as wilderness. The mounting public demand for forest products and forest use increased the anxiety which a natural distrust of the bureaucracy instilled.[64]

Following almost a decade of discussion and debate, the Wilderness Act was finally passed in 1964. Timber harvesting and mechanized recreation were barred from wilderness areas. As a concession to the mining industry, mineral exploration was allowed to continue until 1984. No new livestock grazing or major new range improvements would be allowed, but existing grazing could continue. The act gave statutory confirmation to the status of 9.1 million acres that had already been administratively designated as wilderness by the Forest Service. The Wilderness Act also created procedures for review of additional lands for wilderness designation. Wilderness was said to be ''an area where the earth and its community of life are untrammeled by man, where man himself is a visitor who does not remain.'' For the purposes of the act wilderness was defined by a set of characteristics. But as with the term multiple use, the language left great latitude for interpretation.

In practice the best definition of wilderness is probably a roadless area that in some way is of recreational and environmental concern to the whole nation. Wilderness areas offer a federal parallel to the state creation of ''critical areas'' under state land use legislation of the 1970s. The national parks might be considered early federal critical areas; the creation of a wilderness system allowed the Forest Service to retain its own management control over newer federal critical areas, rather than having to surrender them to the Park Service.

The history of public land legislation is one of conflicting signals; Congress has seldom acted with clear objectives, and events have often produced reversals or contradictions of previous policies. Here again, although Congress enacted a major public land law in 1960 stating its commitment to multiple use, four years later it passed another significant public land law effectively ignoring the multiple-use philosophy and establishing a new single purpose management category. As one observer put it, ''The Wilderness Act is the antithesis of some conceptions of multiple use management and in a sense the Act expressed a lack of faith in the ability of the Forest Service to implement the multiple use requirements.''[65] By 1982, twenty-five million acres of national forests, greater than the total area of the national parks in 1964, had been designated as wilderness. An additional fifty-five million acres of wilderness had been designated within the National Park System and the National Wildlife Refuge System, most of this acreage in Alaska.

Vagueness in congressional directives to administrative agencies often reflects the necessity for political compromise and the fact that congressmen themselves are unsure how to proceed. Vague legislation often amounts to a push for the agencies to move in a general direction, but it is up to the agency and the affected interests to work out the details. The Multiple-use Sustained-yield Act and the Wilderness Act both fit this pattern. The Wilderness Act especially precipitated a major controversy over its implementation.

RARE I and RARE II

The Wilderness Act required that the Forest Service review 5.4 million acres of primitive areas then under consideration for wilderness and make a recommendation to Congress as to whether these areas should be placed within the wilderness system. The Forest Service subsequently determined that almost all such areas were in fact suitable and should be designated as wilderness.

Although not required, the Wilderness Act also included provision for further wilderness review of roadless areas in the national forests. In 1967 the Forest Service decided to inventory such areas, the initial step in the first Roadless Area Review and Evaluation (RARE I). There was little follow-up, however, until 1971, when outside pressures finally forced the Forest Service to act. Having moved very slowly for four years, the Forest Service now rushed to complete the inventory. A total of fifty-six million acres was identified as roadless. Of this acreage, 10.7 million acres were selected in 1972 by the Forest Service for intensive wilderness study.

The study procedures followed by the Forest Service provoked outcries from the environmental and recreation communities. The Forest Service had used a strict standard of judging signs of previous human presence in an area; minor structures or roads were enough to exclude an area from any consideration for wilderness, no matter how otherwise isolated and wild the area might be. Large potential wildernesses were sometimes cut up into pieces by the presence of old and barely discernible roads. In 1972 the Sierra Club and other environmental organizations brought suit against the Forest Service to prevent any commercial activity in roadless areas until acceptable environmental impact statements had been completed. Apparently having doubts about its own position, the Forest Service agreed to this request rather than fight it. The effect was to bar timber harvesting and other development activities from nearly one third of all Forest Service land.

By the time the Carter administration entered office in early 1977, the wilderness review had bogged down. Large acreages were left in limbo, available neither for wilderness nor for other uses. To resolve questions more rapidly and at a national level, a new wilderness review procedure was established: RARE II. The new review began by redoing the basic inventory. This time the Forest Service granted wider flexibility in allowing evidence of previous development, so long as these signs of human presence did not too severely impair the potential for wilderness experience. For example, areas previously cut over for timber could be included if they had returned to a condition characteristic of areas that had never been cut. Special standards were provided for the eastern national forests, a step much sought by recreationists. This process eventually resulted in the identification of 2,919 individual roadless areas containing a total of sixty-two million acres. The review also sought to ensure that the overall wilderness system included adequate representation of different types of ecosystems and land forms and that wilderness was distributed so as to provide adequate accessibility for different populations.

In 1979 the Forest Service released a final environmental impact statement that recommended fifteen million acres of new wilderness, thirty-six million acres of nonwilderness (to be managed under multiple-use principles), and further planning on eleven million acres.[66] Although recreationist critics considered RARE II an improvement over RARE I, it was still judged harshly. The Sierra Club and the Natural Resources Defense Council (NRDC) attacked it as inadequate, biased, and illogical. In their view the Forest Service had decided to emphasize "speed before quality."[67] Both groups argued that the only thing to do was to put most of the land into the further-study category.

The tribulations of the Forest Service in conducting its wilderness review were no doubt partially due to management mistakes. But they were also due significantly to deficiencies in the agency's basic approach to wilderness, which reflected the broader problems of public forest management discussed earlier.

In his insightful book on the Forest Service, Glen Robinson closely examined the problems the Forest Service had experienced in conducting RARE I.[68] The issue was an emotional one; every little battle tended to be elevated to a grand contest of ideology: "Contention between preservationists and multiple-use advocates is quickly escalated into a grand debate over wilderness vs. nonwilderness values, which in turn becomes an even more wide-ranging debate over the character of modern civilization. For some preservationists, each battle is but a larger holy war and has a symbolic significance far beyond any measurable objective. So, too, for some of the opposition."[69] Another factor making things difficult for the Forest Service was the strength of local feelings accompanying each wilderness dispute.

Partially because the wilderness concept is vague, it was not possible to say definitively that one area was wilderness and another not. Among potential wilderness preserves there were large differences in the other resource values foregone by wilderness designation; some potential wilderness areas in the overthrust belt of the Rocky Mountains offered the possibility of finding extremely valuable oil and gas, while others had little if any commercial potential. Such factors make the wilderness issue, at least in part, a question of resource allocation, that is to say, an economic question. According to Robinson, the Forest Service's reluctance to employ economic analysis was a serious impediment to a satisfactory wilderness review. In this regard he found that "the Forest Service has not made much use of economic analysis in its primitive area review process until recently. Even now [1975] one senses it is groping somewhat in deciding just how and how much an economic analysis (beyond crude thumbnail calculations) will aid in decision-making."[70]

Some observers consider that the designation of a wilderness area actually constitutes a religious statement—that wilderness areas are the churches or cathedrals of environmental religion. Indeed, a strong religious motive is explicit in the writings of John Muir, founder of the Sierra Club in 1892. Muir often referred to the wilderness as his "temple" where he sought refuge from the trials of urban life.[71] Partially for this reason, some proponents contend that wilderness is "priceless" and cannot be subject to economic valuation. Nevertheless, such contentions must be taken as largely rhetorical: society obviously has a limit on the sacrifices it will make to create more wilderness; indeed, medieval society similarly could not afford unlimited expenses for its cathedrals. Many other benefits of wilderness are of a much more mundane sort—hiking, fishing, hunting, and so forth.

In short, wilderness does have a value, if one more difficult to fully determine than many other values. Some portions of the value can be estimated in a formal way despite the fact that the benefits have a non-market character. It is often easier to determine the costs of wilderness:

loss of timber harvests, minerals, intensive recreation, and other excluded activities. These costs may well be minimal in many potential wilderness areas, greatly simplifying the task of deciding whether wilderness designation is appropriate. Although they would have been controversial under any circumstances, the Forest Service's unwillingness to subject wilderness decisions to economic analysis further politicized these decisions, the same consequence seen elsewhere of a lack of economic analysis. Decision makers were required to proceed with little hard information, exacerbating the pressures to make wilderness decisions as a symbolic—perhaps even religious—gesture.

The Economics of Timber Harvests

Harvesting timber makes a positive contribution to national economic output only if the value of the timber is greater than all the costs of harvesting it. On lands where this is not the case, more resources are used up in obtaining the timber than the output is worth. The social loss is increased when valuable recreation and other nonmarket uses of forest land are displaced by uneconomic timber harvesting.[72]

It is sometimes suggested that unprofitable timber should nevertheless be harvested in order to restrain increases in (or help drive down) the price of timber. Production of unprofitable timber, however, will act to raise the prices of other goods. By drawing off resources that would more economically be used in nontimber sectors, less production takes place in these sectors; the supply declines and prices rise. Timber price rises are thus simply displaced to price rises of other goods.

Marion Clawson, among many others, has found that Forest Service timber investments and harvests have often been economically irrational—that "the pattern of expenditures by regions and by forests strongly suggests that too much money is being spent on poor sites and not enough on good ones."[73] In particular Clawson reported that "the Forest Service has made timber sales on poor sites, where continued timber management is uneconomic, and has incurred costs for cleaning up the site (more for aesthetic than for silviculture reasons), which were in excess of the value of the timber sold. It is difficult to justify timber management that costs more than it returns, especially since nontimber values are as likely to be reduced as to be increased thereby."[74]

Clawson concluded that by concentrating timber management efforts on the best areas and sites and adopting other measures to use its resources more effectively, the Forest Service could simultaneously increase greatly the volume of timber, wilderness, and other outputs. Indeed, he estimated—probably optimistically—that with more efficient management of national forests, the amount of wood grown annually could be increased on an economic basis by a factor of two or three, wilderness areas expanded by a factor of three or four, and outdoor recreation visits by a factor of two or three.[75] The conflict between timber harvesting and recreation thus could be greatly reduced simply by ceasing to harvest timber on uneconomic lands. In fact the Sierra Club proposed in 1977 to intensify harvests on some highly productive timberlands in exchange for abandoning harvesting altogether on lands with much lower productivity.[76]

The response of the Forest Service to these criticisms was to acknowledge that many timber sales were uneconomic but to defend them nevertheless. In 1980 Assistant Secretary of Agriculture Rupert Cutler reported that Forest Service calculations showed almost 22 percent of the volume of timber harvested in 1978 did not generate enough public revenues to cover public costs.[77] Cutler, however, cited the Multiple-use Sustained-yield Act provision that the goal of Forest Service management is ''not necessarily the combination of uses that will give the greatest dollar return or the greatest unit output.'' Moreover, timber harvesting may promote multiple uses and recreational benefits from wider road accessibility. Cutler also argued that even unprofitable timber sales increase the supply of timber, lower timber prices, and maintain employment. The same could of course be said for any form of production, public or private, no matter how wasteful or unprofitable.

The Forest Service has defined its main timber objectives in terms of volume of wood harvested. The absence of an economic orientation has left a vacuum that instead was filled by physical output measures. Harvesting of uneconomic timber allowed the Forest Service to reach its timber harvest goal for the year. Field personnel often believed they would be judged by the volume of timber harvested, not by its quality or profit. The problem of using the wrong output measures, to be sure, is widely observed in large bureaucracies of all kinds.

But the chief explanation for the maintenance of uneconomic timber harvests has been political pressure from local timber areas. Local timber companies bid what the timber is worth; it is the Forest Service—and indirectly the national taxpayer—that absorbs the harvest deficits. Local communities and mill workers also benefit from income and jobs generated by timber harvests. Hence, local pressures have typically offered strong support for the continuance of uneconomic harvests, although some recreationists and environmentalists in the area have objected.

In a political context, economic analysis tends to serve as pressure for a national perspective. The historic reluctance to employ economics is partially a reflection of a long tradition in public land agencies of deference to local concerns. Traditionally, the Forest Service has proclaimed a management philosophy of shifting decision making as much as possible to the field. In an earlier era when public management costs for national forests were small and many decisions concerned solely the allocation of land among local uses, this local delegation may well have made good sense. However, the rapidly growing costs of forest management have required the assertion of outside constraints, especially since local areas pay so few of the costs. The local incentive is simply to press for further services whose costs will be borne by someone else.

Harvesting of Old-Growth Timber

As discussed previously, the role of the Forest Service as supplier of last resort left it after World War II with large inventories of old-growth timber; in the case of softwoods much larger than those of any other type of ownership. Facing strong pressures to increase supplies, the Forest Service did raise its harvest levels substantially and would have gone further had it not encountered strong opposition from recreational users.

The possession of large old-growth forests required the Forest Service to decide how best to draw down this one-time inventory. Traditional forestry principles, however, offered little guidance. Going back to Pinchot, forestry principles were derived from European circumstances in which few old-growth forests existed. The chief issues for European foresters had been the level of timber investment and how long to let the forest grow before harvesting: the rotation age. The management of a huge stock of timber in vast virgin forests was a wholly unfamiliar problem.[78]

The Forest Service—indeed the entire forestry profession—proved very slow in recognizing the differences between the European and American circumstances. Having learned a particular gospel, foresters attempted to apply it in all circumstances. Thus the allowable cut was set by the Forest Service at the level of long-run sustained yield, even on forests where a large old-growth inventory was found. This harvest policy was eventually enshrined as the "nondeclining even-flow" policy. Specifically, it required timber harvests from a national forest to be set at the maximum level achievable, below which future harvests would never be allowed to fall.

The Forest Service initially defined the long run as the period of the first rotation—usually about one hundred years. The nondeclining even-flow policy then set the allowable cut to equal the maximum sustainable harvest over the duration of the rotation. However, because there was so much old-growth timber in the national forests, much higher harvesting levels could be sustained for the first rotation than for subsequent rotations. Studies by the Forest Service in the late 1960s revealed that a significant drop-off in harvests at the end of the first rotation would occur.

Because this seemed to violate the spirit of the nondeclining even-flow policy, even if it would not occur for one hundred years, the Forest Service decided in 1973 to adopt an even stricter harvesting standard: harvests must equal the maximum nondeclining even flow of timber that could be sustained indefinitely. In areas with ample supply of old-growth timber, this resulted in a constant even flow of timber at the level of long-run sustained yield. In other forests the harvest might start off lower and then rise to the long-run sustainable level. But a harvest higher than long-run sustained yield was precluded, even where the subsequent drop might only be to the level of long-run sustained yield. This was in fact feasible in a number of federal forests with large inventories of old-growth timber.

The public land agencies have justified the even-flow policy partially as a means of promoting community stability. However, this implicitly assumed that private and state timber harvests were also being maintained at an even flow. As will be recalled, private timber has generally been harvested ahead of federal timber—indeed, for good economic reasons. But private supplies in the Pacific Northwest have been greatly depleted and will remain low until second-growth forests become available. In such circumstances an even-flow policy for public forests can perversely become a destabilizing rather than a stabilizing influence.

Forest Service harvest policies for old-growth timber were questioned as early as the late 1950s. A study prepared by the Forest Service examined harvesting issues for the forests in the Pacific Northwest (the Duerr Report).[79] One alternative provided for a five-decade acceleration of timber harvests to twice the levels that would be achieved under the even-flow policy. Over the full rotation (eleven decades), total timber harvests would be increased 27 percent over the even-flow policy. The only liability would be that in decades six through eight harvests would drop to half the even-flow levels. Although this drop might be made up by private harvest acceleration, it created the possibility—however far in the future—of substantial local income and employment instability. The Forest Service considered this alternative to be so heretical that it required that the alternative be dropped from the final version of the study eventually published in 1963.

By the early 1970s timber supplies had tightened further, prices had risen sharply, and Forest Service harvest policies were receiving much wider attention. The price of timber was identified as an important contributor to a surge then occurring in housing costs. Timber prices were one of the few housing-cost elements that the federal government might directly influence. Pressures thus grew to find additional supplies of public timber, which resulted in the creation of the President's Advisory Panel on Timber and the Environment. The panel examined the even-flow issue and in one of its reports concluded that timber harvests could be accelerated by 30 percent in certain forests heavily stocked with old-growth timber. The panel reported: "Even flow restrictions clearly result in a substantially lowered allowable cut than would be the case if full recognition were given to the fact that a typical western national forest is frequently overstocked with old-growth timber and the fact that this overstocking can be harvested over a period of time without any reduction in the amount of second growth timber that can be grown in subsequent rotations."[80] Similar concerns that conservative federal timber harvesting policies were driving up timber prices unnecessarily were expressed in 1977 by the Council on Wage and Price Stability.[81]

Concern for the inflationary effects of federal harvest policies again arose in the spring of 1978 when inflation rates jumped suddenly. In April President Jimmy Carter announced a new inflation control program, including as one element new efforts to contain rising housing prices through expanded federal timber sales. The secretaries of agriculture and interior were instructed to report on ways of increasing federal timber harvests. In preparing the report, internal administration debate focused on the possibilities for departing from even flow as a way of increasing timber supplies. To make such a departure more acceptable, a constraint was proposed that future harvests never decline below the even-flow level. Even-flow proponents were put on the defensive because they were forced to argue that current timber harvest increases should be rejected even where they did not require any future declines in timber harvests below those already planned (under even flow).

The strongest opposition to departures from an even-flow policy came from the Council on Environmental Quality. The council and to a lesser extent the Forest Service argued that the National Forest Management Act of 1976 did not allow departures from an even flow. The greatest support for departures came from the economic agencies (Council of Economic Advisors and the Council on Wage and Price Stability) and the Interior Department. Interior Secretary Cecil Andrus had himself been in the timber business and took this issue into his own hands to an unusual degree. In June 1979 the president announced that he was directing the departments of Agriculture and Interior to "use maximum speed in updating land management plans on selected lands with the objective of increasing the harvest of mature timber through departure from the current nondeclining even-flow policy."[82]

Once again the Forest Service found itself being overridden by an outside institution. In the case of wilderness and environmental protection of fragile areas, it was by environmentalists and the courts; on even flow and the harvesting of old-growth timber, it was by other agencies in the executive branch and by the president. In each instance the Forest Service proved unable to adjust to new ideas and clung to ill-conceived policies until finally outside forces compelled change. Although the Forest Service had aimed to be a vanguard agency, it had long since become defensive and reactive and slow to see new requirements and forces being brought to bear on it.

As in so many other cases, the fundamental problem in its approach to harvesting old-growth timber lay in the absence of an analytical and skeptical tradition. For bureaucratic and other reasons the agency found it very difficult even to ask the right questions about the harvesting of a large one-time timber inventory. The Forest Service also promoted even flow partially because it saw this policy as a popular and easily explainable interpretation of sustained yield management to the public; in short, it sounded good. An even-flow policy was also easy to administer since the guidance to the field for determining timber harvests followed a simple mechanical rule. The fact that even flow produced nonsensical results was perhaps not initially recognized; in any case, once the policy was officially decreed the Forest Service stubbornly defended it against all criticism as though it were defending the one true faith.[83]

Public Forest Mythology

An examination of the track record of public forestry in the United States—now more than three quarters of a century old—reveals some major shortcomings. The public forests contain natural assets of high value, which have conferred many wonderful benefits on the American public. The nation has succeeded in harvesting large amounts of valuable timber and in creating a system of national parks and wildernesses. The national forests have become prime recreational grounds for millions of hikers, fishermen, hunters, and other recreationists. However, these impressive gains have often been achieved against the main precepts of public forestry, rather than with their assistance.

The Forest Service for years issued dire warnings about timber famines that in every case proved to be false alarms. It warned that public regulation of private harvests was the only way to achieve forest regeneration, only to see parts of industry exceed the Forest Service itself in regeneration success a few years later. The Forest Service persisted for years in promoting scientifically inaccurate and misguided information about the impacts of water and fire in the national forests. The agency also misread the future by almost always resisting creation of new national parks from national forest lands, arguing against preservation of large areas from commodity uses.

After pushing the Multiple-use Sustained-yield Act into existence, the Forest Service did little to give this vague concept more substance; instead it used the act as an ever-handy justification for just about any Forest Service policy or action. After initially appearing to promote wilderness, the Forest Service cooled to the idea when the concept appeared to limit the agency's prerogatives. In the face of rapidly growing public demands for more recreation, the Forest Service instead persisted in harvesting timber in roadless and other recreationally valuable areas, even when that timber is uneconomic to cut. The nondeclining even-flow policy advocated by the Forest Service led to obviously silly and unreasonable timber harvesting implications.

The Forest Service still reflects in many ways the character initially given to it by Gifford Pinchot, who saw his role as one of promoting scientific forest management in the United States. In achieving his mission, however, he behaved not as a scientist but as a proselytizer. When challenged, Pinchot did what was necessary to advance his aims, and scientific caution did not necessarily get in his way. Those who agreed with him would later argue that his actions were necessary means to defeat the powerful and self-seeking forces that opposed him: the timber companies, stockmen, and others. Pinchot was a man of action who should be judged by his success in creating the Forest Service, not by the consistency of his thought. As one friendly observer put it, his "genius lay not in silviculture but in progressive reform politics."[84] It took a man of immense political talent because Pinchot, after all, was trying to sell "a socialist approach to forestry—public ownership in operation—in an age when rugged individualism, laissez-faire capitalism, and minimal federal regulation were the accepted political norms."[85]

But as so often happens, the means became the end. The Forest Service never adopted the self-critical and questioning attitude characteristic of science; it showed declining fervor but never really called off the moral crusade. To skeptical outsiders Forest Service policy making often seems to bear a closer resemblance to moral affirmation than to hard analysis.

In reviewing the history of Forest Service policies, it seems clear that a prime criterion has often been to create a suitable image in the public eye. Early opponents were portrayed as villainous perpetrators of "forest devastation" who were pushing the country into a "timber famine." In setting its own policies, the Forest Service characterized itself as following the principles of "multiple use," "sustained yield," and "even flow," all of which may sound laudable but in practice are vacuous or even misconceived. Until recently the Forest Service had shown a genius for such favorable publicity as the Smokey the Bear campaign. In reciprocation, until recently at least, the public has showered good will on the Forest Service, which ultimately was translated into large budgets and congressional deference.

The fact that the Forest Service was a purveyor of very appealing myths did not make much difference so long as Forest Service management remained largely custodial, a situation that lasted up until World War II. One might even say the Forest Service performed a valuable public service in this regard, storing the lands for future, more important uses. But since then there has been a widening discontent with the management of the national forests. The earlier foundations satisfactory for a custodial role proved inadequate to meet a new era of intense competition among valuable uses of the public lands.

The criticisms of Forest Service mythology are part of a wider criticism of the ideas of the conservation movement. The term "conservationist" has great popular appeal. As Scott Gordon noted, it is "replete with honorable and admirable connotations, designating one who is unselfish, and forward-looking, rational and public spirited, energetic and self-denying." Nevertheless, this critic concludes, much as others have, that "a great deal (perhaps the greater part) of what has been done in the name of 'conservation policy' turns out, on subjection to economic analysis, to be worthless or worse."[86]

The Forest Service has never found a satisfactory alternative to its founding conservationist gospel. As support for conservationist ideas has eroded, the defenses against political intervention in national forest affairs have fallen. Indeed, as previous discussion has indicated, over the past years management decisions regarding the national forests have become more political. The criterion for a good decision has typically been to achieve a satisfactory balance of user pressures. Some political scientists contend that this is as it should be. Rejecting a scientific basis for government policies, the proponents of "interest-group liberalism" see the governing process as appropriately and inevitably one of interest-group bargaining and agreement.[87]

As Clawson, Krutilla and others have argued, the best hope for reviving scientific forest management for those who find such a view unsatisfactory lies in economics. Economics seeks to provide an objective measure of the value of each forest resource use. Then rather than weighing the claims of public forest users by their political power and influence, economic decision making would weigh these claims by their market prices or estimated social values. Similarly, the use of economics would attempt to put management of the public forests on a businesslike basis. Instead of managing to produce a maximum profit, however, the wider standard of total social value would be maximized, taking account of nonmarket outputs as well as ordinary commodity outputs.

Prospects for Economic Forest Management

One cannot be optimistic, however, that a vision of a new, economically sophisticated Forest Service is achievable—even making the dubious assumption that some broad agreement on this goal could be reached. There are both internal agency obstacles and external political constraints. Either alone is probably sufficient to ensure that future decision making for the federal forests will continue to rely primarily on factors other than economic analysis. In short, achieving the progressive goal of scientific managers may be an impossibility.

It would not be enough simply to introduce some economists into the Forest Service. There have in fact previously been economists in the agency, but they have had little influence. In order to make economic concerns a central element in agency decision making, more drastic steps are necessary. The leadership positions of the agency have to be occupied by people who are either economists themselves or for whom economic reasoning is second nature. Yet this would amount to a revolution in the selection and advancement processes of most public agencies. Short of extreme outside pressures, it is hard to imagine how the existing leadership would make way for such a new economist cast— most of whom would have to be brought in from outside.

To be sure, skills in economic analysis have not traditionally commanded much of a premium in public forestry because the rest of the world has not asked for them. Under the original conservationism public forestry was to be practiced by expert professionals insulated from politics. But it never turned out that way. Rather, the Forest Service has always operated in a highly charged political environment. Much of the appeal of forestry mythology has been as a way of rallying support to protect Forest Service independence. This effort achieved some success in the early history of the agency but became less feasible over time. Now, like most government agencies, the Forest Service is pushed and shoved by the many interest groups that stand to benefit or lose from its policies. Indeed, it may be that the Forest Service has ended up with the worst of both worlds; it has frequently abandoned scientific analysis for popular imagery, but still cannot achieve the independence from politics prescribed in the conservationist design.

Hence, even if the Forest Service were to decide to base its management on a much greater use of economics, there would still be no guarantee that the policies eventually adopted would closely reflect this change. If a new, economically sophisticated Forest Service were also less popular and therefore politically weakened—indeed, perhaps as a direct consequence of its turn to economic calculations—it might have less ability to implement its newly efficient plans. The ultimate consequence might be a further breakdown of the barriers to political interference and an even less efficient set of actions carried out on the national forests.

Public forest management thus represents an illustration of a basic dilemma facing natural resource management in the public sector. Professional management is impossible without substantial autonomy from the political forces that characterize democratic government. Yet the achievement of such autonomy is itself a highly political task; the necessary political actions compromise both the claim to independent professionalism and the professional quality of management decisions. Progressives sought to establish the idea of management by experts as a generally accepted governing principle. However, this claim to expert authority was never broadly accepted by the American public as legitimate.

Conclusion

The failure of the progressive model, combined with grave doubts as to the efficiency or equity of interest-group politics, raises the possibility of more radical solutions. One option would be to transfer at least the prime timber growing lands to the private sector.[88] Private management would have much more of the autonomy from politics that is necessary to implement scientific management of the forests. Indeed, rather than Forest Service management, the results of Weyerhaeuser management over the years, for example, have probably come much closer to the original vision of Gifford Pinchot and other conservationists. Private management of divested public timberlands would probably not mean transferring the lands to many small firms; rather, it would probably involve creating several new major corporations (or expanding existing ones). These corporations might be established through the issuance of new stock and its sale to the public.

However, the accountability of the large corporation to market forces is not always very great—especially in the short run. Nor are the political mechanisms for regulating corporate behavior always efficient in achieving social goals not reflected in market incentives. These concerns seem particularly important on lands with marginally profitable timber that conversely have high recreation and environmental values. This circumstance characterizes perhaps the majority of current Forest Service lands. Hence, privatization might be suitable for only a limited portion of Forest Services lands; transfer to state and local governments might be the best option for the majority of the lands.

Such public forest issues have not been fully aired since the progressive era. Major changes in social values have occurred since that time, changes that the Forest Service has often had great difficulty comprehending. The time is overdue for a reexamination of fundamental assumptions and purposes with respect to federal forest ownership.[89]

Notes

1. Herbert Kaufman, *The Forest Ranger* (Baltimore: Johns Hopkins University Press, 1960).

2. Samuel T. Dana, *Forest and Range Policy: Its Development in the United States* (New York: McGraw-Hill, 1956): 77.

3. *Ibid.*

4. George Perkins Marsh, *Man and Nature*, reprint (Cambridge, Mass.: Harvard University Press, 1965).

5. Dana, *Forest and Range Policy*: 82.

6. Cited in *ibid.*: 101.

7. Samuel P. Hays, *Conservation and the Gospel of Efficiency: The Progressive Conservation Movement, 1890–1920* (Cambridge, Mass.: Harvard University Press, 1959): 264.

8. Gifford Pinchot, *Breaking New Ground* (New York: Harcourt, Brace and Co., 1947): 125.

9. 30 Stat. 34–36, 43, 4 (1897).

10. Pinchot, *Breaking New Ground*: 190.

11. *Ibid.*: 261.

12. Hays, *Conservation and the Gospel of Efficiency*: 41–42.

13. *Ibid.*: 2.

14. *Ibid.*: 267.

15. Pinchot, *Breaking New Ground*: 284.

16. Dwight Waldo, *The Administrative State: A Study of the Political Theory of American Public Administration* (New York: Ronald Press, 1948): 30.

17. Pinchot, *Breaking New Ground*: 284.

18. *Ibid.*: 258–60.

19. *Ibid.*: 260.

20. *Ibid.*

21. Cited in Henry Clepper, *Professional Forestry in the United States* (Baltimore: Johns Hopkins University Press, 1971): 135.

22. Cited in John Ise, *The United States Forest Policy* (New Haven, Conn.: Yale University Press, 1920): 30.

23. Cited in Clepper, *Professional Forestry in the United States*: 135.

24. Cited in *Ibid.*: 136.

25. Cited in Michael Frome, *Whose Woods These Are: The Story of the National Forests* (Garden City, N.Y.: Doubleday, 1962): 59.

26. Clepper, *Professional Forestry in the United States*: 137–38.

27. *Ibid.*: 145.

28. Sherry H. Olson, *The Depletion Myth: A History of Railroad Use of Timber* (Cambridge, Mass.: Harvard University Press, 1971): 104.

29. *Ibid.*: 96.

30. *Ibid.*: 75.

31. Ashley L. Schiff, *Fire and Water: Scientific Heresy in the Forest Service* (Cambridge, Mass.: Harvard University Press, 1962).

32. *Ibid.*: 5.

33. *Ibid.*

34. *Ibid.*: 120.

35. Cited in *Ibid.*: 139.

36. *Ibid.*: 146.

37. *Ibid.*: 144.

38. *Ibid.*: 162.

39. *Ibid.*: 169.

40. Harold K. Steen, *The U.S. Forest Service: A History* (Seattle: University of Washington Press, 1976): 113.

41. Remarks of Murl Sturms, Chief of Forestry, Bureau of Land Management, cited in David R. Barney, *The Last Stand: Ralph Nader's Study Group on the National Forests* (New York: Grossman Publishers, 1974): 19.

42. Clepper, *Professional Forestry in the United States*: 137–138.

43. *Ibid.*: 138.

44. U.S. Department of Agriculture, *A National Plan for American Forestry: The Report of the Forest Service of the Agriculture Department on the Forest Problem of the United States* (Washington. D.C.: Government Printing Office, 1933): I: 41.

45. Cited in Clepper, *Professional Forestry in the United States*: 150.

46. *Ibid.*: 291.

47. *Ibid.*: 290.

48. Edward C. Crafts, *Forest Service Researcher and Congressional Liaison: An Eye to Multiple Use*, an interview conducted by Susan R. Schrepfer (Santa Cruz, Calif.: Forest History Society, Oral History Office, 1972): 125.

49. U.S. Department of Agriculture, Forest Service, *Timber Resources for America's Future* (January 1958).

50. See U.S. Department of Agriculture, Forest Service, *A National Plan for American Forestry: Timber Resources for America's Future; Timber Trends in the United States* (February 1965); idem, *The Outlook for Timber in the United States* (October 1973); idem, *The Nation's Renewable Resources—An Assessment, 1975* (June 1977); and idem, *An Assessment of the Forest and Rangeland Situation in the United States* (January 1980).

51. U.S. Department of Agriculture, Forest Service, *Timber Resources for America's Future*: 96–97.

52. *Ibid.*: 102.

53. Marion Clawson, "Forests in the Long Sweep of American History," *Science* (June 15, 1979): 1171–72.

54. Public Law 86–517: see 16 U.S.C., sec. 531 (1976 ed.). For the history of this law, see Edward C. Crafts, "Saga of a Law: Part I," *American Forests* 76, no. 6 (June 1970), and Edward C. Crafts, "Saga of a Law: Part II," *American Forests* 76, no. 7 (July 1970).

55. *One Third of the Nation's Land: A Report to the President and to the Congress by the Public Land Law Review Commission* (Washington, D.C.: Government Printing Office, 1970): 45.

56. Crafts, *Forest Service Researcher and Congressional Liaison*: 80.

57. *One Third of the Nation's Land*: 43.

58. Glen O. Robinson, *The Forest Service: A Study in Public Land Management* (Baltimore: Johns Hopkins University Press, 1975): 16.

59. John V. Krutilla, "Adaptive Responses to Forces for Change," paper presented at the Annual Meetings of the Society of American Foresters, Boston, Mass., 16 October 1979: 6.

60. *Ibid.*: 5.

61. *Ibid.*: 7.

62. John V. Krutilla and John A. Haigh, "An Integrated Approach to National Forest Management," *Environmental Law* 8, no. 2 (Winter 1978): 383.

63. *Ibid.*: 383.

64. Robinson, *The Forest Service*: 158.

65. James L. Huffman, "A History of Forest Policy in the United States," *Environmental Law* 8, no. 2 (Winter 1978): 277.

66. U. S. Department of Agriculture, Forest Service, *Roadless Area Review and Evaluation: Final Environmental Statement* (January 1979).

67. "Comments of the Sierra Club and the Natural Resources Defense Council on the United States Department of Agriculture, Forest Service's Draft Environmental Statement on the Roadless Area Review and Evaluation (RARE II)," in USDA, *Roadless Area Review and Evaluation*: V-141.

68. Robinson, *The Forest Service*: 161–89.

69. *Ibid.*: 167.

70. *Ibid.*: 173.

71. See Roderick Nash, *Wilderness and the American Mind* (New Haven, Conn.: Yale University Press, 1967); also William Dennis, "Wilderness Cathedrals and the Public Good," paper presented at a symposium on "Natural Resource Economics and Policy: Explorations with Journalists," Center for Political Economy and Natural Resources, Montana State University, Bozeman, Montana, 15–19 June 1981.

72. See John Baden and Richard L. Stroup, eds., *Bureaucracy versus Environment: The Environmental Costs of Bureaucratic Governance* (Ann Arbor: University of Michigan Press, 1981); and Richard L. Stroup and John Baden, *Natural Resources: Bureaucratic Myths and Environmental Management* (San Francisco: Pacific Institute for Public Policy Research, 1983).

73. Marion Clawson, *The Economics of National Forest Management* (Washington, D. C.: Resources for the Future, 1976): 78.

74. *Ibid.*: 86.

75. Marion Clawson, "The National Forests," *Science* 191, no. 4227 (20 February 1976): 763.

76. Statement by Brock Evans, Director, Washington office, Sierra Club, before the Senate Subcommittee on Interior of the Appropriations Committee regarding the Forest Service budget for fiscal year 1978 (19 April 1977).

77. Letter from Rupert Cutler, Assistant Secretary of the Department of Agriculture for Natural Resources and Environment, to James G. Dean, editor of *The Living Wilderness*, 13 March 1980.

78. R. W. Behan, "Forestry and the End of Innocence," *American Forests* 81, no. 5 (May 1975), and idem, "Political Popularity and Conceptual Nonsense: The Strange Case of Sustained Yield Forestry," *Environmental Law* 8, no. 2 (Winter 1978).

79. U.S. Department of Agriculture, Forest Service, Pacific Northwest For-

est and Range Experiment Station, *Timber Trends in Western Washington* (Portland, Oreg.: August 1960).

80. *Report of the President's Advisory Panel on Timber and Environment* (Washington, D.C.: Government Printing Office, April 1973): 80.

81. U.S. Council on Wage and Price Stability, *Interim Report: Lumber Prices and the Lumber Products Industry* (October 1977).

82. Memoranda to the Secretary of Agriculture and the Secretary of the Interior from the White House, June 1979. For further details on this policy debate, see Robert H. Nelson and Lucian Pugliaresi, "Timber Harvest Policy Issues on the O&C Lands," in Robert T. Deacon and M. Bruce Johnson, eds., *Forestlands: Public and Private* (San Francisco: Pacific Institute for Public Policy Research, 1985).

83. See Thomas Lenard, "Wasting Our National Forests," *Regulation* (July/August 1981).

84. Behan, "Forestry and the End of Innocence": 38.

85. *Ibid.*: 38.

86. Scott Gordon, "Economics and the Conservation Question," *Journal of Law and Economics* 1, no. 1 (October 1958): 110–11.

87. See Theodore J. Lowi, *The End of Liberalism: Ideology, Policy and the Crisis of Public Authority* (New York: W. W. Norton, 1969).

88. See Richard Stroup and John Baden, "Externality, Property Rights and the Management of the National Forests," *Journal of Law and Economics* 16, no. 2 (October 1973); Phillip N. Truluck and David J. Theroux, eds., *Private Rights and Public Lands* (Washington, D.C.: Heritage Foundation, 1983), and articles on "Land Use and Resource Development," *The Cato Journal* 2, no. 3 (Winter 1982).

89. See Robert H. Nelson, "The Public Lands," in Paul R. Portney, ed, *Current Issues in Natural Resource Policy* (Baltimore: Johns Hopkins University Press for Resources for the Future, 1982). See also Robert H. Nelson, "Making Sense of the Sagebrush Rebellion: A Long-term Strategy for the Public Lands," paper prepared for presentation at the Third Annual Conference of the Association for Public Policy Analysis and Management, Washington, D.C., 23–25 October 1981. A shortened version of this paper is found in chapter 8 of this book and in Robert H. Nelson "A Long-term Strategy for the Public Lands" in Richard Ganzel, ed., *Resource Conflicts in the West* (Reno: Nevada Public Affairs Institute, University of Nevada, March 1983).

Chapter 3

Uneconomic Analysis: Scientific Management on the Public Rangelands

Samuel Hays characterized conservationism as the "gospel of efficiency," but it is economics that has long advertised itself as the true science of maximizing efficiency in use of the resources of society.[1] Forestry, rangeland science, and other professional disciplines, economists argue, instead typically seek to maximize the one object of their professional concern: forest products in the case of foresters, rangeland forage in the case of rangeland scientists. These professions fail to take account of the necessity for society to make tradeoffs among all the possibilities for economic benefit. Hence, economists argue, society must look to economic tools and methods as the one best hope of finally realizing the scientifically efficient management of the public lands.

Indeed, as chapter 2 describes, the comprehensive use of economics as the basis for public land decisions has been proposed by a number of observers as the best way of giving operational meaning to "scientific management" or "conservation." If this proposal were adopted, agency economists would first estimate the total social benefits and social costs of alternative land management actions; the action finally selected by agency administrators would then be the one calculated to maximize net social benefits minus costs.[2]

This chapter addresses this proposed means of giving operational content to the progressive model by examining the Bureau of Land Management's (BLM) use of economic analysis in public rangeland management in the 1970s and early 1980s (an exercise in which I par-

This chapter is a newly edited and shortened version of "Economic Analysis in Public Rangeland Management," in John Francis and Richard Ganzel, *Western Public Lands* (Totowa, N.J.: Rowman and Allenheld, 1984).

ticipated as advisor, consultant, and reviewer at the secretarial level of the Interior Department). The BLM rangelands include around 170 million acres—about 9 percent of the land area of the lower forty-eight states—that are grazed each year by around two million cattle, as well as sheep and goats. Together these livestock consume roughly nine million "animal unit months" (AUMs) of forage.

The familiar political and institutional obstacles to scientific analysis were all encountered in this exercise, in addition to many technical obstacles. Economic analysis was often unable to produce the definitive scientific conclusions needed to defend controversial management decisions sure to be attacked fiercely in the political arena. There was also a new and more surprising problem: at least under existing laws and public expectations, and with strong political pressure being applied from all sides, the development of scientific data and analysis proved very expensive. Indeed, the following dilemma arose: because the public rangeland resource has a low economic value, bearing the costs of scientific management may itself not be scientifically justified. In short, if economics is considered part of the scientific equation, the attempt to practice scientific management—at least as it has traditionally been understood—may raise inherent internal contradictions and thus be impossible.

This is one more reason why a fundamental rethinking of public land management is necessary today. It also suggests a turn toward relying more heavily on the old-fashioned method of trial and error. If the actual users of the land had secure rights to the future benefits of the land, these users might be best situated to understand its problems and to manage it in an informed and skillful way at a reasonable cost in relation to the results achieved on the land.

Rangeland Science versus Economics

Following the precepts of the scientific management philosophy, a profession of range science was created to advance rangeland expertise, eventually resulting in the founding of the Society for Range Management in 1948. On the public rangelands the progressive prescription for scientific management has generally consisted of the application of the principles of range science, as taught by the members of the profession of range management.

As they state it, the management objective of range professionals is to maintain a high and permanently sustainable level of productive capacity for the rangelands. Before the emphasis of recent years on a variety of range uses, this was usually considered to consist of maintaining a high sustained yield of forage available for domestic livestock grazing. Thus, a long-time leading textbook defined range management as: "the science and art of planning and directing range use so as to obtain the maximum livestock production consistent with conservation of the range resources."[3] Later, the need to allocate forage for use by wildlife, watershed, and other purposes was recognized. A more contemporary version of this same text states, "Prior to the 1960's range research was designed primarily to maximize forage production for domestic livestock. Current trends in range research are geared to optimize the functioning of the entire range ecosystem."[4]

The basic philosophy of a member of the BLM is that "as resource managers, our first consideration is to preserve and improve the production potential of the land while using its resources."[5] The major BLM statements presenting its range management program in one way or another have included achievement of a high sustained yield of forage production as the fundamental objective of BLM management. A programmatic grazing environmental impact statement (EIS) released by BLM in 1974 stated that "the specific objectives of the livestock grazing management program are to maintain and improve vegetative resources through management actions and supportive measures, to aid biological processes which will result in improved vegetative conditions and greater stability of soil, a sustained yield of livestock forage, more productive wildlife habitat and enhancement of aesthetics."[6] The goal of a high sustained yield of the resource is held not just by BLM, but by Congress and most other leaders in public land management. The Federal Land Policy and Management Act of 1976 directs that "management be on the basis of multiple use and sustained yield."[7] The Public Rangelands Improvement Act of 1978 states a policy to "manage, maintain and improve the condition of the public rangelands so that they become as productive as feasible for all rangeland values."[8]

By pouring ever greater resources and investment into the range, society could in fact increase its productive capacity greatly. For example, much of the range could produce at far higher levels if only water could be supplied. Reclamation efforts have had just this objective, with spectacular results in some areas such as the Imperial Valley in California, a former desert. Less drastic, the forage output could be greatly increased by physically removing existing low-productivity shrub and plants that have resulted from past overgrazing and replacing these plants with more productive species. There are many such vegetative treatments available. Even without efforts of this kind, fencing and water facilities could be installed to give more precise management of livestock movements in small areas.

In practice, however, few if any rangeland managers propose doing everything possible to raise the productivity of the rangelands. They recognize full well that there must be a limit to social expenditures on rangelands. The proposals by range scientists of a goal to maximize forage production thus seem to have mostly a rhetorical function. They fulfill a perceived need for some sort of formal statement of purpose, even while avoiding the difficult issues that would be raised by more analytically precise and meaningful statements. These issues involve tradeoffs between the commitment of the resources of society to rangeland purposes and to other social needs.

In the 1970s economists sought to fill the gap left by the inability of range scientists to provide a practically useful statement of the objectives of range management. In a very general way, economists argued, it is not difficult to discern what the actual objective of rangeland management should be: maximization of the net value to society obtained from the rangelands. Once the concept of net social value is introduced, consideration of costs is required. The fundamental deficiency in the objective to achieve as high a sustained yield of forage as possible, measured in physical terms, is that it fails to consider costs. In this manner the biological concept espoused by rangeland scientists avoids altogether the necessary task of setting priorities among competing uses of the resources of society.

Net social value will increase as long as further investments or other expenditures for the rangelands yield greater social benefits at the margin than the marginal costs incurred. Hence, maximization of net social value leads to the rule that society should continue to spend more on the rangelands until the added social costs begin to exceed the added social benefits. In applying this rule, benefits and costs must include not only marketable inputs and outputs but also all nonmarket benefits and costs. The latter include environmental consequences, aesthetic values, option values, and a number of other benefits never encountered in direct-market transactions.

While economists are few and far between in BLM, the economics profession is well represented in other parts of government, most importantly in the Office of Management and Budget (OMB). Other budget and policy analysis offices within the Interior Department also take an economic rather than a biological view of scientific management. Since each profession professes to have the objective truth, the disputes between economists and range scientists sometimes look a little like a religious war. There is a long tradition of bitter disagreements between OMB and the public land agencies.

OMB preaches, along with other economists, that achieving a high sustained level of rangeland production is not a satisfactory goal in itself. It cannot provide objective, nonpolitical grounds for public rangeland management. OMB sees the attachment of the public land agencies to biological concepts as an attempt either to stake unlimited claims on public resources or, more likely, to preserve maximum administrative discretion and to leave the field open for political maneuvering. OMB thus sees itself as the genuine defender of scientific professionalism. The public land agency biological concept is, as OMB regards it, an imposter behind which hides the real opponent, the surrender of the public lands to domination by various special interest groups. In the case of BLM the early history of domination of the agency by ranchers after the Taylor Grazing Act of 1934 helped to confirm OMB in this view.[9]

OMB thus has put strong pressures at times on the public land agencies to perform more economic analysis. It has sought to resist interest group politics in favor of a greater role for professional expertise, which in its view must in matters of resource allocation be economic expertise. Economic analyses should justify the allocations of the public rangelands among different uses, show whether the benefits of proposed investments exceed the costs, and give the scientific basis for other agency decisions.

In the face of limited success OMB has often responded by taking the attitude that it will try to restrict public land agency budgets to the most promising items and, as one OMB official put it, "cut our losses on the rest."[10] OMB pressures on occasion have also helped to push the public land agencies into greater efforts to conduct economic analysis.

Early Applications of Rangeland Economics

An early major use of economics in public rangeland management was to determine a proper grazing fee. Largely due to OMB insistence, a major study of western livestock grazing was conducted in the mid-1960s.[11] This study examined fees on privately leased grazing lands and the adjustments in the private fee necessary to derive a comparable public land grazing fee. The fee system developed using this economic approach was adopted in 1969 over strong rancher opposition.[12]

The public land agencies did not significantly oppose this application of economics because it did not infringe on any of their important decision-making prerogatives. Range science itself did not offer any theory of the correct grazing fee. The agencies saw higher fees as a step toward assertion of greater management control. A higher fee also would make OMB happy, might relieve some of the conflict between OMB and the agencies, and thus might lead to higher budgets. If agency economists could be helpful in raising the fee, as proved to be the case, their contribution would be favorably received within the agency.

The next major application of economics to rangeland problems was a study led by the Forest Service that involved seven other agencies in the departments of Agriculture and Interior.[13] The study examined the different sources of range forage in the United States, public and private, and alternative means of achieving various levels of total forage production nationwide. It made extensive use of systems analysis and linear programming methods to handle the large masses of data and complex calculations required. The study closely adhered to traditional prescriptions of scientific management. It was comprehensive, looking at the efficient allocation of forage production from the perspective of the nation as a whole. It set a clearly defined objective, a given level of total forage production, and then examined various alternatives for achieving this objective. Finally, it had a clearly defined basis for selection of the preferred alternative, minimization of the total cost to the nation of achieving whatever level of total forage production was selected.

The results, published in 1972, were disconcerting, however. According to the calculations, livestock grazing was economically unwarranted in many areas in the western United States. Other regions had higher potential for investment in forage production at lower costs. Within the West, grazing should be concentrated in limited areas with high investment potential and should be discontinued in many other areas.

For example, the study calculated the lowest cost, most efficient way to meet a projected total forage demand of 320 million AUMs from grazing in the year 2000. Because investments and intensive management would be concentrated on the most productive grazing lands, the total area grazed in the United States would fall by 49 percent, from 835 million acres in 1970 to 429 million acres in 2000. Although the acreage grazed would decline in every region, it would fall by the largest amount in the West, from 86 percent of western rangelands grazed in 1970 to only 23 percent in 2000. Associated with these shifts would be changes in the composition of forage output as described in the study.

The production of animal unit months on the Western Range ecogroup would remain essentially unchanged at 56 million. Production on the Western Forest ecogroup would decrease from 11 to 8 million animal unit months while on the Great Plains it would drop from 93 million to 80 million. These changes would take place in the face of an overall increase in animal unit months of 50 percent. The remaining ecogroup, Eastern Forest, would produce the increase. Production in this ecogroup would increase from 53 million to 175 million animal unit months, a gain of 226 percent. This again represents a major shift in the location of grazing.[14]

These were radical conclusions based on a seemingly scientific approach—minimize costs to achieve a given objective. They were also clearly unacceptable in political and institutional terms. Hence, the Forest Service set about constraining the extent of changes that could occur in seeking to minimize overall forage production costs. One alternative included limits on the intensity of investments and on the acreage that could be newly converted to forage production. The intent was, as the study acknowledged, to pick constraints that "were deliberately restrictive and to a large extent prescribed the distribution of grazing," essentially preventing any radical departures from the status quo.[15] With such constraints added, instead of a 49 percent decline in total acreage grazed nationwide, the decline was only 5 percent. The savings in forage production costs were also much less. The unconstrained solution produced a 59 percent reduction in average forage costs, from $4.03 per AUM to $1.66 per AUM. When constraints were imposed to maintain existing patterns of forage production, however, there was only a 19 percent decline in costs.

It might be thought that the economically preferable option that also yielded higher total production would be more environmentally harmful. However, because grazing was eliminated from so much land under this solution, it also had fewer adverse environmental impacts. The unconstrained economic maximizing solution thus was preferable in terms both of economic and environmental impacts; under the assumptions of the study, it represented the scientifically rational pattern of grazing. The public land agencies, however, had no interest in following up on this analysis.

In deciding to be more practical and to constrain the least-cost calculation to stay within acceptable bounds, the Forest Service made a decision that departed from the scientific realm and became political. The new constraints specified by the Forest Service for its model in essence showed the degree of change that might be politically tolerable over the next decade or two. Forest Service professionals did not have any scientific basis for these changes in the grazing allocation model; in fact, there probably was no such basis. In effect what had been a scientific modeling question had been transformed into a political analysis.

As this example illustrates, one of the major weaknesses of the progressive scheme for government has been its unrealistic portrayal of the relationship between science and politics. When confronted with politically unacceptable scientific results public land managers consistently either ignored the results or altered the science to conform to their perception of political reality. The goal of scientific management has been a rhetorical device, not an operational guide.

Benefit-Cost Analysis

Public land managers see economists as a clearly different breed. In opening a conference of BLM economists, the Director of the BLM Range Division remarked, "I'm a little uncomfortable when I'm around economists because I don't really understand their language."[16] Deep down the true BLMer feels that "it is morally, ethically, and professionally right to institute management practices that stop erosion, grow better forage and vegetation, and improve rangeland condition and trend. We should not have to economically justify these management practices."[17]

Economists thus tend to be placed in a slot separate from the rest of the agency. They are called on when society in general demands an economic justification for an agency program but otherwise are not expected to play much of a role in formulating agency policies. If they expect to fit in, they come under strong pressures to tailor their economic analysis to provide the results desired by superiors.

Responding to growing public concerns, BLM in January 1975 submitted a report to the U.S. Senate concerning conditions on BLM lands.[18] In terms of use of economics the report was significant in that it contained one of the first BLM efforts to perform a benefit-cost analysis for its range program. BLM estimated long-term total benefits of about $400 million and costs of about $225 million for a full-scale program of range rehabilitation.

The economic analysis, however, had been done after the fact and had basic deficiencies. For instance, the analysis included increased retention of soil and soil stability as one major benefit and increased future productive capacity of the land as measured in future forage production as a second major benefit. Since a primary purpose of increasing soil stability is to increase future productive capacity of the land, the same benefit had in effect been counted twice.

By 1975 OMB could see growing pressures to make more investments on the public rangelands. It suspected, however, that many if not most of these investments would not be economically justifiable. At a minimum it preferred that money spent should be allocated first to the investments with the highest payoffs; even if most projects were not justified, the least bad should be undertaken first. Hence, OMB requested that BLM analyze the benefits and costs of proposed new range investments. Policy and budget offices at the secretarial level in the Interior Department had concerns similar to those of OMB and agreed that BLM should undertake some economic analysis of its range investments. As a result an interagency work group was formed to examine the question of the extent to which the benefits of range investments were greater than their costs.[19]

From BLM's point of view the primary purpose in making benefit-cost estimates was to show OMB and other concerned parties that investments on the public rangelands could be paying propositions. In this objective the undertaking was successful, somewhat to the surprise of some participants. A later BLM survey of the benefit-cost studies done up to 1979 indicated that 80 percent of investment plans for individual rancher allotments showed benefits greater than costs.

In a number of cases the initial benefit-cost results had been less favorable but the allotment management plan (AMP) had later been modified to improve the benefit-cost ratio. Although this might appear to be an abuse of the process, it showed that BLM was searching for the best investments to include in AMPs. Ideally, many possible investments would be examined until one with a high payoff could be selected.

Many areas of public rangeland had been seriously overgrazed and had potential for significant forage increases if properly managed. For ranchers such forage increases translated into income boosting growth in their herd size and resulting beef and lamb production. In some cases range investments improved forage quality as well as quantity, causing increased calving rates and more rapid calf and cow weight gains on the range, both of which would be valuable to ranchers.

There may have been a tendency in some cases to be too optimistic. This would not be surprising; even with the best of intentions, agencies often see their proposals through rose-colored glasses. For example, in early applications of the benefit-cost analysis, improvements in calf weights and calf/cow percentages were one of the most significant gains projected from the range investments. Yet within two years there was sufficient doubt about the actual existence of such gains that BLM analysts recommended that, as a general rule, they should not be included as benefits.[20]

Analyzing Investments

Although BLM had initially been skeptical about the usefulness of benefit-cost analyses, it gradually adopted a more favorable attitude. As long as there were not enough funds to make all investments, it made sense to allocate the available funds to the investments with the highest returns. Moreover, the exercise of requiring field personnel to specify economic impacts of investments on ranchers and to estimate the values of nonmarket outputs produced a healthy critical attitude toward many investment plans. It led to better investments from a range science as well as an economic efficiency standpoint. In 1976 BLM decided to require benefit-cost analyses of all range investments. In transmitting the benefit-cost procedures for field use BLM Associate Director George Turcott explained the purposes of the newly required analysis.

> Economic analysis at this stage will provide considerable assistance in: 1) determining whether proposed AMP's [allotment management plans] are economically feasible; 2) providing a basis for consideration of other alternative levels of management and investment; and 3) providing one additional method of comparing AMP's.
>
> Following the ES [environmental statement] process, the results of the economic analysis should be reviewed to determine whether, for environmental reasons, the proposed action has been modified or changed to the extent that such changes will affect the AMP economic analysis. After review, the results of the economic analysis should be arrayed with environmental and other information to assist the decision maker in comparing and analyzing the proposed action and alternatives and selecting a final decision, determining priorities, scheduling implementation, and programming/budgeting.
>
> It is imperative that AMP's for the grazing ES program be of the highest quality and represent the Bureau's best effort in placing before the public our proposals for the range program. To meet the test for quality, AMP's must be not only technically and environmentally acceptable, but also realistic, feasible, and economically justifiable.[21]

Although many BLM range managers still regarded economists with suspicion, the benefit-cost analyses were on occasion used by managers to help them form their decisions, a rare role for economic analysis in the history of public land agencies. For instance, in the Rio Puerco EIS for grazing the proposed action included consolidation of certain allotments in order to create larger pastures and thereby to hold down on costs for building new fencing and water facilities. Ranchers much preferred individual allotments and pressured BLM to abandon the consolidation plan. In explaining why consolidation was necessary BLM cited the economic benefits. "There are several justifiable reasons for combining allotments," including "economics—each AMP had to arrive at a benefit-cost ratio approaching one to one."[22]

By 1979 a number of the first generation of grazing EISs had been released. With a large number of proposed investments entering the pipeline OMB once again expressed its doubts about the economic merits of investments being proposed for funding. BLM responded to OMB's questioning by reemphasizing the role of benefit-cost studies. A new set of criteria for making range investments was developed in which the benefit-cost ratio played a prominent role.

Thus the acceptance of economics in rangeland decision making increased in the public land agencies during the 1970s. In 1979 the secretary of agriculture issued a statement on range policy in which he stated the goal to "administer the range resources of the National Forest System for the benefit of the American public through cost-effective management and development of the range."[23] A 1979 rangelands symposium gave a prominent place to economics in the summary report, stating the need to "apply economic analysis so that the better, more cost-effective conservation and other practices can be applied. Widespread application of practices on a cost-effective basis could lead to more responsive and favorable public consideration of budget requests for range and associated conservation programs."[24]

Nevertheless, economic concepts still occupied a distinctly secondary place to the biological concept. In 1979 the BLM Range Division published a major policy paper assessing the future of rangeland policies.[25] The paper scarcely mentioned the need for benefit-cost or other economic analyses. Indeed, to the extent that the results of economic analysis are expected to be the actual determinants of decisions, the economist theatens the professional land manager in the role of decision maker. Land managers who suspected economists of seeking this authority naturally were less than supportive of economic studies.

Public land agencies also tend to see their role as advocating as much as they can get and OMB's role as resisting them. The biological approach to range management is more congenial to this view, since the goal sought is maximum productivity of the range. Economic analysis in effect asks the agency to curb its appetite voluntarily. Another major obstacle is simply the technical problems of economic analysis, especially in circumstances where there are many nonmarket benefits and costs.

Technical Problems

In examining an investment a business would estimate the increase in its revenues and then compare them with costs incurred. Differences in the time stream of revenues and costs are taken into account by discounting future revenues minus costs to a lump sum "present value." A benefit-cost analysis by a public agency follows the same procedure but "social benefits" substitute for private business returns and "social costs" for private business costs.

In a typical business analysis revenue projections would be based on an estimate of future sales. Costs also could often be estimated in a straightforward manner. But in the public sector social benefits and social costs frequently are much more difficult to estimate. For range investments costs usually do not pose as great a problem, but benefits are often a major challenge.

Much of the benefit of a range investment typically consists of increased forage provided to livestock. One way to evaluate this forage would be to use the public grazing fee. But this fee has in fact long been much below what most economists believe is the true economic value of public rangeland forage. The availability of BLM forage determines the feasible total size of the operation for many ranchers. Hence it might be possible to value the increased availability of public forage by valuing the increase in size of the ranch made feasible by this greater forage. A common practice in the West is to appraise ranches by the number of livestock the ranch will support; a ranch might typically be worth around $1,000 per "animal unit" in the herd. Thus if an increase in availability of BLM forage due to a public investment would make possible a twenty-animal-unit increase in ranch herd size, the added forage could be valued at $20,000 over the long term.

But almost all economic studies of the returns and costs to ranching have concluded that ranch values greatly exceed any reasonable estimate of the capitalized value of the net income that can be earned from ranching. One researcher concluded that the economic returns to ranching were so low that one must view "cattle ranching as a consumer item comprised of many components, including the utility obtained from consumption of such intangibles as 'love of land' and 'love of rural values.' "[26]

The most direct method would be to evaluate new forage at the going lease rate for private forage in the area. In the 1980s such private forage typically was leased for between $5 and $10 per AUM. Available data on private lease rates, however, are often for forage with important differences from public rangeland forage. Moreover, the role of public forage varies greatly according to individual ranch circumstances. In the Southwest, where the public range may be the sole source of forage and where livestock grazing occurs all year long, there will be a closer correlation between public forage availability and livestock numbers and rancher returns. In other parts of the West, however, public land forage typically provides only a portion of the total forage needs; hay and private lands supply the rest. In these circumstances the forage on the public lands can vary from critical to incidental to the ranch operation. Forage supplied at particular seasons may be especially valuable; public land grazing in the early spring is often much sought by ranchers because it relieves them of the need to purchase expensive hay.[27]

These considerations suggest that the only accurate way to evaluate specific forage increases may be to examine the economics of each individual ranch. Revenues and costs could be projected, with and without the availability of greater public land forage. But the public land agencies lack information on the details of individual ranch budgets and operations. Ranchers might be unwilling to provide it, perhaps regarding efforts to acquire it as an infringement on their privacy. Moreover, it would be very costly to survey and analyze individually each of the thousands of ranches using public rangelands.

One might then classify ranches by various ranch types. For each basic type a model of the ranch operation, including revenues and costs, could be constructed. By adding extra forage at a certain time of year the effects on ranch operation and ranch income could be calculated through use of the model. This approach is particularly suited to linear-programming techniques. It still suffers, however, from the defect that individual ranch differences are not fully accounted for; certain ranches may not fit any of the generalized ranch types.

Different approaches will produce different answers, no one of which appears definitive. The BLM state economist for Wyoming reported in one instance that "the BLM estimate of the return per AUM was $2.85.

The University of Wyoming, on the other hand, estimated the returns to be $10.67 per AUM for cattle and $14.91 per AUM for sheep. . . . Without a clear and concise explanation of the divergence between the two values . . . economic impacts derived from BLM values are unacceptable to the academic community.''[28]

Recreation Benefits

Evaluation of recreation benefits on the public lands is still more difficult. There are two main techniques.[29] First, a survey can be made of recreational users to ask how much they would have been willing to pay and still participate in the recreation activity. The major drawback of this "contingent value" approach is that responding to a survey and actually paying are much different things. The wording or phrasing of the question may produce large differences in response. If respondents fully understand the purpose of the question, they may choose to answer strategically; hunters may overstate the value of hunting, hoping to justify greater wildlife expenditures. Other hunters may be offended by the question and refuse to give any answer.

Another method relies on an actual demonstrated willingness—the expenditures of time and money by recreationists who have traveled to a particular site. Based on examination of trips to different sites, an estimate can be formed of the willingness to pay for recreational experiences. Two major drawbacks of this approach are the uncertain value put on time spent traveling—for some it may be all pleasure—and the fact that the same trip often combines a number of destinations, making it difficult to say what the correct share is for any given trip segment.

A third and less common method of evaluating recreation is to find comparable private recreation experiences that are being marketed. There are many places where private landowners are able to control access to hunting and charge for such access. In some cases landowners control key entry points into areas of public lands and impose substantial charges to pass their gateway point. Where such prices can be found, they provide a good estimate of the willingness to pay for the recreational product. Not many studies of such private recreation markets have been done, however, partly because the professional reward structure in economics gives a higher weight to use of complex statistical and other analytical methods, as compared with actual field investigations.

There has been much more work by economists to apply the survey and the travel-cost methods of estimating recreational use values. The quality of travel data available, combined with the degree of judgment required, however, have caused the actual estimates to vary widely. Some analysts still use improper methods—including counting of hunter expenditures in the local economy—in estimating hunter-day values. For a deer hunter-day, it is possible to find values ranging from $10 to $100 per hunter-day. Large variations can also be found for other types of hunting and fishing. Although some of these variations are valid reflections of local variations in hunter-day values, the greater part is no doubt due to differences in data or technique of the researcher.

Compared with hunting and fishing, there is much less information about values for activities such as rock hounding, bird watching, or ordinary hiking. There is almost a total absence of accepted methods for estimating a value where this value is placed on the existence of the species. Yet for the nation as a whole the total value of antelope may be as much in the knowledge of people throughout the country that antelope are commonly found in the West as in the hunting of antelope by individual hunters. For some species, such as wild horses and burros, the "existence value" of their presence on the public range is the only value—at least under current law that prohibits commercial or private use. The values of a wilderness area, archeological site, historic site, and a number of other public rangeland features have the same quality. A significant portion of this value is due to existence: the value is derived by people who may never visit the public lands.

Similar issues are encountered in the third main area of the benefits of range investment—watershed impacts. Some watershed benefits can be valued fairly easily; reduced flooding may allow predictable reductions in expenditures required to repair flood damage to roads or other structures located downstream. Reduced sedimentation may lengthen the useful life of downstream reservoirs. Changes in water yields may be evaluated at existing prices where water rights have been bought and sold in the area. But where the impact is a contribution to river salinity and is only a small part of a much larger waterway system, it is very difficult to estimate the value of this salinity reduction. The same is true of sediment released into a much wider system.

While estimates of hunter and other recreation day values do not inspire much confidence, they do provide hard data in comparison with existence values, option values, and some of the other less direct, nonmarket values of the public rangelands. Taking all these analytical difficulties together, it must be recognized that the benefits of range investments will be a rough approximation. A further major uncertainty affecting the results of the economic analysis is the choice of the proper discount rate. In recent years government agencies have used discount rates varying from 4 to 10 percent (in real terms), which can dramatically affect the economic conclusions reached.

Use of market prices and estimation of "willingness to pay" in benefit-cost analysis also raises some basic philosophical questions not mentioned thus far. The same output has a higher value if it is consumed by a person with a higher income, because that person would be willing to pay more for it. Hence, other things equal, if public benefits are estimated by private willingness to pay, as they usually are, public outputs will be oriented to higher income groups. This is particularly troublesome when there is no charge imposed for these outputs—a common circumstance for recreation and other pubic land benefits.

The accuracy of benefit-cost estimates depends, of course, on their data and the caliber of the analyst using it. One might ask: why not simply improve the accuracy of benefit-cost estimates by putting greater resources into them. But the exercise of conducting benefit-cost studies can itself be subject to economic analysis; in some cases it may simply be too costly relative to the benefits of economics for rangeland management. In short, in some circumstances—which may be encountered rather frequently on the public rangelands—economic analysis may itself not be economic. If scientific management includes the requirement to be economically viable, such circumstances will involve a basic contradiction—the unscientific practice of scientific management—in the very concept itself.

The Economics of Rangeland Planning

Consider a case where a decision must be made and the worst possible result would be a loss of $10,000, while the best possible result would be a gain of $20,000. In this circumstance it can never be economically rational to spend more than $30,000 in information gathering and analysis. In fact such expenditures normally should be much less than $30,000.

In theory agencies should keep spending more on information and analysis until the resulting expected improvement in the decision is worth less than the marginal cost. A little effort often goes a long way, but the rate of return on further information and analysis may fall rapidly. If society's stake in the decision is not large, in many cases it will be economically rational to do only "quick and dirty" studies.

Until the 1970s there had not been a great deal of money spent on studies of the public rangelands of the United States, partly reflecting the considered low value of their outputs. When the courts mandated a set of site-specific EISs for the BLM rangeland program in 1975, however, a sharp increase in federal spending for rangeland studies soon followed (see also chapter 5).

The 1975 court order in the case *Natural Resources Defense Council (NRDC) v. Morton* determined the basic guidelines for the bulk of the funds to be made available for future rangeland studies.[30] First, the money would be spent in a site-specific fashion for 212 (later reduced to 144) separate analyses of certain public range areas where livestock grazing was occurring. The court specifically rejected a "programmatic" or national focus for future rangeland studies. Second, the focus of the studies would be on management decisions: how much livestock grazing, how much forage for other uses, and what investments to make. Federal Judge Thomas A. Flannery directed that the EISs should "discuss in detail the environmental effects of the proposed livestock grazing, and alternatives thereto, in specific areas of the public lands that are or will be licensed for such use."[31]

The orientation toward management decisions largely dictated that the grazing EISs would have to take the form of a land use plan. Initially, BLM prepared two separate documents, a formal land use plan and then a grazing EIS. The land use plan was intended to be completed before the grazing EIS was begun. As matters turned out, however, the preparation of the grazing EIS raised so many questions not covered in earlier planning efforts that a whole new round of planning had to be undertaken. The process for preparing grazing EISs thus became, de facto, the land use planning process.[32] In 1979 BLM resolved this issue by combining the grazing EIS and the land use plan into one document.

The land use planning system developed by BLM in the 1970s required large amounts of data and analysis. It reflected the widely held philosophy that planning must be truly comprehensive; it must analyze all the issues, and the decisions made must resolve these issues. The basic idea was to provide a full blueprint for the future. Such a system is expensive, and the court order effectively decreed that large amounts of money would have to be spent.

Preparation of grazing EISs did in fact turn out to be very expensive. A BLM study of nine of the first EISs completed found that $5.7 million had been spent in direct preparation costs, an average of $630,000 per EIS.[33] The direct costs were, however, only a fraction of the total EIS costs. For example, these costs did not include most of the inventories and land use planning required to lay the groundwork for writing the EIS. The same BLM study estimated that the direct preparation costs of the EISs were only about 10 percent of the total costs associated with completion of each grazing EIS. On this basis the nine EISs together could have cost as much as $50 million, or more than $5 million per statement. Seven million acres were covered by these grazing EISs, so the total cost per acre may have been as high as $7 or $8 per acre.

There exists a limited market in grazing rights to public land in which one rancher may sell his rights to another rancher. In this market the rights to public land grazing have typically sold for anywhere from $30 to as much as $100 per AUM. Since the average AUM on BLM land requires about fifteen acres, then even using the highest purchase price of $100 the permanent grazing rights probably would be worth no more than $7 per acre. Hence, for the first nine grazing EISs, if costs are completely accounted for the total costs involved in grazing EISs may well have approached the total value of the forage being studied. To put the matter another way, if the government had instead used the EIS money to buy out grazing rights to public land, it might have been able to buy out a significant part of the grazing rights in the EIS areas for no more than the costs to prepare the EIS.

The costs of the first generation of EISs were higher than later ones and BLM's estimates of indirect or supporting costs for EISs may well have been too high. But there is a strong case that the early expenditures on grazing EISs far exceeded what could be justified on any economically rational approach to decision making. All the BLM grazing EISs probably ended up requiring as much as $100 million in direct preparation costs and considerably more if all the inventory, planning, and other associated indirect costs are included. The resulting sum is at least as great as the total expenditure for range improvements authorized in the Public Rangelands Improvement Act of 1978 over the twenty years from 1980 to 2000.

As the levels of funding for preparation of early grazing EISs and associated activities rose, the money available for on-the-ground improvements fell. In part many new improvements could not legally be undertaken under the court order until a grazing EIS had been completed in an area. In 1977 budget discussions the assistant secretary for Policy, Budget, and Administration in the Interior Department pointed out that from 1975 to 1977 funding for on-the-ground capital improvements had declined from $8.3 million to $5.8 million per year, while "paperwork" expenditures for inventory, planning, and EIS writing had risen sharply from $3 million to $13 million.

The question raised in these Interior budget discussions was whether adequate rationale existed for the greatly increased expenditure for information gathering and analysis: "In practice due to the difficulty in determining whether or how much decison making is improved and how to value such improvement, there often exists a tendency to make activities such as inventories, planning and environmental analysis ends in themselves." The theoretical necessity of considering benefits and costs of information and analysis was also raised: "Greater expenditures for information gathering can be justified the more important the decision is and the more is at risk in making it." Interior budget analysts showed particular skepticism with respect to the large amounts of expensive inventory data BLM was proposing to collect: "It is important to ask certain questions relating to whether such a level of inventory effort is needed."[34]

These doubts, however, carried little weight in the face of the prevailing enthusiasm in the late 1970s for planning the rehabilitation of the pubic range. By 1980 BLM expenditures on rangeland inventories alone equalled $26.1 million, more than the total revenues collected from grazing fees. A number of observers by then were questioning the expenditures on information gathering and analysis for the early grazing EISs. Three years after the court order, the NRDC, disappointed with the results of the large expenditures being made under its court suit, concluded that "the Bureau has expended very substantial sums of money and manpower on these EISs but has produced little or nothing to show for it." NRDC stated further that "the BLM has so far failed to complete a single, adequate EIS concerning livestock grazing."[35]

In NRDC's view the basic problem lay in BLM's managerial deficiencies: "We believe that the EIS effort to date has been characterized by mismanagement, misrepresentation, unnecessary delay and the failure to comply with the most rudimentary standards for the contents of grazing EISs under NEPA [National Environmental Policy Act]."[36] Moreover, backing away somewhat from its own previous assertions, NRDC now felt that inventory and other data were not the problem: "The evidence reveals that the inadequacy of the draft EISs released to date by the BLM were caused by its failure to address the issues which are central to proper grazing management, rather than insufficient data."[37] BLM had prepared a new Challis grazing EIS in large part in order to include high quality soils and vegetation data. But NRDC still doubted the extent to which improvements in the analysis for the Challis EIS had resulted. With respect to new soils data, for example, NRDC observed that despite its much greater availability, "nothing is done with this data."[38]

BLM's internal evaluations also indicated that conceptual, personnel, and other deficiencies sometimes led to a failure to employ information and analysis.

> Evaluation reports indicate that such deficiencies contribute to superficial treatment of significant issues surrounding decisions relating to the use of the Public Lands, and to the compilation of uninterpreted data whose implications for resource decisions are obscure.
>
> Guidance as to what constitutes analysis, as well as what constitutes analytical procedures for social information is uneven, often rudimentary, and in some cases, nonexistent. This uneven guidance creates a situation which one BLM Regional Economist noted as often leading to "inappropriate utilization of existing data, and at times, lack of awareness of the existence of such data."[39]

BLM also examined why information and analysis might not be used by managers. One problem was that the way in which managers formed decisions was very imperfectly understood, making it difficult to know what information and analysis would be of help to them.

> Interviewers revealed that managers found it difficult to articulate just how they used information of any sort, but it appears that several factors act to shape the output of the [information] conversion process. Most prominent is that managers' own values appear to "filter" decisions through a "screen" of local values and preferences. Managers tended to reflect local community attitudes, values, and preferences in their decision making process. Larger concerns did have weight, particularly in decisions related to energy development, but local values and orientations predominated. Such "filtering" is expectable, since the backgrounds and values of managers in BLM are substantially congruent with those of the communities of the rural West.[40]

Despite the large demands being placed on it, rangeland science had not progressed to the point of even clearly knowing the right questions to ask. A 1976 report on rangeland issues prepared for the Council on Environmental Quality (CEQ) indicated that "research on rangelands and their management has generally been scant and disorganized, with narrowly based objectives. The rangeland area to research is so vast, the need so great, and the money available so small that an organized approach has been impossible."[41] The CEQ report indicated that major gaps in basic knowledge of rangeland biology existed: "Fundamental knowledge of plant response to grazing is incomplete and fragmented. We have not progressed beyond the hypotheses of Stoddart and Smith's

(1943) first edition of their range management text. In fact, we have not even tested many of the hypotheses they proposed because intuitively they feel good.'' Even the concepts of rangeland trend and condition, on which much is based in management, have a suspect theoretical foundation: "Techniques for measuring range condition are imprecise at best, even today."[42]

The 1979 Rangelands Symposium noted above offered some similar reflections. There were suggestions in the summary statement of the need for a basic rethinking of the concept of rangeland condition: "Not all the range data base is solid; much is weak, with improvement needed in how data are collected, the kinds of data to collect, and how to handle data. Questioned were some of the concepts basic to determination of range conditions." A number of other range subjects were critically in need of much more basic research. Having the greatest immediate practical implications, the biological response of rangelands to various management systems was simply not understood very well. Moreover, BLM faced "other technical problems . . . [including] the increasingly important need to have available sound methods for measuring resource interactions and tradeoffs. As competition increases for the many resources of the range, knowing how to predict the effects of multi-resource management systems upon each of the components of the ecosystem will become increasingly important."[43] With a weak foundation of basic knowledge, any new management systems proposed in grazing EISs were likely to show a hit-and-miss pattern of success.

The lack of a solid scientific foundation meant that despite all the expenditures for inventories and analysis BLM was unable to provide definitive estimates of such critical matters as the carrying capacity of the range or the likely forage response to new grazing systems. The pouring of money into grazing EISs, combined with a shaky scientific base of knowledge about rangelands and with a natural resource of modest economic value at stake, raised at least some eyebrows. One range scientist considered that the EISs were "pure busywork carried out in the name of decision making, but serving only to divert energy, attention and effort from management functions to useless paperwork."[44] A commenter on the Challis draft supplemental EIS wondered whether "much more could be accomplished if less were spent on EISs and more were spent on on-the-ground improvements."[45] An economic consultant called in to examine the economic analysis in three grazing EISs concluded that this analysis was reasonably well done. The real economic problem was the expense of preparing grazing EISs themselves.

The entire ES preparation and review process is appallingly tedious and costly. The public and courts should be made aware of the incredible costs of research, printing, coordination, review, correcting, reprinting, and even monitoring, so that these costs can be placed in perspective with the real impact of the BLM's proposed actions. The government is spending millions of dollars to prepare impact statements for projects with economic impacts which can hardly be measured.

The government not only spends money on the ES process that is disproportionate with the potential disruptions to people and the environment, but ultimately this kind of governmental functioning is discouraging to the public as well as those in government employment.[46]

Economists find that many other professional groups tend to make their own concerns an end in themselves (and perhaps economists themselves exhibit this fault). Society must set priorities, however, and choices must be made among many alternative ways of spending resources. It is impossible to regard any one end as the ultimate goal in itself.

Thus in the 1970s OMB and Interior Department economists argued that the BLM goal to maximize the biological productivity of the rangeland was misconceived. Maximizing forage production as an ultimate goal did not acknowledge that beyond some point further expenditures in raising forage outputs simply were not worth it. Further inquiry showed that land use planners and other advocates of increased data gathering and analysis for the rangelands were making a similar error. They tended to make planning inventories, data, and analysis the ends in themselves. There was no conceptual construct by which one could say: This amount of planning, this amount of analysis, this amount of inventory is enough.

All this opened up a whole new field of economic inquiry in the 1970s—the economics of information as applied to the public rangelands. As in studying other economic questions, it was usually difficult to say just how much information was enough. Yet even to ask the question was often significant. An environment in which spending on data and analysis was regarded as virtually free and unconstrained tended to produce much too much data and analysis.

The New BLM

Traditionally, BLM has been seen as an agency dominated by livestock interests. However, the growth of recreational use of public rangelands and the emergence of the environmental movement led in the 1960s to the development of strong counterweights. Paul Culhane argued that BLM was thereby newly free to pursue policies in the public interest because it now had interest groups pressing from all directions. As Culhane put it, "The Forest Service and BLM thus find themselves in a very powerful position. . . . The agencies, whose commitment to multiple use demands a balanced course of action, can play their more extreme constituents off against each other to reinforce the agencies preferred middle course. By using both extreme elements in their constituencies, the bureau and service generate a multiple clientele for their multiple-use mission."[47]

To be sure, Culhane seemed to assume that multiple-use management constitutes a form of professional management in the public interest. More plausibly, multiple-use management actually means interest group competition and accommodation. The lack of objective standards in multiple-use management leads to protracted political bargaining before any decisions can be reached. The court decision mandating grazing EISs set the framework for the 1970s bargaining over future rangeland use. The bargaining process, however, did not yield many decisions. Rather, the most obvious consequence was to greatly lengthen the time and expense for negotiation. The new BLM gave far more attention to the process of mediating conflicts among the multiplicity of interest groups. Inventories, planning, environmental impact statements, and public participation efforts have all been central elements in this costly bargaining process.

A new breed of BLM manager more suited to these emerging tasks began to show up in the 1970s in increasing numbers. The old BLM manager was typically trained as a professional range manager at a western state university. The new BLM employee was more likely to have been trained in some other social or physical science. Of those working on the early grazing EISs, 4 percent were economists, 3 percent were outdoor recreation planners, 4 percent were archaeologists, 7 percent were fisheries and wildlife biologists, 3 percent were hydrologists and geologists, and 3 percent were soil scientists. Range conservationists, the mainstay of the old BLM, were 20 percent of the EIS preparers.

The change in BLM tasks has also required BLM to bring in new people at high levels. A 1980 article described the divisions emerging between "western managers who had come up through the ranks of the agency, starting at low levels in various mud-on-their-boots field jobs, and the Department of the Interior Washington hierarchy, many of whose members have backgrounds as professionals, staff advisors, aca-

demics and lobbyists rather than as managers with field experience."
One old BLM employee complained that "those guys know pencil
work a lot better than dirt work" and that this "preference was starting
to inundate us out in the field."[48]

Environmental groups saw these developments in a more favorable
light: "If a government agency can have a renaissance, the BLM is
becoming one of the best examples. Starting in the 1960s with a rise in
environmentalism the agency began to discard its lethargy. Now revitalized by FLPMA, the agency is enjoying larger budgets and new responsibilities. While its programs, and many of its line managers, reflect the
cowboy and miner orientation of the agency, many of its new wildlife,
recreation and wilderness specialists are challenging it from within."[49]

For the older BLM employees, who were accustomed to managing
by professional judgment and were oriented to on-the-ground results,
the large resources devoted to grazing EISs became an unfortunate
symbol of the new BLM. Many of the social scientists and other recent
BLM employees thought little better of the bureau. They found it difficult to connect the huge amount of work going into grazing EISs with
any direct policy consequences and wondered whether there was any
real purpose. BLM found that among EIS team participants, "11 percent categorically state that they believe that the EIS they were working
on would not be of significant value in BLM resource management," a
further "63 percent expressed doubt that it would be of value or felt
that it would only be of limited value," and only "26 percent stated
that it would [be of value]."[50]

The study concluded that "the range EIS program is suffering serious
morale problems." Only 2 percent of BLM employees working on a
range EIS described their experiences as "greatly satisfying" and only
17 percent as "usually satisfying." On the other hand 43 percent described the experience as "sometimes frustrating" and 16 percent as
"totally frustrating." Twenty-two percent said it was "O.K."[51]

Below-cost Grazing

A striking feature of the public rangelands is their low economic
productivity. There are some BLM rangelands where a square mile (640
acres) is necessary to provide sufficient forage for one cow for one
year. More typically, an area larger than one hundred acres is required;
the average BLM rangeland will support one cow for one month on
about fifteen acres. Livestock grazing occurs on most of these range-

lands because grazing is the only land use feasible. The total capital value of all grazing permits on BLM rangelands may not be much more than $1 billion.

In 1981 BLM spent about $70 million for direct rangeland outlays. This did not include rangeland outlays with a specific wildlife or recreation propose. Expenditures in this latter category constituted about $55 million, most of which also involved rangeland. Thus, total direct rangeland expenditures in 1981 were on the order of $125 million.[52] Moreover, BLM, like most organizations, must maintain a large overhead for the support of its direct program activities. This overhead includes the cost to BLM of operating area, district, state, and Washington offices, as well as the Denver Service Center. Adding in the overhead of all this brings the total 1981 cost of BLM rangeland management to around $230 million per year—about what would be expected for an agency with a total resource management budget in 1981 of $454 million and for which rangeland management takes up much of its attention.

Annual expenditures of $230 million for rangeland management cannot be justified by the economic value of the activities occurring on public rangelands. The government itself collects only about $15 to $30 million per year in grazing fees, plus perhaps another $1 million per year in recreation and wildlife fees. To be sure, the full value of grazing as well as of recreation and wildlife activities on public rangelands both greatly exceed the amounts actually collected by the federal government. But even if livestock grazing is worth four times the fees that the government collects, the total annual value on BLM lands would still be around only $100 million.

The public benefits of recreation and wildlife activities on the public rangelands are considerably larger. BLM estimates that total recreation visitor days in 1981 equalled 64 million for all BLM lands. Valuing these conservatively at $5 per day, the total value of recreation visits would have been $320 million in 1981, easily exceeding the level of BLM rangeland expenditures. Most of the recreation on public rangelands would have occurred, however, whether or not BLM had made any expenditures on behalf of recreation. Indeed, only about $10 million was actually budgeted in 1982 directly for recreational purposes.

A significant part of the BLM expenditures for wildlife are justified by the need to reconcile domestic livestock grazing with wildlife demand for forage and habitat. If the domestic livestock were not present, very likely far less would be spent on wildlife by the federal government. For example, wild horse and burro management becomes contentious and expensive because of the direct conflict with forage availability for livestock. In the absence of livestock grazing on federal rangelands, the federal government might well turn wildlife programs over to the western states.

In short, the expenditures made on BLM rangelands frequently involve domestic livestock issues even when they ostensibly involve other resources. Yet the economic values derived from livestock grazing fall far short of the public expenditures for the rangelands. Politically, it would, of course, be impossible to eliminate livestock grazing. But if the recent levels of rangeland costs were to be taken as given, elimination of grazing would be the only economically rational course. It is analogous to the argument for elimination of below-cost timber sales on the national forests.

Conclusion

To be sure, rather than eliminate grazing, it can well be argued that the better answer is to cut the costs of public rangeland management. The costs for rangeland management have been so high because of the philosophy of scientific management. Scientific rangeland management is expensive for several reasons. First, range conditions and management are site specific. One good study is not enough for all rangelands; rather, many separate and expensive studies for varying sites and conditions are necessary. Second, as noted above, range science often does not produce definitive management prescriptions on which a broad professional consensus is easily achieved. Lacking objective scientific answers, rangeland decisions become political. Then, instead of accepting government decisions, each party is likely to demand further technical analysis in hopes that the next round of studies will lend greater support to its case. Third, scientific management has tended to be associated with centralized decision making, adding large overhead costs to the already substantial field expenditures for inventories, planning, and other elements of rangeland study.

This combination of circumstances confronts the government with the following dilemma. The public land agencies cannot practice scientific management—at least as it has traditionally been understood—without a large commitment of funds to research, formal planning, data gathering, and other scientific studies. But if the practice of scientific management is to include economic science, as it should, this commitment of funds often cannot be economically justified for a low-value resource such as the public rangelands. The economic values of the rangeland and the gains from greater scientific information simply will not be large enough to justify the expense. In short, the proposal by economists to give real content to scientific management by using economic analysis may instead lead to a dead end.

Rather than traditional notions of scientific management, rangeland decisions might instead proceed more incrementally. Management practices could be adopted allotment by allotment, perhaps varying according to different individual theories of rangeland system response and according to economic circumstance. Separate allotments could be testing grounds for diverse management approaches. If subsequent experience showed that one management practice was working well, it could then be adopted on a wider basis. Individual ranchers, and others who are able to acquire rangeland information at low cost because they experience the rangeland as part of their daily routine, could assume a much greater decision-making role.

Such an approach means the decentralization of public land management. It means redrawing the boundaries of ownership and control on the public lands to give new authority in managing the public lands to ranchers, local wilderness users, and local communities. It means rethinking the system of de facto rights that has grown up on the public lands, giving greater formal legitimacy to these rights. All of this, to be sure, will require a willingness on the part of the wider public to depart from a century of increasing centralization of public land management and from the progressive design on which this centralization has been based.

Notes

1. Samuel P. Hays, *Conservationism and the Gospel of Efficiency: The Progressive Conservation Movement, 1890–1920* (Cambridge, Mass.: Harvard University Press, 1959).

2. See John V. Krutilla and John A. Haigh, "An Integrated Approach to National Forest Management," *Environmental Law* (Winter 1978); also Richard M. Alston, *Forest Goals and Decision Making in the Forest Service* (Ogden, Utah: Intermountain Forest and Range Experiment Station, U.S. Forest Service, September 1972).

3. Laurence A. Stoddart and Arthur D. Smith, *Range Management* (New York: McGraw-Hill, 1943):2.

4. Laurence A. Stoddart, Arthur D. Smith, and Thadis W. Box, *Range Management* (New York: McGraw-Hill, 1975): 2.

5. Bureau of Land Management, New Mexico State Office, *New Mexico Allotment Management Plan Handbook, BLM Manual Supplement*, (Albuquerque: 10 October 1969): 14.

6. Bureau of Land Management, U.S. Department of the Interior, *Livestock Grazing Management in National Resource Lands: Final Environmental Statement* (Washington, D.C.: December 1974): I-1.

7. Public Law 94–579, Sec. 102(a)7.

8. Public Law 95–514, Sec. 2(b)(2).

9. See E. Louise Peffer, *The Closing of the Public Domain: Disposal and Reservation Policies, 1900–50* (Stanford, Calif.: Stanford University Press, 1951); Phillip O. Foss, *Politics and Grass: The Administration of Grazing on the Public Domain* (Seattle: University of Washington Press, 1960); and Wesley Calef, *Private Grazing and Public Lands* (Chicago: University of Chicago Press, 1960).

10. Memorandum from Office of Management and Budget to Interior Deputy Assistant Secretary for Policy Development and Budget, 29 August 1975.

11. See Earl E. Houseman, et al., "Special Report on Grazing Fee Survey," Statistical Reporting Service, U.S. Department of Agriculture (Washington, D.C.: 29 November 1968).

12. See *Study of Fees for Grazing Livestock on Federal Lands: A Report from the Secretary of the Interior and the Secretary of Agriculture*, 21 October 1977.

13. U.S. Department of Agriculture, Forest Service, *The National Range Resources—A Forest Range Environmental Study*, by the Forest Range Task Force, Forest Resource Report No. 19 (Washington, D.C.: Government Printing Office, December 1972).

14. *Ibid.*: 79.

15. *Ibid.*: 82.

16. Comments of Max Lieurance, chief of BLM Range Division, at BLM Economics Workshop, Salt Lake City, 22–23 May 1979.

17. "Program Decision Option Document on AMP Feasibility Analysis," Bureau of Land Management, 6 November 1975.

18. U.S. Department of the Interior, Bureau of Land Management, *Range Condition Report*, prepared for the Senate Committee on Appropriations, January 1975.

19. I was a participant on this task force. It was one of the first assignments I received after joining the Office of Policy Analysis in what was then the Office of the Assistant Secretary for Policy Development and Budget of the Department of the Interior in May 1975.

20. "Forage and Livestock Valuation Methods," committee report from the Range Economics Workshop of the Bureau of Land Management, Tucson, Arizona, 19–23 March 1978.

21. BLM Instruction Memorandum No. 76–455, from Associate Director George Turcott on "Allotment Management Plan (AMP) Economic Analysis," 26 August 1976.

22. U.S. Department of the Interior, Bureau of Land Management, *Final Environmental Impact Statement on the Proposed Rio Puerco Livestock Grazing Management Program* (May 1978): IX-8.

23. Secretary's Memorandum No. 1999, "Statement of Range Policy," Secretary of Agriculture, 25 October 1979: 3.

24. Interagency Ad-Hoc Committee on the Sense of the Symposium, "The Sense of the Symposium on Rangeland Policies for the Future," a report to the assistant secretary of Agriculture for Conservation, Research, and Education, the assistant secretary of the Interior for Land and Water Resources, and the Council on Environmental Quality, 1 June 1979: 7.

25. U.S. Department of the Interior, Bureau of Land Management, *Managing the Public Rangelands, Public Review Draft*, November 1979: 1.

26. Arthur H. Smith and William E. Martin, "Socioeconomic Behavior of Cattle Ranchers, with Implications for Rural Community Development in the West," *American Journal of Agricultural Economics* 25 (May 1972): 217.

27. See *Study of Fees for Grazing Livestock on Federal Lands*.

28. Memorandum from Roy Allen (BLM Wyoming State economist) to Bob Browne, "Methodology Used for Assessing the Economic Impacts in the Sandy Grazing Environmental Impact Statement," 29 August 1978: 2.

29. See John F. Dwyer, John R. Kelly, and Michael D. Bowes, *Improved Procedures for Valuation of the Contribution of Recreation to National Economic Development*, prepared for the Office of Water Research and Technology, U.S. Department of the Interior (September 1977).

30. *Natural Resources Defense Council (NRDC) v. Morton*, 388 F. Suppl. at 841 (1974).

31. *Ibid.*

32. See Christopher K. Leman, "Formal Versus De Facto Systems of Multiple Use Planning in the Bureau of Land Management: Integrating Comprehensive and Focused Approaches," in National Resource Council, National Academy of Sciences, *Developing Strategies for Rangeland Management* (Boulder, Colo.: Westview Press, 1984).

33. U.S. Department of the Interior, Bureau of Land Management, *Grazing Environmental Statement Review Report*, 30 April 1979.

34. Budget issue paper on "BLM Inventory, Planning and Environmental Analysis Expenditures for the Public Rangelands," transmitted by deputy assistant secretary for Policy, Budget, and Administration to assistant secretary for Land and Water Resources, 22 June 1977.

35. "Plaintiffs' (NRDC) Summary of the Evidence in Opposition to the Federal Defendant's Notice of Proposed Deviation," in *NRDC v. Andrus* (formerly Morton) 28 February 1978: 7.

36. *Ibid.*: 4.

37. *Ibid.*: 20.

38. NRDC comments on the Challis Draft Supplemental EIS, reprinted in U.S. Department of the Interior, Bureau of Land Management, *Final Supple-

mental Environmental Statement on a Revised Range Management Program for the Challis Planning Unit (November 1978): A-232.

39. Bureau of Land Management, Office of Program Evaluation, *Special Evaluation, Social Economic Analysis in Bureau Decision Making* (1979): 6.

40. *Ibid.*: 15.

41. Thadis W. Box, Don D. Dwyer, and Frederick H. Wagner, "The Public Range and Its Management," report to the Council on Environmental Quality, 19 March 1976: 43.

42. *Ibid.*: 32, 42.

43. "The Sense of the Symposium on Rangeland Policies for the Future": 6.

44. Boysie E. Day, "Range Management, An Ecological Art," in Rangeland Policies for the Future, proceedings of a symposium, 28–31 January 1979, in Tucson, Arizona (Washington, D.C.: Government Printing Office, 1979): 92.

45. Comment of the Idaho Farm Bureau Federation on the Challis Draft Supplemental EIS, reprinted in *Final Supplemental Environmental Statement on a Revised Range Management Program for the Challis Planning Unit*: A-216.

46. "An Evaluation of the Economic Analysis Contained in Three BLM Grazing Environmental Statements," prepared for the Montana Public Lands Council and Old West Rangeland Monitoring Project by T.A.P., Inc., 2 April 1979: 18.

47. Paul J. Culhane, *Public Lands Politics: Interest Group Influence on the Forest Service and the Bureau of Land Management* (Baltimore: Johns Hopkins University Press for Resources for the Future, 1981): 336.

48. Doug Gill, "BLM Exodus Highlights Schism," *The Denver Post*, 6 April 1980: 66.

49. Bernard Shanks, "BLM, Back in the Spotlight after Years of Neglect," *High Country News*, 26 January 1979: 5.

50. *Grazing Environmental Statement Review Report*: 32.

51. *Ibid.*: x, xi.

52. Robert H. Nelson and Gabriel Joseph, "An Analysis of Revenues and Costs of Public Land Management by the Interior Department in 13 Western States—Update to 1981," Office of Policy Analysis, U.S. Department of the Interior (September 1982).

Chapter 4

The Illusion of Planning:
The Origins of the BLM and Forest Service Land Use Planning Systems

The new legislative framework established in the 1970s for the public lands included the Federal Land Policy and Management Act of 1976 (FLPMA), which consolidated numerous authorities and gave the Bureau of Land Management (BLM) a mandate to manage the public domain in permanent federal ownership. The National Forest Management Act of 1976 (NFMA) similarly provided the Forest Service for the first time with clear legislative authority for its existing forestry practices and gave guidance on a number of other important matters. On one of the most important issues, the grounds on which public land managers should decide among competing uses, Congress directed in both FLPMPA and NFMA that the managers should follow the instructions of land use plans.

Land use planning as mandated by FLPMA and NFMA is to include frequent consultation with the public and wide opportunity for affected groups to comment on plan options and proposals. In seeking such heavy public input the new planning process departed from the original progressive design for a strict separation of administration and politics. In the end, however, following all the comment, the basis for land use plans should still be science—including all the physical and social branches of science. It would still be the professionalism of scientists that would ensure that managers acted objectively ''in the public inter-

This chapter is a revised and edited version of selected portions of an unpublished paper, ''Basic Issues in Land Use Planning for the Public Lands,'' prepared for the Office of Policy Analysis, U.S. Department of the Interior, April 1980.

121

est." The National Environmental Policy Act of 1969 (NEPA) required the government to "utilize a systematic, interdisciplinary approach which will insure the integrated use of the natural and social sciences in the environmental design arts in planning and decision making." Seven years later FLPMA repeated virtually the same language. The NFMA similarly states that "the new knowledge derived from coordinated public and private research programs will promote a sound technical and ecological base for effective management, use, and protection of the nation's resources." A "committee of scientists" was required under NFMA to advise the Forest Service on the development of its planning system.

To begin the planning process, Congress mandated the systematic conduct of inventories and other data gathering. Continuing in the scientific management model of rational decision making, various alternatives should be formulated, each subject to a comprehensive economic and environmental analysis. Based on the full evaluation of each alternative, a final decision should be made. A scientific approach is also evident in the emphasis on the "principles" of public land management. Although "multiple use" and "sustained yield" are hardly precise, land managers have often referred to these principles as though public land management decisions can be made by applying them to reach a well-defined decision, that is, in a scientific way.

Planning and zoning laws earlier in this century sought to protect the public interest by requiring that government zoning actions be "in accordance with" a comprehensive land use plan. The Federal Coal Leasing Amendments Act of 1976 required that coal leasing actions be "compatible with" a comprehensive land use plan. Other legislation is less explicit about requiring accordance or compatibility but contains the same strong implication.

The congressional mandates for land use planning did not require the development of whole new planning systems. The Forest Service had been preparing formal land use plans in one form or another since the early 1960s and BLM since the latter part of the 1960s. To some extent Congress was simply further encouraging land use planning, giving it a more formal status. The agencies themselves did not resist a formal statutory requirement to do what they were already doing.

One might think that Congress would have investigated how land use planning was faring on the public lands before making it a legal requirement. Yet there is little evidence that Congress applied any close scrutiny. If it had, it would have discovered that these systems were already experiencing many major problems and that land use planning was thus far largely considered within the public land agencies to be unsuccessful.

Congress mandated land use planning as an affirmation of the basic progressive ideal of scientific management, not because land use planning had already demonstrated a record of effectiveness. Management of the lands should be scientific, and the preparation of land use plans would ensure that decisions were grounded in science. The managers of the public lands should be experts, and the preparation of land use plans would be entrusted to social scientists, planning professionals, and others with appropriate technical skills. Politics should not intrude in professional matters; adherence to a formal plan would ensure that professional voices prevailed. This at least was the theory, if not necessarily the result, as events would prove. In this respect the laws requiring land use planning were like many other congressional actions over the two-hundred-year history of the public lands—driven by a high social ideal of some kind, but with little grounding in the real world.

Like earlier public land laws, while failing to realize the declared purposes, the FLPMA and NFMA mandates for land use planning also had other unintended (or at least unstated) consequences. Land use planning did not create a rational decision process but it did serve to redistribute political power. Environmental and recreation groups were able to manipulate the legal and procedural handles created by planning to obtain greater influence over public land decisions. The planning requirements of FLPMA and NFMA in this respect had practical consequences similar to NEPA.

In the second half of the nineteenth century, Congress sought to create a rational system of land disposal through laws such as the Homestead Act, the Desert Land Act, the Timber and Stone Act, and others described in chapter 1. These laws mostly failed in their intended purposes, but they did serve the very practical aim of transferring large areas of public land into private hands. In the last quarter of the twentieth century, Congress has sought again to create a rational decision-making process for the public lands. Again, in terms of the goal sought, Congress failed. And again there was an important practical result, the transfer of much greater authority over land management to private recreational and environmental groups.

To be sure, the land was not literally conveyed to these groups, but in wilderness areas, critical areas, wild and scenic rivers, and a host of other new protective zones, recreational and environmental groups acquired effective control over future uses. If the control over use is the essence of a property right, it might be said that the late twentieth century witnessed the creation of a whole new set of private rights to public lands, a new form of unplanned and unintended disposal of the public lands. In the cases of both the late nineteenth and late twentieth centuries, private rights came into existence largely through the manipulation of laws that could never succeed in their stated purposes but did serve to accomplish other, perhaps socially useful if unintended, purposes.

Chapter 4 focuses on the failures of land use planning in terms of the stated scientific management goals of planning. It leaves aside for the moment (see chapter 5) the issue of the broader political and practical significance of the legislative requirements for land use planning. It is worth keeping in mind, however, that so much support for planning may have persisted, despite repeated planning system failures over the past twenty years, because the real function of planning was to redistribute political power in accord with the interests of newly powerful environmental and recreation groups in American society. In terms of this unstated purpose, planning did in fact have some major successes.

Forest Service Plans

The Forest Service was the first public land agency to develop a comprehensive planning system for its lands. Until the 1960s Forest Service planning was largely along individual resource lines; timber, recreation, livestock forage, and other plans for particular resources were prepared. As long as available resources were abundant and conflicts among uses few, this approach worked satisfactorily. The enactment of the Multiple-use and Sustained-yield Act in 1960, however, reflected the growing conflicts among uses, particularly between recreational uses and traditional commercial activities such as timber harvesting and livestock raising.

The Forest Service therefore began in the 1960s to prepare a "multiple-use plan" to provide a better mechanism for resolving conflicts. One such plan was prepared for each ranger district. The plans were prepared using a zoning scheme; each zone would have particular management rules, principles, and procedures. For example, "travel and water influence zones" were identified in areas that saw heavy public use and required special management consideration for their environmental and aesthetic values. Zones were created along roads for highway beautification. Other special areas involved unusual archeological, geological, botanical, and scenic features.

The traditional planning along individual resource lines was not eliminated: it continued in the form of "resource development plans" prepared for the entire national forest. For example, the timber harvest plan set the allowable annual cut for the national forest and prescribed timber sale, road construction, and other management practices. The various plans for each of the resources were to be coordinated at the district ranger level through the multiple-use plans. If harvesting timber conflicted with another use, such as fishing, the multiple-use plan might impose particular limitations on timber harvesting to mitigate the conflict, or it might eliminate timber harvesting altogether.

Despite the considerable effort that went into multiple-use planning, the traditional approach of planning by individual resources continued to dominate Forest Service decision making. As Glen Robinson assessed the matter:

> In theory, multiple-use guides and plans provided a general framework of integrated planning within which individual functional [resource] plans were developed. Individual functional plans were thus theoretically subordinate and were developed from or at least were subject to the multiple-use planning documents.
>
> The reality was something else. In practice, multiple-use guides and plans became little more than guidelines for coordinating the more or less autonomous functional plans. As guidelines for multiple-use coordination they were not perhaps without some utility. The underlying concept of the system of zoning classifications, such as scenic zones, travel-influence zones, water-influence zones, and the like, as well as special management prescriptions for each zone, provided a framework for coordination among functions and a more balanced consideration of the different resource uses. However, their practical importance for some time has been a matter for some skepticism. In most cases the guidelines were little more than common sensical directives.[1]

Partly in response to concerns about the dominant role that the individual resource plans were continuing to play, the Forest Service reworked its planning system in the early 1970s. The aim was to assemble genuinely comprehensive plans that reflected an equal consideration of the claims of each national forest use. Rather than develop a timber plan, a recreation plan, and a grazing use plan and then reconcile any conflicts found to exist, the new concept was to develop a plan that from the beginning took full account of all resource interactions.

The resulting planning system, introduced in 1971, was a three-tiered system. Covering the widest area were "planning area guides," which served as management guides below the regional but above the individual national forest level. At the national forest level another new kind of plan was prepared, called the forest land use plan. However, this plan did not identify the specific uses of land; its purpose was to set a policy framework for "unit plans" covering still smaller areas. The forest plan prescribed "coordinating requirements" to be used in the resolution of conflicts among the various unit plans within a national forest.

The unit plan thus was the heart of the new planning system; it specified the intended uses and management practice for lands within the unit boundaries and represented the point at which a map of future land uses was actually drawn. Unit plans cut across ranger district boundaries as units were laid out to include areas with common resource management problems.

Although a main purpose of unit planning was to diminish the role of resource-by-resource planning, the Forest Service continued to prepare functional plans, now called resource management plans. Contrary to the expressed intent, these plans in fact continued to be the primary focus for decision making. As a 1978 study of land use planning in the Forest Service, done for the Stanford Environmental Law Society, found, "many old line forest officers were strongly committed to the separate functional orientation of the Resource Management Plan and resisted making specific decisions in the Unit Plans."[2]

The new planning system required that "information available at the national level accurately reflect the resources and the social, economic, and environmental situation in all of the national forests." The Stanford study, however, found that this was another major problem because "in practice, this has not been the case." A land use planning system should include a mechanism for translating policies devised at the national level to the field level. Such a procedure, however, ran against a long-standing Forest Service tradition allowing wide regional and field decision-making authority. As a result the study reported that "this is where the process most often breaks down." National policy directions were "often of such a general nature and so vaguely phrased that the local plans retain a great deal of flexibility."[3]

The old issue from the progressive era of the politics-administration dichotomy came up again. Like virtually any agency, the Forest Service in practice must pay close attention to politics. Hence the scope for economics and other processes of rational decision making is limited: "If the process is rational, it is not so in the economic sense of the word despite the appearance of a scientific approach."[4] The Stanford study questioned whether it could ever be reasonable to expect current planning to bind future political officers, even though this might defeat much of the purpose of planning to provide longer-run guidance.

Other vagaries of the political process also affect long-term policy decisions. A new administration with a professed sensitivity to environmental values has taken office since the 1975 Program was developed. There is a serious question whether long-range land use planning, which involves a present commitment of resources according to a set of decisions made about the future, is compatible with a political system where values and policy directions are constantly changing.[5]

In the Forest Service, like most agencies, budgeting has been undertaken much longer and has a much stronger institutional base than the formal land use planning system. Unless the connections between the budgeting planning system and the land use planning system are carefully worked out, the danger exists of having in effect two planning systems that produce competing directions for agency policy.

> In the past, Forest Service [budget] requests have not been related to a comprehensive plan in which the interrelationships between program requests are made explicit. There is an obvious tension between this year-to-year, politically sensitive control of the budget and the long range commitment of resources by means of a conscious plan. The result has been a haphazard approach to funding which has not recognized that project relationships within the program change at various levels of funding. An example on the local level is that the allowable cut, which is based on the amount of timber which can be grown in a given year, is artificially inflated by including timber yields which can only be achieved if certain programs, such as pre-commercial thinning, are funded and executed.[6]

Should planning and budgeting be better coordinated, a fundamental question would still arise: How can meaningful planning for the future occur without committing the agency to specific future funding levels? Yet under long-standing processes for formulating the federal budget, neither the executive branch nor the legislative branch is willing to make binding budget commitments for the long run. Even though this may frustrate hopes for planning—planning that the Congress has directed the agency to undertake—the reality is that the Forest Service will continue to face substantial future budget uncertainties.

The common planning problem of vague guidance still beset unit plans. The General Accounting Office reported in a study of Forest Service planning that:

> In addition to not providing specific and quantified resource goals and targets, many land use plans we reviewed did not identify or set priorities for specific management activities required to develop the various re-

sources. For example, a plan may have allocated certain lands to recreation as the primary use. A variety of resource activities can be undertaken to develop recreation—such as establishing trails, campgrounds, and picnic areas. However, these activities were rarely included in plans. Without identifying the activities needed and the priority in which they were to be done, the plans did not provide a basis for programming and budgeting multiple-use activities.[7]

Reflecting this and other problems, GAO concluded in 1978 that the land use planning system was not providing the basis for most Forest Service decisions.

> The land management planning system is to provide a framework on which to base credible program decisions and budget requests. These should be in line with decisions made in land management plans. Although some land use plans have formed the basis for program decisions, we found that most of the forests' program decisions stemmed from other sources, such as individual resource plans, personal knowledge of district staff, crisis situations, and various directions from higher management level.[8]

Although NFMA did not require it, the Forest Service decided, following the new law's enactment, to undertake yet another basic restructuring of its planning system, the second within seven years, and the third overall. Two of the basic planning documents of the previous system, unit plans and area guides, were eliminated. There were still three tiers, but the tiers were now at the national level, regional level, and national forest level.

At the national level, the basic plan was prepared under the mandate of the Forest and Rangelands Renewable Resources Planning Act of 1974 (RPA). Under a program to be reformulated every five years (the Forest Service version of a "five-year plan"), it set basic goals for national levels of production and use of various resources extending well out into the future.

The regional plan served as an intermediate step between national program goals and the individual national forest. The regional plan was also responsible for setting a variety of land management policies to be followed throughout the region. For example, the plan could indicate the general manner in which tradeoffs should be made among competing land uses or what environmental constraints were to be imposed.

The lowest planning level was the national forest. National forest plans provided the specifics of how particular parcels of land were to be used. Instead of the former approach of a set of unit plans within a single national forest, these plans would now simply be consolidated to become one overall land use plan for the forest.

Putting the focus on the entire national forest, however, offered less opportunity for developing specific details about how each particular piece of land would be used. It raised the old danger of plans filled with generalities and long-run projections without much practical consequence. Environmental organizations, for example, wondered whether plans for national forests would have enough specifics to assess the environmental impacts likely to occur within each forest:

> This approach to planning may create legal problems in light of the requirements of NEPA. The Forest Service apparently intends to prepare an EIS for the Forest Plan in order to satisfy these requirements for all actions in the forest. While this will promote efficiency objectives, it may be viewed skeptically in light of the fact that many of the more narrowly focussed Unit Plan EIS's were attacked for inadequate discussion of impacts.[9]

There could also be a problem for the new planning system in balancing the need for local flexibility with adequate accountability to national and regional policies.

> The Regional Plan may also establish specific program objectives for each national forest subject to the plan. This might involve setting actual numerical targets of timber production, grazing acreage, recreation sites, etc. The difficulty with this approach is that in some cases it will inhibit self-determination at the local level unless it is clearly understood that the planning objectives may be modified if the environmental, social, or economic tradeoffs are too great. In theory, all of this information has been aggregated and evaluated at the regional level. However, in practice, only a relatively modest degree of detail can be collected and realistically considered, even when lower-level plans have been previously prepared. Regional Plans are simply not geared for the close scrutiny of the forest resources.[10]

As the Forest Service attempted in the late 1970s to implement the land use planning requirements of NFMA, it was still trying to find a workable system of comprehensive land use planning. Its fifteen years of struggle to develop such a system had not been successful; one approach had followed another, only to reveal that planning was still not working. Indeed, the 1980s and 1990s would not prove much different.

In 1994 the Forest Service is still facing many of the same difficulties and tensions that beset its planning efforts in the 1960s and 1970s. Wide discontent is heard inside and outside the agency concerning the results of its formal planning.

The Legacy of Scientific Management

The limited success of the Forest Service in land use planning is perhaps best understood in the light of Forest Service history. The Forest Service was created to serve the mission—as originally preached by Gifford Pinchot—of scientific management. The goal of the forestry profession was to apply scientific management to the nation's forests, private and public. Forest Service personnel were to be recruited from the best schools of professional forestry and be immersed in a culture in which scientific professionalism was the prevailing ethic.

By the 1960s, however, growing environmental concerns and recreational use of national forests were forcing the Forest Service to contend with problems about which professional forestry had little to say. Forestry was essentially about managing forests for sustained yields of timber over the long run. The profession had little to offer—had not even much considered the issue—concerning how to allocate the resources of the forests among competing land uses. This was in large part an economic concern; the fundamental issue addressed by the members of the economics profession, and for which economic methods are designed, is how to allocate the scarce resources of society among competing uses. Thus the Forest Service might have looked to economists—as some people in fact suggested—for help in this matter.

Another profession, however, also seeks to provide the correct answer to the allocation of a social resource among competing uses. This is the profession of land use planning.[11] Indeed when resolving conflicting uses of the forests became a major concern, it was to the approach and the methods of the land use planning profession that the Forest Service largely turned. Land use planners and economists had traditionally existed in separate professional worlds; land use planning, for example, focused on the development of maps of future use and made little use of economic analysis in deciding the appropriate future pattern of use.

To be sure, the land use planning profession by the 1960s was actually entering a period of considerable self-doubt.[12] Urban land use planning was about to undergo a major transformation in its purposes and methods. The verdict on most municipal land use plans, done in large numbers since the 1930s, was that they historically had mostly been ignored and were unsuccessful—much as Forest Service plans would later be.[13] Yet while some people in the Forest Service may have been aware of these developments, this awareness did not penetrate very far into official Forest Service thinking. The Forest Service planning system was on the whole an orthodox extension of municipal land use planning as it had been practiced in urban settings for many years to the new circumstances of the national forests.[14]

When early national forest planning did not work very well, the Forest Service did not respond by questioning fundamental assumptions. Rather, it upped the ante. If existing planning was not succeeding, then more inventories, more alternatives, more systematic evaluation of alternatives, more coordination among different plans, more public participation, and so on, must occur. Criticized because unit plans did not ensure comprehensive coordination among all national forest uses, the Forest Service moved the focus of planning to the entire forest. Because forest plans were not fully coordinated to meet regional goals, a single regional plan with specific prescriptions for each national forest plan was necessary. If regional plans did not cumulate to a suitable national target, a national program must establish production targets for each of the regions. The ultimate result of such thinking was that there could be only one truly comprehensive land use plan: the national plan for the national forests.

Any adjustment at one level, however, will set off reverberations for all the rest of the system. Indeed, the achievement of a fully consistent and economically feasible set of production outputs is an exceedingly complex task. Even if a consistent overall plan can be developed, the creation of local incentives to ensure its implementation over the whole system poses still further, major difficulties.

The problems of setting and achieving comprehensive targets and quotas are the same as those that bedeviled the national economic planning systems of Eastern Europe and other socialist countries for many years. Early in the twentieth century the advocates of socialist planning assumed, without ever giving adequate thought to the matter, that there would be no great coordination problems in national economic planning.[15] They soon learned otherwise. The Forest Service experienced related problems and learned similar lessons much later in the century. Yet, partly because Congress requires it, the Forest Service continues to search for a workable comprehensive planning system, even after repeated failure.

In developing regulations in the late 1970s for its planning system, the Forest Service looked for help to a seven-person "Committee of Scientists." In the proposed planning regulations published in May 1979, the committee offered a full discussion of its thinking. It stated, not surprisingly, that it had high hopes for the new planning system. Yet the committee also acknowledged that there were a number of important conditions that must be satisfied for land use planning to work as intended. Otherwise—and the committee warned that this was a real possibility—land use planning would turn out to be a complicated and expensive system without much real impact or benefit.

The necessary conditions for successful planning were essentially an updated statement of progressive-era precepts of scientific management. The Committee of Scientists once again strongly embraced the old politics-administration dichotomy. Congress had passed the legislation and now the Forest Service must be left to administer it, free of special-interest pressures and other inappropriate political interference. Separate conduct of wilderness reviews and other functional planning, oriented to specific resources and uses, the committee noted, was a major threat to the goal of true comprehensiveness in the new planning system. Indeed, planning was in danger of being undermined because there were a number of ongoing or proposed activities that were inconsistent with the formal planning process. As the committee observed,

> Wilderness is not the only resource that gives rise to proposals for separate treatment. Proposals to increase the amount of timber cut on the National Forests have been made periodically, most recently through the President's anti-inflation effort. If the RPA/NFMA planning process is to achieve its potential, and the credibility essential to acceptance, it must be allowed to work. It must be allowed to run through at least one full iteration, from the National Assessment Program to the development of regional and forest plans and back to the National Assessment Program. Such a cycle cannot be completed before 1985, and, of course, it is not realistic to expect political forces to refrain from efforts to intervene in the process over that long period of time. In our view, Congress itself must prevent downgrading of its own legislative design for management of the National Forests.[16]

The Committee of Scientists also stated in strong terms that the new planning system would be undermined if the Forest Service funding needs that emerged from plans were not met fully by the executive branch and Congress in the budget process: "We can only hope that Congress intended to fund fully the efforts it demanded."[17] One area in which the Committee stated that much greater resources were required was the gathering of monitoring and evaluation data on the national forests. But the committee also expressed doubts as to whether the proposed funding would actually be forthcoming:

> Forest Service budgets and personnel are insufficient to support either the monitoring process that Congress envisioned in drafting RPA/NFMA, or the yet more comprehensive requirements of the draft regulations. If the monitoring and evaluation process is to succeed to the degree required for the success of RPA/NFMA, then special administrative and budgetary attention must be devoted to it. The Committee is fearful that this will require more awareness and sensitivity than existing processes of the Federal and Congressional budgetary bureaucracy allow.[18]

Similar doubts were expressed by the committee concerning the likelihood that necessary human resources would be available: "Even with shifts in hiring emphasis and internal retraining, we feel that it is unlikely that the agency can produce the appropriate mix in time to develop the first set of forest plans, given current restraints on personnel ceilings in existing workloads."[19] Indeed, despite the surface optimism, the report of the Committee of Scientists read as a statement of how in an ideal world planning would accomplish great things. The Committee also recognized, however, that the real world was a much different place. By the committee's own reckoning, comprehensive land use planning, which was subject to political interference and was facing budget and personal limitations, operating in competition with individual resource planning processes, lacking complete inventory and other information, and facing other practical constraints, was likely to be a "hollow exercise."

As events played out, the committee was accurate in the warning it delivered. Forest Service planning has in fact tended to serve more a public relations than a real decision-making purpose. Since the real world constraints were (and are) not about to go away, land use planning in the national forests has often been the hollow exercise feared. Perhaps the time has come to recognize that the chronic failures of land use planning are not due to any lack of effort or skill in implementation; rather, planning problems have a more fundamental cause: the failure of the basic concepts of scientific management on which Forest Service planning designs have been based.

BLM Land Use Planning

BLM also had a planning system under development for many years, beginning in the mid-1960s. Unlike the Forest Service, the first two planning systems designed by BLM were based heavily on the use of economic methods. As mentioned above, economics and land use planning are alternative and competing professional schemes for resolving the same issue, the allocation of the resources of society among competing uses.

In the first planning system, begun in 1964, every proposed BLM project was to be evaluated in terms of benefits and costs. In order to calculate benefits each resource output would be valued at a specific "resources product value." These values were to be obtained if possible from prices in private markets where the resource was being sold. In other cases administratively determined values, such as the values prescribed in Senate Document 97, Supplement One, giving guidance for evaluating the economics of water projects, could be used. The planning for BLM rangeland was to be incremental and case by case in the field, consisting of the economic evaluation of individual projects currently under consideration and as they were proposed in the future—and in this regard in contrast to the attempt of land use planners to develop a comprehensive map of the future.

The proposed planning system, however, was rejected by BLM leadership. A former director of BLM planning wrote a review in which he explained that "the given reason was failure of end product market values to reflect all the values (social, environmental, etc.) inherent in each resource. The underlying reason, I feel, was often fear that a specific resource could not compete in so tough an analytical arena." The BLM field was also opposed to this system: "Many field offices tried and the reaction was adverse because of both the value concept and the difficulty of using the analytical model."[20] Inevitably, there was a sense of arbitrariness in the social values assigned to many of the benefits, especially those that had no direct market counterpart.

A second BLM planning system, still involving use of economic methods, was a product of the efforts then under way in the mid-1960s to establish a planning, programming and budgeting system (PPBS) for the entire federal government. Various output categories linked to PPBS—for example, acres of rangeland improved, board feed of timber cut, numbers of wildlife sustained—were to be defined. Each proposed BLM project would be characterized in terms of its contribution to these basic output categories. The BLM field offices were then to consolidate individual project analyses into "program packages" of cumulative impacts, output category by output category, to be forwarded to the Washington office.

The whole system was to be automated in order to allow various combinations of projects, outputs, and costs to be surveyed rapidly at the national level. In theory at least, the political leadership of BLM and the Interior Department could then manipulate the final selection of projects to achieve what they believed to be the optimal combination for the nation. One main goal of the designers of the system was to achieve more uniform national standards on public land decisions instead of leaving most decisions to local officials who were often exposed to powerful local political pressures.

This second planning system was also eventually rejected by BLM leadership. Not surprisingly, it faced strong opposition from the field. One lesson learned by BLM planners was that "the possibility of much more centralized and detailed program planning bothered the field greatly—how could they possibly indicate, in a program package writeup, all of the subtle factors that should be considered in a decision on funding a package? And how could they live with the uncertainty of not knowing when a package might be authorized? They wanted to keep the package type decisions at the field level with more general funding level decisions made at higher levels."[21]

The Problem of Balancing Local and National Claims on Resources

As noted with respect to Forest Service planning, a fundamental problem is to balance local and national (or regional) needs. Local officials have the knowledge of opportunities available and of local impacts. However it is difficult for a local official to relate these local impacts to broader regional and national considerations. Even if local officials are aware of the national stake in a local decision, strong political pressures at the local level create powerful incentives to disregard the national interest.

The first planning system proposed by BLM resolved this problem by decentralizing decisions and moving them to the local level. Yet national values and priorities were still represented through nationally specified input and output prices. Given the resource impacts of a proposed project, field employees could assess the desirability of the project by calculating its net social value, based on costs and output values set nationally.

This system in effect simulated a market system. In the private market each producer reacts in his own interest to the going prices for inputs and outputs. These prices effectively indicate the value of the resources used and the value to consumers—at the margin at least. In the United States, because there are national markets for many public land products, market prices often show national values. Unless there are major external effects not captured in the price system, maximizing revenues minus costs serves to maximize net national benefits.

BLM rejected the first planning system, however, because the field was opposed to the loss of its discretion, in particular the ability to accommodate local community values. Also, the managers of range, timber, and other resources did not want to have to place an explicit economic value on a resource. Explicitly valuing the resource would have made them subject to a wide range of local and other challenges. They preferred instead that the values be kept implicit in the traditional broad discretion available under "professional judgment."

Defeated in their first attempt, BLM planners tried the second approach noted above. If the field would not accept and work with nationally prescribed resource values, the decisions themselves would be moved up to the national level. This was the purpose of the program packages to be fed into an elaborate computer system that allowed central handling of large amounts of data. At the national level, confronting the full menu of options transmitted from the field, top officials of the public land agencies could reshuffle the data into whatever combinations they wanted. The field would then carry out the national decisions as they were directed.

Once again, however, the field resisted, and with good reason. Many of the BLM decisions in the field could not be put into any easy format; they involved individual problems or opportunities arising in response to specific circumstances. How could many thousands of field decisions be aggregated in a way that the special circumstances of each decision would not be lost? How could the translation of necessarily highly aggregated and abstract decisions from the national level down to the field level not yield large distortions? As one participant in the BLM debates put it, "One of the basic tenets of PPBS as described by the Budget Bureau was to move program decision making to a higher level and thus overcome the personal whims or vested interests of lower level bureaucracy. This sounded fine in theory, but it was a little unsettling to think that specific land use arrangements would be decided, within a portion of a district, on the basis of package data only and at a point thousands of miles away."[22]

BLM Adopts Land Use Planning

After two unsuccessful efforts to build a planning system grounded in economic methods, BLM planners finally did what the Forest Service had done and turned to a whole new approach, which was prescribed by the profession of urban land use planning. Some BLM planners had contacts with the land use planning school at the University of Wisconsin; later, this school provided training for BLM planners. Basic concepts of land use planning, including conducting extensive inventories, projecting demand, analyzing alternative land uses, studying how various use arrangements could meet projected needs, and preparing a formal land use plan for the future, were all incorporated into the new BLM system. This third planning system was adopted by BLM in 1969.

The new planning process started off with the preparation of what at the time were called economic profiles and district management profiles. These documents included studies of population and employment trends, existing uses of the public lands, the contribution of the public lands to the local economy, the local social environment, and projected future demands on the public lands. A unit resource analysis was conducted for each "planning unit" identified by BLM. There were seven basic resource types—lands, energy and minerals, livestock forage, timber, watershed, wildlife habitat, and recreation. For each of these resources the unit analysis identified the current situation and future resource opportunities and capacities, subject only to the requirement that they be technically feasible.

The next step was to apply economic, social, and other policy filters. The result would be a design developed individually for each resource to maximize the social benefit from that resource. Thus there would be an ideal forage maximizing proposal, a similar proposal for timber, one for recreation, and so forth for each of the seven resources. The planning system then shifted to a whole new mode of operation, an explicitly adversary process in which BLM employees designated as proponents would advocate these resource-specific proposals to the extent of their persuasive powers.

In this process on-the-ground conflicts among resources would be identified. For example, a range conservationist would typically advocate doing everything possible to increase forage supplies for livestock grazing. A wildlife habitat specialist would act similarly. After examining all the interactions and options the responsible field official, the district manager, would calculate the tradeoffs involved and reach a decision on the overall land uses to receive priority. The cumulative result of all these decisions would be the comprehensive land use plan. BLM called this plan a "management framework plan." It was developed in the field at the level of the district office. Except in special cases, it was not reviewed at higher BLM levels.

After the land use plan had been formulated and the basic allocations of parcels of land among specific uses decided, the planning process went back to specify further details in the management of the individual resources. For each resource "activity plans" would be developed to implement the overall recommendations of the management framework plan.

This planning system was accepted by BLM after the first two had been rejected in significant part because it neutralized the main opponents of the earlier system. The field was placated because the responsibility for preparing and approving the plan remained at the district level within each state. The basic problem of how to ensure compatibility of local decisions with national values and priorities could not be solved. It was simply pushed to the side and left to another day. Since then critics of BLM planning have regularly complained that lack of national accountability is a major failing.

The BLM managers of grazing, timber, and other specific resources had also opposed the earlier planning designs. These managers were accustomed to doing their own plans focused on the specific forage, timber, recreation, wildlife, or other resources for which they were responsible. The new planning system, however, also gave a large role to resource-specific plans. Planning started off with a set of proposed "functional" plans; these plans were then reconciled if they raised unavoidable conflicts over the use of particular lands. The final planning result was a detailed set of functional plans developed for each resource: "resource program activity plans."

From one perspective the new BLM planning system was a success because it did not greatly disrupt existing arrangements and thus was likely to be accepted. From another perspective the planning system was a failure because, on the bottom line, it did not really change very much. Outwardly, a whole new land use planning system was being created, but in practice the actual influence of planning on the traditional decision-making process would not prove to be very great. A number of subsequent studies of BLM land use planning in the 1970s documented that formal plans were not really having a significant impact.

In 1975 the Office of Audit and Investigation of the Interior Department reported in a study of BLM planning that "in our discussions with district personnel, we were often told that the districts have not been able to implement most of the dynamic MFP [Management Framework Plan] decisions for various reasons including lack of authority, shortages of personnel, and limited funding." Many of the plans studied contained "obsolete and/or . . . unreliable information." The study reported that only limited follow-up was undertaken by BLM. Two plans that were closely studied "were found to be of such poor quality that they were determined to be useless for management decision making." For another plan, "many of the decisions and rationale are very general, and may not provide adequate guidance for present and future actions."[23]

The internal Interior study concluded that two of the most important reasons for the poor quality of plans were lack of inventory data and the failure to determine well ahead of time the primary policy issues to be resolved by the plan ("preplanning"). Another major problem was the failure to specify in plans how management should proceed in the interim period between plan issuance and the time, well into the future, when many elements of the plan could realistically be implemented, given budget and other constraints.

In 1976 an internal study by BLM's own Office of Evaluation criticized the plans on much the same grounds. The overall findings based on a sample of BLM plans were as follows:

A. With regard to MFP (management framework plan) III and its utility, both in guiding day-to-day decision making and as a base upon which to prepare activity plans and regional ESs, the most serious, widespread problem is the absence of specific resource allocation decisions and supporting reasons. Specificity in terms of "what," "where," "when," and "how" for various land resource uses and major management practices is generally lacking. Many so-called decisions are merely broad policy statements, standard operating procedure or "motherhood" declarations of continued cooperation and coordination. A reason given for a MFP III decision is typically a restatement of technical rationale for an activity recommendation rather than a convincing explanation of the decision based upon the demands, conflicts, and tradeoffs involved.

B. MFP III decisions in many cases fail to resolve or even relate to major issues and problems in the planning area.

C. A common phenomenon in an MFP is to defer critical resource allocation decisions to some time in the future—either activity planning or as situations arise on a "case by case basis".

D. Seldom does MFP III address the issue of interim management. This is particularly troublesome where, for example, range condition is known to be poor and/or declining, and MFP III proposes to do nothing pending implementation of allotment management plans (AMPs) which, realistically, may be years away. Related to this is the failure of MFP III to establish priorities for implementation of decisions based on resource condition, relative values involved, severity of conflict, etc.[24]

As the internal report noted, the greatest obstacle to effective BLM planning was the resistance of many BLM field managers. This resistance was based on a number of field concerns and motives.

> Where the team observed poor quality plans, the managers involved either did not understand the planning process, were not committed to it, or both. Some common perceptions of this latter category of managers are listed below. They were expressed during interviews and, in most cases, were clearly reflected in the planning documents themselves.
>
> A. That "flexibility" in the planning system allows for wide variation in quality. For example, a District Manager may feel he is merely exercising proper "management flexibility" if he chooses not to document the reasons for his MFP III decisions.
>
> B. That MFPs should yield only very broad guidelines—nothing specific.
>
> C. That the activity plan is the appropriate place to make resource allocations and set priorities (as in days of old—before URA [Unit Resource Analysis]/MFP).
>
> D. That resource allocations made in the past (e.g., range adjudication) are not subject to change in an MFP.
>
> E. That the MFP should not constrain activity planning or limit "management flexibility."
>
> F. That specificity, rigorous conflict identification/analysis, generation of alternatives, and making tough decisions lead to controversy; and controversy must be avoided at all costs (White Hat Syndrome).
>
> G. That if controversy breaks out, they cannot count on support from above.
>
> H. That planning (with possible exception of activity planning) is a luxury the Bureau really cannot afford. It is something that has gotten way out of control and seriously hampers accomplishment of "important work."
>
> I. That maintaining *status quo* until an activity plan can be implemented will minimize the risk of controversy. For example, in the case of range, interim management may require reduced stocking rates, change in season of use, etc.
>
> J. That their plans are generally passing state office review now, so they must be good enough.
>
> K. That planning appears to bear no relationship to the allocation of funds. There is no apparent "reward" for planning.[25]

A third study of BLM planning, by the General Accounting Office in 1977, elaborated on these problems: "Land use planning recommendations are often too broad to be useful in resolving multiple use conflicts and allocating land according to the best uses. Lack of specific resource inventory data and the unwillingness or inability of planners to confront land allocation and resource management issues, which are sometimes controversial, appear to be the major causes.''[26] One BLM plan studied by GAO included guidance for range management as follows:

> Coordinate grazing seasons for livestock grazing compatible with identified wildlife needs.
>
> Implement an allotment management plan with a sound and acceptable grazing system.
>
> Coordinate all land treatment proposals with wildlife, watershed, and recreation activities to assure that 11 multiple use conflicts are mitigated.[27]

Partly because comprehensive BLM land use plans had such little impact, the more important planning in BLM continued to be done along resource lines. Reliance on resource-specific planning was also a consequence of a series of EISs that BLM was required to prepare. In 1975 BLM was directed by a federal court to prepare a set of EISs across the West examining the impacts of livestock grazing. In total 212 EISs were scheduled (later reduced to 144), stretching out over a thirteen-year period to 1988. BLM was also required by the courts to prepare a series of district-level EISs for its timber program in western Oregon. Regional coal program EISs were also undertaken, beginning in the mid-1970s. In each of these instances the proposed action for the EIS was developed along resource lines—so many units of livestock grazing, so many board feet of timber sold, so many million tons of coal leased. Planning for a newer BLM land use category, wilderness, also took place separate from the formal planning system. The Federal Land Policy and Management Act of 1976 required BLM to conduct a wilderness review on a separate track, not as part of the formal land use planning process.

In the cases of livestock grazing, timber, and coal, when the time came to prepare an EIS a whole new round of comprehensive land use planning had to be undertaken virtually everywhere. The recommendations in the existing land use plans for such resources were much too general or otherwise inadequate to provide an acceptable proposed action for a grazing, timber or coal EIS. After the land use plan was prepared, the proposed action for the EIS would again focus on the specific resource, such as grazing.

The resource-specific orientation of the EISs did not, however, preclude consideration of other uses. Thus a livestock grazing EIS might propose an amount and type of grazing, but this question could not be fully addressed without also analyzing the amount of forage to be made available for wildlife. Similarly, the proposed board feet of timber to be sold, or the proposed tons of coal to be leased, depended on first deciding which areas of public land would be declared unsuitable for timber harvesting or mining—usually because of conflicts with recreation or for environmental reasons.

The most consequential planning system for BLM in the late 1970s thus amounted to an informal system where one dominant use was identified as the major concern in a particular area, driven by court-imposed EIS requirements. Other uses were also considered, however, and in some parts of the planning area the dominant grazing, timber, coal, or other use could even be excluded altogether.

The focus on a dominant use led to much criticism, leading to still further major revisions in the BLM planning system. Partly in response to the passage of FLPMA in 1976, BLM undertook to rewrite its planning system regulations once again. Final regulations were eventually issued in the summer of 1979. The most important change was to abolish the resource orientation of EISs. Instead, the proposed action for the grazing, timber, or other EIS would consist of the land use plan covering all resources.

BLM also adopted with minor changes the Forest Service nine-step process for planning:

1. identification of issues
2. development of planning criteria
3. inventory data and information collection
4. analysis of the management situation
5. formulation of alternatives
6. estimation of effects of alternatives
7. selection of preferred alternatives
8. selection of "resource management plan" (in place of the old "management framework plan")
9. monitoring and evaluation

This fourth BLM land use planning system also made a greater effort to address the policy issues of greatest public concern. "Scoping" meetings with the public were held to try to better predict where future controversies would arise and what the genuinely important issues would be in the future—always a difficult task. This new element in planning showed some recognition that perhaps it would be impossible ever to achieve full comprehensiveness. Perhaps land use planning should attempt to identify those particular issues for which important decisions were most likely to be required soon or those land areas where future-use opportunities were most likely to arise.

Compared with municipal land use planning, the federal government had the advantage of owning the land being used. BLM thus had a greater ability to control land uses than say a city government would have in areas where almost all the land was private. By urban standards the public lands should have represented a golden opportunity to put planning methods into successful practice. Nevertheless, the core problems of comprehensive land use planning, as experienced earlier on private land in metropolitan areas—lack of much impact on traditional decision making, long-range plans that ignored more important short-run questions, the impossibility of achieving true comprehensiveness, the serving of mainly a public relations function— were all encountered in BLM land use planning in the 1970s.

Conclusion

Changes made in BLM planning, especially the promulgation of the new planning regulations in 1979, sought to address its problems. Comprehensive land use planning in the United States, however, has had a long history of renewed high hopes followed by further disappointments. Today there is still wide discontent with the results of land use planning by the public land agencies. At a 1994 conference at the University of Colorado a top official of BLM said, "We recognize that our planning systems have been a pretty bad failure."[28] Once again, there is much talk of the need for major changes in planning procedures and basic revisions in approach. This cycle is apparently destined to continue until perhaps some day Congress and other top officials will be forced to come to terms with a more basic problem: the failure of the core concepts on which scientific management, including the design for land use planning, have been grounded.

Many strong proponents of planning have favored it not because they had a clear idea of how planning would make for better decisions, but because they have believed in planning as a virtuous undertaking. Seeing the big mistakes, the wastefulness, the confusion, the parochialism, and the many other liabilities of existing government, they have believed that there must be a better way. For them, planning grounded in the scientific method has stood for the possibilities of a rational world serving the interests of all the people.

The members of the legal profession have been particularly prone to think in this fashion. For them, planning also fills a critical niche in an abstract lawyer's argument. As legal thinking goes, government has large powers; these powers are subject to many potential abuses; there must therefore be strong guarantees that government will act fairly and responsibly; and the best way to ensure this result is to require that government actions follow an objective scientific plan prepared by professional experts. After the plan is prepared the judiciary must then be prepared to require that agencies act in accordance with the plan. It all makes for a precise legal logic and a well-defined set of precedures to follow, if it seldom has much correspondence with the real world.

The truth is that if the agencies had adopted and actually followed controlling systems of land use planning, as mandated by Congress in 1976, this would have represented a revolution in public land governance. Among the radical consequences, it would have dispossessed the members of Congress of much of their traditional power in public land matters, substituting the expert judgments of members of the land use planning, forestry, economic, and other professional groups within the agencies. The political influence of grazing, environmental, hunting, mining, and many other parties that have traditionally played a large role in public land decisions also would have been drastically curtailed.

Of course it is also true that, whatever they said about planning in the abstract, Congress, the interest groups, and the other holders of power actually had no intention of abdicating their traditional roles. If they supported planning as an ideal, they undermined it as a reality. They strenuously resisted in practice whatever steps would have been necessary to make planning a decisive force in public land management. Planning was necessary to the vision of scientific management. Short of abandoning the progressive faith, it would be necessary to have a planning process. But planning should not actually control the final decisions, because that would threaten too many people.

The FLPMA and NFMA mandates for land use planning, to be sure, did have some significant practical impacts, although not of the sort espoused in planning theory.[29] The exercise of planning created a new set of legal and other requirements that could be manipulated by groups outside the public land agencies to exert greater leverage over internal agency decisions. In this sense planning transferred political power to those parties—in many cases recreational and environmental groups—with the skills and resources to take advantage of this opportunity. The existence of significant political beneficiaries explains in part why the very expensive and cumbersome process of planning has been continued despite the manifest failure to realize the stated purposes of scientific management.

We may perhaps be reaching the point, however, where our traditional scientific management fictions can be abandoned. It may become possible to acknowledge that the very progressive aims are misguided. We may have to face the fact that almost all public land decisions are to a considerable degree decisions about social values. Contrary to the progressive assumption, there is no separation of politics and administration, fact and value, science and religion. In the end all the important decisions thus become political decisions.

Perhaps the most important question for the future will be the new source of political legitimacy. What will make a land use decision socially and politically legitimate if the authority of science no longer can? The key changes in the future will be changes in the political regime. In short, the working out of a new political constitution for the public lands is a task that confronts the next generation in the twenty-first century.

Notes

1. Glen O. Robinson, *The Forest Service* (Baltimore: Johns Hopkins University Press for Resources for the Future, 1975): 266–67.

2. Benjamin W. Hahn, J. Douglas Post, and Charles B. White, *National Forest Management: A Handbook for Public Input and Review* (Stanford, Calif.: Stanford Environmental Law Society, 1978): 98.

3. *Ibid.*: 82–83.

4. *Ibid.*: 83.

5. *Ibid.*: 88–89.

6. *Ibid.*: 92.

7. General Accounting Office, *The National Forests—Better Planning Needed to Improve Resource Management* (Washington, D.C.: General Accounting Office, 1978): 12.

8. *Ibid.*: 14.

9. Hahn, Post, and White, *National Forest Management*: 103.

10. *Ibid.*: 100–101.

11. See Mel Scott, *American City Planning Since 1890* (Berkeley: University of California Press, 1969).

12. See Robert H. Nelson, *Zoning and Property Rights: An Analysis of the American System of Land Use Regulation* (Cambridge, Mass.: MIT Press, 1977).

13. See Richard Babcock, *The Zoning Game: Municipal Practices and Policies* (Madison, Wis.: University of Wisconsin Press, 1966).

14. See F. Stuart Chapin, *Urban Land Use Planning* (New York: Harper and Brothers, 1957).

15. Michael Ellman, *Socialist Planning* (New York: Cambridge University Press, 1979).

16. U.S. Department of Agriculture, "Proposed Guidelines for Land and Resource Management Planning in the National Forest System," *Federal Register*, Vol. 44, no. 88 (4 May 1979): 26605.

17. *Ibid.*: 26610.

18. *Ibid.*: 26607.

19. *Ibid.*

20. Robert A. Jones, *Developing a Planning System for Public Domain Lands: An Analysis of Organizational Change in the Bureau of Land Management*, master's thesis, Program in Urban and Regional Planning, University of Wisconsin at Madison, July 1971: 12, 20–21. (Robert Jones was closely involved in the development of BLM planning in its early years and then was for many years—until the early 1980s—the director of the BLM planning office in Washington).

21. *Ibid.*: 20–21.

22. *Ibid.*: 22.

23. U.S. Department of the Interior, Office of Audit and Investigation, *Audit of Bureau of Land Management Multiple Use Planning System* (Washington, D.C., August 1975): 31, 21, 23.

24. Bureau of Land Management, Office of Evaluation, *Summary of Evaluation Team Findings, Analysis, and Recommendations* (Washington, D.C.: December 1976): 1.

25. *Ibid.*: 2–3.

26. General Accounting Office, *Study of Bureau of Land Management's Land Use Planning System* (Washington, D.C.: General Accounting Office, October 1977): 11.

27. *Ibid.*: 9.

28. Remarks of Mike Penfold at the Second Annual Western Public Lands Conference on "Who Governs the Public Lands: Washington? The West? The Community?" School of Law, University of Colorado, Boulder, Colorado, 28 September 1994.

29. For an analysis of how formal land use planning yielded a similar outcome in urban areas where the land is privately owned, see Nelson, *Zoning and Property Rights*.

Part III

The New Range Wars

Introduction

In the late nineteenth century, battles among cattlemen, sheep herders, and other parties commonly erupted over access to the western range. Cattlemen fought with homesteaders who were seeking to fence in the lands. This free-for-all resulted from the absence of property rights and well-established procedures for determining the use of the land. It was in the national forests that the government first imposed controls over use of the grazing commons. Following the establishment of the Forest Service in 1905, a grazing fee was charged for the first time in 1906. On most remaining public lands, the era of open access did not end until 1934 when the Taylor Grazing Act was passed into law. In implementing the act permits to graze certain numbers of livestock in particular areas and at particular times were parceled out by committees of local ranchers. In order to qualify to receive a permit, ranchers had to own nearby ''base'' property and show that they had a recent history of grazing on the public rangelands.

Nevertheless, while the Taylor Act divided up the rangelands among livestock grazers, it did not yield a clear allocation among all the competing users of rangeland forage. Livestock would still be in competition with deer, elk, wild horses, and other potential consumers of the available forage supply. Livestock grazing damaged many riparian areas, reducing the usefulness of these areas as fisheries and wildlife habitat. Off-road vehicle users were in conflict with wilderness advocates over control of points and types of access to public lands. In recent years pressures have arisen not only to curtail grazing; some environmentalists have sought the elimination of livestock grazing from the public lands altogether.

The public rangelands are thus today still open in the sense that few rights to the use of the lands are legally secure; potential new users can

149

press further claims at any time. Rather than with guns, the battles to control use are now fought with political instruments. The winning side will be the one that prevails in the court of public opinion and ultimately in the halls of the executive, legislative, and judicial branches. If any one use loses out, it does not have any legally recognized grounds to receive compensation for its loss. It is in short a new type of commons and a new type of range war, a political war for control over public lands.

Beginning in the late 1960s this war heated up when the environmental movement initiated a new round of challenges to existing rangeland uses. Chapter 5 examines how in late 1974 the Natural Resources Defense Council won a major court case that required the reopening of the existing allocation of rangeland resources for reconsideration. Environmental groups sought significant reductions in livestock grazing, achieving some limited successes during the Carter administration. Although cattle and sheep ranchers lost ground in the second half of the 1970s, they counterattacked under the banner of the "Sagebrush Rebellion," the subject of chapter 6. Chapter 7 describes a third episode in the new range wars, the stillborn efforts of the Reagan administration to eliminate the grazing commons and to establish formal property rights through the privatization of some portions of the public range.

Chapter 5

NRDC v. Morton:
Judicial Policy Making in Public
Rangeland Management

For most of public land history few of the important decisions were made by the judiciary. All this changed, however, in the 1970s. As in other areas of environmental policy, the judicial branch began to rival the Congress and the executive branch in influence over public land policy. At one point most of the livestock grazing, timber harvesting, and coal leasing programs of the Interior Department were functioning under judicial oversight. The federal courts had ruled that the department was required to prepare either a "programmatic" environmental impact statement or a comprehensive set of local statements to cover all the lands. Until a satisfactory statement was completed for an area no significant actions could be undertaken without the approval of a federal judge. More recently, the revolution in federal forest management in the Pacific Northwest has been driven by federal court decisions relating to the protection of the spotted owl.

The courts had been willing to defer to the administrative decisions of the public land agencies as long as judges accepted the authority of their expert professionals. Congress also granted wide administrative discretion in governing statutes such as the Multiple-use and Sustained-yield Act of 1960. As faith in the independent professionalism of the public land agencies eroded, however, the federal courts—and Congress as well—responded with increasingly detailed administrative in-

This chapter is a slightly revised version of an article "NRDC v. Morton: The Role of Judicial Policy Making in Public Rangeland Management" in the *Policy Studies Journal* (December 1985).

structions. Legislators and the courts, although finding that scientific management in its existing circumstance was a failure, then often turned around and mandated that the agencies redouble their efforts. Rather than question the basic progressive design, they seemed to assume that the problems had been in the execution. The National Environmental Policy Act of 1969 (NEPA) was a new form of prescription for scientific decision making in government. Although there were also requirements for greater public input, the new legislative framework of the 1970s for the public lands was essentially a new mandate for scientific management. The courts and Congress were saying that there should be more data, better analysis, and a wider range of alternatives considered, all leading to management decisions driven by comprehensive scientific planning. In the 1974 case of *Natural Resources Defense Council (NRDC) v. Morton*, the judiciary attempted to mandate that the Bureau of Land Management (BLM) follow progressive precepts more faithfully on the public rangelands.[1]

For many years the reputation of BLM was instead of an agency dominated by ranchers and other commodity interests. When Grant McConnell in the 1960s criticized the capture of American government by private groups, he singled out BLM as an example. McConnell found that "public authority was for practical purposes in the hands of the ranchers—more particularly of the larger and previously more influential ranchers." McConnell was of the opinion that "in probably no other public program of substantial size are the elements of private power and control so easily visible or so stark."[2]

Not long after his appointment as secretary of the Interior in the Carter administration, Cecil Andrus indicated his desire to shake up the "Bureau of Livestock and Mining"—his interpretation of "BLM." Andrus was responding, however, more to past reputation than to the 1970s reality—something that he later acknowledged. By the mid-1970s BLM had already moved away from its traditional livestock orientation and was courting a new environmental constituency. Its reasons for doing so were several. Perhaps most important, BLM sought greater independence to manage the public rangelands according to its professional standards; an environmentalist counterweight to rancher pressures would help to create the necessary maneuvering room.[3] BLM range professionals generally sought to reduce levels of livestock grazing and to make investments and take other actions with the goal of increasing long-run rangeland productivity.

Environmentalism in the 1970s also had become a powerful political force in its own right; for BLM there were major political points to be earned from accommodating environmentalists. Hunters, hikers, and other ordinary recreationists were increasingly competing with ranchers in making demands for use of the public rangelands. BLM itself was hiring new employees who brought new attitudes to the job; some of the older BLM employees also were receptive to the new public mood of concern for the environment.[4]

The focal point for the 1970s battle for control over the range was *NRDC v. Morton* No other legislative, executive, or judicial action of that decade had as much impact on rangeland management. As in many other court suits of the 1970s environmentalists emerged victorious, tacitly allied with BLM. Ranchers emerged battered and bruised, wondering what had happened to their old comfortable relationship with the agency. They were forced to fight a rear-guard action and hope for another day—which was eventually to come in the 1980s.

Scientific management in the end proved no more successful in this case than in the past. The main difference was that new political and value judgments were now being made in the name of science. *NRDC v. Morton* was the leading vehicle by which the growing environmental movement, supported by sympathetic judges and allies within the federal bureaucracy, attempted to reshape public rangeland management in accordance with environmental values.

This chapter relates the story of *NRDC v. Morton*. It is a story not only of public rangeland management but also of a much broader subject—the policymaking role played by the judiciary in the American political system.

A New Era

By the early 1970s a new tone was heard in BLM pronouncements. Livestock grazing was no longer seen as a consistently positive influence on the range; there was a greater willingness to examine its harmful effects. Ranchers and other members of the professional agriculture community soon detected BLM's new attitude. In 1973 BLM released a draft environmental impact statement (EIS) for its entire range program. The Council for Agricultural Science and Technology (CAST), representing a number of agricultural science organizations, commented that "we believe that the BLM Draft Environmental Impact Statement is biased against livestock grazing."[5] The Wyoming Department of Agriculture observed at one point that "the last two sentences are much too biased against livestock grazing as it concerns critical wildlife habitat.''[6] The Forest Service found that ''parts of the statement are quite negative toward grazing. We suggest the statement emphasize more strongly the positive aspects of BLM grazing policies. We think the Bureau is being 'sold short.' ''[7]

Another document finding harmful effects of past range management was the Senate Range Condition Report, prepared by BLM in response to a 1974 request by the Senate Appropriations Committee. BLM found that:

> general rangeland condition reached its most critical level at about the time of the passage of the Taylor Grazing Act. Subsequent administration and management of grazing have slowed the rate of decline but have not reversed it except on approximately 25 million acres (16 percent) under intensive management and in some localized areas. As a result, over 50 million acres (33 percent) are in poor or worse condition—an area roughly equal to all the lands in the State of Utah.[8]

BLM then employed the Senate Range Condition Report to justify its plans for a new program of large-scale investment on public rangelands. Following the report's issuance, BLM Director Curt Berklund testified to the House Interior Subcommittee on Public Lands that based on the report, ''Analysis of data shows that range conditions are deteriorating except under intensive rangeland management practices. Significant decline may continue. BLM believes the best solution for significantly correcting these deficiencies is acceleration of the intensive management and development of a program to arrest deterioration and increase the productivity of the public lands for a multitude of uses.''[9]

There were still significant obstacles, however, to a major investment program to improve the public rangelands. The Office of Management and Budget (OMB) was skeptical that many range investments could earn adequate economic returns. Ranchers also had reason to be doubtful; they recognized that a major rangeland improvement program would very likely include increased BLM control over livestock grazing activities. Ranchers also believed that BLM was substantially exaggerating rangeland deterioration in order to promote a bigger budget and expanded agency responsibilities. Although their absolute numbers were small, ranchers still commanded great weight in Congress on matters of immediate concern to them.

With legislative and executive prospects uncertain, BLM found that the courts could be a big help. This was a novel approach for BLM; until the 1970s court decisions had not been much of a factor in public rangeland management. BLM almost certainly did not orchestrate this judicial strategy. But when the opportunity presented itself, BLM moved quickly to take advantage.

NRDC v. Morton

NEPA was signed on New Year's Day, 1970. Although the act seemed innocuous at first, it had major consequences for federal agencies because of a series of bold court decisions. In 1971 BLM decided to prepare "programmatic" EISs for its grazing, timber, and coal programs. A programmatic EIS examines an entire program from a national perspective; it thus does not purport to, and in fact could not, consider local impacts in any specific way. By 1973 BLM had prepared a preliminary draft programmatic EIS for its grazing program that was circulated for public comment.

NRDC was founded in 1969 by graduates of the Yale Law School and supported by the Ford Foundation. It soon included a collection of exceptionally capable young lawyers from the best law schools, several of whom had been Supreme Court clerks. NRDC was to play a central role in public land management—as well as a number of other environmental policy areas—throughout the 1970s.

In its response to the preliminary draft programmatic EIS issued by BLM on range management, NRDC made it clear that it could not accept a programmatic EIS as sufficient compliance with NEPA for the grazing program. While not objecting to the programmatic EIS per se, NRDC wanted a basic reappraisal of public rangeland management. It believed this could be accomplished only by a much larger number of EISs, each carefully scrutinizing the impacts of livestock grazing in a particular locality. NRDC made known its intentions to sue if BLM did not agree to prepare site-specific EISs on the grazing program. When BLM rejected this request, NRDC went ahead and filed suit in Federal District Court in Washington, D.C., in October 1973.

NRDC was straightforward about its objectives. It considered that BLM had:

> managed and continued to manage the public lands in a manner which primarily promotes and benefits grazing of privately owned domestic livestock. Livestock grazing and the attendant management practices have had significant adverse environmental effects on the public lands, including reductions in types and populations of fish and wildlife, accelerated ero-

sion, deterioration in soil quality and water quantity and quality, fundamental changes in plant ecology, and the impairment of aesthetic and recreational uses.[10]

NRDC hoped to use the NEPA requirement to force a better balance
between livestock grazing and other uses. In some areas NRDC believed that if an analysis was objectively done, livestock grazing would
probably be eliminated altogether; in its view BLM allowed "grazing
in areas unsuited to livestock because of their value as critical watersheds or their low precipitation, excessive slope, fragile soil conditions,
lack of vegetation, unusual aesthetic, scenic and recreational values and
critical fishery and wildlife habitat."[11] In any case grazing should be
curtailed in many areas to improve the range and to make greater provision for the other uses; NRDC was of the opinion that BLM was permit-
ting "grazing of excessive numbers of stock."[12]

Despite NRDC's strong criticisms of agency management, it did not
take long for some members of BLM to see a common interest. A pivotal event was the release in April 1974 of a draft BLM report on livestock grazing in Nevada, the state with the largest amount of rangeland
under BLM management. The BLM report detailed a series of criticisms of past agency management and laid out a new concept of BLM
as an organization providing for many types of rangeland uses.

In September 1974, as the court suit for the programmatic EIS was
moving toward decision, BLM issued a press release on the Nevada
report, stating that its conclusions applied to other states as well. The
press release dwelt at length on the inadequacies of past BLM management, in many ways a remarkable confession by the normal standards
of bureaucratic behavior. BLM's release stated:

> The Nevada evaluation report was prepared by a team of BLM resource
> managers with expertise in range, watershed, wildlife, and recreation. It
> identifies 11 principal problems arising from present grazing administra-
> tion practices. These are: (1) livestock grazing systems in allotment man-
> agement plans have not adequately considered other multiple uses (wild-
> life, recreation, etc.) in the planning stages; (2) land-use planning should
> be completed on critical areas as soon as possible, so that action plans can
> be implemented on the ground; (3) significant increases in livestock graz-
> ing use have been authorized that cannot be supported by documented
> studies showing existing forage resources; (4) forage was allotted for live-
> stock use without due consideration for wildlife, wild horses, and wild
> burro needs; (5) there was excessive livestock grazing in some areas; (6)
> reservation of grazing privileges in excess of any reasonable forage pro-

duction potentials was carried on the books for future livestock use; (7) the Bureau's intensive livestock grazing management program (Allotment Management Plans) is not being effectively implemented. This has resulted in adverse impacts on the range resource; (8) range improvement projects, such as seedings and other vegetative conversions, have not been followed by proper grazing management techniques; (9) the increasing density of pinyon-juniper stands has caused a loss of under-story forage for all grazing animals including wildlife; (10) protection and enhancement of historical and archaeological values have been diminished for the benefit of the range program; (11) BLM District Offices have inadequate staffs to correct deficiencies in the grazing program. It is not unusual for a single employee to be responsible for the administration of multiple-use programs on a million acres or more of public land.[13]

The immediate purpose of the BLM press release was probably to make a case with OMB and Congress for a larger budget and more personnel. But whatever the immediate purpose, it should have been no surprise to BLM that its release of the Nevada report would provide a major boost to NRDC's grazing suit. In fact, within two weeks NRDC sent a letter to the judge handling the case, Federal District Judge Thomas A. Flannery, requesting permission to introduce the Nevada Report as additional evidence. The NRDC letter stated that "in general, the report is highly critical of the BLM's current administration of livestock grazing in Nevada and reveals that widespread and significant resource degradation is resulting therefrom."[14] The letter further quoted at length from BLM's own Nevada report on the details of mismanagement.

On 30 December 1974 Judge Flannery issued his opinion. Granting NRDC's request, he directed that BLM must prepare a series of site-specific EISs on its grazing program. In his decision it was clear that he was much concerned that the public rangelands were rapidly deteriorating. Three times he referred to the Nevada report to document rangeland decline. At the key point in his decision he stated that "a recent Bureau of Land Management report entitled Effects of Livestock Grazing on Wildlife, Watershed, Recreation and Other Resource Values in Nevada (April 1974) documents the serious damage being wrought on the environment."[15]

Judge Flannery recognized that carrying out his decision would require major new resources. This could not be an excuse, however, for the agency to "ignore or pay mere lip service to the NEPA requirements." He indicated that if necessary Congress would simply have to come up with the money: "The issue of any shortfall in performance by the agency will become a matter for discussion within the pertinent committees and bodies of the legislature.''[16]

In his decision Judge Flannery directed that BLM work out with NRDC a schedule for complying with the court order. The Interior Department decided not to appeal the decision, implicitly accepting much of Judge Flannery's and NRDC's contentions. Settlement was reached on 11 April 1975, under which BLM agreed to prepare 212 EISs, each analyzing the impacts of the grazing program in a particular area. A schedule was worked out under which BLM would prepare the mandated EISs over a thirteen-year period stretching to 1988.

The court order to prepare environmental impact statements provided a procedure whereby BLM might take more active control over range management. BLM was mandated to examine alternative types of range management and to select a proposed action. The emphasis in a number of these alternatives would shift from predominantly livestock grazing to a new orientation including other uses as well. Political pressures from environmental groups and the public expectations created by an extended process of EIS preparation and review, including widespread public participation, gave BLM hopes that it would have new room with which to select alternatives less favorable to livestock interests.

The Ranchers' View

The real losers of the court case thus were the ranchers, not BLM, as reflected in the decision of the Interior Department not to appeal the case. Ranchers themselves recognized this, as shown in their independent decision to appeal the case as separate intervenors. Rancher attorneys stated:

> Viewing the events that led up to the filing of the instant suit many permittees felt besieged on two fronts: On the one hand NRDC was actively engaged in trying to run them off the range; on the other, BLM, which is normally charged with fostering their interests under the Taylor Grazing Act, was preparing to give in to NRDC's demands by voluntarily preparing EISs . . . While the permittees did not feel that the suit was collusive, it was apparent that it was nonadversarial in nature.[17]

Ranchers could see that BLM stood to benefit in funds and manpower from the court decision.

The forward momentum of BLM's range improvement program slowed and certain factions within BLM began searching for a method of obtaining increased funding in order to expand their regulatory activities beyond those permitted by the Taylor Grazing Act. The present NRDC suit was seen by some persons within BLM as one scheme for revamping BLM's management programs and increasing its control of the public lands through increased funding and personnel. BLM personnel reasoned that if BLM voluntarily prepared EIS's, or better, was ordered by a court to prepare EIS's in regard to grazing permits, then BLM's position in requesting large increases in its budget allotments from Congress would be greatly strengthened.[18]

At heart ranchers saw "BLM's maneuvers as an attempt by an increasingly centralized bureaucracy to extend its powers over an industry struggling for survival."[19] In the old days ranchers had kept BLM on a very short leash. Now, perhaps, the tables were being turned.

Ranchers also believed that BLM had misrepresented the actual state of the range and the effects of past management. Indeed, shortly after Judge Flannery issued his opinion BLM released a revised version of the Nevada report. The uproar over the report had caused BLM to give it further scrutiny, and to retract much of what it had previously said. The agency had now decided that the data base in Nevada was inadequate for making accurate judgments about the effects of grazing.

Attorneys for stockmen had hired Dillard Gates, former director of the rangeland program at Oregon State University, to critique the Nevada report. Although this critique was not available to Judge Flannery until after his decision was announced, Gates was severely critical of the scientific merits of the Nevada report: "It is difficult to understand how major changes in BLM policy or management could be made on the basis of a report resulting from an admittedly cursory look at the problem, that is poorly documented, [is] extremely biased, lacks objectivity, and reflects at best a superficial understanding of range ecology."[20]

An Example of Judicial Policymaking

Judge Flannery's decision in *NRDC v. Morton* was ostensibly a matter only of preparing adequate studies of the environmental impacts of livestock grazing. In a number of ways, however, the decision imposed key policy and administrative directions on the executive branch and even on the Congress. It was part of a trend of judicial activism in the

1970s. From the viewpoint of the Interior Department, Secretary Thomas Kleppe commented in 1976 that "increasingly, today's priorities for the national resource lands are directed by the National Environmental Policy Act and in many cases by the courts."[21]

Judge Flannery made fundamental budget decisions in *NRDC v. Morton* that are normally reserved to Congress with the advice of the executive branch. The preparation of environmental impact statements is expensive; a conservative estimate is that all the EISs mandated under the court order eventually will cost $100 million; a more likely figure is $200 to $300 million, depending on the allocation of costs. The total BLM budget for rangeland management in 1973 was $24 million.

The court made a second basic decision of a legislative or executive character. The EISs were to be written to analyze future livestock grazing within each EIS area; hence a plan had to be prepared for livestock grazing throughout the area. The capacity to allocate forage to livestock could not be determined without knowledge of wildlife, watershed, and other forage requirements. In effect, therefore, the court had mandated preparation of land use plans for each of the 212 EIS areas. The legislative character of this requirement is evident in the fact that Congress itself included requirements for preparation of land use plans as major provisions in the Federal Land Policy and Management Act, the Federal Coal Leasing Amendments Act, and the National Forest Management Act, all passed in 1976.

In the Federal Coal Leasing Amendments Act, Congress required completion of a land use plan before any future coal leasing could take place. It did not, however, impose such a requirement for grazing or other uses. But in *NRDC v. Morton* the court had already imposed this requirement with respect to public rangeland improvements. Judge Flannery had enjoined implementation of any new allotment management plans, the main vehicle for BLM range investments, until the EIS (i.e., land use plan) required under the court order had been completed. This effectively prohibited any new major rangeland initiatives for periods that could last up to thirteen years.

The court's wide-ranging injunction was not necessarily mandated by NEPA. BLM had instead proposed to conduct individual "environmental assessment reviews" for each investment. Only where these reviews indicated significant environmental impacts would a full-scale EIS be prepared.

The court ban on major investments until an EIS was prepared resolved important administrative questions. Even within a small area in the field, conditions normally vary considerably from site to site. The potential for investment will often be much greater at one site than another. Hence if BLM were to rank all its investment possibilities, a selection of investments from many areas would typically be found among the highest ranking investments. Only in unusual circumstances would they be clustered in the same area. From the standpoint of rational use of investment funds, the best investments should be taken first and then funds may be allocated to poorer investments.

The court order, however, made such economic rationality impossible because major investments were not to be undertaken in an area until the EIS had been completed. Instead the court order effectively specified that investments must come up for funding priority in the order that EISs were finished. Thus the goal for a more economically rational pattern of investments was subordinated to the goal of completing a land use plan in each area before undertaking any investments.

BLM stated that completing the EISs would require it to delay implementation of management practices on many areas considered to be critical and requiring immediate action. In making this tradeoff the losses from making some investments within an area prior to completing a full plan for the area should be considered. This is turn depends on the degree of interrelationship among investments at different sites within the same planning area and the amount expected to be learned about potential investments through the planning process. The remaining key element in the tradeoff is the degree of inefficiency caused by making poor investments ahead of better investments. Whether Judge Flannery was correct in his decision or not, it is clear that he was making a complex administrative decision in which many factors should be weighed.

A final important matter included in the court order was the establishment of the number and locations of future BLM planning areas, that is, the boundaries of the 212 EIS areas. This critical matter had to be resolved in a few months of negotiations between BLM and NRDC and the planning areas had to be approved by the court. Once agreement was reached, the planning areas were set in concrete and could be changed only by again obtaining approval of the court, as was necessary in 1978.

In the case of the BLM grazing program the court decision had a greater impact on future BLM policy than any legislation or any Interior secretary decision of the 1970s. There is considerable irony, however, in the context in which such court policy decisions were made. The court was ostensibly deciding on whether BLM was adequately complying with EIS requirements intended to show all significant alternatives and the impacts of these alternatives. The EIS process was to involve wide public participation and bring agency decision making into the public light. Yet in making the most fundamental range policy decisions in the 1970s the court itself ignored all these precepts.

Because basic policy issues were cast as a legal question of adequate EIS compliance, the true alternatives to the directions imposed by the court order never surfaced or were analyzed explicitly. There were of course no public hearings or meetings; the parties to the litigation were the only ones participating directly in the case. The level of analysis developed by the court and the litigants was well below the standards to which the courts were then holding executive agencies under the NEPA process. Policymaking by the courts, in short, violated many of the mandates then being imposed by these same courts on policymakers in the executive branch.

The NEPA requirement in this case thus did not change the character of old-style policy formulation as much as it shifted it to a different arena, the courts. This had a major impact on the policy adopted, however, because the courts (i.e., Judge Flannery) had their own ideas about appropriate public range policies. In his decision in *NRDC v. Morton* Judge Flannery also announced his intention to continue to monitor agency compliance with the court order. He thus took on an administrative role similar to that of the judiciary in supervising school busing programs, mandating prison reforms or enforcing legislative redistricting. This was no short-term assignment, since it was to be at least thirteen years before completion of the mandated EISs.

Scientific Disagreements

NRDC hoped in 1975 that its court victory would lay the foundation for a permanent new regime in public rangeland management. This did not happen.[22] As the 1970s moved forward rangeland policymaking shifted back into traditional legislative and executive forums. Here livestock groups were able to reassert much of their old influence, although partially checked by the new political strength of environmentalism.

This was not the only reason, however, that *NRDC v. Morton* did not live up to the expectations of those who sought it. The judge's decision was implicitly based on an assumption that rangeland science had reached a level of development where professionals could agree among themselves on the true management needs of the public rangelands. Strongly conflicting professional views about the real circumstances of the rangelands were, however, evident even at the time of the decision. Then, when BLM later announced its new range management plans, sharp disagreements soon became evident not only among lay observers, but among range professionals themselves.

For example, contrary to BLM assertions of only a year or two before, prominent range scientists came forth to testify that rangeland conditions had actually been improving for the past forty years, since the Taylor Grazing Act of 1934.[23] No one seemed to be able to say with any professional assurance what the proper scientific course of rangeland action should be. The inevitable result was to politicize the process and to help frustrate any hopes that the extensive rangeland planning required by *NRDC v. Morton* would lead to agreement on necessary management changes.

NRDC v. Morton illustrates the hazards of court intervention in complex administrative areas based on little information. The court's decision had a major impact on BLM as an organization, and greatly helped increase its budget and to shift the composition of BLM staff expertise toward wildlife, recreation, and the environmental sciences. The decision also set the context for rangeland policy debates for the next decade, promoting the polarization that later became evident. Indeed, *NRDC v. Morton* was probably the single most important event in setting off the "Sagebrush Rebellion" in 1979 and 1980. But the decision did not do much to improve the public rangelands, nor did it do much to settle the basic questions of how rangeland improvement can best be achieved or where it is most needed—even while it was costing very large sums of money, relative to the value of the range resource.

Conclusion

NEPA assumes that it is possible to objectively set out alternatives and then to analyze the consequences of these alternatives to facilitate a scientific decision. Strong political and value judgments, however, inevitably influence the selection of alternatives. What was not considered in the follow-up to the *NRDC v. Morton* decision was as important as the matters that were studied. In this way Judge Flannery and his environmental and bureaucratic allies clearly showed what was most important in their value systems.

In matters of land policy the central question is often the system of property rights and other means of control over future use of the land. In the nineteenth century this issue was at the heart of debates over disposal of the public lands. In the twentieth century, although disposal was halted, new systems of private rights emerged with, for example, the enactment of the Taylor Grazing Act of 1934. Like many ordinary property rights to private land, these de facto rights have been challenged and in some cases attenuated. There are also basic questions of federalism relating to the relative roles of federal and state governments in public land management.

These issues, however, were never seriously addressed in the extensive NEPA litigation of the 1970s. As in many other policy areas, NEPA proved to be a vehicle for grazing politics in a new form. And those with political power in the NEPA forum were not interested in analyzing alternative property right institutions or in determining how governing responsibility for the public rangelands might be reallocated. Thus it was possible to spend hundreds of millions of dollars over fifteen years in analyzing the basic management regime for the public rangelands without ever seriously addressing the most fundamental management question of all: who will have the rights to control the use of these lands. It would be left to another day and another forum to take up this issue. Both the Sagebrush Rebellion and the privatization movement would seek fundamental changes in these matters.

Notes

1. *Natural Resources Defense Council (NRDC) v. Morton,* 388 F. Suppl. at 840 (1974).

2. Grant McConnell, *Private Power and American Democracy* (New York: Knopf, 1966): 210–11.

3. For a view that public land managers have achieved substantial independence, see Paul J. Culhane, *Public Land Policies: Interest Group Influence on the Forest Service and the Bureau of Land Management* (Baltimore: Johns Hopkins University Press for Resources for the Future, 1981).

4. See Bernard Shanks, "BLM, Back in the Spotlight After Years of Neglect," *High Country News,* 26 January 1979.

5. U.S.Department of the Interior, Bureau of Land Management, *Livestock Grazing Management on National Resource Lands: Final Environmental Statement* supplement no. 1, comment no. 45 (Washington, D.C.: DOI, January 1975).

6. *Ibid.:* supplement no. 1, comment no. 33.

7. *Ibid.:* supplement no. 1, comment no. 4.

8. Quoted in *Range Condition Report,* prepared for the Senate Committee

on Appropriations by the Bureau of Land Management (Washington, D.C.: BLM, January 1975): v.

9. Statement of Curt Berklund, Director, Bureau of Land Management, before the Subcommittee on Public Lands, Committee on Interior and Insular Affairs, United States House of Representatives, on Grazing on Natural Resource Lands (undated): 7.

10. Complaint for declaratory judgment and relief, filed by Natural Resources Defense Council and five other plaintiffs, U.S. District Court for the District of Columbia, 30 October 1973: 1.

11. *Ibid.*: 11.

12. *Ibid.*: 11.

13. "BLM Reports on Conditions on Western Rangelands," Department of the Interior News Release, 3 September 1974: 1, 2.

14. Letter to the Honorable Thomas A. Flannery, U.S. District Court judge, from the Natural Resources Defense Council, 18 September 1974: 2.

15. *National Resources Defense Council v. Morton*, at 840.

16. *Ibid.*: at 840, 841.

17. Supplemental Points and Authorities in Support of Motion for "Summary Judgment in *NRDC v. Morton*," presented by defendants-intervenors (Pacific Legal Foundation), 11 April 1974: 14.

18. *Ibid.*: 12, 18.

19. *Ibid.*: 14.

20. Quoted in brief for defendants-intervenors-appellants (Pacific Legal Foundation, et al.) in *NRDC v. Morton*, appeal from the United States District Court for the District of Columbia, May 1975: 44.

21. Remarks of Secretary of the Interior Thomas S. Kleppe before the Society for Range Management, Omaha, Nebraska, 17 February 1976, Department of the Interior News Release, 17 February 1976: 2.

22. For further details on the implementation of *NRDC v. Morton*, see Robert H. Nelson, *The New Range Wars: Environmentalists versus Cattlemen for the Public Rangelands*, Office of Policy Analysis, U.S. Department of the Interior, 1980.

23. See Thadis W. Box, Don D. Dwyer, and Frederick W. Wagner, "The Public Range and its Management," a report to the Council on Environmental Quality, 19 March 1976.

Chapter 6

The Schizophrenic West:
Why the Sagebrush Rebellion Died

Federal ownership of vast areas of western land is an anomaly in the American private enterprise system. Not surprisingly, it has been the target of periodic challenges. One, known popularly as the "Sagebrush Rebellion," was a movement in the late 1970s and early 1980s to transfer much federal land to the states. The second was the Reagan administration's proposal in 1982 to sell large areas of public lands into private ownership—a process sometimes called "privatization."

Both the Sagebrush Rebellion and the privatization movement generated wide debate but few consequences. Indeed, both were effectively defunct by 1983. Matters seemingly returned to normal with the federal government expected to retain its hold on the public lands after, at most, minor adjustments in boundaries.

This chapter gives a brief history of the Sagebrush Rebellion. It concludes that its momentum was largely dissipated not because the problems of public land management are minor or have been resolved, but because the Sagebruth Rebellion was caught up in critical internal contradictions. It exposed a long-standing schizophrenia in western attitudes toward the federal government. The West has long been on the one hand the region of the country most dependent on the federal government and on the other hand the region most scornful of federal authority. As Wallace Stegner once said, the basic attitude of the West is "get out, and give us more money."[1] It creates a love-hate relationship that complicates the task of understanding the true wishes of the West and making any basic changes in public land management.

This chapter is a slightly revised version of an article entitled "Why the Sagebrush Revolt Burned Out" in *Regulation* (May/June 1984).

The contradictions in western attitudes became apparent, and lethal, as soon as proponents of the Sagebrush Rebellion made significant efforts to move from rhetoric to action. In the future those who want to reform federal land ownership will need a sounder base of ideas—a better ideology, if you will. They will have to abandon some myths about the role of the public lands in the West, some myths that westerners themselves hold dear.

The Origins of Western Dependence

Historians and other writers on the West have often noted that while the West sees itself as the land of rugged individualism (and votes more conservatively than the rest of the country), it also benefits from large infusions of federal spending in many forms. Although the narrow strip of Pacific coastline from San Diego to Seattle has secured a wealthy and diverse economic base, the intermountain West, the Rocky Mountains, and the western Great Plains are still significantly dependent on federal support. Paradoxically, it is in these very areas of greatest dependence that the western individualistic ethic flourishes best. Today the federal government owns around 50 percent of the land in the West, including 83 percent of Nevada and 44 percent even of California, a leading urban state.

Throughout the nineteenth century and well into the twentieth, the federal government promoted the development of the West. Federal funds built the dams and aqueducts that supply the West with critical water supplies and the high-speed highways that link its cities. Defense and space programs have fueled the growth of western economies. Federal employment provides a major part of the employment base in some rural areas.

The federal government has also assumed the financial burdens of managing western public lands. Western ranchers, for example, benefit from federal willingness to bear the costs of administering grazing rights and making investments on public rangelands. The federal government gets far less revenue from grazing lands than it spends to administer them. In 1981 the costs of Interior grazing administration were somewhere between $100 million and $200 million, depending on the assumptions made.[2] By comparison grazing fees amounted to only $25 million, about half of which were earmarked to benefit ranchers through the Range Improvement Fund.

Although there was never any formal document, the federal government and western states for many years effectively had a compact with the following implicit terms. First, the federal government paid most of the cost of western water projects and other public works and of maintaining western land. Second, the West consented to the federal ownership of these properties and the resulting federal control over much of what goes on in the region. Third, this federal power was kept under substantial though not complete control by the West's congressional representatives.

This control was greatly facilitated by the importance of the West in the U.S. Senate. Ten ''public land'' states (Arizona, Colorado, Idaho, Montana, Nevada, New Mexico, Oregon, Utah, Washington, and Wyoming), with 8 percent of the population of the United States, have 20 percent of the votes in the U.S. Senate. These senators also tend to accumulate seniority: in 1984 when the Republicans controlled the Senate, seven committees were chaired by Republicans from the public lands states.

In the 1970s, however, cracks began appearing in this traditional arrangement for several reasons. For years members of Congress from other regions had voted support for western economic development on the belief that western growth was good for the nation as a whole. By the 1970s, though, many eastern and midwestern economic interests had come to see the growth of the West as a threat to their own industrial success.

A second and equally important factor was the growth of the environmental movement. The West itself, like the rest of the country, is internally divided on the proper balance between economic development and environmental amenities. Traditional ranching, mining, and farming pursuits have become less important with the influx of retirees, scientists, government workers, and other white-collar employees. These later groups place a higher value on recreation and environmental quality and do not necessarily welcome the arrival of new industry as a sign of progress.

Environmentalists objected to many aspects of the federal role in the West. They began to challenge federal support for water projects, cheap transportation, and other means of promoting western economic development. They challenged the use of public lands for such activities as livestock grazing, timber harvesting, and coal mining and called for more in the way of creating wilderness areas, protecting endangered species, establishing of wild and scenic rivers, and setting aside archeological and historic sites. They were joined increasingly by those who sought to protect eastern industry and, on some of the public works issues, by those favoring budget cutting as well. Table 6–1 shows how Congress responded to these concerns with a flurry of legislation, starting with the Wilderness Act of 1964, most of which significantly affected public land use in the West.

The strength of these new forces is illustrated by the resistance to the growth of western coal production. National environmental groups joined with midwestern and Appalachian coal miners and other eastern mining interests to seek to limit the development of western coal. This coalition succeeded in attaching provisions to the 1977 Clean Air Act amendments that made little sense except as an attempt to block growth of western coal production.[3] Later, for the same reason, this alliance helped stop legislation promoting coal slurry pipelines.

The environmental movement had perhaps its greatest successes in the federal courts. As described in chapter 5, in the 1974 case of *Natural Resources Defense Council (NRDC) v. Morton,* a federal judge in effect ordered the Interior Department to conduct a massive thirteen-year review of the status of livestock grazing on the public lands in relation to other uses. The first land use plans completed by the department under the court order proposed significant cuts in grazing, which were the aim of the environmental groups that brought the suit. Ranchers were outraged. To add fuel to the fire, the case had been decided by the U.S. District Court in Washington, D.C., far from the lands at issue. The *NRDC* case became perhaps the single most important event in precipitating the Sagebrush Rebellion.

Another key cause of the rebellion, it is often said, was the Federal Land Policy and Management Act of 1976. That act declared an intent to retain most public lands in federal ownership, mandated land use planning as the basis for management decisions, and generally provided the first formal legislative charter for the system of lands overseen by the Bureau of Land Management (BLM). Nevertheless, the changes it made in public land management were more symbolic than substantive, largely consolidating and formalizing policies that had been put into place well before 1976. For example, the era of disposal of the public lands had pretty much ended with the Taylor Grazing Act of 1934, although the 1976 act made it official. It might also be noted that the act was endorsed and in significant part developed by western leadership. In any case, as a symbol of changing times and as representative of the body of legislation shown in Table 6-1, the act came to represent for many in the West the new and unwelcome federal policies on western issues.

Western-federal relations deteriorated further when the advent of the

TABLE 6-1 -- KEY ENVIRONMENTAL LEGISLATION WITH PRESERVATION OBJECTIVES

Law	Year	Main Preservation Provision(s)
Wilderness Act	1964	Created national wilderness system
National Historic Preservation Act	1966 (amended in 1980)	Expanded scope of historic preservation; directed federal agencies to examine impacts on historic properties
Wild and Scenic Rivers Act	1968	Created national wild and scenic rivers system
National Trails System Act	1968	Created national trail system
Bald Eagle Protection Act	1969 (amended in 1972)	Forbade killing of bald and golden eagles and protected habitat
National Environmental Policy Act	1969	Required study of environmental impacts associated with major federal actions
Wild and Free-roaming Horse and Burro Act	1971	Provided for federal management and protection of wild horses and burros
Endangered Species Act	1973	Barred federal actions that would jeopardize an endangered or threatened species
Eastern Wilderness Act	1975	Extended wilderness system, creating first eastern wilderness areas
Federal Land Policy and Mangement Act	1976	Required wilderness review of BLM lands
Surface Mining Control and Reclamation Act	1977	Required restoration of mined land to original condition
Endangered American Wilderness Act	1978	Added 1.3 million acres of new wilderness
National Parks and Recreation Act	1978	Made important additions to the wild and scenic rivers system, national scenic trails system, and national wilderness system
Public Rangelands Improvement Act	1978	Set goal to restore rangelands to earlier productivity
Archeological Resources Protection Act	1979	Required permits to site excavations and artifact removal; provided other protections for archeological resources on federal lands
Alaska National Interest Lands Conservation Act	1980	Established large new parks, wildlife refuges, wilderness areas, and other "conservation system units" in Alaska

Source: Paul R. Portney, ed., *Current Issues in Natural Resource Policy* (Baltimore: Johns Hopkins University Press for Resources for the Future, 1982).

Carter administration brought staffers of environmental groups into key policymaking positions in the White House and the Interior Department. The Carter administration proposed in 1977 to cancel a ''hit list'' of western water projects already under construction and to make water users pay a higher share of the costs of future projects. It proposed strict enforcement of an existing 160-acre limit on the size of farms that could receive low-cost water from the Bureau of Reclamation, curtailed grazing and limited the use of off-road vehicles on public lands, moved forward aggressively in reviewing public lands and forest areas for wilderness designation, proposed legislation to replace the Mining Law of 1872 with a leasing system, and effectively extended for another four years a moratorium on the leasing of federal coal that by 1977 had already lasted six years.

Carter administration officials were somewhat taken aback by the depth of resulting western antagonism. In their view they were simply asserting broader national and also western interests against more parochial western interests. Indeed, some argued that they were still faithfully representing western needs; it was just that true western needs had shifted toward recreational and environmental constituencies and away from livestock, mining, and other development activities. As Undersecretary of the Interior James Joseph put it in 1979,

> the old interests which have for so long dictated public land policies have lost control. Many of you have been saying for years that more than stockmen have a stake in how the public lands are grazed; more than miners have a right to suggest how, when and where mining will be done on the public lands; more than loggers care—and may rightfully comment on how our timber resources are managed.
>
> There is nothing particularly mysterious, I now believe, in what is being called the ''Sagebrush Rebellion.'' Indeed, it is the time-honored response of the fellow who upon finding he can no longer dictate the rules of the game decided to take his ball and go home.[4]

No doubt there is some truth to this interpretation. President Carter's policies, however, managed to alienate not only the old-timers but the newcomers as well—especially since some of his proposals, like the gigantic synthetic fuels program, threatened environmental as well as traditional western interests. It was a ''new politics'' Democrat, Governor Richard Lamm of Colorado, who charged that ''with regard to public lands, and issues related to public lands, the Carter administration was a western nightmare."[5] By 1979 a *New York Times* headline proclaimed: "West Taking South's Place as Most Alienated Region."

An Economically Maturing West

During these years the financial and other assistance contributed by the federal government was becoming less important to the West. In the first place the West had become the fastest-growing region of the country. From 1970 to 1980 the two states with the most rapid population growth in the country were Nevada (64 percent) and Arizona (53 percent). Five mountain states placed in the top ten. In 1980 Alaska, California, Nevada, and Wyoming placed among the half dozen states in highest per capita income. Wyoming's per capita income increased by 197 percent from 1970 to 1980, the fastest in the country. Some of the mountain states still lagged behind the U.S. average, but their economies were catching up rapidly.

With this growth came a richer base for state taxation. Most western states impose severance taxes on production of oil and gas, coal, timber, and other key resources and also receive a major share of the royalties the federal government collects on resources it owns. Partly as a result of the Organization of Petroleum Exporting Countries (OPEC) price hike of 1973-74, these revenue sources rose sharply in the 1970s. As Table 6–2 shows, three states—Alaska, Wyoming, and New Mexico—are particularly well endowed. Wyoming and New Mexico in 1980 collected $571 and $465 per capita respectively in these levies.

The economic gains of the West in the 1970s and 1980s fed the flames of rebellion in several ways. First, they increased eastern pressure against federal public works and subsidies for western development. The West could hardly expect its poorer cousins in the Midwest to keep on sending checks; if anything, perhaps it should consider sending checks back. Second, as other sources of income grew relative to federal subsidies, some westerners began to conclude that perhaps the financial and other gains were no longer worth the trouble of having to deal with growing federal restrictions. Finally, the burden of land management costs no longer looked so frightening. To take the clearest example, the federal Bureau of Land Management spent $35.6 million in 1981 managing public lands in California that amounted to 17 percent of the state's total area. If the state had taken over management of BLM land and had spent the same amount on management, it would

TABLE 6-2 --STATE REVENUES FROM NATURAL RESOURCES
INCLUDING FEDERAL SOURCES
(millions of dollars)

STATE	1970	1975	1980
Alaska	$942.4	$ 84.5	$1,389.5
Arizona	9.7	12.1	33.0
California	62.3	167.1	431.0
Colorado	9.0	44.1	99.2
Idaho	5.8	10.3	29.3
Montana	18.1	38.0	151.5
Nevada	1.5	1.8	20.5
New Mexico	85.8	174.0	604.6
North Dakota	4.8	9.5	117.5
Oregon	62.3	95.3	278.7
Utah	10.4	20.5	51.3
Washington	15.8	47.2	100.8
Wyoming	31.4	65.3	269.0
Total	$1,259.3	$769.7	$3,575.9

Source: U.S. Department of the Interior, Office of Policy Analysis, *Past and Projected Revenues from Energy and Other Natural Resources in 13 Western States,* September 1981.

have added only one-tenth of 1 percent to its 1980 budget of $32.8 billion.

The Rebellion Stirs

Proposals for the federal government to transfer public lands to the states have arisen sporadically for at least 150 years, most often in times of sectional conflict. In the 1830s John C. Calhoun proposed ceding federal lands to the states in order to weaken the power of the federal government and thus the threat it posed to slavery and other southern interests.

Another push for cession arose in the second decade of this century, led this time by westerners. Among the sources of conflict was the newly created national forest system, which removed more than 150 million acres from the public domain; the fledgling Forest Service stirred rancher resentment by beginning to charge fees for grazing in national forests. In 1913, 1914, and 1919 meetings of western governors passed resolutions asking Congress to transfer the remaining public land outside the national forests to the states.

In 1930 in the wake of another bitter conflict between ranchers and the Forest Service over grazing fees, a commission appointed by President Herbert Hoover recommended transferring the surface rights on federal lands to the western states. The states rejected the offer, however, saying that they did not want the surface rights unless they got the mineral rights as well.

Western resentments flared anew after the Taylor Grazing Act in 1934 imposed new controls on public land users and in particular extended the system of grazing permits and fees to all public lands. After World War II proposals for major tenure changes emerged again, not just to transfer grazing lands to states—the thrust of a bill introduced in 1946 by Senator Edward Robertson of Wyoming—but also to provide for sale of such lands directly to rancher-users in what would today be called privatization.

The recent Sagebrush Rebellion thus falls into a familiar pattern.[6] Like past efforts, it was precipitated by a period of increasing federal control over public land users. Once again, the greatest irritant to westerners was controls on livestock grazing on public lands. Ranchers led the Sagebrush Rebellion as they had led previous movements. And the outcome was also similar: the federal government responded not by divesting the land, but by making management concessions to conciliate western interests.

The rebellion of the 1970s more or less began in Nevada, a state that has long shown a particularly strong interest in the question, no doubt because it is the state with the highest percentage of federal land ownership. In 1970 the Public Land Law Review Commission rejected a formal request by Nevada for a land grant of six million acres to be selected over twenty years, along with a similar request from Arizona. In 1976 a Nevada state commission urged the state attorney general "to assert, in the normal course of litigation, all possible claims the State of Nevada has to the public lands within its borders." Two years later the state legislature formally asserted a claim to public-domain lands within the state. Other western states joined in 1978 in forming the

Western Coalition on Public Lands, for which the Nevada Legislative Counsel Bureau agreed to serve as a clearinghouse.

It was not until 1979 that the rebellion made it into the national headlines. In June of that year the Nevada legislature enacted the "Sagebrush Rebellion Act," which flatly declared the public-domain lands in Nevada to be the property of the state, specified steps for state management of the lands, and provided support for litigation to achieve the purposes of the bill.[7]

The legislature asserted in the bill that the vast extent of federal land holdings in Nevada—97 percent or more of five counties and 83 percent of the state as a whole—was unconstitutional. It based this claim on several legal theories, the most important being the "equal footing" constitutional doctrine, which requires that in certain matters affecting basic state sovereignty all states must be admitted to the Union on equal terms. Nevada saw its basic sovereignty reduced by its status as little more than some scattered urban islands surrounded by a sea of federal land.

When Nevada gained statehood in 1864, so the state argued, it joined the Union with the implicit understanding that this challenge to its sovereignty would eventually end: the federal government would dispose of its land-holdings according to the practices of that time. (In most of the states admitted to the Union prior to 1864 the majority of federal land had in fact already been sold, homesteaded, or otherwise divested.) The subsequent federal decision to hold onto the land, Nevada claimed, was an after-the-fact violation of the statehood agreement that left its sovereignty fundamentally impaired.

Thus far, the courts, along with virtually all legal scholars, have rejected these arguments; even the Sagebrush rebels have not seemed to take them very seriously.[8] No doubt it is partly the archaic sound of the claim. But more important, informed national opinion simply has not been convinced that it would be desirable on policy grounds to divest federal lands to the states.

After Nevada passed its "Sagebrush Bill," the legislatures of Utah, Arizona, New Mexico, and Wyoming followed suit in 1980. Sagebrush bills also passed the California and Washington state legislatures, but the California bill was vetoed by Governor Jerry Brown, and in Washington voters turned down in a later referendum provisions on which the bill was contingent. Sagebrush legislation gained strong support and active consideration—if not final passage—in virtually every other western legislature as well.

Presidential candidate Ronald Reagan for his part said in the summer of 1980, "I happen to be one who cheers and supports the Sagebrush Rebellion. Count me in as a rebel." President-elect Reagan later promised, "My administration will work to ensure that the States have an equitable share of public lands and their natural resources."

Some western representatives in Congress began to lend a legislative hand. In 1978 Senator Jake Garn (Republican, Utah) introduced a bill authorizing the secretary of the Interior to convey public lands to states that applied for them. In 1979 Senator Orrin Hatch (Republican, Utah) and Representative Jim Santini (Democrat, Nevada) introduced bills providing for cession to the states of ordinary federal lands.

In May 1981 Hatch and Santini again introduced land transfer bills, both of which required that lands be managed by the states under multiple-use principles. The Hatch bill applied to both BLM and Forest Service lands, while the Santini bill was limited to BLM lands. These Sagebrush legislative efforts, like the legal challenges, never made any real progress.

Political Co-optation

Many key western political leaders in fact embraced the Sagebrush Rebellion more as a symbol of western unhappiness with federal management practices than as a genuine policy proposal. They adopted the pragmatic and time-honored course of using the rebellion as an occasion to work for concessions in federal land management practices.

One important westerner who held this view was James Watt. Asked at his confirmation hearings before becoming secretary of the Interior whether he favored large-scale transfers of land to the states, Watt replied:

> I do not think that is needed. That is not the first order of priority, certainly. What we must do is defuse the Sagebrush Rebellion. The Sagebrush Rebellion has been caused by an arrogant attitude by the Department of Interior land managers, who have refused to consult and include in their decision-making process State and Local governments and land users. The law says they must, I realize, and you have been an author of that type of legislation. Yet the fact remains that they have not. (January 7, 1981)

As secretary of the Interior, Watt adopted what he called the "good neighbor" policy. It involved several elements. First, Watt sought to expedite a variety of "in lieu" and other land transfers to the states that had long been in the works but had never been completed, potentially involving up to five hundred thousand acres of land. Moreover, he announced, Interior would consider transferring other federal lands to western states on a selective basis if the states could identify specific reasons why they needed the land. In many cases the lands would be transferred at a highly preferential price, although not for free. All these transfers could be accomplished within the limits of existing law.

Western governors eventually identified 973,000 acres that they were interested in acquiring. By 1984 BLM had in fact transferred about 65,000 acres to states and local governments under follow-ups to the good neighbor policy. Direct BLM land transfers to the states under other procedures also rose sharply over the rate of transfer of the 1970s.

Finally, Watt pledged to make federal land managers in the West much more responsive to western concerns and needs. Indeed, this latter effort was to prove highly successful in dissipating the momentum of the Sagebrush Rebellion.

The Rebellion Runs into Contradictions

The rhetoric of the Sagebrush Rebellion suggested that federal land ownership was being forced on the western states by a domineering federal government. But the West had long ago become politically strong enough that, by taking a united stand, it could have successfully demanded transfer of the federal lands. The reality was that the West had until recently found the rewards of federal ownership to be worth the annoyances; in fact, it was still of two minds on the issue.

This reality set in when it came time to fill in the specific details of transfer proposals. Western ranchers, for example, benefit from the federal presence in various ways. Most important, informal understandings have evolved over fifty years or more that effectively give them the right to graze certain public lands at less than market rates. If the lands were transferred to the states, these arrangements would be up for renegotiation. What assurances would ranchers have that state land administrators would be bound by the de facto property rights embodied in past federal practices? Indeed, several western states impose grazing fees on state-owned land that are significantly higher than federal grazing fees.

Thus, when the government of Utah proposed "Project Bold," a large-scale exchange of state land for federal land, it ran into opposition from the ranchers grazing on federal land. The *Salt Lake Tribune* reported in October 1981 that:

During their successful crusade for state legislation to take over all BLM lands, the "rebel" cattlemen denounced BLM land management practices and actual or threatened cutbacks in grazing permits. They contended the state could do a better job of management and Utah revenues would increase.

However, in the Project Bold meetings, they opposed state takeover of the proposed BLM properties, voicing fears that the state, as new landlord, might not honor their present federal grazing permits.

In a complete reversal, the feds are now the good guys and the state is apparently not to be trusted. For instance, a rancher at one of the meetings said, "BLM has been very cooperative and has put half of the revenue back into the land."[9]

In New Mexico, where Sagebrush legislation was also enacted, one rancher complained in a letter to the *Albuquerque Journal* that:

> The State Land office has a philosophy of "optimizing the dollar return," all right. Dollars are the only language they speak up there. Any communication with them must be accompanied by a fee. Every year the high leases get higher with no consideration given to what is on the land that year or how many cattle can, or are, grazing on the land. If we had to pay as much to lease the BLM portion of our ranch as we do for our two sections of state land (which are some of the least productive on the ranch) we would go out of business.[10]

It might seem odd that ranchers would not wield as much political clout in state legislatures as they did at the federal level. Of course, with the rapid population growth of the West, livestock interests have diminished in political power in state legislatures. Moreover, tapping the federal till often seems virtually costless, whereas western state budgets have come under close scrutiny after periodic taxpayer revolts.

Ranchers were not the only group with second thoughts about the rebellion. Mining interests also wondered what would happen to their easy access to land for mineral exploration, along with the huge number of existing mining claims on federal lands. State land administrators might also reverse the federal policy of free access and begin charging mineral royalties for gold, copper, nickel, and other "hardrock" minerals.

The other possibility—that states would continue to manage public lands as the federal government had done—raised a different sort of threat, this time to the budgets of the less wealthy states. Studies commissioned by Governors Scott Matheson of Utah and Richard Lamm of

Colorado, among others, showed that the fiscal impacts on the states would be negative. Table 6–3 shows the fiscal situation in 1981, assuming for the purposes of analysis that the states would incur the same management expenses and collect the same total revenues on BLM land as would the federal government. As the table shows, ten of the thirteen western states would have had to absorb added financial burdens, some as high as $10 million to $25 million per year. The adverse fiscal impact would be much greater if the federal government transferred only surface rights and kept its current share of mineral revenues; in that case the thirteen western states would have experienced a new fiscal burden totaling $214 million in 1981.

Recreationists, unlike livestock operators and miners, did not have to reverse their original position to oppose the Sagebrush Rebellion; they had never supported it in the first place.[11] But their opposition sprang from the same fundamental reason as that of the others. Hunters, hikers, and fishermen had free access to public lands under the existing system. Although the federal government has from time to time considered vari-

TABLE 6-3 -- REVENUES TO STATES FROM PUBLIC DOMAIN LAND
(thousands of dollars)

State	Net State Gain (Loss) from Transfer, All Land	Net State Gain (Loss) from Transfer, Surface Only
Alaska	$ (66,947)	$ (23,800)
Arizona	(15,115)	(15,882)
California	(4,089)	(25,193)
Colorado	(6,324)	(17,828)
Idaho	(23,025)	(42,821)
Montana	(9,815)	(14,855)
Nevada	(18,835)	(26,323)
New Mexico	107,328	(13,076)
North Dakota	43,629	35
Oregon	(6,106)	(4,352)
Utah	(2,411)	(18,040)
Washington	(878)	(739)
Wyoming	114,055	(11,469)
Total	$ 111,463	$ (214,346)

Source: Robert H. Nelson and Gabriel Joseph, *An Analysis of Revenues and Costs of Public Land Management by the Interior Department in 13 Western States--Update to 1981*, U.S. Department of the Interior, Office of Policy Analysis, September 1982.

ous proposals to charge fees on general recreational use of public lands, it has never adopted any of them. Who could say what would happen under state ownership? State ownership might also prove to be simply a transitional stage on the way to private ownership. Even if it did not, recreationists might find themselves paying some market-clearing price or facing no-trespassing signs.

Conclusion

The responses of public land users to the Sagebrush Rebellion all had a common thread. Over many years by dint of much political effort these groups had won recognized entitlements to use parts of the public lands in certain ways. In some sense they had established what amounted to property rights, some held individually, such as grazing rights, and others collectively, such as wilderness and other recreational rights. If they were to be persuaded to give up these rights, or at least subject them to new uncertainty in the rough-and-tumble of state politics, they would have to be shown some clear countervailing benefit from state ownership. The Sagebrush rebels were never successful in showing—indeed, hardly tried to show—that these benefits in fact existed.

Political movements need both interest-group support and an ideological base if they are to succeed. While the Sagebrush Rebellion had interest-group support, it never had a well-developed ideology. Leaders of the Sagebrush Rebellion could effectively rouse the troops, but they could not present a consistent theory to explain why state ownership would serve the state's own interest, the broad national interest or the general cause of fairness. Thus they could rebut neither the perception in the rest of the country that the rebellion mainly served the narrow sectional interests of the West nor the perception in the West that the rebellion would endanger the benefits the West traditionally has received from the rest of the country.

These circumstances reflected the absence of intellectual and academic enlistees in the Sagebrush Rebellion. For many people the rebellion appeared as an emotional, populist movement that could not attract the support of "serious" thinkers. In the end, although the Sagebrush rebels opened a useful debate in the West on land tenure, they did not persuade the region's opinion leaders or most of the key western members of Congress.[12] Within the Reagan administration, a different cause—the cause of privatization—soon took center stage.

Notes

1. Wallace Stegner, *The American West as Living Space* (Ann Arbor: University of Michigan Press, 1987): 15.

2. Robert H. Nelson and Gabriel Joseph, "An Analysis of Revenues and Costs of Public Land Management by the Interior Department in 13 Western States, Update to 1981," Office of Policy Analysis, U.S. Department of the Interior (Washington, D.C.: 1982).

3. Bruce A. Ackerman and William T. Hassler, *Clean Coal/Dirty Air: or How the Clear Air Act Became a Multibillion-dollar Bailout for High-Sulfur Coal Producers and What Should Be Done About It* (New Haven: Yale University Press, 1981).

4. Prepared remarks of James A. Joseph, Under Secretary, U.S. Department of the Interior, before the Department of the Interior Executive Briefing (Washington, D.C., 14 November 1979): 14.

5. Richard A. Lamm and Michael McCarthy, *The Angry West: A Vulnerable Land and its Future* (Boston: Houghton Mifflin, 1982): 239.

6. John Leshy, "Unraveling the Sagebrush Rebellion: Law, Politics and Federal Lands," *U.C. Davis Law Review*, vol. 14, no. 2 (Winter 1980).

7. A. Constandina Titus, "The Nevada 'Sagebrush Rebellion' Act: A Question of Constitutionality," *Arizona Law Review*, vol. 23, no. 1 (1981).

8. Richard M. Mollison and Richard W. Eddy, Jr., "The Sagebrush Rebellion: A Simplistic Response to the Complex Problems of Federal Land Management," *Harvard Journal on Legislation*, Vol. 19, No. 1 (Winter 1982).

9. "Antogonists Swap Roles," editorial in *Salt Lake Tribune* (October 16, 1981).

10. Letter from Janaloo Hill to *Albuquerque Journal*, "Rebellion Would Finish Ranchers," (December 12, 1979).

11. John G. Francis, "Environmental Values, Intergovernmental Politics, and the Sagebrush Rebellion," in John G. Francis and Richard Ganzel, eds., *Western Public Lands* (Totowa, NJ: Rowman and Allenheld, 1984).

12. Bruce Babbitt, "Federalism and the Environment: An Intergovernmental Perspective of the Sagebrush Rebellion," *Environmental Law*, Vol. 12, No. 7 (Summer 1982).

Chapter 7

Selling Other People's Property: Why the Privatization Movement Failed

Socialism and American progressivism are cousins. Both became important political forces in the late nineteenth and early twentieth centuries; both are grounded in the concept of the scientific management of society; and both have experienced a severe erosion of faith in the last few decades of the twentieth century. The most visible political manifestation of the decline of socialism has been the wave of privatization of former state-owned businesses that spread around the world, beginning in the 1980s and accelerating in the early 1990s. Privatization is a major activity today in France, China, Mexico, Brazil, India, Russia, and many other countries. In the United States, where basic transportation, communications, and electric power functions were more likely to be closely regulated than government owned, the deregulation movement, beginning in the late 1970s, was the policy equivalent to privatization in other nations.

The United States did, however, have a few government-owned businesses such as Conrail that it could privatize. Yet the greatest opportunity for privatization was the public lands, perhaps the most "socialized" sector of the U.S. economy. Indeed, a movement did emerge in the early years of President Ronald Reagan's administration to sell off portions of the public lands. However, unlike the deregulation movement, and the privatization movement of other nations, this effort met with little success.

This chapter is a revised version of an article entitled "The Subsidized Sagebrush: Why the Privatization Movement Failed" in *Regulation* (July/August 1984). Some portions of the original article that were duplicative of materials covered in other chapters have been deleted.

In contrast to the populist supporters of the Sagebrush Rebellion, the privatization movement on the public lands started with a small group of intellectuals with respectable credentials who developed their arguments in both scholarly and popular outlets.[1] They argued their case not as a matter primarily of western resentment of federal authority, but on grounds of national economic efficiency and well-being. Some saw privatization as a modest way for the federal government to rid itself of parcels that it did not need or could not easily manage. Others saw it more sweepingly, as a challenge to the root premise of government ownership and management of large areas of public land. Similiar to the arguments for deregulation of transportation, communications, banking, and other U.S. economic sectors, this group believed that public management inevitably led to such problems as the "capture" of federal land agencies by private parties and the use of clumsy command-and-control management techniques. Both groups of privatization advocates could point to a large economic and environmental literature (parts of which overlap) on the failures of public land management.[2]

Public Land Failures

Both BLM and the Forest Service operate their surface lands at a big loss. For example, it costs BLM four to five times more to manage grazing land than the land generates in revenues. The Forest Service lands cost $1.8 billion to manage in 1980 and brought in total revenues of only $0.9 billion. The latter deficit is particularly striking given the nature of forest economics. One of the main expenses of ordinary forest owners is the cost of carrying capital—paying a mortgage or foregoing revenue while waiting for a stand of trees to grow to optimal harvest age. The Forest Service, however, pays no capital charges, and most of the timber it harvests has come from "old growth" forests on which it has never had to invest much money. According to Sterling Brubaker of Resources for the Future, "No one has ever established" that these discrepancies are matched by the value of environmental or other non-marketed outputs of the land. "In fact, it seems implausible for much of the land, which is without any special distinction."[3]

Marion Clawson, one of the leading students of public land management, concluded that the management record of the Forest Service was "unacceptable," perennially "rejecting economic considerations or economic analysis as applied to the national forests."[4] The problem was not an isolated matter in Clawson's view, but an inherent defect arising from the Forest Service status as a politically oriented body.

Many of those who have generally supported federal retention of the public lands have acknowledged that a limited degree of privatization would produce more rational patterns of land ownership. Federal and nonfederal lands are closely intermingled in many areas of the West. For example, large swaths of western land are held in "checkerboard" ownership with the government and private owners claiming alternating sections of a square mile each—a legacy of the railroad land grants of the nineteenth century. Yet land uses such as livestock grazing and coal mining call for larger blocks of contiguous lands.

Many federal holdings in the West are even smaller than one square mile. Some are in the midst of an urban area, others are surrounded by private rangeland, and many are far from other federal holdings. There is little if any prospect that the federal government can manage these small parcels effectively. Indeed, the owners of the surrounding private land already typically graze their stock on these federal islands as though they were extensions of their own property.

The director of the Bureau of Land Management in the Carter administration, Frank Gregg, in 1982 advocated a major effort to resolve this problem.[5] He proposed rationalizing land ownership patterns by identifying parcels that should remain in federal multiple-use management; by evaluating and, where desirable, facilitating large-scale land exchanges; and by identifying those public lands that might best be disposed of, either as trading stock for consolidating existing federal areas or by outright sale. While Gregg would doubtless not have described his "house-cleaning" proposal as a wholesale privatization scheme, it would have resulted in sales of at least several million acres of federally owned lands and possibly as much as twenty to thirty million acres.

From Idea to Action

In 1981 the idea of privatizing public lands had a well-developed theoretical rationale but hardly any political constituency. Its base of support consisted of a few professors at places like Johns Hopkins University, Montana State University, and the University of Washington. These advocates undertook to transform the Sagebrush Rebellion into a movement to transfer federal lands not to the states for free, but into private ownership. By the fall of 1981 they had achieved a respectful hearing among some key Sagebrush rebels. Indeed, in early 1982 rebel leader Dean Rhoads, a Nevada rancher and state assemblyman, stated that "[w]e've shifted positions drastically," in part because "we've had to face the hard fact that the Federal Government was not going to give one-third of America to the States for nothing." Rhoads called for privatization subject to the caveat that "if lands are sold, traditional rights and uses should be retained, such as recreation and hunting and fishing, to be managed by states."[6]

The new movement soon found adherents within the Reagan administration. In October 1981 William Niskanen, a member of the President's Council of Economic Advisors, criticized the financial losses and inefficiencies of public land management and suggested selling "much of" the public land estate. A few months later, as a result of a meeting between presidential counselor Edwin Meese and President Reagan, it was decided that an effort to sell substantial areas of public lands would be included in a broader plan to sell off unneeded federal property.

In February 1982 the Cabinet Council on Economic Affairs presented to President Reagan a proposal for "promptly developing a program to dispose of unneeded public lands," a program that would have to be tentative because it would most likely require "sweeping revisions in existing federal laws and regulations."[7] On February 25, 1982 Reagan signed an executive order establishing a Property Review Board that reported directly to the White House to identify unneeded lands, buildings, and other facilities throughout the government and establish procedures for their sale. On the same day Director David Stockman of the Office of Management and Budget (OMB) testified to Congress that the public land part of the overall sale program would focus on "residual BLM land and limited Forest Service lands" and made it clear that national parks and other special areas were to be excluded. Explaining the reason for the property review program, he noted:

> Some federal holdings that were initially acquired at low cost have substantially appreciated in value because of changing land use patterns. The Government has not responded to changing market demands for alternative uses of land and structures as have private sector owners of real property. Government agencies continue to maintain operations on high value sites even though these operations could be relocated to lower cost areas without any negative effects on the program.[8]

As an example he noted that BLM owned an 8,900-acre parcel five miles from the center of gold-plated Palm Springs, California. Stockman estimated that the Forest Service had at least 150,000 acres in "isolated ownerships, road right-of-way, and unintentional trespass situations" that could be sold.[9]

Stockman made it clear that a basic purpose of the program would be to obtain revenue for the government. He tentatively proposed a revenue target from sales of surplus federal buildings and lands (other than those of the public land agencies) of $1 billion in 1983 and $2 billion a year in later years. He also indicated an intent, beginning in fiscal 1984, to raise an added $2 billion a year from sales of BLM and Forest Service lands. Thus the program was supposed to raise about $17 billion in revenues over the next five years, around half of which were to come from public land sales. The five-year target of $17 billion was later used by the administration and was picked up widely in press reports.

Stockman's testimony already showed the conflicting objectives that were to beset the privatization effort. On the one hand the effort was defended as a way to clean house and improve the efficiency of government management. On the other hand it was supposed to raise large amounts of revenue with the purpose, as other administration statements made clear, of reducing the federal deficit. Yet the land plots that were most suitable for sale on efficiency grounds were not always those that would fetch the highest price tags. Moreover, the steps needed to gain political acceptance for the sales, such as excluding numerous categories of land and minimizing the likely disruptions resulting from land sales, all tended to lower the revenues the federal government could expect to receive.

The Interior Department's Response

The Property Review Board in early 1982 asked Interior, along with other federal agencies, to draw up plans for future land and property sales. Interior's plans, formally approved by the Property Review Board in May 1982, were based partly on field office canvasses classifying public lands into three categories. The first category included national park and wilderness areas, areas with known or suspected valuable mineral reserves, and areas that would be permanently retained by the federal government. The second category consisted of land suitable for immediate sale or transfer. These lands were limited in total acreage and unlikely to provoke much controversy. They included urban sites potentially usable for residential or commercial development, small parcels of rangeland amid nonfederal holdings, and lands with significant commercial, industrial, or farm potential. The third category consisted of land the department had marked for further study, which included, in the case of grazing lands, examining such alternatives as long-term leasing instead of outright sale.

Tables 7-1 and 7-2 show the land classified by acreage, estimated sale values, and state. Previous BLM land-use plans, mostly dating back before the Reagan administration, had already identified some 2.7 million acres suitable for sale with an estimated value of $2 billion. A further 1.7 million acres with an estimated value of $439 million were also deemed to be suitable for sale but could not be sold until existing land use plans were amended. The 4.4 million acres in these two categories added up to less than 3 percent of the 175 million acres of BLM

TABLE 7-1

LANDS IDENTIFIED BY THE INTERIOR DEPARTMENT FOR SALE

Type	No Change in Land Use Plan Required		Changes in Plan Required	
	Acres	Value ($ millions)	Acres	Value ($ millions)
(1) Lands in urbanizing areas or with residential, commercial, or industrial value	485,989	$1,626	103,834	$100
(2) Farmable lands	451,202	130	294,34	84
(3) Lands uneconomic for federal management	1,525,642	253	1,255,598	242
(4) Lands no longer needed for federal purposes; disposal would serve other public purposes	244,180	67	92,769	10
TOTAL	2,707,013	$2,076	1,746,543	$436

Note: Surface value only (does not include mineral value).
Source: Interior Department estimates, 30 April, 1982.

land in the contiguous forty-eight states. Twenty percent of the land identified for sale was in Nevada, 15 percent was in Wyoming, and 14 percent was in Arizona. The Nevada land amounted to only 1.5 percent of lands in that state held by the federal government.

The field offices also identified another twenty-seven million acres of BLM land in fragmented ownership situations and put it in the "further study" category. Of these, 7.5 million acres were held in railroad checkerboard patterns, 9.6 million acres were located in townships (six-by-six-mile squares) in which BLM owned less than 20 percent of all township land, and another 9.6 million acres were located in townships in which BLM owned 20 to 40 percent of the land.

Interior Secretary James Watt was not one of the proponents of the privatization program. For one thing it had originated outside Interior and thus raised a turf challenge. Moreover, because of its emphasis on revenue raising, it largely displaced his "good neighbor" policy of free or highly preferential land transfers to state and local governments, although the program would have given grandfather status to existing state applications for transfers. Watt also probably sensed the political liabilities that were soon to become apparent as the program developed.

Thus, at a White House press briefing, after again reassuring the press that "the National Parks, the wilderness areas, the refuge areas, the

TABLE 7-2

LAND IDENTIFIED IN 1982 BY THE INTERIOR DEPARTMENT
FOR SALE, BY STATE
(thousands of acres)

States	Urban	Farmable	Uneconomic for federal management	No longer needed, etc.	Total
Arizona	57.8	75.6	475.9	2.9	612.2
California	111.4	47.8	133.7	27.2	320.1
Colorado	20.8	19.2	347.5	2.2	41.1
Eastern states	12.5	0.9	42.4	0	404.4
Idaho	8.9	170.7	114.9	0.5	295.0
Montana	1.6	27.3	375.5	0	404.4
Nevada	275.5	241.4	154.0	214.1	885.0
New Mexico	30.8	5.2	409.0	3.5	448.5
Oregon	9.7	58.2	185.9	0.5	254.3
Utah	18.1	20.1	91.0	4.1	133.3
Wyoming	42.7	79.1	450.5	82.0	654.3
TOTAL	589.8	745.5	2,780.3	337.0	4,452.6

Source: Interior Department estimates, 30 April, 1982.

conservation areas will not be for sale,'' Watt emphasized that ''at this time, we have no parcels of any real size that we are singling out. There will not be massive land transfers under this program.''[10] In later statements Watt added that no more than 5 percent of public lands would be sold. Since there are about seven hundred million acres of public lands, the cap on sales was widely reported in the press to be thirty-five million acres—even though the Interior Department had actually identified only 4.4 million acres of prime prospects for sale at that point. Even the higher figure, however, was not much higher than might well have resulted from Frank Gregg's proposal for a general house-cleaning of western land patterns.

Belated efforts by the Reagan administration to minimize the scope of the proposed land sales were of little avail. Whether the figure was 35 million acres, representing only 5 percent of the public lands, or 4.4 million acres, representing a minuscule figure smaller than one percent, it seemed to many easterners to be a very large absolute amount of land. Furthermore, it would obviously take a lot of land sales to achieve the stated revenue target of $17 billion over five years (which included sales of other properties along with public lands). To the press, moreover, a massive sale program made a better story than a modest one.

In July 1982 a front-page story in the *New York Times* opened with the statement, ''The Reagan administration has begun what could be the most extensive transfer of public property and resources to private control in recent American history.''[11] The next month a *Time* magazine cover story on the ''land sale of the century'' reported, ''The scope of the proposed sales is enormous . . . Both President Reagan and his Interior Secretary James Watt are convinced that the U.S. owns far more land than it needs or can manage. And both believe that unneeded land should be turned over to private owners.''[12]

As a result of such press coverage the idea became firmly implanted in public attitudes that privatization was about to cut deeply into public land holdings, a seemingly drastic policy change that was to occur with little advance planning or debate.

The Rise of Opposition: Stockmen vs. Stockman

The Cabinet Council had warned that ''altering present policies, either selling the lands or raising user fees, would likely generate considerable controversy.'' Among the potentially hostile groups were ranchers (unless they were allowed to buy the land for well below market value); environmental groups fearing large-scale development and a shift in environmental protection values; local communities that had been receiving federal lands for "public purposes" at less than fair-market value; private landowners fearing that large federal land sales would drive down the price of their own land; and hunters, fishermen, and other recreational enthusiasts who had enjoyed free access to the land. The most powerful opposition came from what might be called the Subsidized Sagebrush. Not only were ranchers benefiting from below-market grazing fees, but in many cases they had literally invested in those rights by buying them from other ranchers. Grazing rights on public land are often attached to particular parcels of private land (and water), which consequently sell at a substantial premium, in some cases amounting to half or more of the private land value.

If public land was to be sold at full market prices, one of two things would happen. Existing public land users might buy the properties, in which case there would be a large financial outflow from western states to the federal government, or outside buyers might come in to buy the land, in which case existing users would either be displaced or pay high rents. Either way, existing users would lose. Even the sales of urban federal lands and other odd parcels might depress the local market for existing private lands—which in some areas is artificially boosted by the unavailability of nearby federal lands. Moreover, urban sales might have set a precedent for much larger land sales at full-market value prices at some point in the future.

Privatization, like the Sagebrush Rebellion, also threatened to disrupt the political structure of the West. Most of the special political character of the West derives from the fact that nowhere else is the federal government so closely involved in matters of solely state and local concern. For example, in the 50 percent of the West that is federally owned, federal land managers play the role that local zoning authorities play elsewhere. If the federal managers left the scene, state governors, state legislators, and local officials would suddenly become more powerful figures. All of the relevant interest groups, which have built up a great deal of capital in learning how to deal with the existing system at the federal level, would lose this investment and have to learn a new political system.

As these factors became more apparent, whatever early western support for the privatization effort had existed turned quickly to opposition. Ranchers and other traditional western land users joined with environmentalists and other national interest groups to derail the entire privatization effort. The *Nevada State Journal* reported on May 5, 1982 that "leading sagebrush rebels" in that state were seeking "to put as much distance as possible between their cause and privatization."[13] Mining and livestock industry spokesmen sought to dispel what they said was the myth that ranchers and miners wanted to buy up federal lands. Actually, said Ned Eyre of the Nevada Cattlemen's Association and Bob Warren of the Nevada Mining Association, their members could not afford to buy the lands they use.

In October 1982 the *Idaho Statesman* reported more reaction.

> "If this continues, it could put a lot of ranchers out of business. People don't realize just how serious this is to stockmen," said rancher Louis Cenarrusa, a brother of Idaho Secretary of State Pete Cenarrusa.
>
> Ranchers could not compete with "tourists and out-of-state interests," who pay high prices for land in Blaine County, rancher Bud Simpson said.
>
> Asked what he could do to stop the Reagan administration's program, [Idaho Governor John] Evans said, "We'll call out the National Guard if necessary. We're not going to be bullied on this."[14]

Public opinion became inflamed by such argument and debate polarized to the point that—distrusting the motives of the land agency administrators—an aroused opposition refused to grant the discretionary powers needed to pursue even the modest sales of 4.4 million acres that were the immediate focus of Interior Department plans. Trapped in a debate over whether to sell millions of acres, Interior managed to lose the ability to sell street-corner lots in Reno and Palm Springs.

The governors of the public land states, who though predominantly Democratic had often found Watt's land policies congenial, began to speak out against the privatization effort. It is interesting to note, incidentally, that western states, while criticizing Interior's privatization efforts, have moved fairly aggressively to sell some of their own lands. Indeed, from a much smaller base they sold much more than the federal government in the years from 1972 to 1981: a total of 192,585 acres, compared with only 67,765 acres for BLM.

Western discontent was of deep concern to the White House. The West had been the bedrock of Reagan support, and his administration had entered office pledging to quell sources of western resentment. Hence the days of privatization were numbered.

The Demise of Privatization

In many ways the privatization effort resembled the Carter administration's "hit list" of water projects. Both initiatives made sense from a national efficiency perspective but foundered because they would have upset western political relationships and land management practices of long standing. Both were pushed by policymakers with strong convictions but little practical experience with public land management. Both were more or less foisted on the respective secretaries of the interior, Cecil Andrus and James Watt, who sustained great political damage in defending programs not of their own devising.

An irony is that it was the privatizers who were defending the principle that public lands must be used for the broadest public benefit. Reducing the federal deficit and paying off the national debt would be of general national interest. The opponents of privatization, despite much rhetoric about the squandering of the public patrimony, drew their greatest political strength from the interest groups that enjoy special benefits from preferential access to public land and influence over public land management.

Momentum is powerful in government, and it was not until the summer of 1983 that the effort to privatize the public lands was officially ended. On July 15, 1983, Secretary Watt announced that he had reached an agreement with Edwin Harper, the chairman of the Property Review Board, to exclude public land sales from the jurisdiction of the board. Watt also pledged in a letter to the western governors that "the mistakes of 1982 are not being, and will not be, repeated. Each governor has been briefed, or his staff has been briefed, on our plans for disposing of the few isolated tracts in the respective States."[15] Watt abolished both Interior's asset management office and the BLM's official liaison with the Property Review Board.

For all the fierceness of the controversy the privatization effort had very little substantive impact.[16] As Table 7–3 shows, land sales through 1983 continued at a level of approximately zero. Less land was sold in the decade from 1974 to 1983 than in any single year from 1950 to 1968. There was no appreciable progress even on the sale of scattered parcels of urban lands and rangelands: those parcels potentially amount to several million acres, hundreds of times more than was sold in 1983.

Incremental Privatization

For a year or more the doings of the Property Review Board made privatization the central issue in public land debates, which were widely covered in the western press. Although this high visibility had the disadvantage of polarizing the issue, it did expose the public to new informa-

TABLE 7-3
SALES OF PUBLIC LANDS BY THE
BUREAU OF LAND MANAGEMENT

Fiscal Year	Parcels	Acres	Receipts
1950	563	65,054	$ 456,259
1955	963	168,013	1,925,975
1960	701	99,225	5,101,297
1965	592	87,061	3.061,158
1968	346	66,632	2,521,132
1969	274	37,877	1,802,126
1970	258	35,150	2,099,849
1971	219	30,113	2,013,823
1972	170	22,005	1,941,520
1973	148	13,669	1,797,933
1974	79	8,691	2,055,637
1975	69	5,105	233,438
1976	84	3,641	584,751
1977	24	1,295	6,480,499
1978	16	709	82,585
1979	86	1,760	6,480,499
1980	159	4,115	7,326,599
1981	111	7,120	2,868,087
1982	55	1,312	1,466,022
1983	223	10,257	8,172,601

Note: Land sales in Alaska are excluded.
Source: Interior Department data.

tion and concepts and in the long term widened the agenda for policy debate.

Students of land tenure have found that new property rights are seldom planned, nor do they proceed in large jumps. Rather, they evolve incrementally in response to the needs and pressures of the moment. Even many instances of "landmark" legislation have simply ratified existing trends and perhaps pushed them along a bit further. The Forest Service, for example, had been creating wilderness areas administratively for forty years before Congress first gave formal statutory recognition to the concept in the Wilderness Act of 1964.

Mining laws on the public lands arose from informal private arrangements worked out in the nineteenth century among western miners, who needed a quick way to resolve potential conflicts in mining claims. Similarly, the Homestead Act of 1862 evolved when the government eventually acquiesced in widespread squatting on public lands. For a long time settlers had honored informal private arrangements whereby, should the government offer the land for sale, the settler in residence had a right to be the sole bidder and thereby get the land for the minimum price, generally $1.25 an acre. Interlopers could be shot for challenging these arrangements.

Grazing rights on public lands also evolved over many years.[17] Much like the squatters, many ranchers worked out informal arrangements to allocate unappropriated areas of public land among contending users. The Taylor Grazing Act of 1934 ratified these arrangements by allocating public land grazing ''privileges'' on the basis of ranchers' historic use of the land and ownership of complementary ''base property.''

Times have changed since the days of the squatters: land users now establish rights to exclude other users from public land by political rather than bodily means. Success has come to depend on political strength, not physical strength: the quick lobbying campaign, not the quick draw. Seen in this light, de facto privatization of the public lands has been occurring throughout this century and proceeded still further in the 1980s.

Wilderness organizations, along with ranchers, showed impressive success in controlling ''their'' chunk of the public land estate. They fended off oil and gas exploration in wilderness areas in highly publicized battles. Hunters, hikers, fishermen, and other recreationists also bolstered their collective access rights to public lands. Reflecting these developments, some supporters of privatization have proposed giving wilderness organizations formal title to federal wilderness areas, thereby recognizing officially that these organizations in effect already hold a sort of collective property right in wilderness areas.

Another recent case of de facto privatization deserves mention. Around half of federal coal lies under private surface lands. As a practical matter it has always been hard to develop this coal against the wishes of the private surface owner. In 1977, in the Surface Mining Control and Reclamation Act, Congress formalized these rights by adopting a requirement that would-be miners obtain the consent of "qualified" surface owners. The practical effect was to transfer a half-share in ownership of nominally "federal" coal to the surface owner. This law had the active support of environmental and other groups that normally are strongly opposed to such privatizing measures.

The rights of state governments over federal lands, like the rights of private parties, advanced bit by bit as well, accomplishing some of the goals of the Sagebrush Rebellion after all. Western state governments showed great strength in the debates over deployment of the MX missile and the siting of nuclear waste facilities. Regional "teams" that include representatives of western states acquired a major decision-making role in the federal coal program.

The federal government agreed to try to make its land use plans consistent with state and local plans. A 1972 law requires that federal actions be "consistent" with state plans for the control of coastal zones. Western state officials have argued that the consistency provisions of the Federal Land Policy and Management Act, which are weaker than those of the coastal legislation, should nevertheless be interpreted with a similar stringency. Some westerners proposed that the actions of public land managers be required to conform to the decisions of local zoning authorities just as if the federal government were a private landholder. In the end it is possible that the states will ultimately have more power over the federal land than if it were privately held.

This might be the most convenient outcome of all for the western states: they make the decisions, while the federal government continues to pay for the administrative apparatus and its management costs. The subsidy, of course, is nothing new; what is new is the further shift of control. It remains to be seen whether this arrangement will prove acceptable to the East and Midwest, which are asked to bear the financial burdens but forgo more and more of their already limited prerogatives of "owning" the land.

But even if the East and Midwest accept this arrangement, the western states are likely to find that they cannot manage federal land very well by remote control, by trying to bind the hands of federal land managers in advance with rigid rules and requirements for consultation with the states. Too much discretion is necessary and the transaction costs will be large.

Since legislation tends to ratify preexisting trends in property rights, the best way to predict the long-run future is to observe the incremental trends of the recent past and present. As we have seen, these trends show less federal control over public lands at the same time that there is more private and more state and local control. In effect privatization and the Sagebrush Rebellion are actually being realized, even if slowly and incrementally and even if the process is obscured by myths and fictions that camouflage its inconsistency with widely accepted political beliefs. In some ways the public and private land systems seem to be gradually converging as state and municipal governments increase their control over the use of private land through zoning and other regulations and as private rights proliferate on public lands.

The speed at which such a new system of public land tenure can evolve depends on several factors. One of the most important is ideology. These evolving processes have not been recognized formally, in part because most Americans are still not convinced that privatization and state ownership are a good idea.[18] Yet the premises of the current public land system are no longer believed either. The public has lost most of its confidence in the notion, dating back to the conservationist ideology of the turn of the century, that management of public resources can be handed over to experts.

If significant changes in public land tenure are to occur, they will probably require combining a popular movement such as the Sagebrush Rebellion with an intellectual base such as that of the privatization movement. For almost the first time in this century there are now academic and other intellectual proponents of major changes in public land tenure, although, of course, the opposition to their views is also strong.[19] Until such ideas can be translated into a strong popular movement, however, they will have little chance of full success.

Conclusion

The advocates of privatization skillfully exposed the deficiencies of public land management. They were less successful in analyzing the transitional problems that would be encountered in any real effort to create a new private property right regime. Some privatizers assumed that matters could be as simple as putting the land up for competitive bid and selling it for the highest offer. This strategy failed, however, to recognize a critical limiting factor. The public lands were already privatized to a greater degree than either the proponents or the opponents of privatization usually acknowledged. There already existed a wide range of de facto private rights—or so the people who used the public lands tended to regard their past privileges—that were grounded in long historic experience.

The lands thus did not stand free and unencumbered. Indeed, to try to sell them to the highest bidder would be like trying to sell someone else's property. The federal government in the nineteenth century had tried to sell land already occupied by squatters, but any bidder in such an auction risked life and limb. There were few such bidders. In the 1980s the federal government never got to the point of being able to offer public land up for sale. In other countries this problem was often resolved by limiting the potential buyers to the existing user and selling government property at a substantial discount. The Thatcher government in Great Britain sold large amounts of public housing on this basis. But the proponents of privatization of public land in the United States never put together a well-developed proposal based on a similar approach.[20] It would also have been at odds with the deficit reduction purposes that were supposedly motivating the privatization effort.

The history of the public lands shows that new laws are most effective when they build on existing developments. The Preemption Act of 1841 granted squatters a prospective right to purchase land only after many retroactive preemption laws had been enacted by Congress. Today there are many informal rights that have developed on the public lands. The challenge for privatization is to recognize these rights, to build on them, perhaps to alter them in some ways, and in this fashion to bring the legal framework into greater conformity with the practices on the land. Any future design for privatization will have to take the existing structure of informal privileges and rights as a starting point.[21]

Notes

1. Richard Stroup and John Baden, "Externality, Property Rights, and the Management of the National Forests,," *Journal of Law and Economics* (October 1973); Phillip W. Truluck, ed., *Private Rights and Public Lands* (Washington, D.C.: Heritage Foundation, 1983); Steve Hanke, "The Privatization Debate: An Insider's View," *Cato Journal* (Winter 1982).

2. Marion Clawson, *The Economics of National Forest Management* (Washington, D.C.: Resources for the Future, 1976); and Marion Clawson, *The Federal Lands Revisited* (Washington, D.C.: Johns Hopkins University Press for Resources for the Future, 1983).

3. Sterling Brubaker, "Land, Lots of Land," *Resources* (February 1983): 5.

4. Clawson, *The Economics of National Forest Management*: 99, 144.

5. Frank Gregg, *Federal Land Transfers: The Case for a Westwide Program Based on the Federal Land Policy and Management Act* (Washington, D.C.: The Conservation Foundation, 1982).

6. Quoted in *Public Land News*, 4 February 1982.

7. Memorandum for the President from the Cabinet Council on Economic Affairs entitled "Federal Property Review Program," 9 February 1982.

8. Statement of David A. Stockman, Director, Office of Management and Budget, before the Senate Committee on Governmental Affairs, 25 February 1982.

9. *Ibid.*

10. Transcript of the White House briefing for reporters by Secretary of the Interior James Watt and Chairman of the Property Review Board, Edwin Harper, 21 May 1982.

11. Philip Shabecoff, "U.S. Plans Biggest Land Shift since Frontier Times," *New York Times* (3 July 1982): 1.

12. Peter Stoler, "Land Sale of the Century," *Time* (23 August 1982): 16.

13. Quoted in Patrick O'Driscoll, "Legislators Blast Federal Land Sale to Pay U.S. Debt," *Nevada State Journal* (5 May 1982).

14. Larry Swisher, "Evans Denounces U.S. Land-Sale Plan," *Idaho Statesman* (7 October 1982).

15. Memorandum from Secretary of the Interior James Watt to all western governors, "Good Neighbor Policy," 18 July 1983.

16. Christopher K. Leman, "How the Privatization Revolution Failed, and Why Public Land Management Needs Reform Anyway," in John G. Francis and Richard Ganzel, eds., *Western Public Lands* (Totowa, N.J.: Rowman & Allenheld, 1984).

17. Gary Libecap, *Locking Up the Range: Federal Land Controls and Grazing* (Cambridge, Mass.: Ballinger, 1981).

18. Joseph L. Sax, "Why We Will Not (Should Not) Sell the Public Lands: Changing Conceptions of Private Property," *Utah Law Review*, no. 2 (1983).

19. Terry L. Anderson and Donald R. Leal, *Free-market Environmentalism* (San Francisco: Pacific Research Institute for Public Policy and Westview Press, 1991).

20. See Robert H. Nelson, "Privatization of Federal Lands: What Did Not Happen," in Roger E. Meiners and Bruce Yandle, *Regulation and the Reagan Era* (New York: Holmes and Meier for The Independent Institute, 1989).

21. See Robert H. Nelson, "Private Rights to Government Actions: How Modern Property Rights Evolve," *University of Illinois Law Review* vol. 1986, no. 2 (1986).

Part IV

Rethinking the Public Lands

Introduction

The new range wars of the late 1970s and early 1980s were fought to a draw. While few matters were resolved, the controversies did at least serve to stimulate interest in the future of the public lands. In the early 1980s Resources for the Future, the Wilderness Society, the Heritage Foundation, and other policy organizations sponsored conferences on this subject. They asked basic questions that had not been addressed seriously for a generation or more: Why are the lands in federal possession? What should be the role of government planning versus the market in managing the lands? How can retention of such large resources by the national government be squared with the private property traditions that generally guide the American economy?

The answers offered surprisingly little support for the status quo. The existing public land system could be explained as the product of many years of history. The continuance of the system could be justified in terms of the great political difficulty of making any major changes. Indeed, the existing users of the public lands often saw themselves as possessing de facto entitlements. They typically fought tenaciously to defend their existing places and patterns of use, sometimes as fiercely as would the owners of private property in defending their rights.

Politically, those who called for any radical changes on the public lands received little support. Nevertheless, in terms of accepted American principles for reliance on a market system or of the accepted principles of American federalism, it was hard to defend existing public land arrangements. On intellectual if not political grounds there was much to be said for examining the options of privatization of substantial areas of federal lands and/or the transfer of sizeable areas of federal land to state and local governments. Well-respected analysts of public land policy such as Marion Clawson of Resources for the Future raised such options and concluded that there was much to be said for a basic re-thinking of existing institutional arrangements.

Chapter 8 examines how the emergence of the Sagebrush Rebellion in the late 1970s raised new options for the future of the public lands, and chapter 9 describes how the intellectual foundations for the management of the public lands had in fact been eroding for many years; there was now a genuine crisis of ideology. These themes are further explored in chapter 10 in the particular context of the Forest Service management of the national forests.

Chapter 8

Making Sense of the Sagebrush Rebellion: A Long-Term Strategy for the Public Lands

The federal government owns 48 percent of the land in the westernmost eleven lower forty-eight states. As shown in Table 8–1, Nevada consists mainly of federal land, which covers more than 80 percent of the total area of the State. Sixty-six percent of Utah and 64 percent of Idaho are also owned by the federal government. Such large federal land holdings in the West have been a source of friction for many years. The Sagebrush Rebellion of the late 1970s and early 1980s was the most recent flaring of resentment (see chapter 6).[1]

Although the Sagebrush Rebellion tended to be dismissed by elite opinion, it was in fact compatible with a number of contemporary trends. Worldwide there is a broad disenchantment today with central bureaucracy and planning. This took an extreme form in the breakup of the former Soviet Union. Old pillars of U.S. industry such as IBM and General Motors have been forced to struggle for their very survival by cutting middle management and decentralizing their operations. The computer and communications revolutions are undercutting the economic grounds for the past concentration of American business in a few large national corporations in each industrial sector.

In looking back on the public debate surrounding the Sagebrush Rebellion, there is a strong sense of positions frozen in the past. Environ-

This chapter is a revised and shortened version of an unpublished paper, "Making Sense of the Sagebrush Rebellion: A Long-Term Strategy for the Public Lands," presented to the annual meeting of the Association for Public Policy Analysis and Management, Washington, D.C., 23–25 October 1981.

TABLE 8-1 - LAND OWNERSHIP, BY STATE (millions of acres)

| State | Original Public Domain Lands | | | Acquired Federal Lands | Total Federal Lands | Total Land in State | Percent Federal |
	BLM Lands	Forest Service Lands	Other				
Arizona	12.6	11.4	7.6	0.3	31.9	72.7	43.9%
California	15.6	19.7	7.4	2.4	45.1	100.2	45.0
Colorado	8.3	13.7	0.9	1.1	24.0	66.5	36.1
Idaho	11.9	19.9	1.1	0.8	33.7	52.9	63.7
Montana	6.3	16.7	2.2	2.5	27.7	93.3	29.6
Nevada	48.4	5.1	7.1	0.2	60.8	70.3	86.5
New Mexico	12.7	8.7	2.9	1.8	26.1	77.8	33.6
Oregon	15.7	14.6	0.7	1.2	32.2	61.6	52.3
Utah	22.6	7.8	3.9	0.5	34.9	52.7	66.2
Washington	0.3	8.8	2.1	1.4	12.6	42.7	29.5
Wyoming	17.5	8.9	2.9	0.6	29.9	62.3	48.0
Total	171.9	135.3	38.8	12.8	358.9	753.0	47.7%

mentalists saw themselves as the heirs to the old conservationists who fought off the timber barons, grazers, and other commodity interests seeking to profit from federal lands at public expense. They sought once again to fight the good old battle to save the public lands. Ranchers and other western interests similarly had been doing battle with the federal government and conservationists for more than seventy-five years. Many saw the Sagebrush Rebellion as simply the latest round in this long-standing dispute.

These old habits seem to have overwhelmed the objective facts of the controversy. Indeed, if one did not know the historical background so well, it might be difficult to predict on which side environmentalists and ranchers would actually stand on the Sagebrush Rebellion. Plausible arguments can be made for why environmentalists should actually have supported a major decentralization of governing responsibility and for why ranchers should have opposed it. Symbolism, memories of past battles, clashes of culture, personal antagonisms and nostalgia often seem to play an especially large role on the public lands.

A Confused Controversy

Contrary to the opinion of many, there are important elements of the environmental movement that represent a strong force for decentralization of governing authority. It is true that the Clean Air Act, the Clean Water Act and other environmental legislation have extended large new federal powers into many areas of American life. Yet environmentalism emerged above all as a set of grassroots protests against development activities typically sponsored or endorsed by higher levels of government. All over the country local citizens successfully fought off proposals for power plants, oil refineries, highways, apartment houses, shopping centers, and many other types of projects. Although environmentalists did not proceed under the banner of any well-developed plan for decentralization, their actions in practice cumulatively gave expression to a powerful new regionalism and localism in American life.

Environmentalists have typically found themselves opposing the market, which is a primary source for central coordination in the American economy. While environmentalists have often given lip service to central planning, they have also typically opposed the results of such planning whenever it did not suit their purposes, as in the successful efforts to defeat the Energy Mobilization Board proposal of the Carter administration. The demands for citizen participation commonly made by the environmental movement act themselves as a powerful force for decentralization. There are likely to be few vigorous proponents at public meetings for policies that serve to advance the national interest, but in which each citizen in the United States individually has only a very small stake.

The appeal of decentralization is brought out in a popular novel, *Ecotopia*, offering an environmental utopian vision.[2] In the novel the Pacific Northwest, extending from San Francisco to Seattle, has seceded from the rest of the United States, cutting off not only political ties but also most economic relationships. In order to build their perfect world, the citizens of Ecotopia had to free themselves from federal domination.

On the other side, the leading Sagebrush rebels, many of whom were members of the western ranching community, actually had a lot to lose from a federal transfer of the lands to the states. Ranchers might well have been exposed to stronger environmental pressures and higher grazing fees under state ownership. Indeed, Congress acted to enhance rancher grazing rights as recently as the passing of the Federal Land Policy and Management Act of 1976 (FLPMA). Ten-year grazing permits were formally mandated for the first time and the existing practice of rancher's first priority on renewal of the permits was legislatively codified. Ranchers were also required by law to receive compensation for investments on public lands, should they for some reason lose their grazing permits. The Public Rangelands Improvement Act of 1978 (PRIA) stated a federal policy of providing necessary funds to make new grazing investments, essentially committing the federal government to trying to protect existing levels of grazing. PRIA also provided a fixed formula for determining rancher grazing fees until 1985, ensuring that the fee would remain low and eliminating the previous discretion of the land management agencies to set an appropriate fee.

The ranchers supporting the Sagebrush Rebellion thus seem to have been willing to set aside the traditional western quid pro quo: continued federal ownership of the public land in return for generous financial and other benefits from the presence of the federal government. Perhaps westerners were deciding that freedom from outside interference and a greater western ability to control the future of their region were more important than they had previously thought. Or perhaps the Sagebrush rebels were simply letting their emotions run. Indeed, the eventual demise of the Sagebrush Rebellion no doubt stemmed in part from a declining ardor for emotional proclamations of western independence and a return to more traditional dollars and cents calculations.

The more cynically inclined might suggest that the Sagebrush rebels never really intended to achieve a transfer of federal lands. Rather, from the first the "Rebellion" may have been merely a practical device to pressure the federal government to be more accommodating of western interests. As Secretary of the Interior, James Watt certainly saw matters in that light.

Ironically, a different rebellion may spring up in the future, an eastern rebellion against the financial burdens of the western lands. With continuing high budget deficits and pressures to cut many urban programs, easterners at some point could demand that the residents of western states take responsibility for paying for the management of public lands within their own states. They might, for example, insist on sharp increases not only in the grazing fee but in recreational access charges and various other user charges. The effect could be to undermine the implicit contract that has made continuing federal management of the public lands attractive to the West.

Thus far most easterners have never examined these matters closely. Many would probably be surprised, for example, to discover the actual distribution of benefits from the oil and gas, and coal and other royalties from federal mineral resources.[3] These royalties in 1992 equalled $865 million, by far the largest source of revenue from federal lands. Under the provisions of the Federal Coal Leasing Amendments Act of 1976 each state receives 50 percent of the total royalties collected from federal mineral leases located within the state. The Reclamation Fund (committed to western water projects) receives 40 percent and the federal treasury receives 10 percent.

Federal royalties, however, are deductible against federal corporate income taxes. Hence, with a 35 percent corporate income tax rate, each dollar of Federal royalty collected can reduce future Federal corporate tax receipts by as much as thirty-five cents at the margin. Balanced against the ten cents that go directly to the federal treasury from each dollar of royalty, the net result can be as much as a twenty-five-cent loss to the U.S. treasury for every dollar of "federal" royalty that is collected.

Admittedly, the Reclamation Fund is somewhat of an accounting fiction, so that payments to the Reclamation Fund as a practical matter probably should be considered a payment to the federal treasury. Moreover, many corporations may not actually pay a 35 percent marginal tax rate on their income. Hence, the net amount actually received by the federal government from its royalty collections from mineral leases is hard to know for sure; it may come out in the end about even or with perhaps a few positive revenues. The federal government has traditionally paid the administrative costs of mineral leasing but in recent years has begun to deduct a portion of these costs before paying the states their 50 percent share of royalty receipts. Whatever the exact final revenue outcome, one thing is certain: the western states will derive significantly greater financial returns from Federal mineral leases than the federal government itself will receive.

The mineral estate is the profitable part of the public estate. Total revenues received do in fact exceed total costs of management before the revenues are distributed among the various parties as designated by law. The same cannot be said for the surface lands. For example, as shown in Table 8-2, federal management of the public domain surface estate incurred total costs in 1978 that were $130 million greater than the total revenues received. When the federal payments to the states and localities of their allotted shares of the revenues from surface activities are also factored in, the overall financial drain on the federal government associated with surface lands becomes greater still.[4]

The federal government thus has little financial stake in continued ownership of the public lands of the West and could in fact stand to benefit significantly from their outright disposal. The management decisions made on the majority of the public lands are essentially local in

TABLE 8-2
1978 Revenues and Costs for the Public Domain Surface Estate in
13 Western States, by State (in thousands)

State	Revenues	Costs	Net Revenues
Alaska	$1,698.9	$28,900.3	-$27,201.4
Arizona	1,356.7	9,564.4	-8,207.7
California	2,511.7	20,058.5	-17,546.8
Colorado	1,321.4	12,217.7	-10,896.3
Idaho	1,775.8	15,619.3	-13,843.5
Montana	1,206.4	10,518.7	-9,312.3
Nevada	3,290.6	14,196.4	-10,905.8
New Mexico	3,102.9	11,462.7	-8,449.8
North Dakota	542.2	43.8	498.8
Oregon	8,756.4	16,249.2	-7,492.8
Utah	1,584.4	12,903.6	-11,319.2
Washington	400.2	565.5	-165.3
Wyoming	3,969.8	9,741.4	-5,771.6
Total	$31,427.4	$162,041.1	$-130,613.7

character: how many cows to graze on which piece of land at which time of year. To be sure, the members of Congress from the West may have a large stake in continued federal land ownership; the presence of these lands allows congressmen to deliver constituent services that get them reelected. The members of the federal bureaucracy in the land management agencies have good-paying jobs that depend on the continued federal ownership of the land. Many members of lobbying organizations in Washington, D.C., might also be out of a job if the lands were transferred to the states. But regarded as a matter of the broad "national interest," there is little federal stake in the retention of most of the public lands. Indeed, if the West should seek their transfer again under some new successor to the Sagebrush Rebellion, the nation would be wise to quickly say yes.

A New Rationale for Public Land Ownership

Sally Fairfax has described public land management as "riding into a different sunset."[5] Beyond the horizon there will have to be new justifications for public land ownership; the old ones persist simply by habit. The process of identifying new goals for the public lands is likely to be incremental, however. Evolution of ideas is gradual; one concept does not lose favor one day and another step into the breach. Thus the intellectual foundations for future public land management are likely to be visible already if one looks closely enough. It is a matter now of recognizing what has become untenable, explicitly discarding it, and then explicitly recognizing what is already emerging.

In fact, an acceptable basic purpose for public land ownership is not hard to discern. Looking behind the continuing formal adherence to outmoded progressive ideas of scientific management, the real reason today for public land ownership is that it protects certain values and provides certain services that the private market neglects or ignores. The most important nonmarket service provided by the public lands is the opportunity to hunt, fish, hike, explore, and participate in other forms of dispersed recreation.

It is important to distinguish such recreation from the broader objective of protecting environmental values. In many cases environmental protection does not depend on land ownership, as suggested by the fact that the Environmental Protection Agency pursues its mission almost entirely by regulation. Taxes or other government financial incentives for private property owners can also be used to protect many environmental values without actual ownership of the resource.[6] Public provision of dispersed recreation, however, makes greater demands. Recreation requires literal entry of a person onto the land, thus requiring actual ownership of the lands (or at least ownership of access rights). Hence, the argument for public ownership is stronger for recreational provision specifically than it is for the broader class of all nonmarket values and services.

Of course, much recreation is provided privately through ordinary market incentives. Disney World did not require any government subsidy. A number of the recreational services now provided on the public lands could be provided by private owners as well. But a good analogy can be drawn here with the highway network for automobiles. Turnpikes between major cities can be provided privately, and have been on some occasions, but not so the general network of city streets. The collection costs and confusions of a pricing system for ordinary city streets would simply be too great (although admittedly advancing technology for monitoring motor vehicle movement could change all this and such technology may not be far off).

Similarly, it would at present be impractical to establish prices for a substantial class of ordinary dispersed recreation—simple hikes in the woods, for example. Much of the pleasure of this kind of dispersed recreation involves the ability to enter into it spontaneously. The marginal costs imposed on society are negligible, if not zero. Provision of such recreational opportunities, as with city streets, is best done publicly.

This is not to say that the government should not impose a fee or charge for dispersed recreation, such as fishing licenses, that would help to cover the average costs of land management. All users of public lands, for example, might be required to purchase a "public land stamp" each year that should be in their possession when they enter public lands. The point is that under such a system a separate charge would not be imposed for each hike in the woods, which would be very expensive and logistically difficult to collect.

The government can provide public recreation opportunities and can establish charging mechanisms to cover its costs of management over large areas—land units covering potentially hundreds or thousands of square miles available for dispersed recreational use—in ways that would be much more cumbersome if a multitude of individual private owners held the same lands. To be sure, an alternative to public ownership would be to create a "recreation condominium" form of collective private ownership that would bring diverse private lands under some form of common recreation management and fee collection. However, there would be major transactions costs and holdout problems associated with setting up any such private collective form of recreation land ownership. It would require a property right institution that does not exist at present and with which current landowners are not familiar. To be sure, if recreation use is of a type that is concentrated in a small area with well-defined access points, these obstacles to private land ownership and private provision of the recreation would not exist.

Many people also believe, of course, that public ownership is desirable because it promotes social equality. Hunting clubs might well spring up on private lands; indeed, in the West property owners with control over entry to public lands in some cases already charge hunters and fishermen $50 a day and more to cross their land. Government, however, is expected to distribute goods and services on an equal basis to each citizen. For many people the public lands are a powerful symbolic affirmation of the egalitarian ideal in a largely private system.

Perhaps more to the point, large numbers of people who now benefit from free recreational access on public lands resist the prospect of having to pay for the same access under a private system. They believe that their long history of past use gives them what amounts to de facto property rights to continue to use the land for hunting, fishing, and other recreational purposes and are prepared to commit great energies to defending these rights. In the past possession has indeed been nine-tenths of the law; new property rights have come into existence by taking possession of land and property and then successfully defending this possession.

To say that the purpose of public land ownership is provision of ordinary dispersed recreation is not, of course, to say that other activities, including more intensive forms of recreation, should be excluded. If these other activities become more valuable, private ownership of the land will often be appropriate. It is also true that government can provide dispersed recreation without public land ownership. Public provision of recreation, for example, could involve arrangements made with private landowners for public use.

The strongest political support in the West for federal land ownership in fact comes down to a belief that for the average voter of average means recreational services will be more amply available at less cost under the current system. Westerners contrast their open access to the public lands with the no-trespassing signs posted throughout the East. As one put it, "I've been hunting and fishing on your land for years—and I've never asked permission. You may not have thought of it before, but if you're an American citizen you own somewhere around 2 and ½ acres of land. We all do. There are roughly 600 million acres of public land in the United States, chiefly in forests and range land, and it belongs to all of us.''[7]

The national parks are visited and enjoyed by millions of Americans every year. The national forests are valued by ordinary Americans above all for their wilderness areas, hiking trails, campgrounds, and other recreational opportunities. Few citizens know or care about the quality of Forest Service timber management, except so far as timber harvests may impinge on endangered species or on recreational use of the land. If traditionally less appreciated, BLM lands have increasingly been used for recreational purposes; for example, the BLM lands that make up much of the southern California desert have been visited by millions fleeing the congestion of metropolitan Los Angeles and San Diego.[8]

A fear echoed repeatedly in western commentary on the Sagebrush Rebellion was that states might well prove to be the go-between, turning lands received from the federal government over to private owners. The result, opponents of state ownership fear, could in fact be a major loss of dispersed recreational opportunity: ''It could be that the forest of No Trespassing signs would be as great as the one of remaining spruce, pine and fir.''[9] Even if state ownership were maintained, state governments might put fewer resources into provision of recreation. As one Idaho newspaper editorial commented, ''Most of us, actually, would probably rather see the great forests and range lands of the West remain the responsibility of the federal government than turned over to the questionable mercies of the states. It is quite clear out here, even if it is not well understood in the East, that the states have neither the money nor the administrative capacity to manage these lands properly.''[10]

At some point, to be sure, growing recreational demands pressing against a limited physical supply of land will create serious congestion. This is already happening in many areas of the West for hunting and fishing. Some wilderness areas are experiencing major overcrowding. Restrictions on use will become necessary if the quality of the recreational experience is not to be degraded. Thus, for such uses the traditional open access to the public lands that has been so attractive to so many westerners will not last forever. Limitations on use will come, whether imposed through a pricing mechanism, a ''time price'' for waiting in line, or some other rationing device. When that happens, there will be a strong argument for using a direct monetary pricing regime, a policy that in many cases would be facilitated by private ownership of the land.

The Federal Role

The western desire thus far to keep the lands in federal ownership is largely pragmatic; westerners simply worry that they would receive fewer recreational benefits if the public lands were transferred to the states or to the private sector. While this concern is understandable, however, it is not sufficient in itself to justify the continuing federal role. The case made above for government ownership of land used for the provision of ordinary dispersed recreation would apply equally to ownership of these same lands by state governments. The question thus should be addressed in a more principled way: are there grounds in economics or federalism to justify federal provision of ordinary dispersed recreation in the West as opposed to its provision by state or other lower levels of government? Provision of recreational services at the federal instead of the state level might be justified in terms of the same economic considerations that have led firms of national scope to emerge in many private industries.

The national scope of many corporations is usually explained by either marketing advantages or production economies of scale. The units of federal recreation systems, however, are often widely separated, and it is hard to see how there could be any substantial economies of joint operation. Conceivably, standard purchasing may be done among a number of federal recreation units, creating greater bargaining power. Some training of personnel and other tasks may also be done on a coordinated basis. Nevertheless, economies of scale do not seem a plausible justification for provision of recreation at the federal level.

Some economists have concluded that the large size of American firms is more attributable to marketing advantages than economies of scale in production.[11] In particular, large corporations like the McDonald's fast food chain benefit simply because consumers come to rely on the brand name as a means of knowing what quality of product they will receive.[12] In the same way designation of lands to be part of a federal recreation system serves to inform members of the public, who may lack information about the scenic and other recreational qualities of the land. The designation as a national park in fact performs much the same function for scenic grandeur and historic significance as the Hilton sign does for hotel service and comfort or the McDonald's sign for fast food.

Similarly, inclusion of lands in the national wilderness system performs an important information service for the public. It tells the public that the lands have met national quality standards for solitude, roadlessness, and other wilderness features. Indeed, the information provided to consumers in this way is sometimes so useful that it attracts large numbers of new visitors to newly designated wilderness areas, ironically threatening the original wilderness quality.

Another reason for federalizing large parts of the nation's recreation system might be to ensure access at low prices to middle and lower income Americans. The rationale for federal provision of recreation would then be much the same as for federalizing other forms of income redistribution.[13] That is, if redistribution were left to local jurisdictions there would be a tendency for the poor to end up located with other poor, the rich with other rich, making it difficult or impossible to achieve redistributional objectives. But the users of federal recreation systems are hardly a deprived population; the benefits of low recreational prices will be obtained by at least as many well-to-do as by poor people.

Certain natural areas have features greatly valued by the whole nation. Some examples are familiar to everyone: the geysers of Yellowstone Park, the Grand Canyon, the Yosemite Valley, and the groves of the oldest redwoods and sequoias. Federal ownership of these areas declares a national commitment to protect and preserve them for future generations. There is little doubt that such protection is a powerful motive for federal ownership of certain national parks and other areas with unique environmental assets.

States, however, would also have strong reasons to protect such areas. The example of Adirondack Park in New York is instructive. In 1885 an article in the *American Naturalist* called for the creation of an Adirondack National Park. The federal government did not follow up, but in 1894 a provision was added to the New York constitution setting aside Adirondack Park for state preservation.[14] The area of land included by New York in the park covered three million acres, 35 percent larger than Yellowstone Park and the largest park in the United States—in fact, about equal in size to the state of Connecticut. New Yorkers have rejected many proposals since then to change the state's constitution to allow timber harvesting and other resource development.

Indeed, one of the strongest proponents of changing the state constitution was Gifford Pinchot, the father of federal forest management. Pinchot was much offended by the restrictions on development of Adirondack Park, considering them a waste of good land and timber. If placed at the federal level, Adirondack Park might well have been included in the forest reserves from which the national forest system later emerged—at first under Pinchot's management. Federal management as part of the national forest system would almost certainly have led to much more intensive timber and other development of Adirondack Park lands. In short, preservation of the largest undeveloped area in the East may well have occurred because the state kept the federal government out and assumed the management responsibility itself for the lands.

In the West recreationists point to management of lands owned by the states themselves as a demonstration that state governments are predisposed to favor livestock, mining and other commodity interests over recreation. This conclusion may be suspect, however, for two reasons. First, existing state lands are typically scattered in small isolated parcels, remnants of old education land grants, making it difficult to manage them effectively for recreation or other environmental purposes.

Second, even if this problem did not exist, the past record still would not be a good indicator of likely future management. The western states are changing rapidly in their demographic and political makeup. The state government of California is probably more oriented toward recreation needs of Californians than is the federal government. In any case management of major new land areas would cause institutional changes to occur at the state level, significantly increasing the visibility of state land management and thus probably creating new political pressures favoring recreational use of state lands.

Taking all these considerations into account, the arguments for federal provision of recreation seem to be strong only for a limited class of recreational areas. The federal government does in fact provide valuable consumer information in designating national parks, historic monuments, wilderness areas, and other categories of special recreational lands. Moreover, it provides widely desired guarantees that the nationally unique features of some of these lands will be protected, that the lands will not be sold off and carved into vacation-home developments.

The number of places with such national assets is limited, however. For less distinctive recreational lands used mainly for ordinary dispersed recreation there is not much case for direct federal ownership and management.

A Land Classification System

The report of the Public Land Law Review Commission in 1970 was much criticized for its recommendation to designate dominant use areas on the public lands.[15] This recommendation was said to be a capitulation to timber, livestock, and other interests aiming to lay claim to the lands for their own exclusive use. The idea of dominant uses, however, has deep roots in public land history. John Wesley Powell in 1878 proposed that western lands be classified according to whether they could best be used for irrigated farming, livestock grazing, timber harvesting, or in other specific ways.[16] In creating separate management systems and approaches for the national forests, National Park System, National Wildlife Refuge System, and Bureau of Land Management lands, Congress has de facto adopted a dominant use approach, matching the management style and public orientation of each agency to the intended park, wildlife preservation, or other primary uses intended for each area.

The Wilderness Act of 1964 authorized a new form of dominant use management. Indeed, the means of implementing land use planning, zoning to permit particular uses in designated areas, involves in essence the identification of a dominant use for each area. Dominant use, of course, does not mean exclusive use, simply that management and planning for an area is focused around a recognition that there is at present a leading use of the area. A main issue for land planners is then how that use will be reconciled with the other uses which will also be allowed.

The main land classifications proposed long ago by Powell—irrigated land, grazing land, and timber land—are still relevant. Since the late nineteenth century, however, as indicated above, recreation has also become a main use of the public lands. Several new land classifications thus must be added to Powell's list: national park lands, wildlife preserves, wilderness areas, wild and scenic rivers, conservation areas, general recreation areas, and possibly other subcategories of recreation. In addition some public lands contain oil and gas or coal, which will constitute the leading use during any period of their active development. Mining of hardrock minerals can also take precedence over other uses in certain areas at certain times.

As Powell indicated, a different management approach and philosophy are likely to be suitable for each classification of land. The national parks obviously have much different management requirements than timber lands, and timber lands require different skills and expertise than grazing lands.

Moreover, there is no reason to assume automatically that public management of land for a given use would be more efficient than private management. This presumption can be traced to scientific management precepts of Theodore Roosevelt and Gifford Pinchot, now long undermined by experience, if still often ritually invoked as a matter of public form. Indeed, the experience in this century of the welfare state and steadily growing federal bureaucracy have effectively reversed the presumption. There exists today agreement across broad segments of

American society that private-sector management is likely to be more efficient than government management and that government ownership and management should exist only where there are particularly strong and compelling reasons for such a government role.[17]

I thus propose a new long-term strategy for the public lands that consists of classifying lands according to their expected primary use and then matching up an appropriate ownership and type of management with each class of land. Brief descriptions follow below of a proposed ownership regime and form of management for each of the major land classifications. The proposals are made in the spirit of providing an example of how this general strategy could be implemented. Obviously, there would be much room for further discussion on the specifics if the broader concept were accepted.

1. National Parks and Wildlife Refuges

Under the strategy proposed here, there would be little change from the traditional approach for the national park system. Existing national parks would be maintained; new ones would be created only where scenic, historic, or other attractions of true national significance exist. Similarly, preserves providing habitat for migratory and other wildlife species of national concern would be maintained, much as the existing system of wildlife refuges has evolved. Changes in the national park and wildlife refuge systems would be incremental. Some individual units of these systems might be turned over to states if it were determined that they lacked any true national significance. Traditional management procedures and acceptable uses in national parks and wildlife refuges could be modified on an incremental basis.

2. Other Recreation Lands of National Interest

Since the 1960s several new categories of recreation lands of major federal interest have been created, including wilderness areas, conservation areas, and wild and scenic rivers. There are now about ninety million acres—an area approaching the size of California—included in the wilderness system. The newer types of federal recreation lands are characterized by either a less demanding standard for identifying sites of federal interest or by the presence of features that have come only recently to be considered of importance to the nation as a whole.

Wilderness and other lands determined to be of national significance could be assembled and placed under a new federal recreation agency—

perhaps a Federal Recreation Service. A good candidate for this role would be the current Forest Service, which has performed best as a provider of recreational services. Indeed, despite the contrary expectations of Gifford Pinchot, the continued popularity of the Forest Service with the public is based mainly on public appreciation for the general recreational services it has provided. The federally retained lands in this category might ultimately include seventy-five to one hundred million acres.

3. Dispersed Recreation Lands of State and Local Interest

Many of the existing national forests do not have wilderness or other features of national importance. They also, however, do not have any high timber, mineral, or other commodity values. The most important use of these lands is in fact dispersed recreational use, predominantly by state and local residents. Much of the national forest system in the Rocky Mountain states—the part that has not been designated as wilderness—would fall into this category. BLM also holds large areas with similar characteristics, including much of its desert lands in southern California. This overall classification includes a large amount of federal land; all told, there might be as much as two hundred million acres of federal land (excluding that in Alaska).

Under the strategy proposed here, the ownership of the dispersed recreation lands classified in this category would be transferred to state governments, which would be expected to manage them for recreation and multiple other uses. The states would be free to decide what mix of uses would be satisfactory. The expectation would be that mining, grazing, timber harvesting (where economically appropriate), and other such uses would continue under suitable environmental controls. As owners of the lands, the states would have to balance the economic gains from commodity uses against any adverse impacts on recreational use.

The federal government might attach certain conditions for transfer of recreation lands to the states. One option would be to restrict the ability of the states to turn the lands over to private parties. Another option would be to require that, if any such transfer later occurred, the rights of public access to the lands would be maintained in public possession.

One type of state transfer to private ownership might be encouraged, however: sale of land to private owners for construction of facilities associated with the provision of intensive recreation. Ski areas, motels, lodges, restaurants, and other recreational facilities might be located advantageously at many sites now within the public lands. Another important broad class of recreational use is second-home development. Such development in many areas could generate land values of $3,000 and more per acre, well above the value of the land in any other use. Second-home development need not be unattractive. The mountains of Switzerland, for example, which are filled with private plots and cottages, rival any area of the world in scenic qualities. In locations where sewer, water, and other basic services can be provided successfully at reasonable cost and where other impacts on the environment are acceptable, the fact that land is not available for private recreational development is one of the greatest inefficiencies of current federal management.

4. Prime Timber Lands

The federal government owns approximately 50 percent of the softwood timber inventory in the United States. Most of this inventory is located in the national forests, although two million acres of prime timber land are managed by BLM in western Oregon. Most economists have been critical of the quality of Forest Service timber management. The Forest Service, for example, often harvests timber on lands where it is uneconomic to do so. Indeed, perhaps no more than 40 million of the total 187 million acres in the national forest system consists of land on which timber production is economically justifiable. A large part of this land is concentrated in the Pacific Northwest in the states of California, Oregon, and Washington. In many other areas where the Forest Service now undertakes timber harvesting, timber sales frequently fail to earn enough revenue to cover the costs of the sale.

It is possible that the Forest Service could be transformed to show a much greater capacity for a businesslike and efficient approach to timber management. Such an approach would limit investments to those practices with adequate returns, would harvest timber only on lands where sales yielded positive net revenues, would harvest old growth inventories of timber to reflect the true capital cost of holding the inventories, and generally would focus on the revenues and costs of various timber management activities. But such a transformation of the Forest Service is in fact unlikely. Ninety years of agency tradition stand in the way.

Efficient timber management of a limited acreage of high quality timber stands would be more likely under the management of newly created timber corporations.[18] Initially, stock in such corporations could be distributed to match the current distribution of revenues from timber operations on federal forest lands. Local counties thus would receive 25 percent of the stock in timber corporations created from national forest lands (50 percent from O&C lands in Oregon managed by BLM), with the remaining 75 percent of the stock going to the Federal government. Federal shares could then be sold gradually over a transition period in the same way that Conrail was privatized through sale of stock to the public. At the end of the transition the ultimate objective would be a private timber corporation, although the local counties could choose to retain their shares.

Even though a public land area may be designated for timber harvesting, it may also provide valuable recreational services to hunters, hikers, and other recreationists. The creation of private corporations to manage some existing federal forests need not foreclose traditional recreational use on the lands; private companies would have many economic incentives to offer hunting, fishing, and other recreational opportunities. If further assurances were desired, special public access provisions might be incorporated in the charters for the new timber corporations. State governments would be the logical parties to enforce such public access rights.

5. Grazing Lands

No other area of public land management has been the subject of as much controversy as the grazing lands. The fierce disagreements have resulted from an inadequate resolution of rangeland tenure, leaving key issues such as the allocation of forage and the level of range investment to be resolved in the turmoil of the political arena.

In areas where livestock grazing is the main use and there are no special recreation values, individual ranchers should be given the responsibility for managing the range. The rancher could decide how many livestock to graze at what seasons and what investments to make. In order to do this, however, the rancher needs secure tenure, something he has never fully received in the past. Ownership of the grazing lands could be transferred to ranchers directly, but a more suitable vehicle would be long-term leasing. Under the strategy proposed here, grazing lands would be leased to ranchers for grazing purposes for say fifty to one hundred years at a time with the preferential option to renew. Unlike the current focus on the amount of grazing allowed the rancher ("animal unit months"), leases would be issued to well-defined areas of land and would be transferable among ranchers without restriction or surcharge.

Such long-term grazing leases would convey the full rights to the lands for livestock grazing, including the installation of grazing systems and investments in range improvements, levels of grazing, and other matters. Under the terms of the lease, however, full public access to the lands for hunting, hiking, and other dispersed recreation would be maintained, as would the rights of federal, state, or other government agencies to install various wildlife improvements or to take other measures to enhance wildlife habitat or watershed conditions. Leases would contain provisions for lease cancellation in unforeseen circumstances, although the government would then have to compensate the lessee for livestock investments and the capital value of the lost livestock grazing opportunity.

The administrative role of the federal government would be sharply reduced from current grazing management to consist mainly of the issuance and renewal of long term grazing land leases. This function could well, in fact, be turned over to a state agency. The federal government might, however, give technical assistance and provide other services to ranchers following the model of the existing extension service relationships between the Department of Agriculture and private land farmers. Enforcement of easements guaranteeing public access on the rangelands and wildlife enhancement measures should be undertaken by state and local officials. Perhaps two hundred million acres of existing public rangelands in the West would come under this classification.

6. Mineral Lands

A basic distinction exists between ''hardrock'' minerals such as gold and copper, which are disposed of under the Mining Law of 1872, and leasable minerals such as coal, which are administered under the Mineral Leasing Act of 1920. In general hardrock minerals are difficult to find and little is known about mining prospects before a discovery is made. Some leasable minerals are found in continuous beds that are already known to exist at a particular site, although finding oil and gas is more like finding a hardrock mineral.

As a general rule, mineral rights to hardrock minerals should be held by the surface owner. Thus, if most dispersed recreational lands are transferred from the federal government to the state, the mineral rights should be included with this transfer. Major coordination and other problems arise where the surface and mineral estates are separately owned. Because hardrock mineral deposits are usually not known to be present beforehand, the act of transferring mineral rights does not usually produce any major windfall gains or losses to the involved parties. For the vast majority of sites no valuable minerals will ever be discovered; the expected value of a discovery at any given site, and thus the market value of the mineral rights, will be small.

Sites already known to have good prospects for oil and gas, existing coal reserves, or other leasable minerals, by contrast, may well have a high current value. The Interior Department has received more than $100 billion over the years from bonus bids and royalties from its offshore oil and gas leasing program. A single coal lease may be worth $50 million.

Under the strategy proposed here the ownership and management of leasable minerals would be turned over to the states. As indicated above, when corporate tax impacts are factored in, federal royalties do not produce much if any net revenue to the U.S. treasury. Hence, maintaining the financial status quo might not require that the federal government retain any interest in leasable minerals transferred to the states. The federal government might, however, retain some overriding royalty or other federal interest in the mineral rights being transferred to make it more politically feasible.

Conclusion

Congress at the end of the eighteenth century adopted a policy of selling the public lands to raise revenue but was frustrated at every step for the next sixty years. Finally accepting defeat by squatters, Congress passed the Homestead Act in 1862, only to see settlement soon move into arid western areas where homesteading of farms was no longer feasible on 160 acres. The Forest Service was created in 1905 to introduce scientific management because it was thought the private sector would not do so, but over the course of the twentieth century it has been the Weyerhaeusers of the world that have set the standard for scientific timber management. The Taylor Grazing Act supposedly ended homesteading, but as it was administered the law actually introduced a procedure whereby ranchers acquired rights to use public rangelands based heavily on past use—that is, a kind of retroactive rangeland homestead law, similar to many previous retroactive confirmations of squatter rights enacted by Congress in the nineteenth century.

This long history of public land laws that did not achieve their purposes—in fact were perhaps just as likely to achieve the very opposite of congressional intent—raises the following possibility. With Congress having passed the National Forest Management Act and the Federal Land Policy and Management Act in 1976, might we be entering a period where the actual outcomes once again will be the opposite of the congressional intent as expressed in those laws? The land use planning and other instruments of federal management required in NFMA and FLPMA have proved no more effective than the requirements of previous public land laws (see chapter 4). Once again, the expressed goals of Congress may have to be abandoned as failures. The principles of multiple use and sustained yield may have to be discarded. Perhaps scientific management will be formally discarded as the official philosophy of public land management. And if all this happens, large-scale transfers of federal forests and rangelands to the states and to the private sector might well occur over the next few decades.

Indeed, the analysis developed in this book suggests that movement in such directions is not only possible, but that it would be desirable.

Notes

1. For an account of rancher efforts to have the federal government dispose of rangelands, see William Voight, *Public Grazing Lands: Use and Misuse by Industry and Government* (New Brunswick, N.J.: Rutgers University Press, 1976). The Public Land Law Review Commission in 1970 recommended limited disposal of certain lands. See *One-Third of the Nation's Land: A Report to the President and to the Congress by the Public Land Law Review Commission* (Washington, D.C.: Government Printing Office, 1970).

2. Ernest Callenbach, *Ecotopia* (New York: Bantam Books, 1977).

3. U.S. Department of the Interior, Office of Policy Analysis, *Past and Projected State Revenues from Energy and Other Natural Resources in 13 Western States: Background Report* (Washington, D.C., 1981).

4. See Robert H. Nelson, *An Analysis of 1978 Revenues and Costs of Public Land Management by the Interior Department in 13 Western States*, paper prepared for the U.S. Department of the Interior, Office of Policy Analysis (Washington, D.C., 1979).

5. Sally K. Fairfax, "Riding into a Different Sunset," *Journal of Forestry*, vol. 79 (1981).

6. See Frederick R. Anderson, et al., *Environmental Improvement through Economic Incentives* (Baltimore, Md.: Johns Hopkins University Press for Resources for the Future, 1977).

7. Ted Trueblood, "They're Fixing to Steal Your Land," *Field and Stream* (March 1980).

8. See U.S. Department of the Interior, Bureau of Land Management, *The California Desert Conservation Area: Final Environmental Impact Statement and Proposed Plan* (Sacramento, Calif.: September 1980).

9. Dan Abrams, "The Rebellion is Getting Hot," *Jackson Hole News* (5 December 1979).

10. "Westerners and the Sagebrush Rebellion," editorial in *Lewiston Tribune* (Lewiston, Idaho: 25 September 1979).

11. See J. Bain, *Barriers to New Competition* (Cambridge, Mass.: Harvard University Press, 1956): 216.

12. See Robert H. Nelson, "The Economics of Honest Trade Practices," *The Journal of Industrial Economics* (June 1976).

13. See Advisory Commission on Intergovernmental Relations, *The Federal Role in the Federal System: The Dynamics of Growth* (Washington, D.C.: June 1981): 111.

14. See Roderick Nash, *Wilderness and the American Mind* (New Haven: Yale University Press, 1967): 119–121.

15. See Michael Frome, "The Environment and Timber Resources," in *What's Ahead for our Public Lands?: A Summary Review of the Activities and Final Report of the Public Land Law Review Commission* (Washington, D.C.: Natural Resources Council of America, 1970).

16. John Wesley Powell, *Report on the Lands of the Arid Regions* (Washington, D.C.: 1878).

17. See, for example, Charles L. Schultze, *The Public Use of Private Interest* (Washington, D.C.: Brookings Institution, 1977).

18. Marion Clawson and Burnell Held long ago proposed the creation of new "federal land corporations" to manage certain public land areas. See Marion Clawson and Burnell Held, *The Federal Lands: Their Use and Management* (Baltimore: Johns Hopkins University Press for Resources for the Future, 1957): 347.

Chapter 9

From Progressivism to Interest-group Liberalism: The Crisis of Public Land Authority

Historically, public land policies have closely followed broader trends of thought (see chapter 1). The nineteenth-century policy to dispose of the public lands fit the prevailing classical liberal ideology and the general expectation of a small role for government, especially the federal government. The turn to federal retention of the public lands occurred as a key element of the Progressive movement that set the stage for the twentieth-century welfare state; indeed, conservationism represented the direct application of progressive concepts to the field of natural resources. The ideas of multiple-use management formulated in the years after World War II were an application to the public lands of the dominant ideology of these decades, labeled by Theodore Lowi as "interest-group liberalism."[1] In this concept the governing process is seen as the achievement of an acceptable balance among contending interest groups, which on the public lands are mostly the multiple users of the lands. The more recent interest in rethinking federal land ownership is part of a broader reassessment in the late twentieth century of the role of government and has many of the same roots as the deregulation movement.

The large extent of federal land ownership is an anomaly in the American system. It violates the principle of trying to decentralize most of the basic governing responsibilities to the state and local level, as

This chapter is a revised and shortened version of a chapter called "Ideology and Public Land Policy—The Current Crisis" in Sterling Brubaker, ed., *Rethinking the Federal Lands* (Washington, D.C.: Resources for the Future, distributed by the Johns Hopkins University Press, 1984).

227

well as the principle of relying on the private sector in most matters. Many arguments for public land ownership would apply equally well to a wide range of existing private property—for example, the need to conserve resources for the future. If such arguments were actually applied uniformly throughout the American economy, the result would be a virtual program for the nationalizing of American industry. Certainly, large areas of private land in the East would also qualify for federal ownership on the grounds commonly given to explain the need for the existing federal lands in the West.

There has been surprisingly little examination of the intellectual case for federal land ownership. The inclination has been to leave the existing division of public and private land ownership unchallenged and to move on to more "pragmatic" subjects. There has always been an element of the American character that disdains matters of social theory and ideology. Yet, it is impossible to function without a guiding sense of direction, an ideology if you will. To neglect such matters is not to deny them influence, but to make the influence implicit rather than explicit. It also runs the risk that attention will constantly be diverted to symptoms, when a basic cure could be achieved. Rather than always bailing the boat, a new design may sometimes be preferable.

The time has come to reexamine the question of public land ownership and to raise fundamental alternatives. These matters have not really been reassessed in any systematic way since the progressive era. This chapter probes some basic issues of economic and political theory as they relate to possible disposal of public land to private ownership, transfer of federal land to the states, and other alternative tenure arrangements.

The nineteenth-century preference for the private market involved not only a confidence in the workings of markets, but also a strong aversion to government. Government was feared as a threat to political liberty. The capabilities of government were also questioned; American democracy was often a rough-and-ready affair, hardly fit for administering details of much complexity or sophistication. Overcoming these attitudes and laying the foundations for a much larger government role in the twentieth century fell to the Progressives. Existing public land institutions are largely a product of the Progressive movement at the beginning of this century.[2]

The Progressive Thesis and the Interest-group Liberal Antithesis

American progressives sought to introduce to government the same methods of modern management that were then transforming the private sector from a world of small entrepreneurs to one of large corporations (see chapter 2 for further discussion of the application of progressive ideas to forestry). Progressives advocated a much more businesslike and efficient basis for government administration. In order to protect professional administrators from political interference, Progressives asserted that there should be a strict separation of government administration from politics. The political process would set the broad policy objectives; after that, professional administrators applying technical management skills would take over and be responsible for implementing these objectives. New Progressive institutions such as the independent regulatory commission were designed specifically with the aim of providing a means of insulating administrators from political interference.

The much greater scope for government advocated by Progressives did not reflect any new-found confidence in political decision making. Progressives, in fact, remained distrustful of traditional politics. However, they believed that the routine tasks of government could be isolated from its harmful influence.

The idea that government administration could be truly scientific played a critical role in this Progressive scheme of thought. Concerned about avoiding abuses of the newly enlarged government powers, Progressives offered assurances that government administration should involve little, if any, leeway for the individual feelings, values, or emotions of the administrators. Science and technology would instead reveal the one correct answer that the experts would apply. Progressives regarded the "special interests" with particular disfavor; such groups sought to distort government decisions to their own advantage and against the valid goal of "the public interest."

Retention of public lands was desirable, according to the Progressive and conservationist ideology, for two reasons. First, some conservationists, such as Gifford Pinchot, contended that the government would do much better than the private sector in achieving the scientific management of natural resources. In part, Pinchot was reacting to the recent rapid depletion of wildlife, forests, and other natural resources by private individuals and companies. The private sector was considered too shortsighted in outlook to achieve a rationally efficient development of natural resources over the long run.

It also appeared, at least from the recent evidence of private sector behavior, that scientific management went hand in hand with large size. As the trust-busting cases showed, another element of Progressivism was its antagonism to large concentrations of private power, another possible threat to American democracy. If scientific management in fact required large organization, then the public sector was preferable to the private sector, or so it seemed to many Progressives. Rather than create one or more new Weyerhaeuser-type empires, Progressives preferred to create the Forest Service instead.

The Progressives thus hoped both to achieve the efficiency of scientific management for government lands and at the same time to prevent large land-holdings that might frustrate traditional American egalitarian and democratic ideals. As Samuel Hays has noted with respect to Theodore Roosevelt's thought, these dual objectives were at times in conflict: "Roosevelt's emphasis on applied science and his conception of the good society as the classless agrarian society were contradictory trends of thought. The one, a faith which looked to the future, accepted wholeheartedly the basic elements of the new technology. The other, essentially backward looking, longed for the simple agrarian arcadia which, if it ever existed, could never be revived."[3]

This tension was not the only flaw in Progressive thought. Indeed, in the post-World War II period a whole host of social scientists, including leading economists and political scientists such as Herbert Simon, David Truman, and Dwight Waldo, established their reputations by showing how government was working in a manner much different from Progressive theory. The administrative and social sciences were finding it very difficult to deliver on their promises to reveal the true laws by which government and society worked. The critical assumption that the administration of government could be kept separate from politics was undermined regularly by events in the real world. Rather than pursuing any identifiable "public interest," government behavior was actually determined largely by interest-group competition.

In contrast to Progressive views, many post-World War II social theorists considered the large role of interest groups to be not only a valid description of the real world, but on the whole to be a healthy development. John Kenneth Galbraith, for example, lauded the happy balance achieved in a system of "countervailing powers."[4] Rather than the classical liberal competition of the free market, proponents of such "interest-group liberalism" instead saw competition in the political arena as the new basic mechanism for resource allocation. As Theodore Lowi explained in 1969, the political philosophy of interest-group liberalism was grounded in the following basic premises:

> (1) Since groups are the rule in markets and elsewhere, imperfect competition is the rule of social relations. (2) The method of imperfect competition

is not really competition at all but a variant of it called bargaining—where the number of participants is small, where the relationship is face-to-face, and/or where the bargainers have "market power," which means that they have some control over the terms of their agreements and can administer rather than merely respond to their environment. (3) Without class solidarity, bargaining becomes the single alternative to violence and coercion in industrial society. (4) By definition, if the system is stable and peaceful it proves the self-regulative character of pluralism. It is, therefore, the way the system works and the way it ought to work.[5]

On the public lands, as noted above, this political philosophy of interest-group pluralism is reflected in the tenets of "multiple-use" management, which seeks a balance among all user groups. The Multiple-use and Sustained-yield Act of 1960 created a formal statutory mandate for multiple-use management of the national forests. In the 1970s new statutory requirements for public participation in public land decision making sought to guarantee that each user group would receive a fair chance to influence management decisions. The guiding vision in all this is that public land policies have been, and very probably will continue to be, made by interactions among competing interest groups.

The ideologies of Progressivism and interest-group liberalism have in common that they specify, and to some degree justify, the role of government. They attempt to provide intellectual legitimacy and in this respect the basis for social authority. Beyond this, they are mostly antithetical. Progressivism seeks to banish interest groups in government; interest-group liberalism puts them at the center of the governing process. Progressivism seeks objective government decisions reached by technical experts using scientific methods; interest-group liberalism simply favors an equilibrium of interest-group pressures. Progressivism advocates comprehensive planning; interest-group liberalism specifies a brokering among interest groups as the primary mechanism for making government decisions.

To be sure, elements of both ideologies are often intermingled in government policy pronouncements—a source of much confusion. Indeed, the original Progressive ideals have never been formally abandoned in public land management. For the record Congress still frequently professes a goal of scientific management of public lands in the public interest. Legislation such as the Forest and Rangeland Renewable Resources Planning Act (1974), the National Forest Management Act (1976), and the Federal Land Policy and Management Act (1976) blends elements of old-style Progressivism (formal comprehensive

planning) and interest-group liberalism (public involvement and participation). Close observers of the implementation of such legislation,
however, often find Progressive elements today to be mostly window
dressing. Instead, the key decisions are actually expected to be reached
in response to interest-group pressures. As the theorists of interest-
group liberalism argued, this may be the only possible outcome within
the existing constitutional framework of American democracy.

The Challenge to Interest-group Liberalism

Having substantially displaced the progressive ideology of scientific
management in practice if not in form, the ideology of interest-group
liberalism itself is now increasingly challenged. A major concern is that
interest-group compromise seldom produces efficient use of resources.
Critics find that interest-group bargaining too often becomes a ''zero-
sum game'' in which efforts are devoted primarily to maximizing individual benefits from government (the act of ''rent seeking''). An analogy can be drawn between the federal Treasury and a common pool
resource. The individual claimant on the Treasury is very unlikely to be
large enough to affect tax rates and thus his own tax payments. His
private incentive thus is to maximize his own claims without regard to
costs. The overall result, however, of all people behaving in this way
will be to ''overallocate'' the federal Treasury, causing budget deficits
and inflation. Budgetary overallocation is the public finance version of
overgrazing the commons.

Government decision making by interest-group competition tends to
favor concentrated over diffuse interests. As a result, government agencies often become the captives of the interest groups most affected by
their actions. The evidence of widespread ''regulatory capture'' played
a major role in promoting the movement to deregulate the Interstate
Commerce Commission, Civil Aeronautics Board, and other government regulatory agencies. The proposal for a balanced budget amendment to the Constitution, whatever its specific merits, reflects a wide
perception that existing political institutions are incapable of controlling the political dynamics created by interest-group pressures.

Such problems are also found in public land management. There is a
low premium placed on efficiency, resulting in high management costs.
At the same time special-interest pressures steadily expand the services
on the public lands but prevent significant charges from being imposed
for these services. The consequences are that public land management

incurs large losses that must be paid by the general taxpayer, much as the overall federal budget chronically shows large deficits.

Examination of public land investments and production levels shows widespread economic inefficiency. The inability of many western water projects to pass elementary economic tests has long been noted. Similar criticisms are now directed at Forest Service timber harvesting: timber investments are based on invalid economic calculations that overstate benefits because of the "allowable cut effect"; timber harvesting occurs over wide areas where harvesting costs exceed revenues generated; and the levels of timber harvests are distorted by the "even flow" and other constraints that have little, if any, economic justification. Perry Hagenstein reported that timber prices in the Pacific Northwest would have been significantly reduced if timber-harvesting levels on the national forests had been determined in response to market incentives.[6] As Hagenstein noted, Forest Service policies of holding down harvests advanced the interests of private timber owners, a result that accords well with interest-group liberal precepts. Perversely, many of the inefficiencies of timber management promoted harvesting in environmentally sensitive areas, compounding the social losses incurred.

Charges imposed for the use of public lands follow the predictable pattern of government decision making in response to interest-group pressures. Users are politically concentrated and thus defeat efforts to impose user fees that would relieve some of the costs now imposed on highly diffuse national taxpayers. Counting those many National Park System units that have no charge at all, the average fee in 1981 for national park visits was a nickel per day. Hunting, fishing, and other recreational use of BLM and Forest Service lands usually does not involve any public charge at all.

The results of interest-group pressures tend to allocate de facto rights to use of public lands among various user groups; Hagenstein refers to these rights as "restrictive arrangements." Historic assignments of uses tend to harden into permanent commitments. Ranchers thus are assured that certain levels of grazing on adjacent public lands will continue; wilderness users are assured that certain areas will be kept free of competing uses. In the case of water, the assignment of rights based on historic use has been made de jure as well as de facto.

In one perspective the fundamental problem of interest-group liberalism is that the creation of property rights is usually not complete: the rights cannot be transferred by selling them to someone else. Hence, efficiency-promoting transfers of rights to higher value uses do not occur. It has been suggested, for example, that wilderness proponents should be able to sell oil- and gas-drilling rights in wilderness areas.[7] The idea is that the revenues from such sales could be used to buy new wilderness lands or to pay for actions that would be more valuable for overall wilderness purposes—as the Catholic Church sometimes finds it necessary to sell a church property to serve the larger purposes of the faith. In the end we all are required to make tradeoffs, however painful it may be or however much we would like to pretend otherwise. Other examples in the water, grazing, and timber sectors could be given, showing social losses resulting from limits on the ability to reassign existing user entitlements.

There is widespread agreement about many of the specific criticisms of public land management: the high cost, the user charges that are well below fair market value, the inefficient investments, the lack of economic analysis and sophistication, and the much greater responsiveness to local and other concentrated interest-group pressures. The greatest differences of opinion concern the solution. Are such problems the result of major failings endemic to the current system of public land management, or are they simply the normal loose ends in any large and complex enterprise? Should we be concerned that the jar is half-empty or thankful that it is half-full? The answers to such questions ultimately depend on the alternatives. The least radical of these alternatives would be to take a series of incremental steps to try to improve the quality of current public land management.

Improved Current Management

Proponents of improving current management of the public lands fall into two camps. If not in quite so many words, one group asserts that current problems actually reflect a failure to implement the Progressive and conservationist prescriptions. Public land management needs to be insulated more fully from political interference, the latest scientific and technical methods need to be applied more diligently, and the professional experts should be given the full decision-making independence they require. The Progressive vision, in short, needs to be revitalized.

Some of the leading proponents of this reform strategy currently are found among the members of the economics profession.[8] In the view of these progressive economists, the original conservationists failed to achieve their aims partly because they failed to understand that public land management is fundamentally an economic problem that includes all nonmarket as well as market outputs in the economic calculations.

Lacking an economic foundation, conservationism became not a true science but an emotional crusade advocating a "gospel," in Samuel Hay's term. But if the scientific methods of economics can be introduced, it will now actually be possible to turn land management over to the experts (that is, economists). In essence, often requiring the use of technical economic methods, the true social benefits and costs of possible public land actions will be calculated, and the one alternative that produces the highest net benefits to society will be selected.

Frequently without realizing that it is an opposite prescription, another group proposes to improve current land management by making it more faithful to the precepts of interest-group liberalism. The objective is not to exclude politics, but to make land management even more political. Such diagnoses of current management emphasize two failings: (1) an attempt to exclude legitimate interest groups (such as environmentalists); and (2) heavy-handed and clumsy tactics in seeking to broker politically viable compromises among the contending interests.

Critics of the Forest Service thus have asserted that the service remains rigidly wedded to archaic concepts of independent management by professional experts and seeks to exclude valid public involvement. In the 1970s and 1980s critics of federal coal leasing by the Interior Department asserted that the department paid insufficient attention to the concerns of western states, environmentalists, and other concerned interest groups. Still others regret the intransigency and divisive behavior of interest groups on both sides of many public land issues and suggest that problems could be solved if only the contending interest groups would be more reasonable, speak more softly, and bargain together in better faith.

Proponents of all these views are often curiously lacking in historic perspective. They commonly do not refer to the debates that have gone on for decades with respect to the ideological merits and failings of Progressivism and interest-group liberalism. Indeed, the fundamental disagreements between these two ideologies—with respect to matters such as the roles of expert professionals, use of scientific methods, and place of politics—are often scarcely noted. Lacking this historic perspective, there is no good explanation offered for why public land management has worked poorly in the past or why matters will be different in the future. There is a strong flavor of wishful thinking, or, more cynically, it may be a good way simply of avoiding any real change and preserving a status quo that is satisfactory to many.

The actual prospects for reviving the Progressive conservationist approach appear dim for several reasons. The prospects in the American political system for greater separation of land management from politics are no greater than they ever were. Indeed, they are probably less today: public willingness to defer to experts depends on confidence in scientific methods and the professions that use them. But in the past twenty-five years there has been a notable erosion of public confidence in professional expertise. In many respects current public attitudes are probably well founded; in my own view the social sciences have made many excessive claims and have been slow to grasp their real limitations.[9]

The prospects for more harmonious bargaining and more productive compromises among interest groups also seem poor. The incentives are simply wrong; the squeaky wheel still gets the grease. Much as bad money drives out good, loud aggressive interest groups drive out soft-spoken moderate ones. The internal politics of interest groups of all political complexions also seem to reward militants and to penalize moderation.

Proponents of interest-group liberalism have assumed, in most cases implicitly, that interest groups would show enough common sense that one way or another they would be able to agree on measures that enlarge the social pie for everyone. The process of debate over the distribution of the pie would not prevent agreement on measures that would make everyone better off. In recent years, however, this expectation has seemed less valid; interest-group bargaining has instead seemed more a zero-sum game where each interest group takes for granted a pie of fixed size. At times it seems to become even a "negative-sum" game, because the lawyers' fees, endless meetings, and other transaction costs of negotiations eat up so much of the product.

Moreover, all this behavior by interest groups individually is "rational," because any one interest group by itself is unlikely to have an effect on the amount of the total social product. The cumulative result, however, may well have been significant social loss, represented in part by inefficient government actions.

As indicated above, the concept of governing by seeking equilibrium among the vectors of all interest-group pressures is troubling in many ways. It offers no standard for judging whether a particular government action is any better or any worse than another—other than the fact that political agreement has been reached. Carried to its extreme and reminiscent of Voltaire's Pangloss, any course of government is rationalized because it simply shows the current distribution of political power. What happened to such old-fashioned ideals as equity, liberty, justice, and efficiency in government?

The best case for focusing on incremental improvements in current public land management is founded on a view that Charles Lindblom described in his famous article, "The Science of Muddling Through."[10] If not exactly a science, muddling through is unquestionably a government tradition of long standing in the United States. Moreover, bitter experience has taught us to be skeptical of any proposals for radical change; the consequences are seldom what the architects had in mind.

Carried to its full logic, however, such incrementalism becomes a formula for stagnation. The hope for broad change of any kind seems to involve a symbiotic relationship between idealism and incremental thinking. The radical visions of idealists are seldom realized but create the social tensions and provide the ideas that steer incremental movement in that direction. One radical change that has been proposed for the public lands is the outright divestiture of most of them to the private sector.

Sale of the Public Lands

One of the major developments in social science over the past several decades has been the invasion by economists of the territory formerly reserved to political scientists—although at one time all such matters were the domain of "political economy." The students of government coming from the discipline of political science have generally reflected a tradition that emphasized descriptive (as opposed to prescriptive) analysis of political institutions. Economists brought two distinctive elements: a long tradition of offering strong policy recommendations (often for greater reliance on the market) and an assumption that political actors behave in a self-interested way (a political analog to the standard economic assumptions about private market behavior). Applying traditional economic reasoning in the context of political institutions, the conclusions have not been favorable to these institutions. For example, the strongest bureaucratic incentives are often simply to expand bureaucracy, not to provide an optimal level of services most efficiently.

Most seriously, if government is employed as an instrument for maximum self- (or group) enrichment, broader social objectives may be lost. Large resources may even be devoted to the competition for government largess. It seems that effective government depends on a large dose of altruistic and genuinely public-spirited behavior by both government administrators (bureaucrats) and the citizens affected by government actions. Yet the supply of such behavior varies greatly in different societies and circumstances; indeed, the trend in the United States in recent years has seemingly been downward as people actually behave more like the economic man of economic theory, including in the political arena.

Another recent development in economics has been a greater attention to the problems of information generation. Rather than a world of perfect information and equilibrium, the real world may be characterized by widespread ignorance and rapid change. In such a world the rewards to planning and conscious design—scientific management—may be less than had once been thought. Chance and happenstance instead seem to play a greater role. The operative mode frequently seems to be trial and error.

Large corporations and other organizations are too often rigid and slow to adapt; innovation is more likely to be the product of new entrants with an old-fashioned entrepreneurial spirit of risk taking. These themes have been emphasized in particular by the writings of "Austrian" economists, following in the tradition of Von Mises and Hayek, who emphasize the merits of the market as an information mechanism.[11] Students of the old socialist planned economies contrast their rigidities with the adaptability and dynamism of western market economies. Studies of formal public planning in the United States similarly find a record of failure and lack of influence.

Proponents of selling the public lands have been strongly influenced by such thinking. Government suffers by comparison with the private sector in two critical respects. First, large government bureaucracies that try to plan formally and precisely will be defeated by the inherent unpredictability of events. Second, in government the general problems of large organization are complicated by the incentives of political decision making. In a world of many narrow interest groups, there is no constituency for efficiency in resource allocation—or often for the goal of true equity either. In short, the assertion of scientific management in government usually turns out to be a fiction.

Such conclusions have comported well with the traditional advocacy by economists of the free market. It is important to recognize, however, that current disposal proponents do not so much advocate the perfection of markets as the imperfection of political resource allocation. If government does most things poorly, especially tasks that are technically and managerially complicated, how can it be expected to manage the public lands efficiently and equitably?

There is indeed much in this critique that describes the historic record of public land management. The greatest problem may well be the difficulty (or perhaps impossibility) of reconciling scientific management with political decision making. A rapidly changing environment in fact does also pose great difficulties for effective planning and conscious design. But it is also true that in a free competition the large corporation—essentially an embodiment of the scientific management approach—has replaced the classic liberal organization of a market of small firms. Indeed, to the extent that scientific management is achievable, the best prospect seems to lie in the large private corporation, not in the large government agency.

The progressive conviction that scientific management can be so scientifically precise as to eliminate wide administrative discretion seems far-fetched. True scientific management requires the application of critical intelligence, still leaving broad discretion for management decision making. It is this necessary discretion that is troublesome in government when the objectives for government actions are often poorly defined and political pressures are so intense. Yet attempts to limit discretion by establishing formal rules and other constraints on government administrators often seem to produce arbitrary and impractical results.

On the public lands the case seems weakest for keeping the government in the business of managing production of public timber, coal, forage, and other commodity outputs—a virtual pocket of socialism maintained within the U.S. market system. In a number of areas there are few public values at stake and greater prospects of efficient management in the private sector. For these lands, a policy of privatization would seem appropriate

To be sure, there is likely to be much opposition. It is said by pollsters that many Americans oppose parts of the Bill of Rights when they are taken out of a Constitutional context. Much the same is probably true of the U.S. capitalist system. The emphasis on private selfishness and competition for profits seems to many Americans to offend their values of community and equality. Indeed, Christianity and capitalism have coexisted over the centuries only with great strains. On the surface at least socialist ideals of government acting for the benefit of all the people appeal more to traditional religious values.

All these concerns are heightened in an economy dominated by large private corporations rather than the small, individual entrepreneurs of classic liberal thought.[12] It is likely that American capitalism could never be accomplished today as an affirmative act, but exists only because it is an historic inheritance. Whatever the conclusions of economists, this tension between the values of the market and other American values creates a major obstacle to any disposal of the public lands.

A narrower and more resolvable objection to public land disposal concerns nonmarket outputs of the public lands for which private incentives may diverge markedly from social goals. The largest class of such outputs involves dispersed recreational use of public lands.

There are four basic reasons why the opportunities available for some forms of recreation might be significantly less under private ownership than socially appropriate. First, collection costs for dispersed recreation spread over large areas at low densities, such as hiking in the mountains, may be too high to justify the opening of private lands to public access on a profit-making basis. Second, such widely dispersed recreational use may have a very low or even zero marginal cost, but private providers would charge a higher price, preventing fully efficient use. Third, some recreation policies such as the establishment of wilderness may create benefits that are realized by people who never directly enter the land. Such "existence values," however difficult they may be to measure precisely, involve a true public good and cannot be captured privately. And fourth, equity arguments can be made against the distributional consequences of private provision of recreation. Hence, retention of some types of recreational lands in public, but not necessarily federal, ownership may often be appropriate. This is most likely to be the case for lands used for dispersed recreation that may involve activities of people spread over wide areas.

Transfer of Public Lands to the States

Some have characterized the third main alternative—transfer of public land to the states—as the worst of all possible worlds. It would keep land management in the political thicket with all the attendant obstacles to rational management. On the other hand it would forgo the key advantages of public management at the federal level: the greater resources to employ sophisticated management methods and the wider scope for coordination. Moreover, the more intense press spotlight and general concentration of critical attention at the national level perhaps spurs more honest and efficient administration at that level.

Nevertheless, the case for transfer to the states has merits that have not been fully aired. In many respects the rights to use public lands have already been transferred to the states; if property is really a bundle of rights, many of the public land "sticks" are already in state possession. Public land managers are often highly responsive to state (and local) pressures. Since 1976 land use plans for the public lands have been legally required to be "consistent" with state and local plans as long as no violation of federal law or policy results.

State ownership of public lands would more directly tie the responsibilities for land policies to those who bear the impacts of those policies. Although the states now have a major management influence, they do not pay the cost. On the other hand national taxpayers do not bear the adverse environmental impacts that may be associated with public land policies they favor. As a rule the separation of responsibility for benefits and for costs makes it more difficult to achieve a happy balance. A great virtue of the market is that both these elements are united in the private producer except to the degree that social externalities are present. Transfers of lands to the states in this respect would be a halfway step toward a market solution.

If the public lands were transferred to the states, it would not necessarily mean that these lands would remain in public ownership. Indeed, one of the merits of state ownership is that it would allow states to experiment with various methods of classifying land for public or private tenures. The concept of the states as laboratories for testing novel policy ideas is an old and honorable one in American political thought. If, as seems likely, there is more than one defensible way to classify land for different tenures, then trial and error among the states may be the wisest course.

Ultimately, like the prospects for disposal of public lands to the private sector, the outlook for transferring lands to the states may depend on matters much broader than the quality of their management. In the early years of the nation most Americans felt a stronger sense of community loyalty toward the states and localities in which they lived than they do now. The great expansion in the role of the federal government was associated with a shift in the progressive era to a much stronger sense of national community. Indeed, some social commentators have suggested that this shift cannot be sustained in the long run and perhaps was undesirable in the first place. The transfer of public lands to the western states could itself be part cause and part effect of a greater future sense of identification with state and local communities.

Public Land Corporations

Yet another alternative, creating public land corporations, seeks in essence to revive progressive ideals in a new institutional setting. BLM and the Forest Service have never been able to achieve professional administration independent from political interference. It may therefore be necessary to provide a more rigid separation of land management from politics. This, in fact, is the basic idea behind creating a public land corporation: to pose a barrier to normal politics that would allow professional administrators to manage the lands in expert fashion. Unlike existing land management a public land corporation would be subject to the discipline that the revenues must exceed the costs. Indeed, the public land corporation would function very much like a private corporation.

In that case, why not simply sell the land to a private corporation? One reason would be that a public corporation would have less finality; if the idea turned out to be a mistake, the public corporation could be abolished more easily than a private corporation. The public corporation, however, would also be susceptible to future political manipulation even if it met all its aims. The risk is that a successful public land corporation would get caught up in political crossfires and then lose its independence from politics. In short, lack of permanent private status avoids some risks but creates others.

A public corporation may seem more acceptable because it could more easily be influenced to support nonmarket values. Yet steps in this direction will require political involvement that again may compromise the objective to achieve professional administration by the experts.

The case for a public corporation is strongest on parts of the public lands where the primary use is for producing a commodity. In particular prime timberlands or intensive recreational lands might be managed in this fashion.

Long-term Leasing of Public Lands

A long-term leasing alternative is similar to the public corporation in that it is a way of avoiding any irreversible commitments. The lease will expire at some point, and the government could then decide not to renew it. To be sure, the objective to turn management over to the private lessee requires a security of tenure inconsistent with frequent review of lessee status. Yet, the more distant the lease renewal and the more secure the tenure, the closer the practical consequence comes to outright disposal. The differences in security of tenure between a one-hundred-year lease and sale of the land are not great.

Leasing is also a broad and flexible concept, which can range from very tight public control over lessee use of the land to almost total lessee discretion. As a practical matter, the former does not differ so much from direct government production of the resource, nor the latter from outright disposal. The differences are largely matters of symbolism—which may be an important political consideration.

Leasing may offer some advantages over disposal in protecting dispersed recreational use of the land. While a lease stipulation may be technically identical to a deed easement on private property, enforcement of the stipulation on a public land lease may be facilitated by the less-proprietary attitudes associated with leasing. In many rangeland areas the recreational use of the land is considerably more valuable than the grazing use, despite the fact that recreation receives less management attention. It would be important not to jeopardize this recreational use by any sale of the land.

Conclusion

Intellectual trends in American life are likely to play a major role in shaping the public land system of the future. Indeed, the environmental movement of the 1970s showed the power of ideas. The creation of the national wilderness system is testimony to the great appeal of the wilderness concept to millions of Americans, many of whom will never visit a wilderness area. The protection of endangered species, involving few direct beneficiaries (human, that is) and having no immediate constituency, still commands strong political support.

Leading political scientists in the 1980s began to reassess the emphasis they had previously put on interest groups in theories of the political process. James Q. Wilson commented in 1981 on "the importance for policy making of the ideas of political elites. A political scientist such as myself, trained in the 1950s when politics was seen almost entirely in terms of competing interests, was slow to recognize the change."[13] It is now many years since the publication of perhaps the most influential statement of interest-group liberalism, *The Governmental Process* by David Truman.[14] In many respects events have confirmed Truman's views, but in others they have not.

If the politics of the future is as much or more a competition of ideas and ideologies as of interest groups, then a key role will be played by intellectuals and other arbiters in ideological matters. The press and other communications media will have an especially critical role as transmitters of new ideas to the public at large.

If an intellectual consensus were to develop for major changes in public land tenure, I suspect that the political process would follow fairly soon. It is speculative to suggest where such a consensus might lie. A few comments can be offered, however, that are already reflected in the observations above.

It is hard to imagine any brand-new ideology emerging that seems definitively to resolve the long-standing questions of the roles of democratic politics, professional expertise, the judiciary, the private sector, and so forth. The current age seems particularly unsympathetic to absolute or single solutions. Rather, each approach is perceived as having its valid points. The objective in reevaluating land management may be to match up different approaches to the specific circumstances of specific types of land. In short, as suggested previously, different areas of public land may have to be classified for different tenures that reflect suitable governing and managerial philosophies.[15]

Thus, lands with few commodity uses and widely dispersed recreation do not involve complex management decisions. The gains from more scientific management of these lands would be less than in other areas; hence, the costs of the democratic politics of interest-group liberalism (that is, multiple-use management) are not so great. Relative to commodity production the private market also fares poorly in providing recreation that is dispersed over a large area. In sum, lands with dispersed recreation characteristics probably should be maintained in public (if most often state or local) ownership.

High-value timberlands in lowland areas with only modest recreational and wildlife use can provide an opposite circumstance. The costs of unsophisticated and inefficient public management of the timber may be high, while the losses to recreation and other nonmarket values resulting from private management may be relatively less than in other areas. Moreover, some private timber companies currently encourage recreational use of their lands. This private provision is likely to rise significantly as recreational demands and values grow. Private ownership and management of commercial timberlands thus may well be indicated. Public rangelands provide an intermediate case, often involving low commodity values combined with low or modest recreation values.

In conclusion the current rethinking of the federal lands reflects broad issues facing all of American society today with respect to the proper role for government. The future of these lands raises questions as large as socialism versus capitalism, or national authority versus states rights. Such matters arise in a particularly pointed way because of the anomalous character of public land ownership. In a nation supposedly committed to private ownership, about 30 percent of the land is federally owned. In a nation supposedly committed to decentralized governing authority, public land management that commonly involves the most local of issues is centralized at the national level.

To be sure, there may be special circumstances that justify giving the federal lands this anomalous status. Perhaps American commitments to private ownership and decentralized government today have become more rhetorical than real. But a third possibility is that existing federal lands are an accident of history sustained through the generalized inertia and gridlock that seem to characterize all of American government today. If the overall political environment in the United States were to change to encourage greater innovation, major changes could occur rapidly on the public lands as a result of the application of basic American political and economic principles.

Notes

1. See Theodore J. Lowi, *The End of Liberalism: Ideology, Policy and the Crisis of Public Authority* (New York: Norton, 1969).

2. Samuel P. Hays, *Conservation and the Gospel of Efficiency: The Progressive Conservation Movement, 1890–1920* (Cambridge, Mass.: Harvard University Press, 1959).

3. *Ibid.*: 268–269.

4. John Kenneth Galbraith, *American Capitalism: The Concept of Countervailing Power* (Boston: Houghton Mifflin, 1956).

5. Lowi, *The End of Liberalism*: 46.

6. Perry R. Hagenstein, "The Federal Lands Today: Uses and Limits," in Sterling Brubaker, ed., *Rethinking the Federal Lands* (Washington, D.C.: Resources for the Future, 1984): 95.

7. John Baden and Richard Stroup, "Saving the Wilderness," *Reason* (July 1981).

8. See John V. Krutilla and John A. Haigh, "An Integrated Approach to National Forest Management," *Environmental Law* (Winter 1978).

9. See Christopher K. Leman and Robert H. Nelson, "Ten Commandments for Policy Economists," *Journal of Policy Analysis and Management* (Fall 1981).

10. Charles Lindblom, "The Science of 'Muddling Through,' " *Public Administration Review* (Spring 1959).

11. Friedrich A. Hayek, *Individualism and Economic Order* (Chicago: University of Chicago Press, 1948).

12. See Alfred D. Chandler, Jr., *The Visible Hand: The Managerial Revolution in American Business* (Cambridge, Mass.: Harvard University Press, 1977).

13. James Q. Wilson, "What Can Be Done?," in *AEI Public Policy Papers* (Washington, D.C.: American Enterprise Institute, 1981): 19.

14. David B. Truman, *The Governmental Process: Political Interests and Public Opinion* (New York: Knopf, 1951).

15. See also Robert H. Nelson, "The Public Lands," in Paul R. Portney, ed., *Current Issues in Natural Resource Policy* (Washington, D.C.: Resources for the Future, 1982).

Chapter 10

Decentralizing the National Forests

The Forest Service today faces a crisis of faith. The reasons are a matter of history. The Forest Service was founded on the idea of scientific professionalism; that is, the national forests should be managed by an elite corps of experts acting in the public interest. The old progressive faith in the capacities of expert professionals, however, is today widely rejected.

The Forest Service faced its first major intellectual crisis when it had to let interest groups into its decision making. By the standards of Gifford Pinchot this was a virtual sacrilege. But in any event the Forest Service somehow made the transition to the age of public meetings and negotiated settlements among interests.

This turned the original clear vision of expert professionalism, however, into a confusing mishmash. In truth the Forest Service was forced to try to blend the incompatible. Still, whatever the logical deficiencies, the agency obviously continued to function.

But then in the last quarter century some new major complications have emerged. New groups, most notably in the environmental movement, are now asserting values they believe are too important for interest-group compromise. There is also a widespread new mood of criticism of and hostility to big government institutions such as the Forest Service. Some libertarians now describe the Forest Service as domestic socialism. From all shades of political opinion there is harsh criticism of the role of interest groups in politics.

This chapter was originally presented as a speech to the Mission Symposium on the Future of the National Forests, San Francisco, California, 13–15 December 1984. An expanded version was later published as ''The Future of Federal Forest Management: Options for Use of Market Methods,'' in Phillip O. Foss, *Federal Lands Policy* (New York: Greenwood Press, 1987).

247

The economics profession, ranging from Milton Friedman on the right to Lester Thurow and Charles Schultze on the left, has been particularly critical of the adverse impact of interest groups.[1] Yet the Forest Service, although founded on a tradition of hostility to interest groups, is now wedded to interest-group involvement. In a way the central problem faced by the Forest Service is that it does not really know how to respond to all these new forces. It is an agency that is having trouble staying in close touch with the times.

The Forest Service should also not be singled out. The other public land agencies all face these problems to one degree or another.

Not seeing any other plausible answer, the Forest Service has treated the new forces of environmentalism and economics as just another set of interest groups. Therefore, the way to deal with them, as prescribed by the old model, is to make some partial concessions, as to the timber industry, for example.

The problem is that environmentalism and economics are not really interest groups. They are sets of beliefs—really ideologies or even quasi-religions.[2] Making a few concessions to a religion may be worse than doing nothing. It may seem to be a corrupt tokenism.

It may also seem to others that the agency lacks conviction and is incapable of understanding what others believe in. Sitting between and dealing with competing ideologies is much different than resolving differences between competing interest groups. This is happening more and more in American politics today. For example, how do you develop a compromise on abortion?

The Catholic Church is weighing in with its views that the economy should be seen as a moral choice.[3] Economic debates may now take on a character of a conflict among religious views. Thus, the Forest Service problems are hardly unique, and it is hardly surprising that the Forest Service is unsure what to do. After all, the agency employees do not receive their primary training in moral philosophy or theology.

What is the answer? Well, there may not be any easy answer. In general, however, the best approach is likely to be seeking greater decentralization of government from the federal to state and local levels. That way there will be greater homogeneity of outlook under the same government, and governments will not have to deal with such sharp conflicts in basic values and beliefs among their citizenry. In other words you do your thing there and I'll do my thing here, and we will try not to interfere with each other too much.

Getting beyond these philosophical issues, what about the immediate prospects for the federal forests? One of the most important new forestry developments is that, after mostly fighting each other for years, environmentalism and economics have found some common ground. The key factor is that in some areas economically efficient actions also turn out to be a major benefit to the environment. This possibility has been highlighted by the below-cost timber debate.

It might be noted that, while this environmentalist-economist alliance is newer in the timber area, fiscal conservatives and environmentalists have been combining forces to try to block inefficient western water projects for a number of years.[4] In some ways they have been remarkably successful: there have been very few new water projects approved since 1976.

Thus, any combining of environmental and economic ideas may create a force to reckon with in forestry. The other key factor is, of course, the national budget situation with its huge deficit. The deficit has been creating great pressures to find ways to reduce costs.

Predictions in political matters are always uncertain. But it seems likely that the demands on the Forest Service to demonstrate the economic rationality of its programs will continue to increase. That simply seems to be the trend of the times.

There are a number of ways in which a higher level of economic rationality could be achieved for the national forests. The suggestions below are divided into four categories: incremental change, major departures, radical change, and divestiture options.

Incremental Change

As the term suggests, "incremental change" in many cases would be a continuation of existing developments. The Forest Service has since the 1970s significantly expanded the amount of economic analysis applied to its programs. Yet despite all the activity there is considerable question as to its actual impact. Outside economists wonder whether economic analyses are not frequently done simply for the sake of doing them. They may be done with great care, but then not heeded when the actual decision is made.

There may be a need for a much stronger institutional presence of economics in the Forest Service. Questions of benefits and costs need to become internalized as a matter of habit. Several among a large number of options that could help to improve the level and quality of economic analysis in the Forest Service are as follows.

1. Give foresters and others not trained in economics more training in the logic and methods of economic analysis.

2. Locate economists in staff positions closer to where the actual decisions are being made.
3. Review methods of economic analysis to ensure that they are generally accepted among professional economists. This would, for example, preclude counting the allowable cut effect in assessing benefits of timber investments.

Major Departures

The next options would involve more substantial departures from past practices. The Forest Service is currently operating under a highly centralized system of planning and economic analysis. Admittedly, this was partly required by Congress in the Forest and Rangelands Renewable Resources Planning Act of 1974 (RPA). But here we have the luxury of at least thinking about making changes in the law.

The apparatus of national goals and central planning dictated by RPA is unwieldy. It suffers from some of the same afflictions found wherever central planning is tried: rigidity, inflexibility, and a lack of sufficient information at the center to know what is really going on in the field. The RPA central planning approach is really a lawyer's concept of planning and economic analysis, not that of an economist. In practice RPA may have to be repealed in order to achieve more efficient management.

So the first major departure needed may be to abandon parts of the planning design implemented under RPA to the extent permissible under the current law or, if necessary, by changing the law.[5] Instead, a more decentralized approach could be adopted. The focal point for decision making would be the individual national forest. National forests would receive substantially greater administrative autonomy.

Of course, it would still be necessary to be accountable to national interests as reflected in national supplies and demands. The two goals of decentralization and national accountability might be achieved under the following scheme.

1. Assess marketable outputs of the national forests at their market value.
2. Value nonmarket outputs by setting prices administratively for them on each national forest.
3. Require that the total social value of the outputs of each national forest, valued as indicated above, must exceed the management costs for that national forest.
4. Subject to this binding constraint, give local managers of the na-

tional forest system units wide discretion to set output levels and decide management costs.

Radical Change

We may have to consider even more radical changes, however, because the actual feasibility of this scheme is in serious doubt. First, the ability to set accurate prices for nonmarket goods such as recreation is questionable. Second, the ability simply to measure the actual physical outputs of nonmarket goods accurately is also in doubt.

If a major decentralization is to be achieved and national accountability preserved, the individual units of the national forest system may actually have to be put on an individually self-sustaining basis.[6] That is, the revenues they collect would have to be enough to cover their costs. They could borrow money but would have to pay it back with interest.

Provision of "public good" outputs of the forests could be supported by grants from state or federal agencies. If, for example, a wildlife project was needed in a national forest unit, the forest manager could go to the state wildlife department, U.S. Fish and Wildlife Service, or some other funding body. Some types of direct recreational users of forests could also pay much higher charges and thus cover the costs of their use. To sum up, this scheme would involve:

1. Allowing individual national forests to set their own charges for use of the forest and also to keep all the revenues.
2. Allowing individual national forests to solicit public funds for projects having public purposes.
3. Allowing national forest units to set their own output levels based on their own revenue and cost calculations.
4. Requiring each national forest unit to receive enough revenues to cover its own costs.

Divestiture Options

In essence, each of the national forests would become similar to an independent public corporation.[7] The line of logic here can be carried even further, however. If it is appropriate to put the national forest system units on an individually self-sustaining basis, one could also go all the way and consider whether some of them should be divested by the federal government. National forest lands could be either sold to the private sector or transferred to state government.

This is not the place to go into the details (see chapter 8). Briefly, however, one possibility could be as follows.

1. Prime timber lands, those with lesser recreational value, could be ˙sold to private timber corporations.
2. Prime livestock grazing lands on the national forests could be leased to ranchers on long term fifty- or one-hundred-year leases.
3. Lands used primarily for dispersed recreation by state and local residents could be transferred to state governments.
4. Lands of major national significance such as national parks, wildlife refuges, and wilderness areas could be retained in federal ownership.

Conclusion

It should be noted that the present period is one of intellectual ferment with respect to the public lands as a whole. The next twenty-five years may well bring greater change in the institutional arrangments for managing the public lands than has been seen since the disposal philosophy was abandoned and the retention philosophy adopted in the progressive era early in the twentieth century. The old progressive philosophy, however, is now surviving mainly on inertia and the lack of any clear successor. The most important public land debates today are really about the shape that this new vision will take in the next century.[8]

Notes

1. See Milton Friedman and Rose Friedman, *Free to Chose* (New York: Avon Books, 1979); Lester C. Thurow, *The Zero-sum Society: Distribution and the Possibilities for Economic Change* (New York: Penguin Books, 1981); and Charles L. Schultze, *The Public Use of Private Interest* (Washington, D.C.: Brookings Institute, 1977).

2. See Robert H. Nelson, *Reaching for Heaven on Earth: The Theological Meaning of Economics* (Lanham, Md.: Rowman and Littlefield, 1991); and Robert H. Nelson, ''Environmental Calvinism: The Judeo-Christian Roots of Eco-theology,'' in Roger E. Meiners and Bruce Yandle, eds., *Taking the Environment Seriously* (Lanham, Md.: Rowman and Littlefield, 1993).

3. Thomas M. Gannon, ed., *The Catholic Challenge to the American Economy: Reflections on the U.S. Bishop's Pastoral Letter on Catholic Social Teaching and the U.S. Economy* (New York: Macmillan, 1987).

4. See Terry L. Anderson, ed., *Water Rights: Scarce Resource Allocation, Bureaucracy, and the Environment* (San Francisco: Pacific Institute for Public Policy Research, 1983); and Richard W. Wahl, *Markets for Federal Water: Subsidies, Property Rights, and the Bureau of Reclamation* (Washington, D.C.: Resources for the Future, 1989).

5. Richard W. Behan, "RPA/NFMA: Time to Punt," *Journal of Forestry*, vol. 79, no. 12 (1981).

6. See also Randal O'Toole, *Reforming the Forest Service* (Washington, D.C.: Island Press, 1988), and John H. Beuter, *Federal Timber Sales*, (Washington, D.C.: Congressional Research Service, report 85–96, 9 February 1985): 125–28.

7. Dennis E. Teeguarden and Davis Thomas, "A Public Corporation Model for Federal Forest Land Management," *Natural Resources Journal* (April 1985).

8. See Robert H. Nelson, "Government as Theatre: Toward a New Paradigm for the Public Lands," *University of Colorado Law Review*, vol. 65, no. 2 (1994).

Part V

Options for Change

Introduction

In the 1990s growing segments of the American public express doubts that the federal government is an effective instrument for achieving public purposes. Poorly constructed laws, numerous layers of red tape and approval, complex regulatory processes, a bewildering diffusion of authority, and many other features of government at the federal level tend to defeat even the most skillful of administrators. The level of popular discontent was shown in the large vote in the 1992 election for the third-party candidacy of Ross Perot and in the election of a Republican majority in the U.S. House of Representatives in 1994 for the first time in forty years.

Current strong demands for change may open the way for basic redesign of the public lands. As the preceding chapters have examined, many of the complaints being made today about American government in general are applicable to public land management. The public lands have contributed significantly to the economic development of the western United States and have provided wonderful recreational opportunities for many millions of people. The managers of the public lands have secured the protection of environmental assets important to the whole nation. Yet there is today wide agreement that, economically and environmentally, the management of the public lands has left a great deal to be desired.

The chapters in this part of this book offer a number of options for major changes on the public lands. Several of them were originally written as internal "think pieces" or memoranda to be read by Department of the Interior and other government officials. Chapters 11, 12, and 13 describe ways in which market forces could be used more effectively in the management of the public rangelands, forests, and coal resources, respectively. Chapter 14 develops four specific options for decentraliza-

257

tion of responsibility for management of portions of federal forests, rangelands, and other surface lands. Finally, chapter 15 raises the possibility of a large-scale rearrangement and transfer of administrative responsibilities that would in essence dismantle the current Interior Department.

Chapter 11

Some Economics of Public Rangelands

The announcement by Secretary of the Interior Bruce Babbitt in August 1993 of a proposal for a new grazing fee and other major changes in public rangeland management set off the latest round in perhaps the oldest controversy on the public lands.[1] As with previous episodes in this long-running battle over livestock grazing, there was more heat generated than light. Bold assertions were made with little empirical support. It was, as public land debates tend to be, above all a morality play concerned with matters of good versus evil.[2] Also, like other grazing battles, this one seems to be yielding little real change, once again showing a public land system in a state of gridlock.

Given the intensity of the public debate, there has been surprisingly little study of the underlying economics of the public rangelands. Controversies flare up in which economic questions are central, the dispute rages in the absence of little concrete information, and then the disputants eventually move on to another subject. The moments of intense public interest, however, yield little in the way of a commitment to in-depth economic and other study. Because of the short-term nature of most political appointments, the results of sustained inquiry typically will not be available soon enough for the current appointee to benefit from them. Also, as noted, many participants in public land debates address them from an essentially moral (if not almost theological) perspective. Hence, when the same issues arise again at some point in the

This chapter is a revised and shortened version of a paper on "Economic Issues in the Multiple-use Management of Public Rangeland," presented to the annual meeting of the Western Agricultural Economic Association, Coeur d'Alene, Idaho, July 9–12, 1989, and subsequently included in Western Agricultural Economic Association, *Papers of the 1989 Annual Meeting, Western Agricultural Economic Association.*

future, the debate is generally little better informed than on the previous occasion.

This chapter describes several of the key economic issues on the public rangelands that seem likely to be prominent again in the next round of rangeland controversy. It also examines potential changes in rangeland tenure and the basic management regime. Possible avenues for research in each area are suggested.

Planning by Policy Analysis

In an idealized world of perfect information—a world in fact often encountered in economic theorizing—the process of economic planning for the public rangelands might well work as follows. The multiple potential uses of the rangelands, many of them competing, would be reviewed and described. A full economic evaluation and assessment of each potential rangeland use would be prepared. If available, market prices would be employed to estimate directly the value to society of each use; otherwise, indirect economic techniques such as the travel cost method would be employed to estimate dollar values. All the environmental impacts relating to each use should be considered and included in this evaluation process. Taking into account all possible rangeland alternatives, the overall set of uses, present and future, that maximized the net social value of the rangelands would be chosen.

This sort of economic planning concept underlies the requirements of the Forest and Rangeland Renewable Resources Planning Act of 1974 (RPA) and other 1970s legislation for the public lands. Nevertheless, such goals for comprehensive planning ignore a critical element. Planning is itself part of the economics of rangeland management. The data and information requirements for the idealized version of comprehensive planning would be very costly to satisfy. At some point the gains from greater information and more precise analysis will fall below the costs of these activities.

A further complication is that many types of information with respect to future events cannot be known with certainty, even at any cost. There will soon be new information to supplant erroneous and incomplete past information that was nevertheless unavoidably incorporated into earlier plans. Yet continuous revision of comprehensive plans to take account of the latest data and information will itself also be costly—indeed sometimes prohibitively so.

On the public rangelands the problem of inadequate information for comprehensive planning is likely to be particularly important because of the low economic value of the resource being managed. On the rangelands the issues are likely to be scientifically complex, but the amount of scientific information that can be collected at a cost that is justifiable will be limited. This is especially true because the character of the scientific problem may vary considerably from region to region and even site to site. Hence, the issue of how to proceed in the presence of frequently sketchy and unreliable information is central to the question of how to plan appropriately for the public rangelands. The economic problem of the rangelands is in the broadest perspective a problem of managing the acquisition and distribution of information and establishing a sequence of decision making that will mesh properly with the requirements and constraints imposed by limited information.

One conclusion is that if comprehensive planning is to be ruled out on grounds of cost, economic planning at any one time may have to be limited to a select set of issues, a set that may fall well short of the universe even of all potentially important subjects. The determination of appropriate topics for study should reflect a number of considerations.

(1) the economic values at stake in a potential future resource decision
(2) the likelihood of a decision in the near term
(3) the costs of obtaining the information needed for successful resolution of the issue
(4) the political pressures and demands that a decision be made
(5) the likely receptivity of the ultimate decision makers to sound and accurate information and analysis.

Rather than trying to be comprehensive, the skillful rangeland planner will have to be able to balance all these considerations in deciding where to focus his or her efforts. It will inevitably be a somewhat subjective exercise that requires combining political wisdom with economic sophistication. The kind of planning that will be necessary can perhaps best be described as "policy analysis" planning. The most effective rangeland planners will not be able to limit their knowledge to any one field of physical and social science; rather, they will have to bring together knowledge from diverse fields in ways that defy any scientific formula. The successful rangeland planner will have to have some of the talents of both the artist and the scientist.

Key Economic Issues

The remainder of this chapter describes some of the policy issues that seem most likely to occupy the attention of the political process in the next few years. It also considers briefly how economists with creative suggestions and supporting analysis might be able to help out.

1. The grazing fee

The grazing fee is perhaps the longest-running economic controversy on the public rangelands. The Forest Service first imposed a fee in 1906. A particularly bitter dispute erupted in the 1920s when the House Committee on Agriculture sought to increase grazing fees by three hundred percent. Since World War II there has been one struggle after another over the proper charge for grazing on public rangelands.

The latest installment began with congressional action in 1978 to eliminate administrative discretion and instead set the grazing fee legislatively. The fee formula selected by Congress was mandated through the end of 1985, after which the matter again reverted to the hands of the Interior and Agriculture departments. When the time arrived the departments chose simply to continue the legislative formula. Critics charge that this method of setting the fee has resulted in unduly low fees and is inadequate in two basic respects: it does not represent fair market value, and it fails to obtain sufficient revenue to cover costs to the government of administering livestock grazing.

Although fair market value may well be much higher than the current grazing fee, the equity case for raising the fee is also subject to some dispute. Past low fees—and a reasonable expectation of continued low fees in the future—have been capitalized in the prices of private ranches bought with federal grazing permits attached. Any inequities resulting from low fees may well have been captured by the original ranch owner, not the current owner. Indeed, the issue is debatable but at least in some ways to raise fees sharply now might be to create a new inequity.

The method used by BLM and the Forest Service to estimate fair market value of federal grazing depends on finding private grazing leases whose prices in the market can be used as a basis for further comparison with federal grazing opportunities. In many cases, however, private leases represent a small number of private transactions in a sea of federal grazing permits. The government charge for grazing, and other terms of the grazing permit, thus become significant factors that can influence the private lease rate itself. Using private lease rates to determine the value of grazing on public land thus may become a circular process. Indeed, the relevance of the very concept of fair market value is questionable in an economic environment where the federal government already holds so much of the resource that no independent market for private leases can be said to truly exist.

Setting one grazing fee for the entire West, or even one region in the West, also means that the fee will not represent the actual fair market value of the particular grazing opportunity available to any one rancher. There is a great variety in the length of time on the public rangeland, season of use, and other circumstances of private grazing on public lands. A fully valid calculation of fair market value might require a complete simulation (necessarily hypothetical) of an entire local grazing market. All the private ranch lands and all the government lands in the local area would have to be entered as inputs for this simulation. The simulation routine would in essence act to lease each parcel of federal land and each parcel of private land as though they were freely available and being offered for whatever the private grazing lease market would bear.

Yet, although such an approach is easily within the capacity of current computer technology, the information requirements would be far beyond the current availability of data and the results would be of highly uncertain reliability. Indeed, there would be little point to making such an effort. The point here is that we really have no way of getting at fair market value in a true sense. It is simply impossible if the institutional and scientific complexity as well as the costs of data and calculation are taken into account.

Hence, despite the assumptions of current law and practice, fair market value may be an unworkable standard for setting the grazing fee. Indeed, the current agency approach to calculating fair market value does not yield fair market value in the accepted appraisal meaning of the term. It is a heroic simplification that has been adopted to deal with what would otherwise be an intractable problem.

We might be best off to simply acknowledge this and give up on fair market value. An alternative method of setting the fee would simply relate the fee to administrative costs; or the fee could be based explicitly on an equity standard determined by what seems ''fair'' to current ranchers. This would have to be a political determination since it would be impossible to assert on the basis of any scientific or technical calculation exactly what is meant by ''fair.''

In any case the greatest economic problem of the grazing fee may not be the magnitude of the fee but the major uncertainties created for both ranchers and government administrators from never knowing for sure what the fee will be. The best economic answer to the grazing fee may be to select some fee—however this may be done, and perhaps even somewhat arbitrarily—and then forget about the fee for a long time to come. Another major misallocation with respect to the grazing fee has been the amount of time it has required of top government administrators, who should have much better things to do.

2. Below-cost grazing leases

The economic controversy with respect to "below-cost" timber sales has now raged for a decade or more in the public forests. By many calculations, including those of the government, federal timber sales often return less in revenue than their associated administrative and other government costs. It has attracted less attention, but federal livestock grazing management also yields much less in fee revenues than the costs of operating the grazing program. For 1983, for example, BLM and the Forest Service estimated their direct costs of the grazing program at $60.9 million, while grazing fee revenues were $24.8 million. It would have required a grazing fee of $2.85 per animal unit month (AUM) to cover grazing administrative costs, as compared with the actual fee of $1.40 per AUM in 1983.

The direct costs, moreover, are only a fraction of the full costs of grazing management, including a proportionate allocation of general BLM overhead to the grazing program and the costs of other activities such as wild horse and burro management that exist in significant degree because of the presence of livestock on the range. Some years ago I estimated the real costs of livestock grazing management to BLM, including the range program proportionate share of BLM planning and budgeting, the Washington headquarters office, and other forms of general BLM overhead.[3] These costs amounted to $125.4 million in 1981, equal to about $12 per AUM. The grazing fee in 1981 was less than 20 percent of these costs.

The costs of public grazing management per AUM exceed not only the grazing fee but also the best estimates of the full market value of current livestock grazing. The fee report submitted in 1986 by the secretaries of Agriculture and Interior estimated a 1983 market value for livestock grazing that ranged from $4.68 per AUM in one western region to $8.55 per AUM in another.[4] These market values were still well below the full cost per AUM of grazing management as I estimated it for 1981.

One economic issue raised by such estimates is whether it might make economic sense for the government to seek to buy out some grazing rights. The savings in management and other costs to the government in the long run might exceed the purchase price of these rights. Such a program could operate on a case-by-case basis, seeking situations where a price could be found acceptable to a rancher that would also yield major savings in management costs to the government. Range economists could usefully devote some of their studies to delineating public rangeland places and circumstances where these conditions would hold.

The government might institute a long-run program with the objective of purchasing much or all of the grazing rights in certain areas or geographic conditions. The price of a BLM grazing permit in the market has typically been around $50 to $100 per AUM. Given that BLM administers somewhat less than ten million AUMs, a simple calculation suggests that the total capital value of all livestock grazing permits on all BLM lands is no more than $500 million to $1 billion. By comparison the true BLM livestock grazing management costs are perhaps $100 million to $200 million per year. Hence, the present value of all future BLM administrative costs that can be largely attributable to the management of livestock grazing is probably around $2 billion—or even more, depending on the discount rate used, the method of allocation of overhead, and other considerations that affect the determination of true cost.

If domestic livestock grazing involves significant environmental costs, then the social benefits of purchasing grazing rights might be even greater. As a first step in this direction economic studies might be undertaken to assess the costs and feasibility of purchasing grazing rights in especially sensitive places such as wilderness areas and riparian zones. It might also be desirable to clarify the legal status of any private nonprofit groups that seek to retire grazing rights in environmentally sensitive areas through purchase. At present, if a rancher were to accept a payment to stop grazing in a particular area of public rangeland, the grazing rights might revert to the government. The government could then reissue the rights to another rancher for continued grazing. A private group such as the Wilderness Society thus finds itself facing legal uncertainties with respect to its ability to buy out and retire the grazing rights in a wilderness area, even if ranchers were happy to sell.

3. Recreational use of rangelands

The federal government spends more on forage production for livestock than it does on recreation and wildlife. BLM reports, however, that in 1987 there were 496.7 million "recreation hours" spent on BLM lands (most but not all of them rangelands). If these recreation hours are valued conservatively at fifty cents per hour, the total dollar value of recreation on BLM land in 1987 would approach $250 million. By comparison grazing fees returned $14.3 million; government estimates suggest a total market value of BLM grazing of perhaps $50 to $70 million. In short, recreational outputs of BLM lands may have a value of three to five times the value of livestock grazing outputs. This multiple will probably become larger in the future.

Economically, a shift in rangeland spending priorities from livestock grazing to recreation could yield a high social payoff. Studies should be undertaken of the benefits and costs of recreational improvements such as campgrounds, hiking trails, scenic overlooks, access roads, visitor centers, and other facilities that might make recreational use of BLM rangelands more accessible and enjoyable. BLM might then take a more active stance in organizing and publicizing recreational opportunities on its public rangelands.

While recreational use of public rangelands has a large total value, the amounts paid by recreational users themselves remain very low. In 1981, total BLM revenues received from recreational and wildlife uses were only $900,000, compared with total direct and indirect costs for these uses estimated at $107 million. Most recreational users of rangelands pay no fee or other charge at all.

There are a number of alternative methods of charging recreational users. One option would be to require people entering BLM rangelands to have in their possession a "public land access stamp"—something like a fishing license. Public land stamps might be sold, for example, for $10 or $20 and might be valid for a full year. In the case of campgrounds and other limited areas with well-defined entry points, recreational fees could be charged at the gate and collected directly on a per visitor basis. There are many alternative fee structures that could be followed. The National Park Service, for example, charges a flat fee per car for entry into its units for as long as a week. It would make more sense, however, to vary the total fee according to the number of adults and children in the car and the number of days of the visit. This approach would be both more equitable and result in significantly higher revenues collected. If BLM moves to impose greater charges for rangeland recreational use, it should tailor its fee structures to be flexible and responsive to actual demands.

In some cases congestion has become a problem on the public rangelands. The presence of too many hunters in a location significantly reduces the quality of the hunting experience. In some recreation areas the enjoyment of the visit is diminished by the large number of fellow visitors. Devising means of controlling levels of recreational visitation is another important economic issue for rangeland planners. Obviously, charging a price is one alternative rationing device; congestion may turn out to be the key factor in some recreation areas driving the government to collect higher fees. To be sure, such a pricing policy is sure to stimulate many complaints from people who see it as inequitable and otherwise objectionable. Charging for access to public lands is likely to be most acceptable if firm assurances can be provided that the revenues will be spent locally on the same recreation lands where the money is collected.

The Federal Land Policy and Management Act of 1976 (FLPMA) required BLM to review its lands for potential wilderness designation within fifteen years. The secretary of the interior makes recommendations to the president, who then makes his recommendations to the Congress, where the final decisions will be made. Decisions on creation of potential wilderness areas should be supported by economic studies of the values of alternative uses that might be lost. Among these, perhaps the most important—and often neglected in wilderness discussions—will be the various forms of recreational use that would be excluded by a wilderness designation.

There are occasional complaints heard from those who have physical handicaps, but the problem is much broader. If someone has to be able to walk more than five miles over a trail to enjoy an area, it will cut out a significant share of the American people. As the population ages and more people are retired and have a lot of time to travel, this consideration is likely to grow in importance.

One option would be to make greater use of land classifications that are less restrictive than wilderness that would still prohibit activities such as timber harvesting and coal mining, which threaten to reduce the quality of recreational enjoyment. Greater BLM use of classifications such as ''conservation area'' on the public rangelands might allow for a wider range of recreational uses within protected areas. Studies might be undertaken of the demographic and income characteristics expected of future wilderness users versus the most likely types of users of lands placed in other types of restrictive recreational classifications. The availability of access roads into a recreation area under a less restrictive classification than wilderness, for example, could have a major impact on the projected numbers, age, and amount of time spent by the users of the area and thus on the calculation of net social benefits under various land classification alternatives.

4. *Withdrawals and the mining law*

Large areas of public rangelands (and forests) have been withdrawn from the application of the mining law.[5] These withdrawals are typically intended to protect the environment of the area from the possibility of mining or to ensure that the land remains available for specific nonmining uses. As a result the potential discoveries that might result from mineral explorations in these areas and, statistically, the "expected" economic value from mining is foregone.

Besides the wilderness review, the Federal Land Policy and Management Act of 1976 also directed that a review of existing land withdrawals be completed within fifteen years. This review has highlighted some of the difficulties of the administration of the Mining Law of 1872, which still governs the disposition of most nonenergy or hardrock minerals on public lands. Under the mining law, if surface uses are fully protected, the mining opportunity must be lost. If the opportunity is left open for mining, then valuable surface assets may be endangered.

There is growing congressional interest in altering the mining law for this and other reasons. Many of the most important economic issues in the design of a new mining law have, however, never been adequately explored. Making a mining discovery is a lot like hitting the lottery. Even when the payoff to the lottery is far more than the price paid for the winning ticket, it obviously does not mean that the overall lottery is a bad deal for the government—even though a lot of politicians and the media seem to think that the operation of the mining law should be subject to a precisely analogous reasoning. They focus on a few big mineral discoveries—the mining law lottery winners—and ignore the much larger number of exploration failures.

Economists need to try to develop better figures on the number of mining explorations, the success rate, the average payoff, and the "expected return" to the average miner. For all we know, it could be negative, as it is for most government lotteries. There may be some good environmental reasons to change the mining law, but the financial side is essentially unknown at this time. Economists also need to delve into the full economic returns to the government from the mining law, because even without a royalty or other direct charge for mining the federal government will normally receive considerable corporate income tax payments from a mining operation—at least if any real profits exist.

Better Economic Incentives through Institutional Redesign

Public land management exhibits significant elements of the institutional immobility, rigidity, and inefficiency that have given large bureaucracies a bad name all around the world. A breakup and revitalization of public land management systems could be accomplished in a number of ways. The study of these alternatives today offers a fertile field of inquiry for rangeland economics.

1. Long-term leasing

Marion Clawson of Resources for the Future has suggested several ways to pursue long-term leasing systems for the public lands. The objective would be to create a more secure tenure and in this way stronger private incentives for efficient and prudent management by ranchers. If incentives can be devised by which most ranchers on their own initiative would want to maintain and conserve the land, the government could limit its close attention to the limited set of ranchers who—out of ignorance, desperation or some other motive—might ignore their own long-run economic interest. Economists should study experiences in the private sector or in foreign nations such as Australia that have given long-term leases on government-owned lands for livestock grazing.[6]

The objective of a more secure tenure might require considerably longer leases than the current ten-year maximum set by FLPMA. If the law were changed, rangeland leases might be issued for a period of, say, fifty years. The government might check the lease every five or ten years to ensure against serious abuses. The lease might come up for renewal in the thirty-fifth year, with a positive decision expected in the large majority of cases. Provision should be made in the lease terms for full compensation of the lessee in the event cancellation prior to lease expiration becomes necessary. Besides fairness to the rancher, the willingness to pay this compensation would serve as a useful economic test for society to ensure that a new use intended for the lands did in fact have a higher value.

Long-term leases for public rangelands might be issued as well to conservation organizations for the purpose of managing and protecting rangeland areas possessing features of special environmental sensitivity. If a conservation organization bought out an existing livestock grazing permit or lease on public rangelands, this organization should have the option to convert the lease to nongrazing status. The cumulative budget for all environmental organizations exceeds $500 million per year. A very small part of this would be sufficient to retire grazing rights over significant areas of public lands, given the modest economic value of these rights. Recreational leases might be issued to hunting and fishing clubs; livestock operators should be allowed to sell their permits to such groups or to sublease the livestock forage rights to them. Long-term rangeland leases of all kinds should include stipulations in the leases guaranteeing open access to hikers and other nonintrusive forms of ordinary dispersed recreation.

2. Contracting, cooperative management and land transfers to states

There are still other types of tenure options that could be explored. The government might sign management contracts for particular areas with ranchers, environmental groups, and other potential land managers. The contracts might set performance standards, perhaps linking future payments by the government to the level of contractor performance. The contracts could be signed for varying periods and could have varying penalties for failure to meet their terms.

Cooperative management agreements represent a related approach to rangeland management. BLM in 1984 established a program to sign cooperative agreements with ranchers of proven management skills.[7] These agreements allowed ranchers to exercise greater leeway in grazing seasons and other decisions concerning the manner of livestock grazing on BLM rangelands. More than twenty-five such agreements were signed with ranchers. An adverse court ruling and criticisms of environmental groups that BLM was giving excessive decision-making authority to ranchers, however, led to the suspension and then the abandonment of rancher cooperative agreements.

A second element of the cooperative management program involved the signing of agreements with nonprofit groups for the management of environmentally significant lands. These agreements were not affected by the court decision and BLM has continued the program, signing more than forty cooperative management agreements with recreational and environmental groups. An effort could be made to revive cooperative agreements with ranchers, and still more agreements could be signed with recreational and environmental groups.

Cooperative management agreements could also be entered into with government agencies. BLM might, for example, sign an agreement with a state government to manage an area of rangeland of particular recreational interest (perhaps as a state park). More radically, although probably within the legal authority granted by FLPMA, a state government might undertake the management of most or all the public rangelands within the state. The federal government would sign an agreement setting terms and conditions and then would limit its rangeland role to overseeing the results. Day-to-day management would be in state hands.

3. Outright sales of rangelands

Still another alternative would be to sell some public rangelands. Some existing public rangelands are already landlocked by surrounding private lands, making effective federal management difficult or impossible. Rangelands in checkerboard areas might be consolidated with private holdings. In other cases public rangelands are found on the fringes of metropolitan areas, where they may soon be valuable as sites for residential and commercial expansion. There are particularly large and valuable holdings of such lands in the Las Vegas metropolitan area, probably worth at least several hundred million dollars.

Public rangelands may also be sought in some cases for second homes, resorts, and other intensive recreational purposes. In many cases the land values in these uses would greatly exceed livestock grazing or dispersed recreation values. If a comprehensive long-run economic plan to maximize the total value of the existing public rangelands were ever actually developed, it would likely include the designation for disposal of several million acres of sites particularly attractive for second homes (or first homes, in some cases).

To be sure, such a program would probably have to overcome strong objections from the residents and owners of private lands near areas proposed for disposal. For one thing many private landowners will fear that their own land values might decline, because of the expanded supply of land for sale. They may also be worried about increased congestion and the arrival of new people, which could change the cultural environment of the community. Under current arrangements the public lands provide many rural communities at federal expense with a large area of their own rangeland "public park."

A broader plan of private sales might seek to sell some of the higher quality rangelands for continued livestock grazing use. Given the low resource value of the rangelands and the high costs that result for all concerned, the current situation of mixed government and private management of livestock grazing may be the worst of all worlds. This divided responsibility could be ended in either of two ways. As noted above, one option would be for the government to buy out the ranchers. The other option would be for the ranchers to buy out the government.

In the latter case the government should probably offer the land at a preferential price that reflects the savings in management costs to the government that would result from disposal and the need to gain the political support of ranchers. A hard-nosed economic calculation might even show that, if all the future grazing management costs to the government from the current situation are considered, the federal government might want to simply give some portions of the rangelands away free of charge to ranchers. The best choice—whether to buy out the rancher grazing rights, sell to the rancher, or give the grazing rights (maybe even the land) away for free—may be much different from one place to another.

Conclusion

Economics has historically had a small impact on public rangeland (and forest) management. This is partly because the key decision makers in rangeland controversies have not been especially interested in their economic aspects. However, it is also because economists have done a poor job of anticipating key economic policy problems and developing useful studies. Even when they have had something to say to policy makers, many economists have been unduly cautious about communicating their results for consideration in the larger policy arena.

These problems stem in part from the Progressive model. According to the precepts of scientific management, expertise and politics should be separate domains. A good professional generates scientific knowledge but is not responsible for disseminating this information to the political arena. Indeed, professional involvement in politics may even taint the professionalism of the participant. Too many economists have also sought to frame their research to fit within the comprehensive information demands of the scientific management framework of rangeland management. When comprehensive rangeland planning did not work, when scientific management proved all too often to be a utopian aspiration, the efforts of economists often went for naught. Their efforts would have been better directed toward the economics of the more narrowly defined policy questions that were likely to arise in future policy debate.

The shortage of effective leadership of economic and other professionals involved in rangeland issues has been an important contributing factor to the barrenness of our rangeland policy debates. When Interior Secretary Bruce Babbitt proposed his rangeland reforms in 1993, they were not grounded in any professional agreement that had been developing over the previous years. As the Progressive prescription for government fades from American life, it will not only be the institutions of public land management, but also our professional structures for generating expert knowledge, that will have to be rethought. These structures, no less than the public land agencies, are products of the Progressive scheme.[8]

Notes

1. U.S. Department of the Interior, Bureau of Land Management, *Rangeland Reform '94: A Proposal to Improve Management of Rangeland Ecosystems and the Administration of Livestock Grazing on Public Lands* (Washington, D.C.: August 1993).

2. See Robert H. Nelson, "Government as Theatre: Toward a New Paradigm for the Public Lands," *University of Colorado Law Review*, vol. 65, no. 2 (1994).

3. Robert H. Nelson and Gabriel Joseph, "An Analysis of Revenues and Costs of Public Land Management by the Interior Department in 13 Western States, Update to 1981," U.S. Department of the Interior, Office of Policy Analysis, (Washington, D.C.: 1982).

4. U.S. Department of Agriculture and U.S. Department of the Interior, *Grazing Fee Review and Evaluation: 1979–1985* (Washington, D.C.: 1986).

5. See John Leshy, *The Mining Law: A Study in Perpetual Motion* (Washington, D.C.: Resource for the Future, 1987).

6. John H. Holmes, "Land Tenures in the Australian Pastoral Zone: A Critical Appraisal," in I. Moffat and A. Webb, eds., *North Australian Research: Some Past Themes and New Directions* (Darwin, Northern Territory, Australia: North Australian Research Unit, 1991).

7. D. Bernard Zaleha, "The Rise and Fall of BLM's 'Cooperative Management Agreements': A Livestock Management Tool Succumbs to Judicial Scrutiny," *Environmental Law*, vol. 17, no. 1 (1986).

8. See Robert H. Nelson, "The Economics Profession and the Making of Public Policy," *Journal of Economic Literature* (March 1987).

Chapter 12

A New Mission for RPA: Improving Market Mechanisms on Public and Private Forests

The Forest and Rangeland Renewable Resources Planning Act of 1974 (RPA) prescribes what is in essence a socialist planning regime for an economic sector that is embedded in a market economy. Indeed, Congress seems to have given little consideration to the possibility that central planning in a market context might be largely meaningless. Congress perceived, correctly enough, that public land management has many major failings. Its motives in enacting RPA probably were not much more complicated than that; since the progressive era, for the faithful of the Progressive gospel, the conduct of comprehensive planning has symbolized the hope for a more rational world.

As products themselves of Progressive thinking, the Forest Service and other public land agencies have been reluctant to inform Congress of the error of its ways. To do so might raise questions about the very Progressive grounds for the existence of these agencies. Although little may come of all the planning now mandated by law, it is better simply to go ahead and do it. This planning is, the public land agencies understand, a necessary part of the ritual of establishing social legitimacy for agency actions in the U.S. political system.

Thus, most of what the Forest Service has done under the require-

This chapter is a revised and shortened version of a chapter originally published as "Improving Market Mechanisms in U.S. Forestry," in Clark S. Binkley, Garry S. Brewer, and V. Alaric Sample, eds., *Redirecting the RPA—Proceedings of the 1987 Airlie House Conference on the Resource Planning Act*, Bulletin 95, Yale School of Forestry and Environmental Studies (New Haven, Conn.: 1988).

ments of RPA has been of little use to decision makers. There is not much to be done with a projection of total national recreational user-days thirty years from now. The planning allocation of some share of this demand specifically to the national forests is not much more helpful.

Perhaps the best answer is to repeal RPA. Another possibility is to think more carefully about what it can mean to do government planning in a market system. This chapter describes how RPA could be transformed to become an instrument for improving the workings of the market mechanism on the forest lands of the United States.

RPA and Markets

In implementing RPA one of the questions asked is the role that private sources can play in meeting RPA calculations of future forest outputs in the United States. The very nature of the question suggests that the private sector is to be treated as another planned source of forest supply, along with federal lands and any other forest owners. Private suppliers are regarded in essence as one more factor to be entered into a set of central planning calculations to ensure that total U.S. forest production requirements are met.

This very approach must be rejected, however, in light of the lessons learned about central planning over the years. Typical liabilities have included a difficulty for planners in keeping up with rapidly changing events; poor coordination between central plans and developments in the field; supply-demand projections that soon prove erroneous; and the susceptibility of plan contents to political manipulation. Many central plans have been rapidly outdated and have ended up being ignored.

By contrast the market provides a more incremental, flexible, and decentralized process for bringing supply and demand into a satisfactory balance. In a market system there is no push to achieve any predetermined output levels. The outputs are simply learned after the fact; it is expected that they will often differ significantly from any earlier projections that might have been used by businessmen, government planners, and other interested parties.

In the 1980s and 1990s there has in fact been a worldwide trend toward experimentation with use of market methods, even where a resource such as a forest may remain in public ownership. The *New York Times* reported that:

It seems that no matter where you look, governments have been turning to market mechanisms—Adam Smith's ingenious invisible hand—to pep up their economies. Economists say there is unusual agreement . . . about the importance of giving freer rein to the market: that overarching mechanism that helps articulate consumer desires, encourages inventiveness and disciplines inefficient producers.

"In remarkably different circumstances, people are learning that one can make market systems work in very useful ways," said Charles Lindblom, a Yale University political economist and author of *Politics and Markets*.

[Nations] have been looking for ways to reinvigorate their economies and avoid the kind of painful stagnation that marked much of the 1970's. They are straining as well to increase efficiency in reaction to greater worldwide competitive pressures. And they are also recognizing that central planning does not work as well once countries achieve a basic level of industrial development.[1]

Instead of its current central planning approach, the mission of RPA could be reoriented to address ways in which the market mechanism could be used in U.S. forestry. Market methods can function in the context not only of privately owned but also publicly owned U.S. forests. Indeed, although the United States is regarded around the world as a land of private ownership and free markets, U.S. forestry is an anomaly in this regard. Almost 40 percent of U.S. forest land is owned by the federal government, and federal forests contain more than 50 percent of the existing U.S. inventory of softwood timber.

The most direct way to introduce market incentives into the management of public forests would be to sell them. Sales might be limited to the commercially most productive and profitable public forests that would justify the most sophisticated forestry practices and bring the highest prices to the government. This option may be rejected for a number of reasons, however, including its political infeasibility.

The federal government could still employ the market mechanism on government-owned forests in a variety of ways. Instead, current Forest Service planning for the national forests usually goes out of its way to ignore market forces. For example, timber harvest levels are driven by the "even-flow" requirement, which is determined entirely by the physical inventories of timber available on a forest. The market for timber could be booming or it could be collapsing, and it would not make any difference for Forest Service timber sales in an even-flow regime. The age of trees that may be harvested is set according to the requirement for maximizing the physical volume of wood over future years, ignoring the discount rate and any economic consideration of the age at which the value of timber might be maximized.

Equally troublesome, the Forest Service often does not allow its lessees and permittees to respond to market forces. Indeed, on all the public lands the federal government typically imposes conditions on its lease holders that are specifically designed to override market incentives. For example, under the Mineral Leasing Act of 1920 and its amendments, leases to explore for and produce oil and gas, coal, and other federal minerals typically contain a "diligent development" requirement. Whatever the market might say, this requirement directs that a lessee begin production within some designated period (often ten years) or forfeit the lease. The law requires that federal coal lessees achieve "maximum economic recovery," whatever the market might say about the marginal profitability of a coal seam. Similarly, timber sales on the national forests and on BLM forests require in almost all cases that the purchaser must harvest the timber within a limited period (not the same for all sales, but no more than seven years).

A philosophy of improving the workings of markets for timber, coal, and other resources on public lands could loosen or eliminate restrictions of these kinds. It would amount not to abandoning planning, but to a different form of government planning. Rather than overriding the market with direct commands and controls, the government would instead redirect its efforts to planning an institutional framework that better permits the market to function.

To be sure, the market does not accomplish all tasks. Information, for example, represents a particular problem for market incentives. Even though some forms of information may be very valuable to many people, the inability to establish an effective property right to information of wide interest may frustrate its private production and distribution. Hence, government involvement may be especially needed in areas such as the collection of broad market data and basic research. It is also true, of course, that the market does not take into account many environmental impacts. Market failings may justify government regulatory involvement, assuming that the government intervention does not itself create greater problems—an assumption that has come to be questioned more frequently in recent years.

The following sections briefly describe steps that might be taken to improve the workings of the market for specific types of forest resources and outputs.

Improving Timber Markets

Subsidized production of natural resources is an old and honorable American tradition. The oil and gas industry for many years benefited from depletion allowances, tax rules for drilling expenses, and other government favors—and still does, if to a lesser degree. The tax advantages to the timber industry are less well known but have also contributed significantly to the profitability of the industry. Another form of government aid is the imposition of tariffs directed against Canadian timber imports, designed to prevent cheap lumber from Canada from undercutting American prices. Abolishing both the income tax and tariff advantages of the timber industry would represent one step toward improving the workings of U.S. forest product markets.

Federal lands have contributed to the support of the timber industry through the practice in many areas of selling timber at prices well below the cost to federal agencies of holding the sales. Eliminating below-cost timber sales would mean that the Forest Service would behave more like an ordinary market participant. It would improve the allocation of public funds within the Forest Service and the economic efficiency with which overall U.S. forest resources were being used. It would also have significant environmental benefits.

The procedures for the sale of federal timber could be redesigned to let market forces have greater impact. For example, the requirements specifying that the timber must be harvested within a certain number of years may be necessary as long as sale payments to the Forest Service are largely deferred until the harvest time and no interest is charged. As a result, without a diligent harvest requirement, the optimal bidding strategy might be to bid very high and then wait until timber prices at some point reach a level high enough to justify the original bid.

If, however, the government were to charge an appropriate rate of interest for any timber sale amounts owed during the interim period between the sale and the harvest, diligence requirements would lose much of their economic justification.[2] If these requirements were abandoned altogether for public timber sales while market interest rates were charged, private timber companies could be given much greater leeway in deciding when they should harvest the public timber they had purchased. Since they could hold federal timber supplies for longer periods, it would be possible for timber companies to accumulate a larger timber inventory. This would permit a closer coordination of their private forest and mill investment decisions with future harvesting opportunities on public lands.

There has been a great deal of discussion over the years that the market works poorly with respect to private forest lands in nonindustrial ownerships. The main problem has been perceived to be a lack of information among nonindustrial owners, many of whom possess only small areas of forest land. These owners may not be aware of regeneration, fertilization, thinning, and other forestry practices that could significantly increase the yields from their lands. They may not even be aware of their own volumes of timber, market prices, and the revenues they could earn from selling timber. Since nonindustrial forests represent about 60 percent of the commercial forest area, any major improvements in the workings of this market could make a significant contribution to U.S. forestry.

Many nonindustrial owners, however, may regard their forest as a consumption item rather than a production item. Given the small size of many nonindustrial holdings, the dissemination of timber market information to widely dispersed owners could itself be costly enough to make the effort economically questionable. Moreover, if private timber owners need better information, there are private mechanisms, such as private contracts signed by nonindustrial owners with timber management advisors and agents, that could serve this purpose.

In a comprehensive study of this issue Marion Clawson offered the conclusion that "the scale of programs aimed specifically at the nonindustrial private forests has been small and questions may well be raised about their effectiveness and their rationale." Without any special new efforts, Clawson found that "non-industrial private forest owners are indeed responsive to prices and that their timber output will increase in the future if wood prices continue to rise."[3]

Improving Recreation Markets

The development of the institutions of a market is itself partly a response to economic forces.[4] A market mechanism involves legal and other costs for enforcing property rights and charging prices. These costs of a market may be justified only when potential prices and profits reach a high enough level. The United States is only now reaching this point with respect to a number of forms of dispersed recreation. As Neil Sampson has said:

What we must do . . . is create new institutional ways for farmers, foresters and landowners to be able to deal with the "people" aspects of recreational use. If owners incur costs, and recreation users reap benefits, there has to be a way for the users to repay the owners, or there simply will not be the amount of recreation that would otherwise be possible. We pride ourselves in this country on our ability to let the free market regulate most of our activities, but this is one [place] where we have not yet invented a market mechanism in many places, and we need to encourage that.[5]

One of the main obstacles to private provision of forest recreation is the fear of legal liability, the threat of high damage awards, and the consequent high cost of insurance. The President's Commission on the American Outdoors reported that "as we held hearings across the country, we heard time and again about the liability crisis. In 1985–1986, liability premiums for recreational providers skyrocketed 200–300 percent—sometimes more."[6] Many states have statutes that seek to protect landowners from lawsuits but only if they do not impose any fees or charges on entrants to their lands. Such laws constitute a major obstacle to the development of private recreational markets.

Many private forest owners have parcels that are too small by themselves for the most enjoyable recreational use. If they joined with other nearby forest owners, however, they might be able to pool their lands to create a recreational unit of an efficient size. Such pooling may require the formation of new cooperative, partnership, or other legal pooling mechanisms, as well as the dissemination of information to landowners concerning the availability of such mechanisms. It might be regarded as a form of recreational land condominium. Just as the joining of many housing units to form a single condominium management unit had to await the availability of appropriate legal mechanisms, so might the availability of new recreational legal arrangements spur wider recreational provision for private profit.

Use of market mechanisms often depends on the existence of enforceable property rights. Government in some cases, however, actively intervenes to block such rights. For example, some states grant automatic public access even to small rivers and streams for fishing, denying property owners the ability to protect the fishery. Excessive fishing and severe depletion of stocks has resulted in some areas. It may be appropriate, especially for smaller streams, to allow landowners full control over fishing access and to charge fishermen for use of these areas.

In Texas the great majority of hunting has for some time been for fee on private lands. Nationwide, however, only 3.1 percent of the land available for hunting in 1980 involved the payment of a fee.[7] Forty-four percent of all hunting land in the United States was public, while 53 percent was private land that did not involve a fee.

Further growth of fee hunting on private forests would be encouraged by providing a more secure property right. Farmers need to know that, if they invest in improvements for wildlife habitat, they will be able to capture some of the benefits of increased wildlife numbers. State wildlife laws may need to be revised to allow landowners greater flexibility in determining when hunters can come on their land and the levels of hunting after owners have invested their private funds to improve wildlife habitat and numbers. Ross Shelton reports that "an extended consistent marketing season plus flexibility in harvest would greatly improve landowners' incentives as well as their prospects of being successful with wildlife enterprises."[8] Tighter and more vigorous enforcement of trespass laws is also a key factor.

New markets for forest recreation may depend on appropriate policies in the public forests as well. Where federal and private forest lands are intermingled, cooperative public-private arrangements to allow fee hunting could be developed. Because some private landowners effectively control access to national forest lands, they might be allowed to charge for this access in return for some sharing of the payments with the federal government or in return for habitat improvements or other public benefits.

Federal agencies have been slow to make public forest land available for intensive recreational uses. Approval of new ski facilities has become a very time-consuming and expensive process in the national forests. Obtaining public land to build a mountain hotel or other resort facility is difficult if not impossible. Use of public forests for second homes is severely constrained. Yet an economic calculation would show in many cases that intensive recreation would have use values in limited areas greatly exceeding those of any other uses of the national forests in these areas.

Improving Livestock Forage Markets

The market for livestock forage on national forest lands is highly imperfect. Because of long historic use and government acceptance, owners of private ranches have acquired de facto private rights to graze their cattle and sheep on particular parcels of national forest. If ownership of property consists of the possession of a bundle of rights, as it is often asserted, one might even say that public ownership of the forage resource of the national forests is a misnomer. Much like split private ownership of surface and subsurface estates, the Forest Service grazing lands also involve a form of split ownership: private possession of certain grazing rights and public (or nongrazing private) possession of other surface rights.

The private grazing rights to the national forests, however, are subject to all kinds of limitations and conditions on their transfer. The Forest Service, for example, acts to limit or prevent altogether subleasing of grazing rights. Subleasing could bring prices as high as $10 or more per AUM. The willingness of the current permit holder to sublease shows that a potential acquirer of the sublease places a higher value on the grazing opportunity. By preventing subleasing the government is in effect requiring that the forage resources of the national forests must be used inefficiently.

Improvements in forage markets on public lands could involve the elimination of various restrictions on trading in grazing rights.[9] Some possibilities in this regard include:

1. Grazing permits to public forests could be transferrable to environmental groups, hunting clubs, and any other party willing to pay the necessary price to purchase them from a rancher. In practice this would mean dropping the use-it-or-lose-it provisions that are traditional to public land grazing. It would allow, for example, the Wilderness Society to buy out grazing rights from willing ranchers in order to retire grazing in national forest wilderness areas.

2. Ranchers or other holders of national forest grazing permits could be allowed to sublease grazing rights to another rancher, an environmental group, a hunting club, or any other party willing to pay an attractive price. There should not be any government surcharge or other restriction on subleasing, in order to encourage the use of grazing lands by the party that can generate the greatest benefit from the use of the lands as shown in practice by the maximum willingness to pay for this use.

3. Ranchers could be allowed to convert livestock AUMs to wildlife AUMs. They might do this, for example, in a case where the rancher converted his operation from primarily livestock to primarily fee hunting. Or a hunting club might purchase a ranch outright and convert its existing public and private forage resources to hunting use. In such cases there would continue to be a grazing

fee, but the fee would be collected on wildlife use of the forage, not livestock use. Collecting revenues for wildlife forage use would be partly a matter of equity and partly a matter of creating financial incentives for public land agencies to support conversions from livestock to wildlife forage use.

4. Any requirements to possess "base property" in order to hold a grazing right on public lands could be eliminated.

5. Public land managers could encourage state "game ranching" and other state programs that allow ranchers to participate in the financial returns from hunting on intermingled private and public forest lands.

Conclusion

The implementation of RPA has been based on a central planning framework. Future national demands for timber, recreation, livestock forage, and other goods and services available from forests and rangelands are to be projected. Supplies are similarly to be projected. In this economic framework the private sector is treated as one element in the total supply picture. Reflecting an outlook dating as far back as Gifford Pinchot's days as chief of the Forest Service, the government role prescribed by RPA is to look for ways to ensure that future total supplies, including private supplies, will come up to the level of total projected demand.

In the 1980s and 1990s, however, countries all over the world that had previously been following such central planning approaches have rejected them as simplistic and infeasible. They have concluded that central planning cannot develop all the information needed and cannot keep up with events, especially in a rapidly changing world economy. Instead, planners have looked to the market as a decentralized, more flexible, and more rapidly adjusting framework for making economic decisions. Economic planners themselves have redirected their efforts, devoting fewer of their own resources to production and consumption forecasts and instead focusing their planning on devising new institutions to create greater market freedom and otherwise to make the market mechanism work more effectively. In many cases this means outright privatization of government businesses and other assets. It is also possible, however, to improve market incentives in the context of public resource ownership.

In the United States the RPA process should be redirected in this fashion, if RPA is not to be repealed altogether. Instead of central planning any continuing version of RPA should focus on planning new and better means of using market methods in private and public U.S. forests. This will require major changes in the way the Forest Service has traditionally approached its planning task. It would be ironic, however, if the United States—known as the leading market economy in the world—should now fall behind even some former communist and socialist nations in studying and applying the use of market methods for public resources.

Notes

1. Steven Greenhouse, "The Global March to Free Markets," *The New York Times*, 19 July 1987: F1.

2. See Robert H. Nelson and Randal R. Rucker, "Federal Timber Sale Procedures: The Need for Reform," *Western Journal of Applied Forestry* (January 1987); also Robert H. Nelson, "Mythology Instead of Analysis: The Story of Public Forest Management," in Robert T. Deacon and M. Bruce Johnson, eds., *Forestlands: Public and Private* (San Francisco: Pacific Institute for Public Policy Research, 1985).

3. Marion Clawson, *The Economics of Non-industrial Private Forests* (Washington, D.C.: Resources for the Future, 1979): 12, 11.

4. Terry L. Anderson and P. J. Hill, "From Free Grass to Fences: Transforming the Commons of the American West," in Garrett Hardin and John Baden, eds., *Managing the Commons* (New York: W. H. Freeman, 1977).

5. Quoted in *The Report of the President's Commission: American Outdoors, the Legacy, the Challenge* (Washington, D.C.: Island Press, 1987): 200.

6. *Ibid.*: 209.

7. John R. Stoll, Christine Sellar, and Rod Ziemer, "Analysis of the 1980 National Survey of Fishing, Hunting, and Wildlife Associated Recreation—Report No. 4: Recreational Use of Public vs. Privately Owned Lands for Hunting," prepared for the U.S. Fish and Wildlife Service (Washington, D.C.: August 1985).

8. Ross Shelton, "Fee Hunting Systems and Important Factors in Wildlife Commercialization on Public Lands," in Daniel J. Decker and Gary R. Hoff, eds., *Valuing Wildlife: Economic and Social Perspectives* (Boulder, Colo.: Westview Press, 1987): 113.

9. B. Delworth Gardner, "A Proposal to Reduce Misallocation of Livestock Grazing Permits," *Journal of Farm Economics* (February 1963).

Chapter 13

One-Third of the Nation's Coal: Planning a Market for Federal Coal Leasing

Coal reserves found west of the Mississippi River represent more than 50 percent of U.S. coal,[1] of which the federal government owns around 60 percent. As recently as 1967 total federal coal production in the United States was only seven million tons, representing a mere 1 percent of total U.S. production. Following the OPEC oil shocks of the 1970s, however, western and midwestern utilities increasingly turned to coal for electric power generation. Western coal was attractive because much of it is low in sulfur content, in some cases enabling utilities to meet federal air quality standards without installing expensive sulfur scrubbing equipment. By 1993 production of federal coal had climbed to the point that it was supplying about 30 percent of total U.S. production.

As it became apparent in the 1970s that federal coal would be supplying a significant share of U.S. coal output in the near future, a fierce battle erupted for control over its development. Several major lawsuits, one of which reached the Supreme Court, were filed by environmental groups opposing federal coal development or seeking major changes in its management. Indeed, the stalemate in federal coal policy proved so difficult to resolve that most new federal coal leasing was effectively suspended from May 1971 to January 1981. Federal coal production

This chapter is a slightly revised version of an article originally published as "Planning a Market for Federal Coal Leasing," *Natural Resources Journal* (July 1983). The coauthor of that article was Donald Bieniewicz of the Office of Policy Analysis in the U.S. Department of the Interior.

could grow rapidly during this period only because many new federal coal leases had been sold by the federal government to coal mining companies in the 1960s. While many policy issues were debated, the greatest controversy concerned the appropriate role of market forces in shaping the future development of federal coal.[2]

A Market Solution

In the private coal market the pressures of competition tend to promote development of lower cost deposits ahead of higher cost deposits.[3] Despite considerable popular belief to the contrary market forces in the form of speculation also act to promote conservation of coal resources for the future. Speculation might aptly be characterized as ''private conservation''; it provides a mechanism whereby future generations can pay current resource owners to conserve the resource.[4] Market processes also tend to put each coal deposit in the hands of the particular producer who values it most highly and can use it most efficiently. Competition among users of coal similarly acts to ensure that the output of a particular deposit is likely to be purchased by the electric utility or other user that values it most highly. Total national resources employed in coal production are then determined by the competitiveness of coal in the market compared with other energy resources or with conservation alternatives.

Until 1971 the federal government leased coal with few controls to any private party requesting the coal. Partly for lack of federal attention the location and pace of development of federal coal was left to private initiative and the pressures of the marketplace. However, this de facto system—it was never explicitly adopted—could not survive the environmental challenges of the 1970s. Moreover, it was incompatible in many ways with the statutory authority under which federal leasing was supposed to take place.

Critics of federal leasing rightly claimed that the market did not take into account many external impacts of coal development. In legislative and administrative actions in the 1970s the federal government tried to respond by adopting various regulatory measures to protect the environment.[5] The most important was the enactment in 1977 of the Surface Mining Control and Reclamation Act.[6] In another important step the Interior Department in 1979 established twenty ''unsuitability criteria,'' which specified circumstances in which federal coal leasing would not be permitted for environmental reasons.[7]

These actions, however, did not satisfy all the objections to a market solution. Large-scale coal development is highly disruptive to the social environment and generally threatens people in the area with a loss of control over their lives. Such forces create strong demands for greater insulation from change, primarily by means of government control and planning of coal development.[8] While such control could in theory be exercised by regulatory mechanisms, many barriers to effective public control over use of privately owned property exist. Some westerners perceive, probably correctly, that their ability to influence the federal government is greater than their ability to control market forces. Through such influence the real costs of redirecting coal development can be shifted onto national taxpayers, who may barely notice these costs. In contrast, if those costs were to be borne at the state level, they would be absorbed by a much smaller group of people, who would be more aware of them.

Full reliance on the market also requires that natural resource holders be able to capture the value gains derived from conservation of the resource—that is, that they be allowed to speculate. Some market critics oppose speculation in principle as morally offensive. Others, however, contend—if only implicitly in most cases—that the returns from speculation are unduly high. Due to high private risk aversion or other reasons, society concedes too much of the value of the resource as payment for the resource conservation service performed by the private speculator. In effect this view argues that it is less expensive for society to perform the speculative function itself through government.

The specific means by which the government sought to eliminate private speculative incentives in the case of federal coal was the diligent development requirement under the Mineral Leasing Act of 1920.[9] However, the act's general requirement for diligent development of leases was not enforced for many years. The Federal Coal Leasing Amendments Act of 1976 eliminated the uncertainty regarding the diligent development requirement by expressly requiring that future coal leases be brought into production within ten years of lease issuance.[10] In the presence of this requirement leasing of more coal than the market can absorb will result in various distortions of normal market workings. In the extreme a company might even open a mine and stockpile the coal, simply to avoid losing the lease for lack of development. As a result the government faces strong pressures to lease only the amount of coal that can be produced in the near term.

Central Planning for Federal Coal

Although the Nixon and Ford administrations sought to employ market approaches, congressional and judicial pressures were moving toward a much more direct government role. In 1977 the Carter administration initiated a system of central planning for federal coal development. This effort occurred in conjunction with a wider trend toward national planning throughout the U.S. energy sector, which was reflected in the creation of the Department of Energy (DOE).

The new coal program developed by the Carter administration began with DOE calculation of individual production goals for each of twelve coal regions of the United States. In six of these regions federal coal was a major part of the total coal resource. Similar to RPA procedures in forestry, the production goals were to be set for five and ten years in the future and were to include both nonfederal and federal coal. Following calculation of the DOE goals, the Interior Department would next estimate the total production (nonfederal and federal) already planned or otherwise likely to occur in each region five and ten years in the future. This production was assumed to require no further federal coal leasing. If the already planned level of production fell short of the production goal, new federal leasing would be indicated. The specific level of leasing would then depend on Interior estimates of the appropriate nonfederal and federal shares in meeting any projected production shortfalls. Finally, the Interior Department would have to select the best federal coal tracts to lease.

The Carter administration recognized that some uncertainties would arise in making such estimates. In hindsight, however, it seems fair to say that the uncertainties were substantially underestimated by Interior officials, at least initially.[11] As part of the plan for federal coal leasing, separate sets of regional coal production goals were prepared by DOE in 1978, 1979, and 1980. This effort yielded rapidly shifting production goals, providing evidence of the difficulties in central coal planning. In an admittedly extreme example the 1990 DOE production goal for the San Juan River coal region in New Mexico equaled fifty-eight million tons when calculated in 1978, dropped all the way to seventeen million tons in 1979, and then rose back to fifty-seven million tons in 1980, all based on the assumptions considered most likely. The 1990 DOE goal set for the key Powder River coal region was calculated at 396 million tons in 1978, rose slightly to 418 million tons in 1979, and then fell sharply to 294 million tons in 1980.[12]

Detailed information is required to calculate accurate production goals for individual coal regions. For example, coal production for the Powder River coal region depends in part on demands from states to the east, such as Wisconsin. The government would need to know how much Powder River coal would be purchased by Wisconsin utilities at various prices. This knowledge in turn would require information on the cost of alternative coal supplies, such as Kentucky or Illinois coal, or alternative energy sources such as nuclear or gas power generation for Wisconsin. The potential for conservation of electric power as power prices rise would be a further important factor. Different transportation and environmental protection costs would affect the desirability in Wisconsin of each alternative.

Moreover, coal prices would not hold steady, but would change as the amounts of coal supplied from each region varied or as the costs of factor inputs into coal production varied. Such information would be required for hundreds if not thousands of other places and circumstances. Any major changes in one part of the system would require a recalculation to take into account interactive effects throughout the rest of the system as well. While such a system can be simulated with the use of high-speed computers, the results tend to be unreliable, especially at a high level of disaggregation.

By the end of Carter's tenure even many of the original proponents of national energy planning in the administration harbored serious doubts. Due in part to the seeming uncertainty in the planning process, actual selection of leasing levels tended to be informed more by considerations of administrative capacity to lease than by central planning calculations.

In seeking more realistic approaches to development of federal coal resources, the Carter coal program gradually shifted toward greater use of market mechanisms. The Reagan administration accelerated this trend. The movement was not toward a free market as such, but toward what might better be called a ''planned'' market.

Because market outcomes do not always correspond to social goals, economists have sought ways of redirecting the market without undermining its basic productive efficiency. While public opinion could change in the future, the political process thus far has clearly dictated that private gains from speculation in federal coal should be minimized. The government is thus constrained by a requirement that it lease only that amount of federal coal that can be developed promptly, given construction lead times and other mechanics for commencing mine production. Some additional coal leasing may be necessary simply to facilitate the assembly of minable properties sufficient for advance commitment of coal reserves to meet utility plans.

The diligent development requirement thus creates a tradeoff between equity and efficiency. An attempt to eliminate even short-term speculative holdings of federal coal would eliminate necessary flexibility in the system and generate large national efficiency losses. Hence, a more pragmatic aim is to prevent only long-term speculation, however it may be defined. Lessees can hold on to federal coal for shorter periods, even while not producing. The length of the permissible holding period will depend on social preferences in trading off distributional impacts versus efficiency of national coal use.

Assuming some social resolution, a planned-market philosophy would seek to implement the tradeoff with a minimum of interference with the underlying market mechanism. Keeping this goal in mind, economists in the Interior Department's Office of Policy Analysis over the years have formulated two basic market plans for federal coal leasing.

Market Plan 1: Intertract Competition

A new design for federal coal leasing was first proposed in 1975 by C. B. McGuire, a Berkeley professor who at the time was on leave to the Office of Policy Analysis. Under this plan the government would first determine how much coal should be leased, preventing large-scale speculative holdings. Government, however, would not determine which specific tracts to lease. Instead, within a sale region all or most tracts deemed suitable for coal development would be put up for bid. Then only the specific tracts receiving the highest bids on a per-ton basis would be leased, up to the specified target leasing level. McGuire called this leasing approach "intertract competition."[13] Separate intertract sales would be held for metallurgical coal and possibly for synthetic coal or other sufficiently differentiated coal types.

McGuire was most concerned with the likely failure of traditional sale methods "to yield a revenue near to true value of the land under optimal exploitation."[14] He noted that bidding competition for individual coal tracts was apt to be weak because there were a great number of potential coal mining tracts, each of which tended to be of interest to a single firm. Bidding competition could be significantly enhanced, however, by putting firms in a position in which they would have to compete with bidders for other tracts as well, in other words, by creating intertract competition.

Interior analysts soon recognized that intertract competition might be equally useful as a tract selection mechanism.[15] Typically, far more coal tracts are available for lease than the government desires to see leased. Without use of a market mechanism the government would have to examine all the potentially leasable tracts and then decide which ones have the highest overall value. The government would be required to make extensive calculations of selling prices for different-quality coal and of the costs of mining and transporting coal at the various potential sites. Under intertract competition, however, coal companies would make such calculations and reflect them in the prices they bid for each lease. A market mechanism in the form of bidding competition among tracts thus selects the most valuable specific deposits to lease, that is, those that receive the highest bids.

The market created through intertract competition would be similar in some respects to the private market for coal supply contracts. In that private market the contracts signed by utilities in any particular year are limited in number, and coal suppliers compete for them. Some utilities ask potential suppliers to submit bids on the price per ton the firm would accept to deliver coal of a specified quality. The supplier making the lowest bid wins the contract. Similarly, in intertract competition the firms pursuing the best federal coal tracts could afford to bid the highest prices per ton and thus win their respective coal leases. Both procedures tend to select appropriate coal sites and obtain appropriate coal prices; both represent use of a selection mechanism that is natural to market processes.

What amounts to a form of intertract competition—although not called that by that name—has been successfully employed to sell Treasury bills. In Treasury Department auctions bills have been sold to the bidders making the lowest-yield offers, up to the total number of bills to be sold as set by the Treasury. The principal difference between Treasury sales and intertract sales is that the bills being sold are identical whereas federal coal tracts are not. Some people have in fact suggested taking intertract bids on a fully standardized tonnage basis, with all tracts adjusted for coal quality differences and mining costs. This procedure, however, would negate many of the tract-selection benefits of intertract competition. Intertract competition is designed to select low-cost tracts in much the same way that a government-established system of marketable pollution permits would select the firms able to reduce emissions at least cost.

Intertract competition has yet to be tested in practice, although the Interior Department had decided to do so in the April 1982 coal lease sale in the Powder River Basin. Intertract competition was to be used to lease two from among four available tracts located near Ashland,

Montana. The regional coal team had ranked the four tracts as having very similar environmental and socioeconomic impacts. In the end, the test could not be undertaken because three of the tracts did not qualify for the sale because of surface owner consent problems. A precedent had been set, however, in that intertract competition had been chosen over administrative tract selection in a portion of a scheduled federal coal lease sale.

Intertract bidding competition has several drawbacks. There is some loss of social control over noneconomic factors related to coal development. It can be argued, however, that the major externalities associated with coal development have been internalized by surface mining laws and other environmental protection measures. Remaining environmental costs could also be accounted for by subtracting estimates of these costs from company bids for each tract and then selecting for lease those tracts with the highest net bids (i.e., the amount bid minus the environmental cost estimate). Some commentators have also been concerned that under intertract competition companies face greater uncertainty about the prospects of winning a tract; in general their bidding calculations become more complex. This problem can be reduced by using oral bidding for sales in intertract competition as the Interior Department planned to do in the Montana sale.

In intertract sales the government must still decide on the appropriate amount of coal to lease. This task is itself amenable to a market approach that Interior analysts called the inventory method. The government would first lease a large enough inventory of federal coal reserves to provide wide competition for upcoming coal supply contracts. The goal might be to lease enough coal to meet coal needs for new coal supply contracts expected to be signed over the next seven to ten years. The trigger for new leasing, once an acceptable inventory level had been reached, would be a drawdown of the inventory as new coal supply contracts were signed. This approach would rely on direct observation of the absorption of federal coal leases in the market to signal the need for new leasing.

The government has in fact already been making its leasing decisions in much this way. Past leasing controversies have often concerned the size of the appropriate inventory. A formal and explicit recognition of this approach should spur more analysis and better understanding of inventory requirements.

The initial buildup of the inventory should also be carefully calculated. Holding several small intertract sales, perhaps spaced several months apart, would probably be better than attempting to establish the full inventory in a single sale. Each small sale would provide useful feedback about the demand for additional reserves and the need for further sales. This strategy would also reduce the range of value among the tracts leased in each sale and thus tend to provide more competitive, higher bids overall.

While intertract competition will make the final tract selection from the eligible set, the government must still determine the tracts in this latter category. Each potential tract must be evaluated to determine the environmental acceptability for leasing, which can be a costly exercise. A market mechanism can be employed in this undertaking as well, however. Companies could be requested to nominate tracts for inclusion in a lease sale but would be required to pay a fee for each nomination. If the tract were actually leased, the winning bidder would be required to reimburse the initial nominator for his fee. Charging a nominations fee equal to the administrative cost of evaluating each nomination would recover the costs to the government, as well as induce firms to focus nominations on tracts that actually have a good chance of being leased.[16]

Postponing environmental and other tract evaluation until after the intertract auction (but still prior to final lease issuance) would be another way to reduce tract evaluation costs. After the auction only those tracts receiving high bids would be evaluated. If this evaluation revealed unacceptable environmental or other consequences, the tract would not be leased and another tract would instead be leased. Bids thus would be accepted contingent on acceptable results of later environmental studies.

Market Plan 2: A Uniform Minimum Price System

Under intertract competition government sets the quantity of coal to be leased and a market mechanism then determines the minimum price required to obtain a coal lease. The alternative would be to set a minimum price and then let this price determine the amount of coal leased in the market. Operationally, government would simply make all or most environmentally acceptable tracts available for lease. Any high bid for a tract that was above the minimum price would be accepted. Separate minimum prices would be set for metallurgical coal or any other special uses for which coal types cannot be substituted.

If the intertract approach is similar to a system of marketable pollution permits, then the price control approach is similar to a system of emission fees. Either strategy is capable of controlling leasing/pollution levels. In fact, in a world of perfect knowledge and zero transactions costs the results would be essentially the same under a quantity or a price control strategy. Which approach is actually preferable must be determined based on administrative feasibility and cost, information requirements, and political acceptability, as well as the cost of resultant leasing/pollution levels that are too low or too high.

The pressure for more rapid mineral leasing led to some use of price control methods in federal leasing of oil and gas on the outer continental shelf (OCS). Around 1970 the minimum bid was set at $25 per acre, or $125,000 for a standard five-thousand acre OCS tract. In 1982 the Interior Department initiated a new policy of "area wide" sales of much greater size. Concurrently, the minimum bid was raised to $150 per acre, or $750,000 for a typical tract. The department explained that "the program will make more acreage available for leasing . . . and will use the market mechanism rather than government decisions to select areas for lease and exploration."[17]

The Interior Department also made a limited move toward a price control method in federal coal leasing. In 1982 the department raised the minimum bid for federal coal leases from $25 an acre to $100 an acre—an action unlikely, however, to create an effective screen for identification of high-value coal sites. Although $100 an acre is a high price for thin-seamed eastern coal, it is quite low for much thicker-seamed western coal.

The appropriate minimum price per ton could be set in several ways. For example, the minimum could based on observation of prices paid in private sales of prime leases or could be set via application of exhaustible resource theory to estimate the size of the present-worth economic rents of coal near its optimal time of leasing. Alternatively, the minimum price could be identified by the lowest bid accepted in an intertract sale, where quantity control is used to set the appropriate leasing level, or by holding a series of small sales, starting with a rather high minimum price per ton and reducing it in each further sale until a leasing level deemed appropriate is reached. Once an inventory of leases is in place, the minimum price could simply be adjusted for changes in the inventory. If the inventory tends to exceed the level desired, the price should be raised. Conversely, if the inventory is too low, the price should be reduced.

A mixture of approaches may in fact be desirable. It is likely for political reasons that tight controls over levels of leasing will be preferred for initial establishment of a suitable inventory of federal leases available for new production. Once that inventory is built up, however, a switch to a pricing strategy would offer some significant advantages. Simply leasing to anyone willing to pay the minimum price would allow reduced administrative effort and provide much faster response time to company coal needs. Such leasing would be drawn from a base of tracts already determined to be environmentally acceptable for development.

The old preference-right leasing system abandoned in the 1970s was similar to this proposed system, although limited to "unexplored" coal regions.[18] This system's main shortcoming was that it used in effect a zero price and thus was incapable of controlling leasing levels during a time of rapidly rising coal resource values.

One means of charging a part of the minimum price would be to include a requirement for payment of an annual rental equal to some percentage of the lease bonus. Thus, for a valuable western lease that obtained a bonus of say $4,000 per acre, a 1-percent ($40 an acre) annual rental might be required, as compared with $3 an acre at present. Such a rental would create a disincentive to speculative lease holdings, provide a steady revenue stream to the states in which federal coal is located, and make it easier for small firms to compete with large firms in bidding for federal coal.

Obstacles to Market Planning

While the federal government has not yet expressly adopted either of the market plans described above, a number of limited steps have been taken in these directions, some of which have been mentioned previously. Perhaps most important, there has been much greater recognition of the difficulties of central planning for federal coal resource management and the importance of moving toward a market mechanism.

A major remaining obstacle to formal market planning is the concern that any explicit calculation of leasing limits will encourage monopoly restrictions on federal coal supplies. Western states, which receive much of the revenues from leasing, might in fact benefit from a restricted federal coal supply and the higher coal prices that would result. Since the market plans described previously involve an explicit limit on leasing, their adoption might end up providing a mechanism for inappropriate restriction of coal supply.

Another set of critics are more bothered by the loss of social control in using a market mechanism to accomplish tract selection. It is impossible under the planned market approaches to maintain tight government control over the social impacts of the coal development process. The natural bureaucratic impulse is toward retaining tight control, in part reflecting a distrust of market unpredictability.

The coal industry has been strongly opposed to intertract competition. In public meetings prior to the 1982 Powder River lease sale, almost every industry representative objected to the proposal for a limited experiment with intertract competition. Coal companies seemed primarily concerned with the potential for stiffer competition and having to pay more to the government. Company attitudes could change, however, if some of the benefits to industry—especially the assurance of a neutral tract selection process—are more widely appreciated.

Conclusion

Government planning can take many forms. Historically, central planners have sought to calculate production goals and then take actions to achieve those goals. On the whole this process worked poorly in the late 1970s in managing federal coal resources—as it has generally worked poorly over the years in all areas of federal land management. Interior planners then sought instead to make use of the market mechanism to guide federal coal development. Use of such a "planned-market" approach maintains federal ownership of the resource but relies significantly on market signals to guide the key decisions of when, where, how much, and in what manner the resource will be developed.

Planning a market is no doubt better than trying to work with production targets and other apparatus of traditional socialist planning regimes. It still raises many of the problems, however, that beset government planning efforts of all kinds. Politicians will still want to manipulate the planning process—no matter that the objects of planning are now instruments of control over the market—to reward constituents. Citizen activists will be no more inclined to accept the authority of economic planners to take market actions that might have an adverse impact on them; they are thus just as likely to litigate. Setting the market parameters correctly may require almost as much supply-and-demand information as setting a proper production target.

Indeed, the planned market approach has thus far had limited success in the management of the federal coal resource. It has proven difficult to persuade Congress to stand aside to let public land managers act to create the conditions for the coal market mechanism to work, and the managers themselves have not necessarily accepted that this is the proper goal of federal coal management. The rapid expansion of federal coal production of recent years has largely occurred on leases that were sold by the government in the 1960s, before government leasing activities were receiving much public attention. Since the early 1970s the main product of the federal coal leasing system has been controversy and gridlock.

Planning a market is the federal coal equivalent of the *perestroika* that the former Soviet Union sought to implement in the late 1980s under the leadership of President Mikhail Gorbachev. In both cases the aim was to have the economic efficiency and other benefits of the market without abandoning the principle of government ownership or making other more radical changes in the system. In the former Soviet Union, of course, *perestroika* was eventually abandoned. Perhaps in the United States as well, the best answer is to sell the federal coal outright. If this is politically or otherwise impossible, however, federal coal management should look to a second-best answer: the planning of the federal coal market.

Notes

1. For basic federal coal information, see U.S. Department of the Interior, *Final Environmental Statement: Federal Coal Management Program* (Washington, D.C.: April 1979), and Interior's annual *Federal Coal Management Report*. See also Office of Technology Assessment, *An Assessment of Development and Production Potential of Federal Coal Leases* (Washington, D.C.: December 1981).

2. For an analysis of the federal coal program during the 1970s, see Robert H. Nelson, *The Making of Federal Coal Policy* (Durham, N.C.: Duke University Press, 1983).

3. The coal market is generally considered to be highly competitive. See U.S. Department of Energy, Office of Competition, *Coal Competition Prospects for the 1980's* (1981); and Antitrust Division, U.S. Department of Justice, *Competition in the Coal Industry* (Washington, D.C.: November 1980).

4. For further discussion of the role of speculation, see Richard L. Gordon, *Federal Coal Leasing Policy: Competition in the Energy Industries* (Washington, D.C.: American Enterprise Institute, 1981): 8–12.

5. For an in-depth review of public lands policy, see Robert H. Nelson, "The Public Lands," in Paul R. Portney, ed., *Current Issues in Natural Resource Policy* (Washington, D.C.: Resources for the Future, 1982).

6. Surface Mining Control and Reclamation Act of 1977, 30 U.S.C. §§1201–1328 (Supp. II 1978).

7. The unsuitability criteria are embodied in the regulations that govern the federal coal management program at 43 C.F.R. §3461.1 (1982).

8. See Council on Economic Priorities, *Leased and Lost: A Study of Public and Indian Coal Leasing in the West* (New York: 1974): 20.

9. Mineral Leasing Act of 1920, 30 U.S.C. §§181–287 (1976).

10. Federal Coal Leasing Amendments Act of 1976, 30 U.S.C. §207(b) (1976).

11. Other federal agencies, in particular the Council on Wage and Price Stability (COWPS), Department of Justice (DOJ), and DOE, did express concern over the way Interior was calculating leasing targets and proposed that such targets be set two to three times higher than the Interior Department numbers. See letter to Frank Gregg, Director, BLM, from Donald L. Flexner, Deputy Assistant Attorney General, Antitrust Division, DOJ, 1979. See also internal COWPS memorandum to Tom Hopkins and Ron Lewis from Jack Campbell, "Federal Coal Leasing: Problems and Solutions" (9 January 1980).

12. U.S. Department of Energy, Leasing Policy Development Office, *Federal Coal Leasing and 1985 and 1990 Regional Coal Production Forecasts* (Washington, D.C.: June 1978); *Work Paper: Interior Updates to 1985 and 1990 Regional Forecasts* (Washington, D.C.: April 1979); and *The 1980 Biennial Update of National and Regional Coal Production Goals for 1985, 1990, and 1995* (Washington, D.C.: December 1980).

13. C. B. McGuire, *Intertract Competition for Western Coal Development*, U.S. Department of the Interior, Office of Analysis (Washington, D.C.: 10 December 1975). See also C. B. McGuire, "Intertract Competition and the Design of Lease Sales for Western Coal Lands," prepared for the session on federal mineral leasing policy, 53rd Annual Western Economic Association Conference, 25 June 1978.

14. McGuire, *Intertract Competition for Western Coal Development*: 1.

15. See U.S. Department of Interior, Office of Policy Analysis, *Bidding Systems for Coal Leasing* (Washington, D.C.: 2 February 1976), and Tom Teisberg and Robert H. Nelson, *Coal Tract Selection and Bidding System Option Paper*, U.S. Department of Interior, Office of Policy Analysis (Washington, D.C.: 5 May 1978). For some critical comments see Wallace E. Tyner and Robert J. Kalter, *Western Coal: Promise or Problem* (Lexington, Mass.: Lexington Books, 1978).

16. For further discussion of a nominations fee approach, see Donald J. Bieniewicz, *Improvements to the Federal Coal Leasing Program Linked to the Use of Intertract Bidding*, U.S. Department of Interior, Office of Policy Analysis (Washington, D.C.: draft 24 April 1981): 28–30.

17. U.S. Department of Interior, Office of the Secretary, *Adoption of Proposed Final Five-Year OCS Oil and Gas Program Announced* (Washington, D.C.: 13 May 1982).

18. Under the preference-right leasing system an applicant could file for a two-year prospecting permit in areas where the presence of coal was uncertain.

To obtain a lease the holder of a prospecting permit had to demonstrate that coal had in fact been found in "commercial quantities." This program was suspended by the Interior Department in 1971 and abolished by Congress in 1976. See Sally K. Fairfax and Barbara T. Andrews, "Debate Within and Debate Without: NEPA and the Redefinition of the 'Prudent Man' Rule," *Natural Resources Journal* (July 1979).

Chapter 14

Four Good Places to Decentralize and Privatize

As Interior policy and budget analysts studied the financial details of public land management in the 1980s, there was surprising agreement that, if the public land surface could be given away for free, the fiscal impacts on the federal government would in many cases be positive. Indeed, given the current distribution of revenues and management costs, there was little financial stake in retaining the mineral rights as well (with the significant exception of oil and gas leasing on the outer continental shelf). In practice public land "ownership" has been transformed into the "right" of state and local governments to receive most of the net revenues and of various user groups to receive federal subsidies.

Thus, the "privatization" campaign of the early 1980s was misguided: the federal government had few if any hopes of selling the majority of the lands for large new revenues. A more realistic hope was

This chapter revises and integrates material from five sources: (1) unpublished concept paper proposing to "Transfer Ordinary Federal Recreation Lands to State Ownership," prepared at the request of and submitted to the President's Commission on Americans Outdoors (1986); (2) unpublished Office of Policy Analysis internal discussion draft on "A Proposal to Transfer the BLM Lands Within the California Desert Conservation Area to the State of California" (1985); (3) unpublished paper (written in consultation with Karl Hess, Jr.) on "A Proposed Project to Implement Market-Based and Decentralized Public Land Management" (1993); (4) Memorandum from Robert Nelson to Merritt Sprague (deputy director of the Office of Policy Analysis) on "A Program to Sell Federally Owned Land in Order to Establish a Fund to Pay for New Federal Land Acquisitions" (January 17, 1991); and (5) Memorandum from Robert Nelson to Robert Hahn (staff member, Council of Economic Advisors) on "Revenue Potential from Outright Sale of Powder River Federal Coal Beneath Private Surface Land" (November 23, 1988).

303

perhaps to escape some of the burden of subsidy. If it could simply give the land away for the long run, the federal government for the short run might even be willing to phase out existing transfer payments and subsidies over some transitional period.

Studies have shown that for most units of the National Park System, the majority of visitors come from within the same state. While similar figures are more difficult to obtain for ordinary BLM and national forest lands, the percentages of state and local users are almost certainly high. States stand to benefit from tourism and other economic expansion resulting from greater recreational use of federal lands in the state. In short, the impacts of most ordinary federal lands are felt largely within the same state.

The federal management of these lands has drawn the federal government into many fierce political disputes about proper land use that are essentially state and local in nature. The federal government is a virtual planning and zoning board for about 50 percent of the land in the West. Involving the federal government in these contentious local matters creates a drain on federal resources and needlessly squanders federal political capital. There is little or no reason that essentially state and local matters should be decided in Washington as opposed to, say, Sacramento.

There is a good case for public ownership of mountains, deserts, and other low-value lands that provide hiking and other ordinary dispersed recreation spread over wide areas (see chapter 8). Although this is often taken to mean that ownership of the land by the federal government is necessary, state governments could assume this public role as well, or better, for many current federal lands.

Unlike dispersed recreation, most concentrated recreation—such as guest ranches or mountain lodges—is better handled privately. Yet federal land agencies have virtually refused to sell off any of their current land for such intensive recreational purposes. States might show a more flexible attitude, recognizing the tourism and other benefits to the state from intensive recreation development. They would also not have the current bureaucratic stake in maintaining the status quo and the jobs associated with existing management practices.[1]

Federal land management has become bogged down in environmental impact statements (EISs), comprehensive land use plans, and other formal documents that have more to do with litigation strategies than with proper planning. This produces more gridlock than either production or environmental protection of the land. The actual benefits in improved land use decisions from all the planning now being done are exceeded by the large social costs of this cumbersome decision-making process. Some estimates suggest that land use planning in the Forest Service involves costs of $200 million per year. State ownership and management would make it much easier to break out of the current procedural gridlock and to install a more sensible and streamlined decision process.[2] Indeed, virtually any major institutional change, if it permitted the system to be redesigned in light of actual current needs and circumstances and break the strangle hold that the weight of the past continues to impose on public land management, would probably be an improvement.

This chapter describes four policy proposals that were raised for informal discussion among Interior Department budget and policy analysts and on a few occasions were heard by the political leadership of the department. They involve possibilities for decentralizing public land management in a limited way. Two of them also involve the disposal of selected areas of public lands. These proposals attracted interest, although never to the point of becoming likely candidates for the Interior Department to implement.

This lack of action did not necessarily reflect on their merits or their potential political attractiveness, if the various sides in public land controversies were willing to take a fresh look at them. Indeed, each side might find that it has more to gain than to lose. The proposals offer potential incremental steps toward a broader stategy of reducing the federal role in managing the lands of the West.

A Proposal to Transfer BLM Lands within the California Desert Conservation Area to the State of California

The California Desert Conservation Area (CDCA) contains twenty-five million acres, one quarter of the land in the state of California.[3] About half of the CDCA is federal land that was historically administered by BLM. Additional federal lands within the CDCA are administered by the National Park Service and the Defense Department—an area increased by 1994 legislation that transferred portions of BLM land to the Park Service.

The CDCA contains some of the most valuable recreation lands owned by the federal government. The lands are in close driving proximity to the many millions of residents of southern California. More than one million people live within the CDCA itself. In 1980 there were fifteen million visitor days to the CDCA, about one for every resident of southern California. If these visits are valued conservatively at $5 per day, the value of recreational use to the CDCA was then about $75 million per year and has no doubt risen since.

Livestock grazing occurs on 4.5 million acres of BLM lands in the CDCA, providing 75,000 AUMs per year of grazing. There are about fifty rancher allotments; the average size of existing allotments is 79,000 acres, reflecting the sparse vegetation in a desert environment. Annual BLM grazing fees are around $150,000. Grazing thus has a far lower value than recreation.

Mining is an important activity within the CDCA. The area has produced 15 percent of the nation's talc, 10 percent of its gypsum, and 5 percent of its iron, as well as most of the United States' borax production.

In 1976 the Federal Land Policy and Management Act directed that a "comprehensive, long range plan for the management, use, development, and protection of the public lands within the California Desert Conservation Area" be prepared by BLM. After wide public consultations and several years of study, BLM issued a proposed plan and final EIS on this plan in September 1980. In April 1981 the Interior Department officially approved the plan. Among its features the plan zoned the BLM lands within the CDCA into four use classifications: controlled use (in essence wilderness), limited use, moderate use, and intensive use. These classifications contained respectively 17, 49, 28, and 4 percent of the BLM land within the CDCA. The planning effort for the CDCA was probably the most intensive and expensive ever undertaken by BLM.

As proposed here, the ownership of the remaining BLM lands within the CDCA could be transferred by an act of Congress to the state government of California. California would have to agree to honor all existing private rights in such lands—in particular, mining claims. California would assume the full responsibility for managing the lands and would bear the costs as well. There would be few restrictions on California's use of the lands or its ultimate disposition of these lands.

As a condition for receipt of the lands, however, the state of California would have to agree to honor existing grazing privileges. If California wanted to eliminate grazing, it could buy out rancher grazing rights. At current capital values for grazing AUMs elimination of all grazing on CDCA public lands would probably cost California no more than $5 million to $10 million.

The mineral estate would be conveyed to California as well as the surface estate. The federal government, however, would retain a 6¼ percent overriding royalty (its current share of royalty receipts) on any future oil and gas production. California would own and manage the oil and gas resource. Federal oil and gas onshore royalties in 1992 for all of California were $33 million.

The great majority of the use of the CDCA is by residents of southern California. It is therefore appropriate that California both bear the costs and make the management decisions for these lands. A closer weighing of benefits and costs is likely when the beneficiary of a decision is also the one who bears the cost.

In 1992 the management of all BLM lands in California and of the total federal minerals estate (a BLM responsibility) in the state cost the federal government an estimated $56 million. Total federal revenues from BLM surface lands and the total federal mineral estate (including national forests) in California were about $60 million. The states currently receive 50 percent of mineral revenues. The estimated federal budget savings in 1992 of transferring all BLM management responsibilities to the state of California, and associated lands and minerals, is about $25 million. Perhaps half of this would be saved by transferring BLM lands in the CDCA alone.

The BLM plan for the CDCA suggested annual BLM costs for implementing the plan at $18 million per year. Surface management revenues are derived mainly from grazing fees and recreation permits and are well below $1 million.

Even though the state would lose in immediate fiscal terms, the prospect of gaining state control over the use of 10 percent of the total land area of California should be adequate compensation. The total state and local budget for California is greater than $40 billion, dwarfing any management costs for the CDCA. Moreover, the many millions of acres of land transferred free of charge to California would probably have a capital value of several billion dollars. At some point, if it wished, the state might sell part of the lands.

Because the highest value use of the lands in the CDCA is dispersed recreation, these lands are less suitable for disposal to the private sector. Politically, the recreational users of the CDCA have a de facto entitlement to continued access to BLM lands. Any proposal that sought to extinguish this entitlement would face wide opposition. Public ownership by the State of California, however, would maintain recreational access.

Unlike BLM lands in other states, grazing concerns are not a major obstacle to realignment of land tenure in the CDCA. The value of grazing is so low in relation to recreation and the number of ranchers that grazing is not a major consideration. Environmentalist and recreationist opposition has been a major hurdle to significant land tenure changes. Such opposition, however, should be less in California; instead, these groups might even support a transfer of BLM lands in the CDCA to the state. In other western states environmentalists and recreationists perceive the political process as still heavily influenced by ranching, mining, and other development interests. The political makeup of California, though, reflects the highly industrial and urban nature of the state. Environmentalists and recreationists in California have as much influence at the state level as at the federal level, and perhaps more.

Mining is an important use, but it requires small acreages of land. Where commercial mineral discoveries are made, these lands could still be transferred to the private sector, as they are at present under the Mining Law of 1872.

In summary, if the federal government wishes to consider the policy option of transferring dispersed recreational land to the states, the CDCA offers in many respects an ideal circumstance. The lands of greatest national interest have already been transferred to the National Park Service. The remaining BLM lands in the CDCA receive heavy use by the citizens of California but for the most part do not involve substantial national values or interests. State ownership would give the state the ability to manage the lands according to state policies; the requirement also to bear the costs would help ensure a realistic relationship between costs and benefits.

A Proposal for a Local-governance Public Land Demonstration Project

There is growing interest on many fronts in the idea of significantly decentralizing the management of the public lands. The Forest Service and the BLM have both come under sharp attack for inefficiency, ineptness, politicization, and other grave failings. Their problems are partly due to the attempt to manage a vast land area with a highly bureaucratic and centralized organization.[4]

The demonstration project proposed here would select one or more appropriate areas and transfer the public land management responsibility for these areas from the Forest Service and BLM to a new local entity. Using a newly created local governance body, both funding and control over use of current Forest Service and BLM lands would be transferred to the local level.

The size of the area suitable for such a demonstration project would have to be worked out with state governments and other concerned parties; the exact boundaries of the area would reflect watersheds and other local ecological features, BLM Resource Areas and Forest Service Ranger Districts. The demonstration area should not be so large that the local character would be lost—in some cases it might be on the order of say twenty-five miles by twenty-five miles. All Forest Service and BLM lands within such a boundary would be brought under new local governance.

Such a demonstration project would also involve the following features:

1. The Forest Service and BLM would determine the share of their current total funding that is being employed within the boundaries of a demonstration project area, including allowances for overhead at higher level administrative units of the land management agencies. This amount of funding would initially be transferred for the use by the new local governance entity. There would be few restrictions on how the funds could be employed.

2. Over the longer run, the goal would be to reduce substantially or perhaps to eliminate federal funding for the governance of the lands within the demonstration area. The transition could take as few as four or five years or, depending on the speed with which user fee and other revenue sources could be developed at the local level, might require as many as ten years.

3. Local governance entities would have the authority to raise funds for land management and other purposes through charging grazing, recreational, and other fees for access and for other purposes. Other than the share going into a national biodiversity fund (see below), the fees collected would be retained by local governance entities.

4. A local governance entity would have the authority to enter capital markets to obtain funding through issuance of bonds and other debt financing.

5. Some share—say 10 or 20 percent—of user fee collections could be set aside for the promotion of biodiversity. A certain percentage—say 50 percent—might have to be spent for biodiversity purposes within the particular local governance unit that collects the revenues. The remainder could be spent in other areas and according to biodiversity priorities throughout the nation that would be

determined by a national biodiversity board composed of environmentalists and other appropriate parties.
6. A key issue would be the selection of the leadership of the local
governance entity. There might be elections of some or all of the
leadership. Certain groups, including the ranching, recreational,
and other main current users of the lands, might be guaranteed
participation in a local governance entity in some fashion. There
might be provision for membership on the leadership of a local
governance entity both of residents living within a demonstration
area and of others who live outside but are current users of lands
or otherwise concerned.

It might be noted that 1988 legislation provided for the Bureau of
Indian Affairs (BIA) to undertake a demonstration self-governance
project to transfer both funding and management responsibility from
BIA to reservation tribal governments. It works in a way similar to that
proposed above for public land management. Under this demonstration
project, as of 1994 a total of thirty tribal governments either had entered
into the planning stage or had completed self-governance agreements
with BIA. In the long run, if the demonstration projects prove successful, the purpose is to largely replace direct BIA provision of services
with direct tribal provision of services.

The effectiveness of local governance will be much enhanced if there
is provision to include a variety of market incentives as part of the local
governing process. Local recreationists and other groups will be able to
work out resource and use issues with less controversy and less conflict
if one user group is able to make payments to another set of users.
For example, if local wilderness proponents within a self-governance
demonstration area can offer to buy out grazing rights of ranchers in
wilderness areas, they could accomplish the goal of removing grazing
through agreements reached voluntarily with local ranchers who would
be adequately compensated. A similar process might be used to remove
grazing from areas of critical environmental concern. Other agreements
could involve monetary payments as part of the negotiation process
within the local area.

It would be necessary to obtain legislative authority to enter into such
a demonstration project. In order to win passage for the legislation it
would be important to have strong support both at the local level and at
the national level. This support would have to include at least some
market-oriented critics of current public land management and some

environmental critics. Otherwise matters would simply become polarized and the current gridlock would continue.

In the long run, if a demonstration project such as that described above showed that one or more local governance models could be successful, this type of approach might provide a mechanism by which both the Forest Service and BLM would someday be largely replaced by local land management entities responsible to a set of property owners and a constituency much more directly concerned with the use and management of the local lands.

A Proposal to Create a Land Acquisition Fund

Current federal land holdings are the product of a history that goes back to the very founding of the United States. As such they represent an extremely wide range of land types, values, uses, locations, and so forth. Although the government has little use for some of these federal lands, it is also interested in acquiring other lands that are now private. For example, the National Park Service has long sought to acquire many of the private land inholdings still found within existing Park System units. Brand new units of the National Park System may require the acquisition of private lands. A greater emphasis on environmental and recreational concerns has also led other Interior agencies such as BLM to want to acquire certain private properties. For example, the creation of a new wilderness area or the designation of a particular area for critical wildlife habitat may cause BLM to seek private inholdings.

Within the Interior Department, proposals have been made for at least the past ten years to raise funds for land acquisitions through the sale of excess federal lands. In one limited case Congress enacted legislation to provide for sale of public lands in a designated portion of the Las Vegas metropolitan area to create a fund to pay for land acquisitions in the Lake Tahoe area. BLM has additional large land holdings in the Las Vegas area that may be needed for commericial and residential purposes in the future and have a potential value of perhaps several hundred million dollars.

The attraction of selling existing lands to create a land acquisition fund includes the avoidance of a need to collect taxes or increase government debt in order to pay for acquisitions, thus reducing direct burdens on the federal Treasury. Many people also believe that new land acquisitions should not expand the federal estate and that the total amounts of private and public land in the United States should stay about the same—a condition that would be met if new acquisitions were matched by new sales. Some current lands do not belong in the federal estate; by linking sales to acquisitions it might become politically feasible to accomplish disposals of select federal lands, disposals that are desirable in their own right.

In the early 1980s any proposals to sell federal lands, whatever the purpose, became closely linked in the public mind with the public land privatization proposal of the Reagan administration and Interior Secretary James Watt.[5] This proposal met intense public opposition and was withdrawn about a year after it was made. Ever since, almost any suggestions to sell federal lands have been tarred with the brush of another "privatization" campaign.

Interior agencies, however, came up with an alternative way of disposing of at least limited areas of federal land. Rather than a sale program, they have developed a much expanded program of land exchanges. When an agency wants a particular piece of private land, it often seeks to acquire it by exchanging an existing piece of public land.

The current owner of the property desired by the government may not need or want any federal land. Three-party transactions may be able to solve the problem. The government transfers some federal land to a third party. The third party then pays the owner of the private land actually desired by the government. Its owner in turn completes the three-way transaction by transferring the land originally sought to the government. Some land brokers have entered the business of trying to facilitate such three-way exchanges.

As a result of such policies BLM land exchanges under the Federal Land Policy and Management Act rose sharply in the 1980s. In 1981 BLM exchanged 37,629 acres and received 15,287 acres in return. In 1989 BLM exchanged 168,112 acres and received 217,987 acres in return.

Exchanges remain, nevertheless, a cumbersome method for acquiring land. It is in effect a barter system. Political pressures seem to have driven the Interior Department into a position where barter is an acceptable way of acquiring land but land transactions become tainted and unacceptable if government hands touch any money.

A land acquisition fund might significantly facilitate acquisitions within the department. When an agency wanted to acquire some land, money would be available in the fund. Assuming the land acquisition had a high enough priority, acquisition would be a matter simply of negotiating an acceptable purchase price.

The potential for federal land sales is substantial. According to estimates made in the early 1980s, there were then more than four million acres of lands already identified as strong candidates for disposal (see chapter 7). These lands had an estimated value of about $2.5 billion. While some of these lands have no doubt already been sold or exchanged, many probably remain in federal ownership.

There are also many other federal lands that could be sold. For example, recent criticisms of the Mining Law of 1872 have brought to light the sales potential of some federal land. After acquiring mining patents for $2.50 per acre, the acquirers have then gone on to sell land near ski resorts and in other attractive locations for prices in some cases approaching $100,000 per acre. Besides the deficiencies of the mining law, another lesson to be learned from these cases is that the federal government is holding on to some very valuable properties that could very well be sold and put to more intensive use in the private sector.

There are admittedly some problems that arise with respect to a land acquisition fund. Within Interior the agencies with the greatest needs to acquire land may be the National Park Service and the Fish and Wildlife Service but the agency with the most land that is suitable for disposal is BLM. BLM is not likely to be enthusiastic about giving up its land to expand the land holdings of other agencies; the bureau has opposed such proposals in the past. Another problem is that OMB might object that a land acquisition fund would be a backdoor spending scheme for getting around the normal budget process (a criticism not as easily made with respect to exchanges, even if the practical effect of making an exchange is the same).

There would no doubt be some heated controversies about whether land sales or purchases by the federal government were being accomplished at true fair market value. Some people will object that virtually any sale of public land is undesirable in principle, while others will take a similar view with respect to virtually any expansion of the federal estate. It is also not clear that land sales are much help in solving the macroeconomic and deficit problems that face the nation. Instead of selling a bond to finance the deficit, land sales will often require a private form of financing to buy the land, still raising the total U.S. indebtedness, as well as pressure on interest rates.

Despite these qualifications the creation of a land acquisition fund is an attractive policy option. It would serve two worthwhile policy goals: federal lands that are not really needed by the government could be sold and put to more efficient use, and it would represent an incremental step toward getting the federal government out of the business of managing ordinary federal lands. The federal government could instead concentrate its efforts on those land units—national parks, wildlife refuges, wilderness areas, etc.—where there is a real national stake. The proceeds of land sales would be used to improve the federal land base in such areas and the potential for effective management.

Politically, a land acquisition fund might offer a viable compromise between those seeking to reduce the size of the public lands and those seeking to expand the public land area. Each side would stand to gain more from the operation of the fund than it would lose.

A Proposal to Sell Powder River Basin Coal Reserves

The federal government owns large amounts of coal that lie beneath private surface lands in the Powder River Basin of northeast Wyoming and southeast Montana. This basin yielded almost 20 percent of the coal produced in the United States in 1987. About 80 percent of this production was derived from existing federal coal leases. Fully 85 percent of the surface acreage lying above leased federal coal in the Powder River Basin consists of privately owned surface land—a figure that is representative of the surface ownership on lands lying above unleased federal coal as well.[6]

Normally, the rationale for holding federal coal is to coordinate the management of this coal with the management of federally owned surface resources. This rationale does not apply, however, for most of the federal coal in the Powder River Basin, because no federal surface is present.

In the past, reflecting the original progressive goal to achieve the scientific management of the public lands, it was also believed by many that federal resource management would be more technically informed and more skillful than private management. Even in terms of the quality of coal management alone, the federal government was supposed to be able to do a better job than would private coal companies.

There is little in the historical record, however, to support this progressive view. Indeed, federal coal management has reflected clashing interest-group pressures, political stalemates, and other factors that have made it very difficult to manage the federal coal holdings in an economically rational and efficient way.[7] When the federal government has chosen to lease its coal, for example, it has typically ended up leasing when the market was low and holding when the market was high. It is also argued that selling federal coal outright would be conceding some of the value of the coal to speculators. This argument assumes that the federal government has a lower discount rate than potential private owners. The current budgetary pressures on the federal government, however, call this assumption into question. Indeed, one main purpose of selling federal coal reserves in the Powder River Basin would be to raise revenues that are much needed at present. The other main purpose for selling the coal would be to improve the quality of coal management through allowing market forces and the market mechanism to work more successfully in the allocation of the coal.

There have been few if any sales of privately owned coal in the Powder River Basin in the last few years. Sales of federal leases have also been rare since the large Powder River sale of 1982. In that sale the federal government received bonus bids of slightly more than five cents per ton.[8] Since 1982, however, coal reserve prices have gone down, along with other energy prices. Recent federal coal lease sales in the West have been few and the scant evidence available shows lease sale prices typically below five cents per ton.

The outright sale of the coal, in comparison to leasing, might generate higher prices because new leases currently require production within ten years, creating a significant risk that the lease will never produce. On the other hand rapid sale of large amounts of coal might depress prices by straining the absorptive capacity of the market.

The potential selling price of federal coal depends on whether existing federal royalties (12.5 percent) are carried over to the coal being sold. Given the very large uncertainties, an order of magnitude estimate is about all that can be done. If the coal were sold with the 12.5 percent royalty continued, it would be hard to predict a sale price any more precisely than a range of from 0.5 cents per ton to 5 cents per ton. If the coal were to be sold without any federal royalty imposed, there would be even larger uncertainties, yielding a possible price range of 1.5 cents per ton to 15 cents per ton.

Using existing coal reserve data (which may not include all valuable deposits), there are approximately forty billion tons of unleased federal surface minable coal in the Powder River Basin that lie under private surface. The direct sale of all this coal thus could yield revenues as high as $6 billion if no royalty were imposed. Given the continued low prices of oil and natural gas, however, it is unlikely that funds of this magnitude would be available to these companies for coal purchase. The low end of the estimated range without a royalty would be $600 million.

If the 12.5 percent royalty were continued, this estimated range would fall to between $2 billion and $200 million. The federal government could in this case, however, hope to receive significant future revenues from coal royalties. The federal government in 1992 received $144 million from federal coal royalties in Wyoming, and most of these royalties were from the Powder River Basin.

Another option would be to sell the rights to the royalty streams from existing federal coal leases that are already producing. This would be somewhat like the sale of loan portfolios, converting a future revenue stream into current revenues. The sale of existing federal lease rights in the Powder River Basin beneath private surface might yield sale revenues in the range of $1 billion to $2 billion.

Two objections would be that the federal government would be encouraging private speculation and that it would be losing control over the land development process and the ability to plan for future land use development (not that this potential has been much exercised in the past).

The other main objections would probably come from those who would fear a loss relating to their existing financial stake in federal coal. State governments at present receive 50 percent of federal mineral leasing bonus bids and royalties. Unless they received a comparable share from coal sales, they would almost certainly resist such sales. Thus, federal revenue potential might be only half the figures mentioned above.

However, Wyoming imposes an effective severance tax of almost 15 percent and Montana has a significant severance tax (taxes that apply to the production of federal coal as long as it is mined by private lessees). It has been argued that these state severance taxes in themselves provide generous funding from federal coal development in the state.

Besides the 50 percent of coal lease revenues going directly to the states, another 40 percent goes to the Reclamation Fund in the federal treasury, which is pledged to support Bureau of Reclamation dams and other projects. The Reclamation Fund is largely an accounting fiction (the revenues really benefit the federal treasury), but some western political leaders would probably also perceive declining revenues to the Reclamation Fund as a political problem if not a real hardship.

Under the Surface Mining Control and Reclamation Act of 1977, the federal government is required to have "surface owner consent" before underlying federal coal can be leased. Private surface owners have been selling these consents for prices of up to $1,000 per acre and sometimes more. Outright sale of the federal coal might diminish consent values, although state law in Wyoming requires surface-owner consent in any case.

Federal law, however, requires consent only of "rancher" surface owners, not of coal company surface owners (who already own much of the surface in the Powder River Basin). If necessary, a stipulation requiring future surface owner consent could be added to the sale of federal coal, but this would diminish the potential selling price.

To some extent revenue gains from sale of federal coal would be offset by federal tax losses because of company deductions of their purchase payments from taxable income. These federal tax losses could eat up much of the federal revenue gain, especially if the states were to receive 50 percent of the coal sale revenue (as the states at present benefit considerably more than the federal government from "federal" royalty collections when all the tax impacts are considered).

Outright sale of Powder River coal could not be accomplished under existing legislation. A major controversy might well result from a legislative proposal to sell the coal, bringing up issues of "privatization" and "give-aways" that have beset the federal coal program in the past and have tended to polarize Congress and public opinion.

Nevertheless, if the federal government is seeking potentially significant new sources of immediate revenue and is willing to accept the controversy, outright sale of unleased and/or leased federal Powder River Basin coal lying beneath private surface land offers such a revenue potential and would offer some long-run coal management benefits as well. It would promote the more efficient long-term development of the coal resources of the United States.

Conclusion

The possibility of making major changes in the institutional arrangements for public land management may not be very great if the changes have to be adopted for all the public lands. It may seem to many people to be too large a risk to adopt a whole new approach for all the lands in one fell swoop. It may be more feasible to experiment with alternative management systems. This chapter proposes four good opportunities for proceeding incrementally toward decentralizing management, privatizing some lands, and in general establishing a new management regime for the public lands.

Notes

1. One recent study shows that state forest lands in Montana often cost about half as much to manage as compared with similar national forest lands located

nearby. See Donald R. Leal, "Making Money on Timber Sales: A Federal and State Comparison," in Terry L. Anderson, ed., *Multiple Conflicts over Multiple Use* (Bozeman, Mont.: Political Economy Research Center, 1994).

2. See Jon A. Souder, Sally K. Fairfax, and Larry Ruth, "State School Lands and Sustainable Resources Management: The Quest for Guiding Principles," *Natural Resources Journal* vol. 34 (Summer 1994); and Sally K. Fairfax, Jon A. Souder, and Gretta Goldenman, "The School Trust Lands: A Fresh Look at Conventional Wisdom," *Environmental Law* vol. 22 (1992): 797–910.

3. Unless otherwise indicated, the data on land uses and values contained in this proposal are current as of 1985, when the proposal was written. Legislation was enacted in late 1994 to transfer a portion of BLM lands in the CDCA to the National Park Service.

4. See Randal O'Toole, *Reforming the Forest Service* (Washington, D.C.: Island Press, 1988).

5. C. Brant Short, *Ronald Reagan and the Public Lands: America's Conservation Debate, 1979–1984* (College Station: Texas A&M University Press, 1989).

6. Coal production, pricing, and other data given in this proposal are current as of 1988.

7. See Robert H. Nelson, *The Making of Federal Coal Policy* (Durham, N.C.: Duke University Press, 1983).

8. See *Report of the Commission on Fair Market Value Policy for Federal Coal Leasing* (Washington, D.C.: February 1984).

Chapter 15

How to Dismantle the Interior Department

The Interior Department is the accumulation of two hundred years of public land history. Over all these years many agencies have been created in response to perceived needs of a particular moment in American history. Yet few of the resulting agencies have been abolished. The momentum of American government is always toward the accumulation of greater responsibility. To eliminate a part of the government is a seeming impossibility.

Most of the agencies within the Interior Department were created as part of the progressive plan for government. The Geological Survey, Bureau of Reclamation, Bureau of Mines, and National Park Service were all established in the progressive era. Although they came into being later, agencies such as the Bureau of Land Management and the Fish and Wildlife Service were still guided by Progressive precepts of scientific management. Yet as previous chapters have examined, the progressive scheme is no longer an adequate guide for American government. Indeed, our task today is to find a new guiding vision and to reshape American governing institutions accordingly.

In the Interior Department this process can at least begin by recognizing that many features of Interior organization and responsibility no longer make sense. In particular the Interior Department is responsible for many things that are properly state and local responsibilities or could be better handled by the private sector. The Progressive precepts that once suggested the need for federal authority in these areas are no

---

This chapter is a slightly revised version of a memorandum from Robert Nelson to Martin Smith, Director of the Interior Department's Office of Policy Analysis, titled "Restructuring the Department of the Interior" (21 March 1986).

longer persuasive. In addition to an outmoded Progressive ideology the main forces supporting the status quo are vested bureaucratic interests and outside interests that perceive change in the department as a threat to their historic benefits from the public lands and other Interior responsibilities. Of course, the power of these groups to block change is great.

This chapter proposes a radical reorganization of the Interior Department and its functions. The changes proposed would cumulatively have the effect of dismantling much of the department. The basis for this reorganization is four, essentially simple principles.

1. Activities that can reasonably be carried out in the private sector should be done privately.
2. Activities that mostly involve state and local concerns should be administered by state and local governments.
3. The federal government should limit its role to activities and concerns that involve major federal interests and responsibilities.
4. Administrative organization at the federal level should place similar functions in the same agency.

The agency-by-agency review below describes how the Interior Department might be reorganized and many of its responsibilities transferred elsewhere: to the private sector, to state and local governments, to other federal agencies, or to new agencies within Interior. Obviously, any short-run attempt to carry out such a reorganization would face great political obstacles. That should not prevent us, however, from at least thinking about what might be done in a world in which these political constraints were not present.

Bureau of Land Management

The Bureau of Land Management (BLM) was created in 1946 from the old General Land Office and the Grazing Service.[1] The General Land Office no longer had any significant function once the era of public land disposal had passed. The Grazing Service served largely as a mechanism for policing grazing arrangements on the public lands that had been worked out among private ranchers before creation of the service. The informal private allocation of the range was unstable, however, and needed a more formal enforcement mechanism. BLM has been searching for a more "public-interest" mission ever since but has never really found one. Its role and responsibilities are almost entirely of a state and local nature; there is little or no reason for federal involvement, other than the accidents of history.

BLM would be broken up and divested along the following lines.

1. Transfer the BLM lands to the states in which the lands are located. Existing private rights to the lands would be protected. Mineral rights would be transferred as well, although the federal government might retain some overriding royalty share for oil and gas rights (to be paid by the new state owner to the federal government). The federal government could assist this transfer and create incentives for the states to take the lands by agreeing to contribute to the management costs for some transitional period.
2. Sell off the mineral rights where the surface is privately owned. Fully half of all federal coal lies under private surface, including the majority of the most valuable coal deposits in the Powder River Basin.
3. Transfer to the National Park Service a limited number of BLM areas identified by the current wilderness review and other review processes as having genuine national recreational, historic, or other significance.
4. Create one or more public timber corporations to take over the management of the O&C timber lands in Oregon. Stock in the corporations would be held by the federal government and the local counties (which now share the revenues). The O&C lands are some of the prime timber lands in the world and require sophisticated management that is best provided by a corporate form of organization. The governmental owners of the initial assignment of shares would be free to sell their shares to private purchasers if they wished. The O&C lands are not part of the public domain—they are revested railroad grant lands—and thus a separate treatment of them is justified by both economic logic and tradition.
5. Abolish the existing BLM.

Bureau of Reclamation

The Bureau of Reclamation (BuRec) falls in much the same category as BLM. It was created in 1902 for a purpose—"a homestead act for the west"—that no longer exists, if it ever did. The nation is today beset by excessive agricultural production and is paying farmers large subsidies to take land out of production. The West today needs more water to meet the demands of its rapidly growing urban populations and needs to transfer water out of low-value agriculture uses, rather than create more agricultural uses.[2]

BuRec would be broken up and divested along the following lines.

1. Transfer water transmission facilities, pumping facilities, and other BuRec assets that are mainly used by identifiable irrigation districts to these districts. In order to sweeten the pot to get these districts to accept all future operation and maintenance responsibilities, some or all of the debt repayment of the districts might be cancelled.
2. Transfer BuRec facilities that have wider state use but still have an impact mainly within a single state to that state. The government might agree to pay some part of the new state management costs for a transitional period.
3. Create a public corporation to manage BuRec facilities that significantly involve more than one state and that thus could not simply be turned over to a state. The management of the corporation would be selected by the affected states (an example of such a corporation is the Port Authority of New York, which is a joint creation of the states of New York and New Jersey). One such public corporation, for instance, might be created to manage the Colorado River system.
4. Sell off power-generation facilities that are not integral to the operation of water-supply facilities. Existing rights of preferential customers would be protected for the duration of their current contracts.
5. Abolish BuRec. Some of its functions would be transferred to the Corps of Engineers where they could be employed in continuing water activities. Other functions would be transferred to EPA where they could be used for engineering work on toxic site reclamation and other appropriate tasks.

Geological Survey

The Geological Survey (GS) was created in 1879 at a time when there were few other research facilities or federal sources of earth science funding and advice, and when the exploration and development of the West was a major national priority. Today, however, there are many alternative institutions capable of providing the services provided by

GS. The separate existence of GS tends to perpetuate and promote an overemphasis on its traditional concerns relative to other pressing national science needs.

GS would be broken up and divested as follows.

1. Transfer the basic research funding and functions of GS to the National Science Foundation (NSF). There, geologic and water science funding would have to compete with other, possibly more important, national scientific needs. The specific research facilities now operated by GS could be transferred to universities, where they would be funded by NSF to the degree that NSF determined was appropriate.
2. Sell the GS map sales and distribution functions to a private operator. The production of most GS maps should be subject to a market test. There is no major public interest in providing subsidized maps to hikers, fishermen, rock climbers, and other typical users, and the production and distribution of such maps should be done in the private sector.
3. Eliminate the federal-state cooperative program of the Water Division. States could buy from private consultants the water studies that they now purchase from GS. The fact that GS provides 50 percent of the cost of these studies creates an undue incentive for states to undertake studies that they otherwise would not pay for themselves.
4. Abolish the GS. Its water quality monitoring efforts could be transferred to EPA, where they probably belong anyway. Its stream flow monitoring could be transferred to states or to other operating agencies that require stream flow data. Any stream flow monitoring required under international or interstate compacts could be done by contract with the private sector.

National Park Service

The National Park Service was created in 1916 and brought together the management of a set of parks that had already been established individually.[3] The Park Service was created to manage parks such as Yellowstone, Yosemite, the Grand Canyon, and other areas of major national interest. Over the years, however, the Park Service has added numerous recreation areas, historic sites, urban parks, national monuments, and so forth. Many if not most of these areas have much less national significance. Their visitors often come largely from the same state in which the Park Service facilities are located. In the 1970s the term "park barrel" was coined to explain the political forces bringing about many of the newer facilities. Private nonprofit groups often do as good or better a job at much less expense to the government (e.g., Mount Vernon or Luray Caverns).

The Park Service could be reduced to a much smaller size, keeping only those limited facilities that are of truly national significance and where there is a clear reason for a federal management role.

1. Transfer to the state national parks in which visitation is 75 percent or more by residents of that state, after which they might well be incorporated into the state park system. A few exceptions might be made where a park serves to protect an ecological more than a recreational purpose and the ecology being protected is of clear national significance (e.g., some of the Alaska parks). During a transitional period the federal government would continue to provide funds for management purposes.

2. Transfer the urban parks, including Gateway, Golden Gate, Cuyahoga Valley, Santa Monica, and Fire Island, either to the state or to the relevant local government.

3. Transfer most historic parks, battlefields, memorials, monuments, historic sites, and other Park Service historic facilities either to local nonprofit groups or to state and local governments. Park Service historic facilities should be retained only where is both a clear national interest and where there is good reason to doubt that state or nonprofit management would be satisfactory. In order to promote the assumption of management responsibilities by nonprofit groups or states, the federal government might continue to provide some of the management costs or provide an endowment as a starting point.

4. Transfer to state and local governments or to nonprofit groups official national recreation areas, national seashores, national lakeshores, national rivers, national scenic trails, national parkways, and other Park Service facilities that meet largely state and local purposes.

Fish and Wildlife Service

The Fish and Wildlife Service can be traced back to the Bureau of Fisheries, which was formed in 1871. Somewhat like BLM, it serves a variety of aims and lacks a clear sense of purpose and mission. Wildlife refuges were originally conceived to be for wildlife purposes, but farming, grazing, hunting, and other activities not allowed in national parks were allowed in refuges. In recent years strong pressures have emerged to treat refuges as another version of the National Park System and to significantly restrict the types of use. Most refuges, however, lack the distinctive features that would make them of major national recreational interest.

The Fish and Wildlife Service would be sharply reduced in size and limited to those few of its activities that involve a wildlife mission requiring federal involvement.

1. Transfer wildlife refuges that involve lands of major national recreational and ecological interest to the National Park Service.
2. Transfer other wildlife refuges that do not protect endangered species or other wildlife of unusual federal interest to state or local governments, where they might well be included within state park systems.
3. Transfer fish hatcheries to state governments, or perhaps in some cases sell them, where the users of hatchery services are able to pay a market price. Federal funds to help pay management costs would be provided for a transitional period.
4. Continue Fish and Wildlife Service management of the national wildfowl programs that involve many states, the endangered species program, international wildlife protective programs, and perhaps a few refuges that serve wildlife objectives of major national interest.

Minerals Management Service

The Minerals Management Service (MMS), unlike most Interior agencies, was founded recently, in 1982. The service is finding it increasingly difficult to exercise management control over the leasing of the oil and gas rights to the outer continental shelf (OCS).[4] Legal handles, political pressures, and other trends are increasingly making the states the copartners in leasing, making for a very time consuming and cumbersome process. The efficient long-run utilization of these areas is more likely to be achieved by giving the states a strong direct interest in seeing them developed.

The Minerals Management Service would be restructured as follows.

1. Transfer remaining onshore minerals management responsibilities such as royalty collection to the owners of the minerals (e.g., states under the proposal made above and Indian tribes).
2. Transfer the mineral development rights in OCS areas with marginal current development prospects to the states, retaining an overriding royalty that would be paid to the federal government on development of these resources in later years.
3. Retain MMS leasing of those OCS areas with significant current development prospects but share revenues from newly issued leases with the states.
4. Sell off the federal royalty streams from existing federal leases on the OCS to private collection organizations.

Bureau of Indian Affairs

BIA was founded in 1824 and was located in the Department of War.[5] Indian tribes were at first treated as foreign nations with whom treaties were approved by the U.S. Senate. Thus, by long tradition, Indian affairs have been considered a federal responsibility. The role of the BIA has long been diminishing, however, as other federal agencies have taken direct responsibility for providing health, housing, and other services to Indians. Tribes themselves have increasingly been administering their own affairs under self-determination policies and contracting approaches.

Those existing trends would be accelerated as follows.

1. Much as Indian health responsibilities were transferred to the Indian Health Service in the Department of Health and Human Services (HHS) in 1954, transfer remaining BIA Indian education responsibilities to the Department of Education, remaining BIA Indian housing responsibilities to the Department of Housing and Urban Development, remaining BIA transportation responsibilities to the Department of Transportation, remaining BIA welfare responsibilities to HHS, and so forth.
2. Transfer the management of tribal minerals, timber, agricultural, and other natural resources to the tribes themselves. The federal government would continue to help pay for the management costs for a transitional period—possibly a quite lengthy one.
3. Abolish much of the superstructure of detailed trust review by

which BIA has long sought to exercise precise control over tribal management and other details of tribal behavior.

4. Reduce drastically the size of BIA and allow it to serve in part as a conduit for federal funds to tribes, in part as a state department for conducting federal affairs with Indian tribes, and in part as an advocate for Indians in the federal government. BIA would concentrate its remaining efforts on providing technical advice and assistance to tribes, rather than engaging in the direct provision of services or the supervision of tribal activities. The tribes themselves would provide the bulk of services to their own members.

Office of Surface Mining

The Office of Surface Mining, like MMS, is a more recent Interior agency, created in 1977. While it has its problems, many of these problems may be unavoidable, or at least are not due to any agency mission and organization designed for the circumstances of fifty or more years ago and that are no longer suited to current requirements.

Bureau of Mines

The Bureau of Mines (Mines) was created in 1910 and is an agency that has outlived its original role and mission. Its activities could either be better performed elsewhere in the federal government or outside the government altogether. Mineral production plays a far smaller role in the economy today than when Mines was created.

Mines would be abolished and its functions transferred as follows.

1. Transfer its information gathering and dissemination functions for the minerals industry to the Energy Information Agency in the Department of Energy or, to the Department of Commerce, or allow private providers who would be willing to undertake some of these functions to do so.
2. Transfer the research and development functions of Mines to the private sector, which performs these functions for most industries. If some research and development functions genuinely justify a federal presence, they would be undertaken by other agencies such as DOE, EPA (for air quality controls), and so forth.

3. The helium stocks owned and managed by Mines would be sold to private operators and owners.

Conclusion

Most of the proposals made in this chapter would require overcoming large political hurdles, and would seem impossible to many people. American politics is, however, in a particularly volatile stage. There is widespread discontent with the workings of government, especially the federal government, even while there is much less agreement on the appropriate directions for change. The crisis of Progressive faith, and the failure of interest-group liberal and other ideas to provide an adequate replacement (see chapter 9), have left the federal government without any clear guiding vision.

In this political climate there is a greater prospect that drastic changes will become politically feasible than many people realize. If change moves in the direction of significantly reducing the scope of the federal government, reversing the trends since the rise one hundred years ago of the Progressive vision of centralized American government, the proposals above offer a concrete design for implementing such an agenda of decentralization and privatization at the Department of the Interior.

Notes

1. Marion Clawson, *The Bureau of Land Managment* (New York: Praeger, 1971).

2. National Water Commission, *Water Policies for the Future* (Washington, D.C.: Government Printing Office, 1973).

3. Ronald A. Foresta, *America's National Parks and their Keepers* (Washington, D.C.: Resources for the Future, 1984).

4. See Robert H. Nelson, "Greasing the Skids for a New Federal Oil and Gas Leasing System," in Terry L. Anderson, ed., *Multiple Conflicts over Multiple Use* (Bozeman, Mont.: Political Economy Research Center, 1994).

5. Francis Paul Prucha, *The Great Father: The United States Government and the American Indians* (Lincoln: University of Nebraska Press, 1984).

Part VI

Private Rights to Public Lands

Introduction

Around the world privatization of government enterprises has become standard policy in many former socialist and other nations seeking to revitalize their economies. Brazil, China, France, India, Japan, and Russia are all busy privatizing. In the United States, a nation commonly regarded as the ''citadel of capitalism,'' however, there has been little willingness even to consider privatization of any significant portion of the public lands. Numerous opponents denounce any such suggestion as a sellout of the public interest to greed and special privilege.

Yet on close inspection the rhetoric of this discussion is often far removed from the reality. Indeed, the very distinction between public and private land is not clear. The use of ordinary private land is often subject in the United States to close government control through zoning and other regulations to the extent that some landowners possess few of the historic prerogatives of private ownership. As previous chapters have described, there are already well-established traditions of private use on public lands that take on much of the character of property rights. It would not be much easier for the Bureau of Land Management to cancel a grazing permit or eliminate a wilderness area than it would be for a local government to significantly alter the existing pattern of residential housing.

To a considerable extent there already exists a system of private rights to public land. The existence of these private rights has important implications for considering any proposal to privatize public land. First, privatization would be much less radical a step in substance than in form. Second, any privatization must take account of the existing private right holders. To sell off a portion of public land in disregard of de facto rights would be much like trying to sell off property belonging to someone else. In fact privatization is likely to be successful only where it

331

serves to formally establish and thus to legitimize private rights to public land that have already come into existence on a de facto basis.

In opposing past privatization proposals the defenders of existing rights have often found that one of their most effective defenses is to charge that the public lands would be given over to special interests. There is considerable irony in the fact that the holders of de facto rights to public lands often protect their turf by brandishing charges of "privatization" against any competitors. Indeed, chapter 16 describes how public lands illustrate an important trend within all of American government, the tendency of new private rights to come into existence along an informal path that begins with a government decision to regulate some type of resource use. As the exercise of government controls gradually comes to be dominated by a particular set of private parties, the controls over use take on more and more of the character of property rights. Once this has happened, the best thing to do then is to formally recognize the private rights.

Privatization by means of formally recognizing existing de facto rights will avoid all the forms of distortion, economic and intellectual, associated with trying to deny that the rights actually exist. It will create a regime of private rights that serves the cause of human freedom and of marketplace efficiency. It will give the owner of the property the long-run incentive to take care of it and in this fashion will also serve the cause of environmental protection. Government ownership of land and other resources has not only failed to achieve economically satisfactory results but in many cases has been detrimental for the quality of the environment as well.

Chapter 16

Private Rights to Government Actions: How Modern Property Rights Evolve

The very idea of private ownership of land was once a radical thought. In medieval Europe the lord of the manor held control over the land in return for military obligations to the king. He could no more sell the land with its obligations than a current general in the U.S. Army could sell his command. Yet by a process that took centuries the feudal system of land tenure gradually evolved into the modern notions of private property and the formal assignment of a set of private rights to the land.

The idea of carving the public lands up into a set of individual properties, or of communal property holdings held privately, if collectively, by residents in a local area, appears about as radical to many people today as private ownership of the manor did to the feudal era. Such an outcome would, however, be consistent with a trend of property right evolution that is occurring in a number of areas of the American economy today. In the past many people have based their expectations for the future property right regime more on their own high hopes than on any clear-sighted analysis. In fact the best way to predict future property rights has been to observe the current direction of events. This chapter examines how the existence of a broad trend in American government for the evolution of private property rights through a transitional stage of government regulation suggests a similar outcome for the public lands, an outcome that would be beneficial both economically and environmentally.

This chapter is a slightly revised version of an article that originally appeared with the same title in the *University of Illinois Law Review*, Issue 2 (1986).

The New Property

George Stigler, conservative former economist at the University of Chicago and Nobel prize winner, and Charles Reich, former Yale University law professor and author of *The Greening of America*, would seem to have little in common. Yet each authored a celebrated article with a common theme: the making of modern government into a new form of property.[1] Indeed, the development of private rights to government actions constitutes the primary mechanism by which new property rights are evolving in the United States today.

In "The New Property" (1964) Reich argued that recipients of government assistance programs should be able to regard their benefits as matters of private right—literally as a new type of "property." As such they should be protected by many of the same judicial safeguards that protect ordinary private property rights. As Reich explained in a later article:

> The idea of entitlement is simply that when individuals have insufficient resources to live under conditions of health and decency, society has obligations to provide support, and the individual is entitled to that support as of right. To the greatest degree possible, public welfare should rest upon a comprehensive concept of actual need spelled out in objectively defined eligibility that assures a maximum degree of security and independence. The concept of equal treatment also inheres in entitlement, and argues against basing eligibility on special statuses, such as maternity.[2]

Elaborating on this concept, Reich in 1966 stated that:

> Among the resources dispensed by government which it would seem desirable to treat as property are social security pensions, veterans' benefits, professional and occupational licenses, public assistance, unemployment compensation, public housing, benefits under the Economic Opportunity Act, Medicare, educational benefits and farm subsidies. Planning with respect to such rights can be done on a general basis; the rights themselves should be distributed to all who qualify for a certain status. Governmental decisions concerning such rights should be and are increasingly subject to the requirements of due process of law; such rights should not be denied or revoked without a full adjudicatory hearing.[3]

Reich believed that he was merely extending into the social welfare arena the same premises that were already widely applied in other areas of government activity. Stigler tended to confirm this view in his 1971 article, "The Theory of Economic Regulation," in which he explained how other government activities can also effectively create new property rights. Stigler focused his attention on government regulation. He found, contrary to accepted regulatory theories, that "regulation is acquired by the industry and is designed and operated primarily for its benefit."[4] Industries desired state regulation because it gave them access to the unique state powers to coerce. These powers "provide the possibilities for the utilization of the state by an industry to increase its profitability."[5] Like purchasers of ordinary goods and services, industries obtained access to the coercive powers of the state by paying "with the two things a [political] party needs: votes and resources."[6] Although Stigler did not use the term "property," the essence of his critique was that the modern regulatory apparatus created a new form of business property right, one designed, purchased, and managed by the regulated industry.

The viewing of government as a form of "property" reflects a fading of the Progressive intellectual vision, a vision that provided the theoretical foundations for modern government. In Progressive political theory—first articulated by Woodrow Wilson, Frank Goodnow, and other Progressive theorists around the turn of the century—the government acted "in the public interest." Rational, scientific methods were used to discover the public interest; expert professionals were responsible for administering government objectively and efficiently; and the final result was free of any private or other special interest domination.[7]

Later students of government, however, came to see this Progressive vision of objective, expert decision making as more myth than substance. Post-World War II political scientists such as David Truman and Robert Dahl found that government conduct was more typically the product of a buffering by private forces.[8] Indeed, the advocates of "interest-group liberalism" sought to make a virtue of necessity, arguing that a happy social equilibrium resulted from political competition among affected interests. John Kenneth Galbraith, for example, wrote enthusiastically about the high economic productivity and social harmony that he believed would result from a modern system of "countervailing powers."[9]

Critics of these views found, however, that modern pluralist politics produced government by and for special interest groups, and that it often served narrow and even private purposes at the expense of broader social goals.[10] Stigler was simply extending this reasoning to its logical conclusion. As private influence grew, government regulation was perhaps best seen as the possession of its clientele groups. Reich also recognized that his views involved a rejection of progressive governing concepts. But he believed that the progressive concepts were unrealistic and that it would be unfair to apply them to the poor and disadvantaged when more powerful social groups were being treated more favorably.

Possession is said to be nine-tenths of the law and, indeed, possession and disputes over possession have had a central role in the evolution of property rights.[11] In earlier eras possession was frequently a matter of physical force—for example, whether a landowner had the physical power to evict a squatter.[12] In the modern era, however, possession relies not so much upon physical as upon political strength. A good part of the domestic political debate of the past two decades has centered around the extent to which private rights to government actions will be recognized or accepted; around, that is, the legitimacy of the "new property." The deregulation movement, for example, showed that to a surprising extent business lacked the political strength to retain the property rights that it had acquired in the regulatory process.[13] In the social welfare area, judicial decisions and legislative actions since Reich's article have established many new private rights for beneficiaries of government income transfer programs.[14] But in the 1980s these rights were challenged as a backlash set in. Some groups, including ordinary welfare recipients, have been unable to retain the full rights they had accrued. On the other side Social Security recipients and certain other groups seem to have established their rights to receive government support even more securely.

Similar battles have been fought in many other areas of government activity. Indeed, virtually every beneficiary of government action, ranging from broadcasting licensees to recipients of cheap government hydroelectric power, has sought to transform the benefits received from a "privilege" into a "right."[15] If a benefit is merely a privilege, then it will continue only so long as government officials determine that continuance "serves the public interest." The recipient of a privilege faces substantial uncertainty and insecurity and is at the mercy of government planners and administrators who base their authority on claims to expert objectivity. Moreover, the beneficiary knows that expert decisions are often much more arbitrary than these claims would suggest.[16] By comparison, when benefits become a "right," they are more certain and secure. Courts offer protection to holders of rights against arbitrary or otherwise unjust government actions. In addition courts place on the government a much greater burden of proving the validity of any revocation of rights. As a practical matter the government may be able to revoke established rights only if the political process devises some form of formal or informal compensation; revocation without compensation may be considered a de facto "taking" of a private property right.

The evolution of private rights to government actions is continuing in many areas. The remainder of this chapter focuses on this process in the specific areas of environment, land, and natural resources, where the past several decades have been a fertile period for the evolution of "new property." Indeed, the pace of this evolution has accelerated as the environmental movement has forced government to confront the growing scarcity of key resources. The fate of the new property—whether government will encourage, restrict, or abolish it—will be a central issue for natural resource policy debates in the years to come.

Government has seldom succeeded when it has sought directly to "privatize" a publicly owned or common property resource. By indirect routes, however, often obscured by public myths and fictions, government has created many new private rights in publicly owned resources. Indeed, these new property rights could prove to be a transitional stage—perhaps even a necessary stage—in the evolution from a common property resource to a system of full-fledged and officially recognized private property rights.

Zoning as Private Property

Zoning provides one of the most important examples of this evolutionary process. Zoning was first established in the United States in New York City in 1916. A product of the progressive era, zoning was justified intellectually in terms of the accepted Progressive theories of the day.[17] Expert, or "scientific," planners would prepare a land use plan for a city. These planners and other city administrators would then use zoning, along with other public instruments such as road and sewer installation, to guide development and to fulfill the city plan. Zoning theories reflected the widespread faith at the time that professional expertise and planning could make American cities both more efficient and more beautiful.

After World War II, however, it became apparent that the land use system was not working as intended. For one thing, local officials seldom consulted local land use plans in making zoning decisions. Zoning had become a discretionary system in which developers typically bargained with local government to gain permission to develop, a practice that had been condemned by the architects of zoning. In this bargaining process zoning typically served narrow, parochial objectives. Indeed,

commentors commonly decried the "private" purposes of zoning actions and called for reforms to restore zoning to the original, Progressive ideal of serving the public interest.[18]

One of the sharpest departures from the zoning ideal in the postwar
era was the development of a widespread "black market" in zoning
changes. In the 1950s and the 1960s local governments were slow to
accommodate the needs of millions of Americans rushing to the suburbs. Developers found that in many cases bribes to local officials were
required to obtain access to land to build new housing to meet burgeon-
ing demands. Marion Clawson in 1966 suggested as a pragmatic solution that municipalities make the process more straightforward by selling zoning changes directly.[19] In so doing Clawson proposed in effect
to acknowledge that zoning changes had already become a de facto
form of property. As a form of property zoning rights should be legally
saleable like other property rights.

Clawson's view, however, was the exception; most leading critics of
zoning in the 1960s, writers such as John Delafons and Richard Babcock, proposed traditional remedies including better planning and increased regional and state authority.[20] It was not until the 1970s that a
new generation of zoning students sought more radical changes. The
need, they believed, was not to try to make zoning practice conform to
a misguided and utopian theory, but to reform zoning theory itself.
These new "property right" theorists called for a drastic rethinking of
the intellectual foundations for zoning. In their view the major defect
of zoning was that the property rights created by zoning had evolved
insufficiently. As Clawson had observed, the greatest difficulty was that
the actual holders of development and use rights could not sell them
legally in the market. As a result necessary and socially desirable
changes in land use were being blocked or had to occur by extralegal
means.

Dan Tarlock first briefly sketched the new property rights theory of
zoning in a 1972 article, "Toward a Revised Theory of Zoning."[21] As
Tarlock noted, a basic purpose of zoning has long been to protect the
amenity levels in high-quality neighborhoods. In effect zoning creates
collective property rights by giving neighborhood residents the ability
to control the use of their neighborhood environment. Zoning thus gives
neighborhood residents much the same controls over land use that other
people, such as members of large condominium developments, gain and
exercise collectively through strictly private means. As a prescription
for a new regulatory system in place of zoning Tarlock suggested that
municipalities recognize the private, protective purpose of zoning, that

they establish new forms of neighborhood private property rights to serve this purpose, and that ordinary market trading be allowed in the rights. As Tarlock explained:

> Under the existing zoning system subsequent users who wish to deviate from the surrounding land-use pattern must "buy" their way in through the political process. Majority approval from an appointed commission or elected local legislative body is required. The process, I have argued, is very costly and produces doubtful efficiency gains. Arguably the costs of administering a zoning system would be decreased and efficiency gains more certain if entrants had to bargain directly with surrounding landowners. The function of the government would be to impose an initial covenant scheme and then let the market or a close proxy determine subsequent reallocations of land.[22]

In undeveloped areas that lacked residents to take possession of these collective, private rights, Tarlock proposed that municipalities simply sell development rights and then let the market govern.[23] That is to say, municipalities would be empowered to sell zoning to such vacant land.

Various writers in the next few years embellished and elaborated on Tarlock's suggestions. In an influential 1973 article Robert Ellickson proposed that states revise their nuisance laws to expressly allow cash payments to help resolve nuisance disputes.[24] If adequately compensated financially, neighborhood groups would have no reason to block entry of a less attractive land use. In a 1977 article Ellickson proposed that municipalities should have the right to impose on undeveloped land a "normal" level of zoning restriction.[25] However, municipalities wishing to "downzone" such land to limit development more severely would be require to buy the development rights from the landowner. In effect Ellickson recommended the purchase and sale of zoning changes, although only in specified circumstances that served a set of equity and efficiency criteria that he prescribed. Economist William Fischel later also advocated that municipalities sell zoning changes to undeveloped land.[26]

The property right theory of zoning has posed a major challenge to, if not undercut altogether, traditional theories of zoning. It has had much less impact on actual zoning practice and on the courts, although the Supreme Court since the 1980s has been slowly expanding the range of circumstances in which compensation for stringent land use controls is required, an important move toward the property rights perspective. In the 1980s individual homeowners in several neighborhoods in Atlanta and in the Virginia suburbs of Washington, D.C., organized to sell their neighborhoods. They sold their lands as a group, typically to developers with large projects in mind, at prices contingent on rezoning to allow more intensive development. In effect these neighborhood residents were selling the zoning rights to all the neighborhood land and physical property, often receiving two or three times the total value of the homes if sold individually. As Harvard law professor Charles Haar commented about the Atlanta situation, "We have finally reached the point where zoning is a form of private property right. . . . We have created a collective property right, in the form of zoning."[27] In the Atlanta cases the neighborhood decided to "sell its zoning as a right of ownership."[28] These collective sales of whole neighborhoods may eventually prove to have been a critical step in the long-run evolution of zoning from a system of government regulation to a formally recognized system of collective private property rights to land.[29]

In summary, zoning is a leading example of how the "new property" is created. The new property begins as a government action (in this case regulation), the government action benefits particular private groups, and these private groups then claim their benefits as matters of private right. When private parties achieve the ability to sell their rights to government actions, as they have begun to do in the case of zoning, the evolution of a full private property right is nearly complete.

Private Rights to Federal Lands

Like zoning, the current federal land system originated in the progressive era.[30] Throughout the nineteenth century the objective of the federal government was to dispose of the public lands. The first step toward permanent retention took place in 1891 when Congress provided for the setting aside of "forest reserves."[31] By 1910 Congress had largely created the current system of national forests and had formed the Forest Service to manage the lands. The first federal wildlife refuge was designated in 1903.[32] By creating the National Park Service in 1916, Congress brought together under common management a number of individual parks that it had earlier established.[33]

The Progressive designers of the public land system had a vision similar to that of the Progressive architects of zoning.[34] Technical experts, including foresters, hydrologists, and biologists, would plan scientifically the future uses of the lands. Professional land administrators would implement these plans "for the greatest good of the greatest number in the long run."[35] Gifford Pinchot and other leading Progressive advocates of public land retention called for the removal of politics from the routine management of the land.[36] Interest group influences in public land management, they believed, corrupted the basic integrity of the system.

Experiences under the Taylor Grazing Act of 1934, however, soon showed the large gap between Progressive ideals and actual management practices.[37] The Taylor Act put the finishing touches to the 150-year era of disposal of the public lands. Instead of disposal, the federal government would now issue permits making "allotments" of public land available to ranchers, based on their historic use and their ownership of nearby private ranching property. Ranchers could graze their livestock on these public land allotments at times and under conditions specified by the permit. The government would also charge grazers a fee, initially calculated simply to cover administrative costs.

Over the years public land managers have almost never revoked grazing permits, and they continue to charge grazing fees well below market prices. A grazing permit attaches to a particular private ranch property, and the existing rancher can transfer it almost automatically to any purchaser of his property. A grazing permit thus greatly increases the selling price of privately owned "base" properties. Ranchers also sometimes sell grazing permits on public lands as independent assets and even sublease them temporarily. A government study reported that the going sale price for federal grazing permits in 1983 averaged $68.00 per month of cattle grazing allowed by the permit. The average sublessee in 1983 paid $6.53 to ranchers for a single month of grazing on federal land, compared with a government grazing fee collected in that year of $1.40 per month of grazing.[38]

In light of their de facto permanency and transferability, rights to graze livestock on public lands have evolved virtually into a form of private property. A leading agricultural economist, Delworth Gardner, proposed in 1963 that the government expressly sanction this evolution. He contended that the government should "create perpetual permits [and] issue them to ranchers who presently hold permits in exchange for those now in use. These permits would be similar to any other piece of property that can be bought and sold in a free market."[39] Gardner argued that the lack of formal recognition of rancher rights, as well as certain procedural obstacles imposed by the government, significantly increased the transaction costs of permit trading. Barriers to permit transfers might keep grazing rights from reaching the rancher valuing them most highly and result in less efficient use of grazing resources.[40]

The case of livestock grazing provided an early and obvious departure from the Progressive design. In other areas of public land management, however, the Progressive vision has also survived more in form than in substance.[41] In practice, public land management has become a balancing of interest-group pressures, and this balancing has received wide acceptance. Congressional mandates for "multiple-use" management have amounted in effect to a Congressional blessing for a system of interest-group negotiation and accommodation.[42] To be sure, this evolutionary process has merely brought public land management into line with the prevailing political practices in other areas of government.

Users of the public lands seek not only the maximum benefit from their use rights, but also the maximum security in their rights of future use. Each user group seeks to convert public land benefits from a matter of publicly granted privilege or public benevolence into a matter of privately held right. Ranchers are not the only group that has succeeded in securing saleable private rights to use public resources. Some years ago public land agencies adopted a permit system to alleviate congestion among rafters and other users of rivers running through public lands. Pressures from commercial river operators have since forced the agencies to provide a virtual guarantee that they will transfer a permit to any purchaser of an existing, permit-holding private river operation. On a number of rivers there is no room for new permits and existing commercial permits have become very valuable, in some cases more valuable than the physical facilities. More recently, permits to commercial outfitters serving hunters and other recreationists on ordinary public lands have reached a similar position of scarcity and have become a new valuable form of property right to use public land.

In 1977 Congress created another lucrative private right to a government action. The Surface Mining Control and Reclamation Act provides that ranchers and other "qualified" owners of private surface land must consent before the federal government can lease federally owned coal underlying their surface lands.[43] Prior to the act the federal government could lease the coal for mining at its discretion and was simply required to compensate the surface owner for damages. In effect Congress in the new law gave private surface owners the right to control federal coal-leasing actions. The Commission on Fair Market Value Policy for Federal Coal Leasing found that some private surface owners were profiting to the extent of selling their consents for prices in excess of $3,000 per acre and for royalties exceeding one percent of the value of the federal coal.[44]

Although transferable rights to use public lands are still the exception, public land agencies in most of their management decisions are captive to particular user groups. Timber harvest areas, wilderness areas, coal mining areas, conservation areas, wild horse areas, critical environmental areas, and various other special categories of public lands are gradually establishing a zoning system on the public lands.[45] And much like urban zoning of private land, the long-run trend of public land zoning is toward a system of collective private rights to use these areas of public lands.

The national wilderness system, for instance, now includes about ninety million acres, including more than fifty million acres in Alaska. The early architects of the wilderness system were high-minded idealists seeking to serve the best interests of mankind. Nevertheless, wilderness management today is moving toward carving out de facto property rights from the public lands for committed wilderness users and the organizations that represent them. At present, groups such as the Sierra Club and the Wilderness Society exercise substantial power to control the uses permitted in wilderness areas; indeed, these groups possess as a practical matter considerably more power than the secretary of the Interior. If property ownership consists of the right to control use, the Sierra Club and the Wilderness Society are already partners with the government in owning wilderness areas. Moreover, the trend is toward a greater private influence. The political muscle exerted by wilderness proponents over the years has demonstrated that their preferences are almost sure to prevail in disputes over wilderness area management. In the 1980s wilderness groups resisted Reagan administration proposals for oil and gas drilling in wilderness areas every bit as effectively as rancher groups have traditionally resisted proposals for higher grazing fees.

Exclusionary zoning in urban areas does not work by directly excluding the undesired uses. Rather, it employs various control devices such as large-lot zoning—typically adopted in the name of some higher social ideal—that have the practical effect of excluding the unwanted uses. In the same way future controls are likely to limit wilderness use in the name of such idealistic goals as preventing excessive congestion and protecting wilderness character. Eventually, controls could well limit wilderness area entry to the existing hard-core users of the wilderness system and effectively set aside preserves of federal land for these private groups.

Prohibitions on roads, trail cabins, and other manmade structures already exclude a large part of the public from wilderness areas. Longtime wilderness users are still concerned, however, that too many people are visiting wilderness areas; perversely, designation as a wilderness area tends to increase substantially the number of visitors. Land managers have already adopted permit systems in some wilderness areas, systems that inevitably favor traditional users who know the ropes and can plan well ahead to obtain entry permits. Wilderness advocates are now beginning to discuss new, stronger measures to inhibit wilderness use.[46] One proposal is to remove the identification of wilderness areas from Forest Service maps. Another restrictive device under discussion among wilderness users is to eliminate trail signs in wilderness areas. These restrictive devices will control wilderness use by creating major obstacles for anyone not already familiar with the particular area. Although not the stated purpose, the practical effect is to make the wilderness the private preserve of existing users.

The tradition of mass public access is much older and stronger for the National Park System than for the national wilderness system.[47] Nevertheless, the same pressures exist to control uses of the national parks. One recreation planner from the old school recently voiced angry opposition:

> If you are a backpacker, resource management scientist, wildlife photographer or nature mystic, you are in luck . . . . But if you want to enjoy a national park in another way, like going car camping with your family, having a drink in a park dining room with a great view, or staying overnight in a bed with sheets at a park lodge, then you don't belong in a national park. In the future, according to this plan, everything should be done to make your visit as unpleasant as possible.
>
> But if the parks are reduced to virtual fiefdoms from which most of us are banned, how will this allow our children and grandchildren to enjoy the parks? Will there still be any national parks left?[48]

Some observers have concluded that the government might best respond to current pressures by transferring the public lands, perhaps free of charge, to the private organizations that currently dominate their use. Thus, in a manner similar to the Gardner proposal for grazing lands, John Baden and Richard Stroup proposed that "lands presently included in the wilderness system be put into the hands of qualified environmental groups such as the Sierra Club, the Audubon Society and the Wilderness Society."[49] Private ownership of wilderness areas would recognize formally the evolving de facto private rights to these areas. Baden and Stroup argue that such a step would facilitate better wilderness management. For example, private wilderness groups might charge significant fees for wilderness entry, fees that are now politically impossible. They could then use the resulting revenues to buy additional lands for the wilderness system and for other wilderness protection purposes.

The Reagan administration proposed in 1982 to sell large areas of public lands to help reduce the national debt. This proposal provoked sharp outcries, many from administration supporters, and the administration quickly shelved the idea. The opponents included a broad alliance of grazers, wilderness users, miners, horse and burro advocates, timber companies, hunters, and fishermen. Indeed, virtually every current user of the public lands opposed the idea. Top Reagan administration officials had naively assumed that public ownership of the public lands meant that the public could use these lands for any fitting public purpose. The administration soon discovered, however, that a wide array of public land users considered themselves as holders of vested rights to continue existing land uses. The administration was unable to sell the lands because in an important sense it did not really own them. The Reagan administration tried to sell someone else's property, and the owners reacted to the threat as vigorously as would any other private owners.[50]

With the evolution of municipal zoning and the development of private rights to public lands, the private land and public land tenure systems are tending to converge, despite a large difference in formal appearance. Consider, for example, a livestock grazing allotment located in a wilderness area on the public lands. The rancher holds the existing grazing rights individually, and these rights are the rancher's de facto private rights. Wilderness users, however, effectively control the rancher's ability to make significant changes in the grazing use. Similarly, individuals own urban homes as private property, but neighborhood home owners effectively control significant changes in land use. In each case individual owners control some elements of land use, while private groups hold collective rights to control other elements of land use.

In sum the labels "public land" and "private land" tend more to obscure than to illuminate the realities of land ownership today. On both public and private land the "new property" is evolving, resulting in new individual private property rights and new collective private property rights. To an increasing degree the two ownership systems now are similar in practice, if not in form.

A Theory of Modern Property Right Evolution

The manner in which the land tenure system has evolved on private land and public land is characteristic of a broader range of circumstances involving "common property" resources. In each case a physical resource such as land is available in limited supply. Initially, access to the resource is open to all, often because, like air to breathe today, there is no scarcity of supply. The first stage in the evolution of a property right is reached when demands for use of the resource grow large enough to create a congestion problem. Excessive use creates conflicts among users, deterioration in the quality of the resource, disincentives to invest in improving and maintaining the resource, and eventually demands for some form of social control. Centuries ago the solution might have been a royal grant of exclusive use rights to the nobility or the sale of newly created property rights to wealthy landlords and merchants. In the United States in the twentieth century, however, the usual response has been government regulation of the use of the resource.[51] The government regulation generally involves a permit system and the allocation of use permits to permittees, usually in a manner favoring historic users.

The establishment of a permit system marks the beginning of a second stage in the evolution of a private property right system. The initial recipients of use rights gain political strength and gradually acquire greater and greater effective security in their use rights. They oppose government attempts to change the terms and conditions of their use rights, as well as attempts by the government to impose significant fees or charges. In the fragmented American political system with its highly decentralized power and great weight of organized user groups, the preferences of existing users generally prevail. At some point the dominant influence of user groups becomes accepted as the norm and existing users have acquired de facto private property rights.

The property rights acquired by users, however, are still seriously incomplete until they are legally tradeable and saleable. The third stage in the evolution of full private property rights consists of achieving such rights of "alienability." At first, sales of user rights may be feasible only if owners sell them in conjunction with other private property, as when owners sell public grazing rights together with private ranch property. In the next step use rights become detached and independently transferable. In some cases independent transfers will remain illegal and transferring parties must hide them from view. In other cases the government may allow or even encourage such sales but may restrict the types of purchasers or impose other conditions. The government may require, for example, proof that the transfer serves a "public purpose." Full saleability occurs when the government officially recognizes the rights of a user to sell use rights without restriction.

The fourth and final stage of property right evolution occurs when the government regulatory agency formally transfers use rights to the private user and then ceases its regulatory activities. At this point the user holds an ordinary private property right, and the laws and procedures applicable to other ordinary private property govern the exercise of this right. As Bruce Yandle has described this overall process,

> Unrestricted public access to a resource leads to scarcity and increased costs. In response to that allocative problem, government regulation emerges to measure and manage those resources. Once the resources can be monitored and measured, transfer to private ownership and subjection of the resource to the allocative efficiencies of the market takes place.[52]

In addition to zoning and public land management the evolution of new rights has reached one of these four stages in the following areas: rights to use surface water in the western United States; rights to pollute the air; rights to use groundwater; rights to ocean fishing in United States waters; rights to pollute rivers and other surface water; and rights to broadcast over the airwaves. Thus far a number of writers have advocated in concept the fourth and final stage: full creation of an ordinary private property right system.[53] Although the fourth stage has not been achieved in any case, the third evolutionary stage—saleability of de facto user rights created by a regulatory system—has been reached in a number of cases.

Broadcasting rights may have reached the most advanced stage of property right evolution: the government generally accepts licenses to use the airwaves as the property of the current licensee and routinely allows sales.[54] Technically, the Federal Communications Commission (FCC) awards broadcast licenses for a limited period and can deny renewal requests by existing licensees. In practice denial has happened only very rarely in the history of the FCC.[55]

Air pollution rights are moving gradually toward the third stage of evolution, direct private saleability. The Environmental Protection Agency (EPA) has encountered substantial difficulties in making command and control decisions for thousands of pollution sources. Reacting to these difficulties, EPA has encouraged the development of market trading in the rights it awards to use a common property resource—in this case, the right to use the air by polluting it.[56] EPA took the first step in this direction by allowing new polluters seeking to enter an air quality region to subsidize reduced emissions by existing polluters in the region. Under this "offset" policy a new polluting source could obtain permission to enter the region if it paid for sufficient pollution reductions elsewhere to offset its own additions to the pollutant load.[57]

As a second step EPA began to adopt a "bubble" policy in the late 1970s, which allowed a firm to exceed allocable emission levels in one part of its facility if it could generate equal or greater reductions from another part.[58] In other words, for purposes of meeting pollution-control laws EPA viewed the whole facility as one source (one "bubble") and ceased applying the control laws separately to each part of the operation. The next step in this policy would expand the bubble to cover not just a single facility but several separately owned plants. The owners of these plants could then buy and sell pollution reductions among themselves in order to achieve overall compliance with EPA standards for the plants as a whole.

Market trading in air pollution rights has generated considerable opposition. Opponents criticize such trading as morally offensive because it recognizes a private "right to pollute," grants undue private windfalls, and abdicates government responsibilities for planning. Nevertheless, after a slow start sales of air emission rights gained in frequency. By 1984 about 2,500 offset trades had occurred. Moreover, several states have approved rules allowing polluters to "bank" emission reduction credits for future use and have taken a number of other steps toward developing full-fledged markets in rights to pollute.[59] In 1990 the acid rain provisions of the Clean Air Act Amendments established a formal market in "allowances" for power plant emissions of sulfur dioxide, a major departure in U.S. environmental policy.

Surface water in the arid western United States offers a further example of property right evolution. Under the prior appropriation doctrine, which governs western water allocation, the government grants each user a right to withdraw water if the water is available and if the user can show an ability to use the water "beneficially." The doctrine also allocates user rights with a priority according to the date of first water use. Traditionally, the system has been based on a philosophy that government permission to use water should not be saleable. Yet a number of sales of rights to use surface water have occurred and there is growing acceptance and legitimacy for such sales. Pressures for more efficient allocation of scarce western water may foster the development of a widespread system of "water marketing."[60] In short, property rights to western water are today in the process of shifting from stage two to stage three in the evolution of a full-fledged, private-property right system.

As compared with surface use rights, groundwater rights are in a less advanced stage of property right evolution.[61] Indeed, in some areas groundwater is still a common property resource and its use remains largely uncontrolled, leading to excessive depletions and conflicts over groundwater use. Responding to such problems, Arizona in 1980 revised its groundwater laws to bring groundwater use under tighter regulation.[62] Several other western states have also taken steps to regulate groundwater use. Groundwater use rights, therefore, are only at the first or second stages in the evolution of full private rights.

The development of new rights to use U. S. ocean fisheries provides yet another example of property right evolution. For many years the government did not control fisheries use, resulting in severe depletion of many fishery stocks. In 1976, however, the United States extended its territorial waters to two hundred miles and adopted the Fishery Conservation and Management Act of 1976 (the Magnuson Act). In so doing the government took the first critical step toward developing a property rights system. The Magnuson Act established eight regional fishery councils and provided for the regulation of domestic and foreign fishing activity within each region.[63] A report of the National Oceanic and Atmospheric Administration, the parent body to the National Marine Fisheries Service, explores possible future management options that include allocating fisheries rights to individual fishermen and developing marketable and perhaps even privately owned fisheries rights.[64]

Since the 1970s government control over the pollution of surface waters has become firmly established. But unlike air pollution, there has been little movement toward establishing markets in water pollution rights. Numerous students of water pollution have recommended that the government adopt systems of saleable water pollution rights. These observers generally have proposed, however, that the government lease these rights on a temporary basis rather than distribute permanent rights that could be bought and sold by private owners.[65]

In all of these circumstances involving a common property resource, society has first chosen government regulation as the preferred means of allocating the use of the resource. In none of the cases did government regulation begin with the aim of developing a full system of private property rights. In each case, nevertheless, the regulatory approach is at one stage or another in an evolution toward a private property rights regime. In some instances government agencies have recognized the great difficulties of a direct regulatory approach and have encouraged the evolution of private property rights. In other instances, however, the government has resisted this evolution. Much of the resistance stems from the continuing stronghold of the Progressive intellectual heritage, which seeks to allocate social resources according to public plans and to achieve the scientific management of public resources by disinterested government agencies. Indeed, a measure both of the strength of the private pressures for a private property right regime and of the practical advantages of such a regime is that the evolution of the ''new property'' has been able to advance as far as it has for these common property resources.[66]

Other New Property

The creation of new private rights to government actions is not limited to circumstances involving the use of common property resources. Indeed, as indicated previously the development of the ''new property'' is a widespread phenomenon in modern government. New property has also arisen in other settings involving the allocation of key economic resources.

One important form of new property is the right to purchase land, natural resources, and other real property at below-market prices. Some occupants of rent-controlled apartments have long been able to move out and ''sell the furniture''—thereby in effect converting their possession of a low-rent apartment into a saleable private right. Holders of rent-controlled apartments also capitalize on their de facto property rights when owners convert apartments to condominiums. Owners often convert condominiums by selling each unit to the existing tenant at a price far below the going market price for the unit. The owner accepts the low price because it provides the best way to eliminate the obligation to provide a low-rent apartment. Such sales in effect allow each rental unit to capture the capital value of the property rights conveyed by the rent-control scheme.

New property exists similarly in the form of rights to buy irrigation water from the U. S. Bureau of Reclamation at highly subsidized rates. The Bureau of Reclamation historically has charged less than 30 percent on average of the true, full cost of delivering its water to irrigators.[67] As states move toward the increased trading of water rights in newly formed western water markets, they and the federal government must decide whether existing recipients of subsidized water will have the power to sell to others the right to continue buying water at the same subsidized rate. If the government decides that it will end the subsidy for new users, it will significantly limit the incentive for beneficial sales of water. Because of the adverse effect on efficient use of western water, most commentators have concluded that the subsidized water rate should be available, in whole or in part, for new water users. If governments adopt this approach, they would make transferable another form of new property: the right to buy government-supplied water at a below-market rate.

Customers of public utilities that receive electricity from government power facilities similarly benefit from prices that are far below going market rates. For example, recipients of power from the Hoover Dam pay rates that are 25 percent or less of normal market prices for electric power. By approving the renewal of these contracts Congress determined in effect that existing utility purchasers had established de facto rights to buy power at the low prices first set fifty years ago. If allowed, holders of these valuable purchase rights could sell them to other utilities at high prices. Indeed, such sales might be socially desirable, although politically difficult to sustain, because they would tend to deliver the power where most needed and would thereby enhance the overall efficiency of the U. S. energy system.

For many years the regulation of natural gas in a similar fashion created de facto property rights to buy gas at below-market rates. Congress effectively recognized these rights when it decided in the late 1970s to move gradually to an unregulated gas market; Congress provided for deregulation of ''new'' gas but left in place a regulatory structure and below-market rates for ''old'' gas.[68] A rationing system, such as the one used for gasoline during World War II, is an explicit and formal way to create a private property right to buy a product at below-market prices. The owner of a rationing ticket can usually sell the property right in a black—or if legal, ''white''—market and thereby capitalize on the value of the government-generated new property right.

Another type of new property emerges when government regulates access to a resource that the government has made artificially scarce. These cases differ from those discussed above in which the scarcity was inherent in some physical circumstance. For example, Interstate Commerce Commission trucking certificates assumed a high market price in the 1970s after the government tightly limited entry into trucking.[69] When deregulation greatly eased entry, however, the market was undercut. Taxi medallions similarly have a high selling price in some cities that regulate the total number of taxis. Airport landing rights can take a similar high value when airport facilities are inadequate to handle existing traffic loads. Indeed, when Secretary of Transportation Elizabeth Dole in 1985 proposed that airlines at four airports have the power to sell their existing landing rights, it was an unusual instance—a sign of a changing intellectual and political climate—in which the government proposed formally to allow the sale of new property.

When government-created scarcities give rise to new property rights, the rights are typically considerably less secure. For one reason or another the government might eliminate the scarcity and thus undercut the value of the right.

When the government finds that private rights to government actions are evolving, it must consider how it should respond. Four options exist, options that correspond to the four stages of property right evolution. As a first option the government could eliminate the private rights. For example, the government could hold frequent competitive auctions for temporary use rights, rather than allocating long-term, permit rights that are in practice virtually permanent. As a second option the government could accept the existence of the private rights but adopt or more strictly enforce laws that prohibit their private transfer and sale. Third, the government could recognize the private rights and allow or even encourage their private sale but could maintain long-run government flexibility by leaving open the possibility that it might later decide to cancel the rights of users. Fourth, the government could formally transfer the new property rights to the current private possessors and give to them all of the legal protections enjoyed by ordinary private property owners.

A Case for Private Property Rights

When government actions create the condition of scarcity—such as a regulatory system that offers some people access to goods and services at below-market prices or offers limited permission to enter a regulated industry—the best government policy will normally be to eliminate the government actions that cause the scarcity. Thus, the government could abolish price controls or deregulate an industry, wiping out the new property rights that have been created by its actions. Nevertheless, this is easier said than done; strong equity arguments also may exist for maintaining long-established government policies, whatever their initial wisdom. For example, a demand for payment of full market rent from an elderly couple that had long occupied a rent-controlled apartment— say, in New York City—would be unreasonable. Hence, some government-generated scarcities, like actual, physical scarcities, may as a practical matter defy elimination.

When the government cannot eliminate the scarcity, it should generally attempt to convert existing de facto private rights into new, formally recognized, and legally saleable private rights. Thus, for example, local governments should replace zoning with a system of officially recognized private rights to control entry into urban neighborhoods. Governments should also replace existing regulatory systems with private rights to graze on public lands; private rights to pollute the air; private rights to use surface water in western rivers; private rights to rent apartments at rent-controlled rates; and various other private rights to government actions. Governments should recognize these private rights as legally valid, freely alienable, and subject to no greater government control than other types of private property. (To be sure, an unusual degree of government involvement may be necessary in defining some of the private rights and in establishing the equivalency of rights transferred from one location for use in another.)

There are major pragmatic advantages to such a policy. The greatest efficiency of property use occurs when the party that most highly values the property uses it. This goal is achieved if the property is freely transferable. On the other hand restrictions on saleability encourage less efficient users to retain their property. Consider, for example, the case of the elderly couple in a rent-controlled apartment that may well have living space for a full family. Assuming this is so, the community could substantially increase the efficiency of the use of its housing stock by allowing the couple to sell its valuable property right in the rent-controlled apartment to a new household with much greater need for the housing space.

As a general matter, creation of a private property regime makes it possible to rely on a market mechanism to allocate scarce resources. In government permit regimes, by contrast, the government has the responsibility to allocate. Government planners, however, are unlikely to possess the information needed to issue efficient command and control decisions and may well lack the incentive to carry out plans with much energy. The record of central planning by government generally compares poorly with the allocative efficiency achieved by private markets.[70]

Social equity goals also can be furthered by formally recognizing and making transferable the private rights to government actions. These private rights often have great value. Yet, as long as the rights are not saleable, holders of the rights cannot convert them into money. This restriction may diminish significantly the effective wealth of the holders, and for no good social reason. Again taking the example of the elderly couple in the rent-controlled apartment, this couple might well benefit from the opportunity to sell their new property. They could move to another, smaller apartment and have considerable money left for a new car, fancy restaurants, or other pursuits in their old age.

Opponents of formal recognition of transferable private rights to government actions generally do not base their arguments on equity or efficiency considerations. Instead, they usually rely on a moral argument or ethical judgment: that the sale of rights to government actions would somehow be "wrong" or "unjust." It would be wrong, for example, for a government to allow the elderly couple above to sell directly to another party its existing right to rent at the controlled rate. Similarly, it would be wrong to allow private ranchers to sell their existing rights to graze on public lands at below-market rates. Such sales would somehow violate the basic integrity of modern governing institutions. They would challenge directly the guiding ideal that legislators enact government regulation to serve the broadest public interest and should not use regulation to enhance narrow private purposes and for private financial gain.

Ancient Property Right Controversies

Students of the long history of private property evolution may recall, however, that increased transferability has often generated strong opposition. Indeed, the history of property is filled with religious, moral, and other principled objections to property sales. Although these objections have taken years, sometimes even centuries, to overcome, the practical advantages of transferability have typically prevailed in the end. In the modern era the right to sell the "new property" may evolve slowly, but it too may gain acceptance in the end.

The difficulty with discussing the evolution of private rights to transfer property, Oliver Wendell Holmes once explained,

> is to convince the skeptic that there is anything to explain. Nowadays, the notion that a right is valuable is almost identical with the notion that it may be turned into money by selling it. But it was not always so. Before you can sell a right, you must be able to make a sale thinkable in legal terms. The most superficial acquaintance with any system of law in its earlier stages will show with what difficulty and by what slow degrees such machinery has been provided, and how the want of it has restricted the sphere of alienation. It is a great mistake to assume that it is a mere matter of common sense that the buyer steps into the shoes of the seller, according to our significant metaphor.[71]

Historically, increased transferability of land has encountered particularly great resistance. Under the medieval land tenure system the possessor of land held it as the servant of a higher lord; a set of mutual social obligations tied the lord and tenant together. This feudal ideal is similar to the idea today that possession of a regulatory permit to use a common property resource must be justified by the service of a greater public interest. In the case of broadcasting, for example, a license to use the airwaves carries with it an explicit public service obligation, much as the feudal system required a medieval serf to perform appropriate services for a lord in return for use of the land.[72]

When a medieval tenant asked permission to sell some land, the tenant challenged the very essence of the social system. A similar challenge occurs today when the possessor of a type of "new property" seeks to sell government-granted rights. One historian described the confused attitudes in the late thirteenth century, a confusion echoed today in discussions over the status of the new property.

> The mortmain laws, the doctrine of uses, the sensitiveness of common law towards seisin and the crisis of 1290 were all effects of the tension between the tenants and lords of military fiefs. The tenants were maneuvering towards freedom of management and disposal. And the overlord, jealous of the fruits of chivalry, countered the moves point for point. As a consequence a land market did not develop easily at high social levels. Socage tenure, on the other hand, was freer. At this level signs of a vigorous land market are evident. The market in socage land was also probably due to the fact that socage was the tenure of the free peasantry. The noble classes would not be moved to sell estates for money: apart from financing a crusade or other military undertaking, there was little cause to convert land to money. The land was the hallmark of aristocracy. The noble would only exchange land for land. But the peasant of the thirteenth century with free money in his pouch faced a prospect of many horizons, and among the fields of the vill the economic historian has discovered evidence of an early, widespread land market.[73]

Like the medieval lord, the modern government has little sympathy with the sale of rights of government actions. Nevertheless, we now know with hindsight that the pragmatic advantages of market trading won out decisively in the medieval era, eventually caused the dissolution of medieval land tenure, and brought about the creation of the modern land market. Today, a new set of legally accepted private property rights may emerge from the "new property." Rather than the opposition of lords and priests, these new property rights must overcome the opposition of their modern equivalents, Progressive administrators and theorists of modern government.

The evolution of new property rights can be aided by myths and fictions that obscure the wide discrepancies between actual property practices and formally stated ideals. The development of medieval usury laws illustrates the possible value of fictions to smooth the path for important property right changes. Money lending for a fee, like the sale of land, was resisted in the medieval period. As historian (and federal judge) John Noonan put it, the "most perspicacious moralists described usury as the great vice which corrupted cities and Church alike and held all men of property in bondage."[74] Nevertheless, this moral view yielded to practical considerations; as Noonan further explained, "Unquestionably the changed economic circumstances were the greatest factor in producing the general later modification."[75] In order to reduce the conflict with received church doctrines, a "large part of the development in theoryconsists in the development of alternative analyses of operations which are often in practice indistinguishable from loans. Instead of treating a credit operation as an illicit loan, the majority of scholastics resolve the transaction into another, lawful contract."[76] Similar practices exist today, as when, for example, a municipality "grants" (i.e., sells) a zoning change upon receipt of a sufficiently high "impact fee" or "park fund donation" (i.e., sufficiently high price).

Historically, private property and transfer rights have generated strong opposition in many societies. Indeed, observers at times have regarded private property as a corruption of the highest ideals of a society. The early Christians regarded the institution of private property as a necessary evil. As historian of ideas Richard Schlatter explains, they held the view that "the natures of men, all of them depraved, make necessary instruments of social domination. The division of property which gives some men a power over the lives of others is one such instrument."[77]

By the thirteenth century economic activity had advanced and the social utility of private property was more widely recognized. The theologians of the age responded to the changing circumstances by developing a more favorable view of private property. For example, St. Thomas Aquinas found some theoretical desirability in communal property ownership but believed that private property had compelling practical advantages. In his *Summa Theologica* Aquinas presented a case for property rights that has a distinctly modern ring.

Two things are competent to man in respect to exterior things. One is the power to procure and dispense them, and in this regard it is lawful for man to possess property. Moreover, this is necessary to human life for three reasons. First, because every man is more careful to procure what is for himself alone than that which is common to many or to all: since each one would shirk the labor and leave to another that which concerns the community, as happens where there is a great number of servants. Secondly, because human affairs are conducted in more orderly fashion if each man is charged with taking care of some particular things himself, whereas there would be confusion if everyone had to look after any one thing indeterminately. Thirdly, because a more peaceful state is ensured to man if each one is contented with his own. Hence it is to be observed that quarrels arise more frequently where there is no division of the things possessed.[78]

In short, in this century the emergence of new property rights to government actions has revived ancient debates and controversies. Attacks on the new property echo criticisms made centuries earlier. If modern property rights evolve as did earlier rights, the new property will eventually become legally recognized and fully saleable. Both economic efficiency and social equity support such an evolution.

Assessing the New Property

The creation of the "new property" is a development of great social importance on two counts. First, the evolutionary process represents the most important mechanism by which new property rights have arisen in this century in the United States. Second, the rise of the new property reflects the failure of the progressive theories of scientific management for modern government.

The U.S. political system has often proven unable to sustain and follow a consistent vision of the national interest. Instead, government policies have tended to become the servants of narrow, often private interests. Occasionally, as in the case of economic deregulation or the environmental movement, a burst of ideological enthusiasm allows broader social concerns to overcome parochial interests.[79] In most areas, however, parochial forces have dominated American politics and have pushed inexorably toward the creation of private rights to government actions.

In many cases the best policy response is to eliminate the government action and thus the corresponding private rights. Modern American government has entered into many activities that do not advance either equity or efficiency objectives. Many other government activities, however, will still be necessary. In the case of these necessary government functions, the only appropriate response would seem to be to try harder, to make a greater effort to introduce rational government planning and analysis, broadly understood.

For a third, important class of government activities, the best response will be the formal acceptance and recognition of the "new property." Government activities in the natural resources and environmental fields often fall within this class because the government regulatory role in these cases involves the allocation of a fixed common property resource among different users. In such cases the government would do well to substitute a formal system of private property rights for the de facto system of private rights that typically is already well evolved.

Private property rights seldom arise from deliberate social planning.[80] They are more likely to emerge almost surreptitiously as the end result of a series of practical expedients adopted to solve on-the-ground problems. Sir Frederick Pollock once noted of the English experience that "the history of our land laws, it cannot be too often repeated, is a history of legal fictions and evasions, with which the legislature vainly endeavored to keep pace until their results . . . were perforce acquiesced in as a settled part of the law itself."[81] Yet, once created and recognized, property rights have often been praised for their social utility. If the "new property" gains formal recognition in the future and becomes another component of the "old property," its evolution will have followed a well-worn path.

Conclusion

The public lands belong to the third category above where the best response to the new property is to formally recognize it and to transform the existing de facto rights into de jure rights. This process is complicated, however, by the fact that there is a wide range of de facto rights existing on the public lands at present, from livestock grazing rights, to outfitting rights, to hunting rights, to wilderness rights, to rights of miners to explore. Sorting out all these rights, determining which rights command higher priorities in which places, protecting other rights from undue infringement, and getting the holders of the various rights to accept all this is a complicated process. Some of the rights may be exercised collectively, and it will fall to local communities to find suitable ways of making the collective decisions for the exercise of the rights.

This book describes why, even though the task is complicated, it is worth undertaking. The public lands are in effect today a commons of nationwide scope. The ongoing battle to assert rights to this national commons has yielded a new form of range war that has been economically wasteful and environmentally harmful. Like the solution to the commons problems of old, the answer today is to draw clearer property right boundaries. The new property on the public lands should transfer the ownership rights to the land to the people who are most directly affected by the actual results on the land.

Notes

1. Charles A. Reich, "The New Property," *Yale Law Journal* vol. 73, no. 5 (April 1964); George J. Stigler, "The Theory of Economic Regulation," *Bell Journal of Economics and Management Science* vol. 2, no. 1 (Spring 1971): 3; reprinted in Stigler, *The Citizen and the State: Essays on Regulation* (Chicago: University of Chicago Press, 1975): 114.

2. Charles A. Reich, "Individual Rights and Social Welfare: The Emerging Legal Issues," *Yale Law Journal* vol. 74, no. 7 (June 1965): 1256.

3. Charles A. Reich, "The Law of the Planned Society," *Yale Law Journal* vol. 75, no. 8 (July 1966): 1266.

4. Stigler, "Theory of Economic Regulation": 3.

5. *Ibid.*: 4.

6. *Ibid.*: 12.

7. See generally Frank Goodnow, *Politics and Administration: A Study in Government* (New York: Macmillan, 1914); Dwight Waldo, *The Administrative State: A Study of the Political Theory of American Public Administration* (New York: Ronald Press, 1948); Woodrow Wilson, "The Study of Administration," *Political Science Quarterly* vol. 2 (1887), reprinted in *Political Science Quarterly* (1941).

8. See Robert A. Dahl, *Pluralist Democracy in the United States: Conflict and Consent* (Chicago: Rand McNally, 1967); David Truman, *The Governmental Process: Political Interests and Public Opinion* (New York: Knopf, 1951).

9. See John Kenneth Galbraith, *American Capitalism: The Concept of Countervailing Power* (Boston: Houghton Mifflin, 1956).

10. See Theodore J. Lowi, *The End of Liberalism: Ideology, Policy and the Crisis of Public Authority* (New York: Norton, 1969); Grant McConnell, *Private Power and American Democracy* (New York: Knopf, 1967).

11. See Carol Rose, "Possession as the Origin of Property," *University of Chicago Law Review* vol. 52, no. 1 (Winter 1985).

12. See John Umbeck, "Might Makes Right: A Theory of the Formation and Initial Distribution of Property Rights," *Economic Inquiry* vol. 19, no. 1 (January 1981).

13. See Martha Derthick and Paul J. Quirk, *The Politics of Deregulation* (Washington, D.C.: Brookings Institution, 1985).

14. John Rohr, *Ethics for Bureaucrats: An Essay on Law and Values* (New York: M. Dekker, 1978): 211–36.

15. See Editorial Research Reports on the Rights Revolution (1978); James Fallows, "Entitlements," *The Atlantic* (November 1982).

16. See Garrett Hardin, *Filters Against Folly: How to Survive Despite Economists, Ecologists, and the Merely Eloquent* (New York: Viking, 1985); Charles E. Lindblom and David K. Cohen, *Usable Knowledge: Social Science and Social Problem Solving* (New Haven: Yale University Press, 1979).

17. See generally Seymour I. Toll, *Zoned American* (New York: Grossman, 1969).

18. Charles M. Haar, "Zoning for Minimum Standards: The Wayne Township Case," *Harvard Law Review* vol. 66 (April 1953).

19. Marion Clawson, "Why Not Sell Zoning and Rezoning? (Legally, That Is)," *Cry California*, Winter 1966–67: 9, 39.

20. See Richard F. Babcock, *The Zoning Game: Municipal Practices and Policies* (Madison: University of Wisconsin Press, 1966); John Delafons, *Land-Use Controls in the United States* (Cambridge, Mass.: MIT Press, 1962).

21. Dan Tarlock, "Toward a Revised Theory of Zoning," in Frank Bangs, ed., *Land Use Controls Annual* (Chicago: American Society of Planning Officials, 1972).

22. *Ibid.*: 147.

23. "For residential development the function of the government should be to define the desired level of amenity primarily in terms of population density in a given area. To avoid the common suburban practice of using low-density zones to exclude the poor and minority groups, minimum-density levels might be established, and developers could purchase the right to construct a certain number of units. Conventional subdivision regulation would be maintained, and developers would have to meet high sanitation and traffic control standards in the design of their projects. Funds from the sale of development rights could be used by governmental units to finance their share of the improvements." Id. at 150–51.

24. Robert C. Ellickson, "Alternatives to Zoning: Covenants, Nuisane Rules and Fines as Land Use Controls," *University of Chicago Law Review* vol. 40 (Summer 1973).

25. Robert C. Ellickson, "Suburban Growth Controls: An Economic and Legal Analysis," *Yale Law Journal* vol. 86, no. 3 (January 1977).

26. William A. Fischel, *The Economics of Zoning Laws: A Property Rights Approach to American Land Use Controls* (Baltimore: Johns Hopkins University Press, 1985).

27. Quoted in "Lake Hearn: The Great Debate," *The Atlanta Constitution*, June 20, 1985 (special DeKalb supplement): 6a, col. 4.

28. *Ibid.*

29. This theme is developed in Robert H. Nelson, *Zoning and Property Rights: An Analysis of the American System of Land Use Regulation* (Cambridge, Mass.: MIT Press, 1977). See also Robert H. Nelson, "A Private Property Right Theory of Zoning," *The Urban Lawyer* vol. 11, no. 4 (Fall 1979); Robert H. Nelson, "Private Neighborhoods: A New Direction for the Neighborhood Movement," in Charles C. Geisler and Frank J. Popper, eds., *Land Reform, American Style* (Totowa, N.J.: Rowman & Allenheld, 1984); Robert H. Nelson, "Agricultural Zoning: A Private Alternative," in John Baden, ed., *The Vanishing Farmland Crisis: Critical Views of the Movement to Preserve Agricultural Land* (Lawrence: University of Kansas Press, 1984).

30. See Paul W. Gates, *History of Public Land Law Development* (Washington, D.C.: Government Printing Office, 1968); E. Louise Peffer, *The Closing of the Public Domain; Disposal and Reservation Policies, 1900–50* (Stanford, Calif.: Stanford University Press, 1951).

31. Samuel Trask Dana and Sally K. Fairfax, *Forest and Range Policy: Its Development in the United States* (New York: McGraw-Hill, 1980).

32. U.S. Fish and Wildlife Service, *Operation of National Wildlife Refuge System—Final Environmental Statement* II-5 (1976).

33. John Ise, *Our National Park Policy: A Critical History* (Baltimore: Johns Hopkins University Press for Resources for the Future, 1961).

34. Samuel P. Hays, *Conservation and the Gospel of Efficiency: The Progressive Conservation Movement, 1890–1920* (Cambridge, Mass.: Harvard University Press, 1959).

35. Gifford Pinchot, *Breaking New Ground* (New York: Harcourt Brace, 1947): 261.

36. *Ibid.*

37. See Wesley Calef, *Private Grazing and Public Lands* (Chicago: University of Chicago Press, 1960).

38. Bureau of Land Management, United States Department of the Interior, *1985 Grazing Fee Review and Evaluation: Draft Report* 10, 51 (1985).

39. Delworth Gardner, "A Proposal to Reduce Misallocation of Livestock Grazing Permits," *Journal of Farm Economics* vol. 45, no. 1 (February 1963).

40. More recently, ranchers have discovered a significant new source of income: sales to hunters of access rights onto public lands. Extensively intermingled public and private land ownership patterns make much public land in the West difficult or impossible to reach without crossing strips of private land. Many owners of strategically located private parcels have begun to charge hunters high prices ($50 to $100 per day) for the right to such access. For some ranchers, access fees from hunters on public lands are beginning to rival their livestock earnings.

41. See Robert H. Nelson, *The Making of Federal Coal Policy* (Durham,

N.C.: Duke University Press, 1983); Robert T. Deacon and M. Bruce Johnson, eds., *Forestlands: Public and Private* (San Francisco: Pacific Institute for Public Policy Research, 1985).

42. Robert H. Nelson, "A Long Term Strategy for the Public Lands," in Richard Ganzel, ed., *Resource Conflicts in the West* (Reno: Nevada Public Affairs Institute - University of Nevada, March 1983). See also Robert H. Nelson, "Ideology and Public Land Policy—The Current Crisis," in Sterling Brubaker, ed., *Rethinking the Federal Lands* (Washington, D.C.: Resources for the Future, 1984).

43. 30 U.S.C. §§ 1201–1328 (1982).

44. *Report of the Commission on Fair Market Value Policy for Federal Coal Leasing* (Washington, D.C., February 1984).

45. Robert H. Nelson, "The Public Lands" in Paul Portney, ed., *Current Issues in Natural Resource Policy* (Washington, D.C.: Resources for the Future, 1982).

46. Dyan Zaslowsky, "Managing the Dream: Recreation, Contradiction and the Pressures of Enchantment," *Wilderness* (Summer 1984): 32–33.

47. See generally Ronald Foresta, *America's National Parks and Their Keepers* (Washington, D.C.: Resources for the Future, 1984).

48. "Conservationists vs. National-Park Visitors," *New York Times* (12 October 1985): 27.

49. John Baden and Richard Stroup, "Saving the Wilderness," *Reason* (July 1981): 35.

50. Robert H. Nelson, "Why the Sagebrush Revolt Burned Out," *Regulation* vol. 8, no. 3 (May-June 1984); Robert H. Nelson, "The Subsidized Sagebrush: Why Privatization Failed," *Regulation* vol. 8, no. 4 (July-August 1984).

51. Nineteenth century examples of the evolution of property rights in the United States are described generally in John R. Umbeck, *A Theory of Property Rights, with Application to the California Gold Rush* (Ames: Iowa State University Press, 1981); Terry Anderson and P. J. Hill, "The Evolution of Property Rights: A Study of the American West," *Journal of Law and Economics* vol. 18, no.1 (April 1975).

52. Bruce Yandle, "Resource Economics: A Property Rights Perspective," *Journal of Energy Law and Policy* vol. 5 (1983): 1–2.

53. See Terry L. Anderson, *Water Rights: Scarce Resource Allocation, Bureaucracy and the Environment* (San Francisco: Pacific Institute for Public Policy Research, 1983); J. Dales, *Pollution, Property and Prices* (Toronto: University of Toronto Press, 1968); A. DeVany, R. Eckert, C. Meyers, D. O'Hara and R. Scott, *A Property System Approach to the Electro-magnetic Spectrum: A Legal-Economic Engineering Study* (1980); Gary Libecap, *Locking Up the Range: Federal Land Controls and Grazing* (Cambridge, Mass.: Ballinger, 1981); Robert H. Nelson, *Zoning and Property Rights*; Phillip N. Trulock, ed., *Private Rights and Public Lands* (Washington, D.C.: Heritage Foundation, 1983); Anthony Scott, "Catch Quotas and Shares in the Fish Stock as Property

Rights,'' in *Natural Resources Economics and Policy Applications: Essays in Honor of James Crutchfield* (Seattle: University of Washington Press, 1986); Vernon Smith, ''Water Deeds: A Proposed Solution to the Water Valuation Problem,'' *Arizona Review* vol. 26 (1977).

54. Milton Mueller, ''Spectrum Fees vs. Spectrum Liberation,'' *Regulation*, vol. 7, no. 3 (May–June 1983). Kenneth Robinson, ''Some Thoughts on Broadcasting Reform,'' *Regulation*, vol. 7, no. 3 (May–June 1983).

55. Information provided to author by FCC staff.

56. Michael H. Levin, ''Statutes and Stopping Points: Building a Better Bubble at EPA,'' vol. 9, no. 2 *Regulation* (March–April 1985). See also Michael Shapiro and Ellen Warhit, ''Marketable Permits: The Case of Chlorofluorocarbons,'' *Natural Resources Journal* vol. 23, no. 3 (1983).

57. Bruce Yandle, ''The Emerging Market in Air Pollution Rights,'' *Regulation* vol. 2, no. 4 (July–August 1978).

58. M. T. Maloney and Bruce Yandle, ''Bubbles and Efficiency,'' *Regulation* vol. 4, no. 3 (May–June 1980).

59. Levin, ''Statutes and Stopping Points.''

60. Terry L. Anderson, *Water Crisis: Ending the Policy Drought* (Washington, D.C.: Cato, 1983); Anderson, *Water Rights*; and Kenneth D. Frederick, ed., *Resources for the Future, Scarce Water and Institutional Change* (Washington, D.C.: Resources for the Future, 1986).

61. Yandle, ''Resource Economics.''

62. See Desmond D. Connall, Jr., ''A History of the Arizona Groundwater Management Act,'' *Arizona State Law Journal* vol. 1982, no. 2 (1982).

63. Lee G. Anderson, ''Marine Fisheries,'' in Portney, ed., *Current Issues in Natural Resource Policy*.

64. Office of Policy and Planning, National Oceanic and Atmospheric Administration, United States Department of Commerce, *Fishery Management-Lessons from other Resource Management Areas* (1985). For a proposal to privatize fisheries, see Fred Singer, ''Free-for-All Fishing Depletes Stock,'' *Wall Street Jounal* (10 October 1985): 32.

65. See generally Allen V. Kneese and Charles L. Schultze, *Pollution, Prices and Public Policy* (Washington, D.C.: Brookings Institution, 1975); Edwin Mills, *The Economics of Environmental Quality* (New York: Norton, 1978).

66. Harold Demsetz states that ''property rights develop to internalize externalities when the gains of internalization become larger than the cost of internalization.'' Presumably, because the ''new property'' for common property resources has emerged, this condition has been satisfied—the benefits of property rights exceed the costs. See Harold Demsetz, ''Toward a Theory of Property Rights,'' *American Economic Review* vol. 57, no. 2 (May 1967). See also Armen A. Alchian and Harold Demsetz, ''The Property Rights Paradigm,'' *Journal of Economic History* vol. 33, no. 1 (March 1973); Eirik Furubotn and Svetozar Pejovich, ''Property Rights and Economic Theory: A Survey of Recent Literature,'' *Journal of Economic Literature* vol. 10, no. 4 (December 1972).

67. United States Department of the Interior, *Water Resource Policy Study, Task Force Reports 15, 15a* (1977). See also Water and Power Resources Service, United States Department of the Interior, *Acreage Limitation: Interim Report 6* (Appendix IV) (1980).

68. See Edward J. Mitchell, ed., *The Deregulation of Natural Gas* (Washington, D.C.: American Enterprise Institute, 1983).

69. Stephen G. Breyer, *Regulation and its Reform* (Cambridge, Mass.: Harvard University Press, 1982).

70. Friedrich Hayek, "The Use of Knowledge in Society," in Hayek, *Individualism and Economic Order* (Chicago: University of Chicago Press, 1948). See also Michael Ellman, *Socialist Planning* (New York: Cambridge University Press, 1979).

71. Oliver Wendell Holmes, Jr., *The Common Law* (Boston: Little, Brown, 1938): 354.

72. One historian commented with respect to feudal bonds: "Nothing could be more misleading than to dwell exclusively on the economic aspects of the relationship between a lord and his men, however important they may seem. For the lord was not merely a director of an undertaking; he was also a leader. He had power of command over his tenants, levied his armies from them as occasion demanded, and in return gave them his protection. . . . Many a Frankish king or French baron if asked what his land brought him would have answered like the Highlander who said 'five hundred men.' " in Marc Bloch, *The Rise of Dependent Cultivation and Seignorial Institutions*, quoted in Carl Johan Dahlman, *The Open Field System and Beyond: A Property Rights Analysis of an Economic Institution* (New York: Cambridge University Press, 1980): 52.

73. Donald R. Denman, *Origins of Ownership: A Brief History of Land Ownership and Tenure in England from Earlier Times to the Modern Era* (London: Allen and Unwin, 1958): 150

74. John Thomas Noonan, Jr., *The Scholastic Analysis of Usury* (Cambridge, Mass.: Harvard University Press, 1957): 1.

75. *Ibid.*: 199.

76. *Ibid.*: 200.

77. Richard Schlatter, *Private Property: The History of An Idea* (New Brunswick, N. J.: Rutgers University Press, 1951): 35.

78. Schlatter, *Private Property* (quoting *Summa Theological, I–II, Q. 105, Art 2, Basic Writings of St. Thomas*): 52.

79. See Derthick and Quirk, *The Politics of Deregulation*.

80. See Anthony Scott, "Property Rights and Property Wrongs," *Canadian Journal of Economics* vol. 16, no. 4 (November 1983). See also Anthony Scott, "Does Government Create Real Property Rights: Private Interests in Natural Resources," University of British Columbia Discussion Paper No. 84–26 (1984).

81. Frederick Pollock, *The Land Laws* (Littleton, Colo.: Fred Rothman, 1979—reprint of 1896 edition): 64–65.

Index

365

About the Author

Robert H. Nelson is Professor of Environmental Policy at the School of Public Affairs at the University of Maryland, College Park. From 1975 to 1993 he was a member of the economics staff of the Office of Policy Analysis of the U.S. Department of the Interior, the principal policy office serving the Secretary of the Interior. He has been a visiting scholar at the Brookings Institution, a visiting senior fellow at the Woods Hole Oceanographic Institution, and a visiting scholar at the Political Economy Research Center. He is presently a senior fellow of the Competitive Enterprise Institute and of the Center for the New West.

He is the author of three previous books—*Zoning and Property Rights*, *The Making of Federal Coal Policy*, and *Reaching for Heaven on Earth: The Theological Meaning of Economics*—as well as many professional articles. His writings have appeared in *The Washington Post*, *Wall Street Journal*, *Forbes*, *Technology Review*, *Regulation*, and many other publications.